D1227361

Cisco® Network Security

Little Black Book

Joe Harris

President
Keith Weiskamp

Editor-at-Large
Jeff Duntemann

Vice President, Sales, Marketing, and Distribution
Steve Sayre

Vice President, International Sales and Marketing
Cynthia Caldwell

Editorial Director
Sharon Linsenbach

Production Manager
Kim Eoff

Cisco® Network Security Little Black Book

Limits of Liability and Disclaimer of Warranty

The author and publisher of this book have used their best efforts in preparing the book and the programs contained in it. These efforts include the development, research, and testing of the theories and programs to determine their effectiveness. The author and publisher make no warranty of any kind, expressed or implied, with regard to these programs or the documentation contained in this book.

The author and publisher shall not be liable in the event of incidental or consequential damages in connection with, or arising out of, the furnishing, performance, or use of the programs, associated instructions, and/or claims of productivity gains.

Trademarks

Trademarked names appear throughout this book. Rather than list the names and entities that own the trademarks or insert a trademark symbol with each mention of the trademarked name, the publisher states that it is using the names for editorial purposes only and to the benefit of the trademark owner, with no intention of infringing upon that trademark.

Paraglyph Press, Inc.

2246 E. Myrtle Avenue

Phoenix, Arizona 85202

Phone: 602-749-8787

Paraglyph Press ISBN: 1-932111-65-4

Printed in the United States of America
10 9 8 7 6 5 4 3 2 1

PARAGLYPH
PRESS

The Paraglyph Mission

This book you've purchased is a collaborative creation involving the work of many hands, from authors to editors to designers and to technical reviewers. At Paraglyph Press, we like to think that everything we create, develop, and publish is the result of one form creating another. And as this cycle continues on, we believe that your suggestions, ideas, feedback, and comments on how you've used our books is an important part of the process for us and our authors.

We've created Paraglyph Press with the sole mission of producing and publishing books that make a difference. The last thing we all need is yet another tech book on the same tired, old topic. So we ask our authors and all of the many creative hands who touch our publications to do a little extra, dig a little deeper, think a little harder, and create a better book. The founders of Paraglyph are dedicated to finding the best authors, developing the best books, and helping you find the solutions you need.

As you use this book, please take a moment to drop us a line at **feedback@paraglyphpress.com** and let us know how we are doing - and how we can keep producing and publishing the kinds of books that you can't live without.

Sincerely,

Keith Weiskamp & Jeff Duntemann
Paraglyph Press Founders

Paraglyph Press
2246 East Myrtle Ave.
Phoenix, AZ 85020

email:
feedback@paraglyphpress.com
Web: **www.paraglyphpress.com**
Phone: 602-749-8787
Fax: 602-861-1941

Look for these related books from Paraglyph Press:

Windows 2000 Security Little Black Book
By Ian McLean

Also Recently Published by Paraglyph Press:

Visual Basic .NET Programming with Peter Aitken
By Peter Aitken

Visual Basic .NET Black Book
By Steven Holzner

Mac OS X Version 10.1 Little Black Book
By Gene Steinberg

C++ Black Book
By Steven Holzner

C# Core Language Little Black Book
By Bill Wagner

I dedicate this book to my wife, Krystal, to whom I fall in love with all over again every day. I love you, I always have, I always will. To my son, Cameron, I cannot begin to put into words how much I love you. You are my world—my purpose in life. To my mother, Ann, thank you for your love and support, and for always being there for me—you will always be my hero. To my father, Joe Sr., thank you for all the sacrifices you had to make, so that I wouldn't have to—they didn't go unnoticed. Also, thanks for helping to make me the man that I am today—I love you.

—Joe Harris

About the Author

Joe Harris, CCIE# 6200, is the Principal Systems Engineer for a large financial firm based in Houston, Texas. He has more than eight years of experience with data communications and protocols. His work is focused on designing and implementing large-scale, LAN-switched, and routed networks for customers needing secure methods of communication.

Joe is involved daily in the design and implementation of complex secure systems, providing comprehensive security services for the financial industry. He earned his Bachelors of Science degree in Management Information Systems from Louisiana Tech University, and holds his Cisco Security Specialization.

Acknowledgments

There are many people I would like to thank for contributing either directly or indirectly to this book. Being an avid reader of technology books myself, I have always taken the acknowledgments and dedication sections lightly. Having now been through the book writing process, I can assure you that this will never again be the case. Writing a book about a technology sector like security, that changes so rapidly, is a demanding process, and as such, it warrants many "thanks yous" to a number of people.

First, I would like thank God for giving me the ability, gifts, strength, and privilege to be working in such an exciting, challenging, and wonderful career. As stated in the book of Philippians, Chapter 4, Verse 13: "I can do all things through Christ which strengtheneth me." I would also like to thank the team, which made this book possible. You guys are a great group of people to work with, and I encourage other authors to check them out. I would like to extend a special thanks to Jessica Choi, my development editor. In addition, I would also like to thank my acquisitions editors, Charlotte Carpentier and Katherine Hartlove, and my project editor, Greg Balas. It was a pleasure to work with people who exemplify such professionalism, and to the rest of the team—Jeff Johnson, my product marketing manager, Peggy Cantrell, my production coordinator, and Laura Wallander, my cover designer—thank you all!

In addition, I would like to thank Judy Flynn for copyediting and Christine Sherk for proofreading the book, respectively, and to Emily Glossbrenner for indexing the book. A big thanks also to Sheldon Barry for serving as the tech reviewer on the book!

Special thanks to my friend, Joel Cochran, for being a great friend and mentor, and for repeatedly amazing me with your uncanny ability to remember every little detail about a vast array of technologies, and for also taking me under your wing and helping me to "learn the ropes" of this industry. Also thanks to Greg Wallin for the late night discussions and your keen insights into networking, and for your unique methods of communicating them in a manner that consistently challenges me to greater professional heights.

Finally, I would like to thank Jeff Lee, Steven Campbell, Raul Rodriguez, Jose Aguinagua, Kenneth Avans, Walter Hallows, Chris Dunbar, Bill Ulrich, Dodd Lede, Bruce Sebecke, Michael Nelson, James Focke, Ward Hillyer, Loi Ngo, Will Miles, Dale Booth, Clyde Dardar, Barry Meche, Bill Pinson, and all those I have missed in this listing for their insight and inspiration.

And last, but certainly not least, I would like to thank my wife, Krystal, for her love, support, and patience with me during this project. To my son, Cameron, thank you for being daddy's inspiration.

Contents at a Glance

Table of Contents

Introduction

Thanks for buying *Cisco Network Security Little Black Book*, the definitive guide for security configurations on Cisco routers.

New business practices and opportunities are driving a multitude of changes in all areas of enterprise networks, and as such, enterprise security is becoming more and more prevalent as enterprises try to understand and manage the risks associated with the rapid development of business applications deployed over the enterprise network. This coupled with the exponential growth of the Internet has presented a daunting security problem to most enterprises: How does the enterprise implement and update security defenses and practices in an attempt to reduce its vulnerability to exposure from security breaches?

In this book, I will attempt to bridge the gap between the theory and practice of network security and place much of its emphasis on securing the enterprise infrastructure, but first let me emphasize that there is no such thing as absolute security. The statement that a network is secure, is more often than not, misunderstood to mean that there is no possibility of a security breach. However, as you will see throughout this book, having a secure network means that the proper security mechanisms have been put in place in an attempt to reduce most of the risks enterprise assets are exposed to. I have tried to include enough detail on the theories and protocols for reasonable comprehension so that the networking professional can make informed choices regarding security technologies. Although the focus of this book is on the Cisco product offering, the principles apply to many other environments as well.

Is this Book for You?

Cisco Network Security Little Black Book was written with the intermediate or advanced user in mind. The following topics are among those that are covered:

- Internet Protocol Security (IPSec)
- Network Address Translation (NAT)
- Authentication, authorization, and accounting (AAA)
- TCP Intercept
- Unicast Reverse Path Forwarding (Unicast RPF)
- Ethernet Switch Security

How to Use this Book

This book is similar in format to a typical book in the Little Black Book series. Each chapter has two main sections: "In Brief," followed by "Immediate Solutions."

"In Brief" introduces the subject matter of the chapter and explains the principles it is based upon. This section does not delve too deeply into details; instead it elaborates only on the points that are most important for understanding the material in "Immediate Solutions." "Immediate Solutions" presents several tasks related to the subject of the chapter and presented in "In Brief." The tasks in "Immediate Solutions" vary from simple to complex. The vast array of task levels provides a broad coverage of the subject.

This book contains seven chapters. The following sections include a brief preview of each one.

Chapter 1: Securing the Infrastructure

Chapter 1 provides insight into enterprise security problems and challenges that face many organizations today in the "Internet Age" and focuses on the configuration of networking devices to ensure restricted and confidential access to them within the enterprise infrastructure.

Chapter 2: AAA Security Technologies

Chapter 2 includes a detailed examination of Cisco's authentication, authorization, and accounting (AAA) architecture, and the technologies that not only use its features, but also provide them. It presents proven concepts useful for implementing AAA security solutions and discusses how to configure networking devices to support the AAA architecture.

Chapter 3: Perimeter Router Security

Chapter 3 describes many of the security issues that arise when connecting an enterprise network to the Internet. It also details the technologies that can be used to minimize the threat of exposure to the enterprise and its assets. The chapter covers features such as TCP Intercept, Unicast Reverse Path Forwarding (Unicast RPF), and Network Address Translation (NAT).

Chapter 4: IOS Firewall Feature Set

Chapter 4 discusses the add-on component to the Cisco IOS that provides routers with many of the features available to the PIX firewall, which extends to routers with similar functionality as that provided from a separate firewall device. It covers features such as Context-Based Access Control (CBAC), Port Application Mapping (PAM), and the IOS Firewall Intrusion Detection System (IDS).

Chapter 5: Cisco Encryption Technology

Chapter 5 presents on overview of encryption algorithms, hashing techniques, symmetric key encryption, asymmetric key encryption, and digital signatures. It discusses how to configure a router to support Cisco Encryption Technologies and presents detailed methods for testing the encryption configuration.

Chapter 6: Internet Protocol Security

Chapter 6 presents an overview of the framework of open standards for ensuring secure private communications over IP networks and IPSec. It discusses how to configure a router for support of the protocols used to create IPSec virtual private networks (VPNs) and details the configuration of preshared keys, manual keys, and certificate authority support.

Chapter 7: Additional Access List Features

Chapter details the use of access lists and the security features they provide. It discusses the use of dynamic and reflexive access lists, as well as standard and extended access lists.

Appendix A: IOS Firewall IDS Signature List

Appendix A provides a detailed list of the 59 intrusion-detection signatures that are included in the Cisco IOS Firewall feature set. The signatures are presented in numerical order with a detailed description of the signature number contained within the Cisco Secure IDS Network Security Database (NSD).

Appendix B: Securing Ethernet Switches

Appendix B presents an overview of methods used to provide security for the Catalyst Ethernet model of switches. This appendix discusses how to configure VLANS, Vlan Access Lists, IP permit lists, port security, SNMP security, and support for the AAA architecture on the Catalyst line of Ethernet switches.

The *Little Black Book* Philosophy

Written by experienced professionals, Paraglyph *Little Black Books* are terse, easily "thumb-able" question-answerers and problem-solvers. The Little Black Book's unique two-part chapter format—brief technical overviews followed by practical immediate solutions—is structured to help you use your knowledge, solve problems, and quickly master complex technical issues to become an expert. By breaking down complex topics into easily manageable components, this format helps you quickly find what you're looking for, with the diagrams and code you need to make it happen.

The author sincerely believes that this book will provide a more cost-effective and timesaving means for preparing and deploying Cisco security features and services. By using this reference, the reader can focus on the fundamentals of the material, instead of spending time deciding on acquiring numerous expensive texts that may turn out to be, on the whole, inapplicable to the desired subject matter. This book also provides the depth and coverage of the subject matter in an attempt to avoid gaps in security-related technologies that are presented in other "single" reference books. The information security material in this book is presented in an organized, professional manner, that will be a primary source of information for individuals new to the field of security, as well as for practicing security professionals. This book is mostly a practical guide for configuring security-related technologies on Cisco routers, and as such, the chapters may be read in any order.

I welcome your feedback on this book. You can either email Paraglyph Press at **feedback@paraglyphpress.com**, or email me directly at **joefharris@netscape.net**.

Chapter 1

Securing the Infrastructure

In Brief

This chapter is made up of two parts. The first part provides insight into enterprise security problems and challenges that face many organizations today in the "Internet Age." The Internet has changed the way people live, work, and play. Even more so, it has revolutionized the way business is conducted and the methods in which businesses communicate. More and more businesses are recognizing that the Internet provides them with a relatively inexpensive medium for conducting business on a global scale. Unfortunately, the Internet is missing a lot of key components, one of which is security. The Internet possesses an unlimited number of possibilities for enterprises, but enterprises must first weigh the risk of conducting business on the Internet against the security measures necessary to protect the business they are trying to conduct. As a result of the Internet, information traffic loads within the enterprise have increased exponentially, and so, too, has the business value of the infrastructure that supports the higher traffic loads, thereby increasing the risk of vulnerability to security breaches.

The second part of this chapter focuses on configuration of Cisco routers to ensure restricted and confidential access to network devices within the enterprise infrastructure. This chapter examines common features used to secure access to physical and logical interfaces and technologies used to effectively manage routing updates and control commonly exploited methods for gaining access into networking devices. It also examines what Simple Network Management Protocol (SNMP) is used for within a network and methods used to secure SNMP access to networking devices. Finally, it examines the HTTP server function that a Cisco router can perform, the security risks associated with it, and the methods used to protect the router if this function is used.

Enterprise Security Problems

One of the major security problems that enterprises face today is that sophisticated and sometimes complicated security defenses are required to mitigate the newest threats posed by intruders and to provide a reduction in business vulnerabilities. Another major hurdle involves choosing whether or not a security solution is the proper fit for the business; a vast number of specialized products in the market only work in certain parts of the network and fail to provide a true end-to-end solution for the business. Security is a complicated subject in theory and in practice, and more often than not, is very difficult to implement, especially when the solution must provide end-to-end security.

To provide the utmost security to your network, you must first have an idea of what it is you are trying to protect. You must then decide what type of intruders you are trying to protect yourself from. Intruders can take on many forms, including the following:

- Current employees
- Former employees
- Employees that misuse the environment
- Competitors
- Thrill seekers

The most common terms used today to identify an individual who uses a computer to engage in mischievous behavior are "hacker" and "cracker." A *hacker* is intensely interested in the innermost workings of any computer operating system. Most often, hackers are programmers. As such, they have advanced knowledge of operating systems and programming languages. They constantly seek further knowledge, freely share what they have discovered, and, almost never, intentionally damage data. Hackers are sometimes referred to as white-hats.

A *cracker* breaks into or violates the integrity of someone else's system with malicious intent. Crackers gain unauthorized access, destroy vital data, deny service to legitimate users, or basically cause problems for their targets. Crackers are sometimes referred to as black-hats.

Types of Threats

The methods hackers and crackers use to gain unauthorized access into network devices are known as threats. Having a security problem is bad enough, but defying any effort to categorically group problems and define methods to protect against them, is the number, nature, and types of security threats that exist today. These defy any effort that attempts to categorically group and define methods to protect against problems. A generalized list of threats follows; the methods used to thwart these threats will be discussed later in this chapter as well as throughout this book:

- *Unauthorized access*—A network intruder can gain unauthorized access to networking devices through a variety of means, three of which are as follows:

  - *Physical*—If attackers have physical access to a machine, more often than not, they will be able to get in. The techniques used to gain access range from accessing the device via the console to physically taking apart the system.

  - *System*—System access assumes that the intruder already has a user account on the system. Proper privileges should be granted to the user such that he or she is authenticated and authorized only to do that which is deemed to be a function of his or her job duties.

  - *Remote*—Remote access involves intruders who attempt to penetrate the system remotely from across the Internet, through a dial-up connection, or on local or wide area network. This type of intruder usually has no account privileges.

- *Eavesdropping*—Eavesdropping is used to capture TCP/IP or other protocol packets, thus allowing the intruder to decode the contents of the packet using a protocol analyzer. "Packet sniffing" is a more common term used to describe the act of eavesdropping. Eavesdropping leads to *information theft*, like stolen credit card and social security numbers.

- *Data manipulation*—Data manipulation is simply the act of altering files on computers, vandalizing a Web site, or replacing FTP files.

- *Protocol weakness*—The most-used protocol in circulation today is TCP/IP. This protocol was designed a long time ago. As a result, a number of its design flaws can lead to possible security problems, such as smurf attacks, IP spoofing, TCP sequence number prediction, and SYN floods. The IP protocol itself is a very trusting protocol; therefore, hackers are free to forge and change IP data.

- *Session replay*—Intruders can eavesdrop on one or more users involved in a communication session and manipulate the data in such a manner according to the hack they are trying to perform.

This list does not by any means include all of the types of security threats. Its purpose is to give you a general idea of the number and types of methods intruders have at their disposal.

Enterprise Security Challenges

One the biggest challenges that IT managers face is choosing from among the vast number of security offerings and vendors in the market space. IT managers must weigh the cost of security products against things such as performance, manageability, and scalability. After sorting through each vendor, IT managers must choose the security solution that most uniquely adapts to and satisfies their business environment. The solution that is chosen must not be overly restrictive and must allow the business to enable new applications, innovations, and services as needed, without unnecessary challenges.

After IT managers choose a security solution that most adequately meets their specific needs, more often than not they find themselves having to develop a design that will allow them to smoothly integrate the solution into a network environment of products developed by different vendors. This usually adds to the cost of implementation and overall operation of the network. On top of that, IT managers must hire skilled security engineers or spend money from their budgets to adequately train their existing engineers to support the new technologies.

After an organization's IT management has recognized the existence of security threats and has directed changes to improve its posture or information security process, they should formulate a plan to address the issue. The first step in implementing this plan is the development of a security policy.

Enterprise Security Policy

Request for Comments (RFC) 2196, *Site Security Handbook*, states that "A security policy is a formal statement of rules by which people who are given access to an organization's technology and information must abide." A security policy should not determine how an enterprise operates; instead, the business of the enterprise should dictate how a security policy is written. Business opportunities are what drive the need for security in the first place. The main purpose of a security policy is to inform anyone that uses the enterprise's network of the requirements for protecting the enterprise's technology and information assets. The policy should specify the mechanisms through which these requirements can be met. Of all the documents an organization develops, the security policy is one of the most important.

Prior to developing the security policy, you should conduct a risk assessment to determine the appropriate corporate security measures. The assessment helps to determine areas in which security needs to be addressed, how the security needs to be addressed, and the overall level of security that needs to be applied in order to implement adequate security controls. A risk assessment is a process whereby critical assets are identified and values are placed on the assets. You determine how much each asset is at risk of being compromised and how much you need to upgrade or add to it to meet your business needs.

To develop a security policy that is not overly restrictive for users, that balances ease of use with a certain level of security, and that is enforceable both technically and organizationally, the policy should contain, at a minimum, some of the topics in the following list:

- *Acceptable use policy*—Spells out what users are allowed and not allowed to do on the various components within the network; this includes the type of traffic allowed on the network. The policy should be as explicit as possible to avoid any ambiguity or misunderstanding.

- *Remote access policy*—Spells out to users acceptable or unacceptable behavior when they have connected to the enterprise via the Internet, a dial-up connection, a virtual private network (VPN), or any other method of remote connectivity.

- *Incident handling policy*—Addresses planning and developing procedures to handle incidents before they occur. This document also creates a centralized group to be the primary focus when an incident happens. The incident handling policy can be contained within the actual security policy, but due to corporate structure, this document often actually exists as a subdocument to the security policy.

- *Internet access policy*—Defines what the enterprise considers to be ethical, proper use of its Internet connection.

- *Email policy*—Defines the acceptable use of the enterprise's email systems, including personal emails and Web-based email.

- *Physical security policy*—Defines controls that pertain to physical device security and access.

After you've completed the enterprise security policy, the last step is to perform regular audits. Audits not only give you a baseline by which to judge what is deemed as normal activity or network behavior, they also, in many cases, produce results that will be the first alert in the detection of a security breach. Noticing unusual events within the network can help to catch intruders before they can cause any further damage.

Securing the Enterprise

The enterprise infrastructure is vulnerable to many different security threats (discussed earlier) from any number of intruders. The solution to the infrastructure security problem is to securely configure components of the network against vulnerabilities based on the network security policy. Most network security vulnerabilities are well known, and the measures used to counteract them will be examined in detail throughout this chapter.

Physical and Logical Security

Physical and logical security include the following:

- Securing console access
- Securing Telnet access
- Setting privilege levels
- Disabling password recovery
- Configuring password encryption
- Setting banner messages

Securing Console Access

It's important to put the proper physical security mechanisms into place. If the proper physical security mechanisms are not in place, an intruder could potentially bypass all other logical security mechanisms and gain access to the device. If an intruder can gain access to the administrative interface of the router, he could view and change the device's configuration and gain access to other networking equipment. The first thing you should do to thwart intruders is to set a console password. If the intruder has already gained physical access to the device, he'll attempt to gain network access through the console port first. The console port supports many different methods for authenticating a user and allowing access, some of which are listed here:

- Console password
- Local user database
- TACACS+
- RADIUS

Securing Telnet Access

Telnet is a protocol that allows a user to establish a remote connection to a device. After connected to the remote device, you are presented with a screen that is identical to the screen that would be displayed if you were directly connected to the console port. Telnet ports on a router are referred to as *virtual terminal ports*. Telnet is really no different from a console connection, and as such, the proper logical security mechanisms should be put into place to ensure that only responsible personnel are allowed Telnet access. Virtual terminal ports support many different methods for authenticating a user and allowing access. Some of the methods are included in the following list:

- Vty password
- Local user database
- TACACS+
- RADIUS

Setting Privilege Levels

Privilege levels associate router commands with each security level configured on the router. This allows for a finer granularity of control when restricting user access. There are 16 privilege levels contained within the router operating system. Level 2 to level 14 are customizable and allow you to configure multiple privilege levels and multiple passwords to enable certain users to have access to specific commands.

Disabling Password Recovery

Setting passwords is the first line of defense against intruders. Sometimes passwords are forgotten and must be recovered. All Cisco password recovery procedures dictate that the user performs the password recovery process from the console port of the router or switch. There are, however, certain circumstances in which the widely available password recovery procedure should be disabled. One such circumstance is an emergency Add, Move, or Change (AMC), whereby a networking device needs to be in a location that does not have the proper mechanisms in place for physical security, thus allowing an intruder a greater chance of circumventing traditional security measures.

Configuring Password Encryption

All Cisco console and Telnet passwords configured on the router are stored in plain text within the configuration of the router by default, thus making them easily readable. If someone issues the **show running-config** privileged mode command, the password is displayed. Another instance when the password can easily be read is if you store your configurations on a TFTP server, the intruder only needs to gain access into the TFTP machine, after which the intruder can read the configuration with a simple text editor. Password encryption stores passwords in an encrypted manner on the router. The encryption is applied to all configured passwords on the router.

Setting Banner Messages

You can use *banner messages* to issue statements to users, indicating who is and who is not allowed access into the router. Banner messages should indicate the seriousness of an attempt to gain unauthorized access into the device and should never reflect to the user that gaining unauthorized access is acceptable. If possible, recite certain civil and federal laws that are applicable to unauthorized access and let users know what the punishment would be for accessing the device without express written permission. If possible, have certified legal experts within the company review the banner message.

SNMP

The *Simple Network Management Protocol (SNMP)* is an application-layer protocol that helps to facilitate the exchange of management information between network devices. SNMP enables network administrators to manage network performance, find and solve network problems, and plan for network growth. An SNMP network consists of three key components: *managed devices, agents,* and *network-management systems* (NMSs). A *managed device* is a network node that contains an SNMP agent and resides on a managed network. Managed devices collect and store management information and make this information available to NMSs by use of the SNMP protocol. Managed devices can be routers, access servers, switches, computer hosts, or printers. An *agent* is a network-management software module that resides in a managed device. An agent has local knowledge of management information and translates that information into a form compatible with SNMP. An *NMS* executes applications that monitor and control managed devices. NMSs provide the bulk of the processing and memory resources required for network management. An SNMP managed device has various access levels. These are as follows:

- *Read-only*—Allows read access of the Management Information Base (MIB) on the managed device

- *Read/write*—Allows read and write access of the Management Information Base on the managed device

- *Write-only*—Allows write access of the Management Information Base on the managed device

Routers can send notifications to NMS machines when a particular event occurs. The SNMP notifications can be sent as a trap or inform request. Traps are unreliable because the receiver does not send an acknowledgment that it received a trap. However, an NMS machine that receives an inform request acknowledges the message with an SNMP response. If the NMS does not receive an inform request, it does not send a response. If the sender never receives a response, the inform request can be sent again. Thus, informs are more reliable.

Cisco IOS software supports the following versions of SNMP:

- SNMPv1
- SNMPv2c
- SNMPv3

Both SNMPv1 and SNMPv2c use a community-based form of security. The group of managers able to access the agent is defined by an access list and password.

SNMPv2c support includes a bulk retrieval mechanism and more detailed error-message reporting to management stations. The bulk retrieval mechanism supports the retrieval of large quantities of information, minimizing the number of polls required. The SNMPv2c improved error-handling support includes a larger number of error codes that distinguish different kinds of error conditions. Error return codes in SNMPv2c report the error type.

SNMPv3 provides for both security models and security levels. A security model is an authentication strategy that is set up for a user and the group in which the user resides. A security level is the permitted level of security within a security model. A combination of a security model and a security level will determine which security mechanism is employed when an SNMP packet is handled.

Routing Protocol Authentication

Routing protocol authentication prevents the introduction of false or unauthorized routing messages from unapproved sources. With authentication configured, the router will authenticate the source of each routing protocol packet that it receives from its neighbors. Routers exchange an authentication key or a password that is configured on each router. The key or password must match between neighbors.

There are two types of routing protocol authentication: plain text authentication and Message Digest 5 (MD5) authentication. Plain text authentication is generally not recommended because the authentication key is sent across the network in clear text, making plain text authentication susceptible to eavesdropping attempts. MD5 authentication creates a hash value from the key; the hash value instead of the actual password is exchanged between neighbors, preventing the password from being read because the hash, not the password, is transmitted across the network.

Routing Filters

Route filtering enables the network administrator to keep tight control over route advertisements. Frequently, companies merge or form a partnership with other companies. This can pose a challenge because the companies need to be interconnected yet remain under separate administrative control. Because you do not have complete control over all parts of the network, the network can become vulnerable to malicious routing or misconfiguration. Route filters ensure that routers will advertise as well as accept legitimate networks. They work by regulating the flow of routes that are entered into or advertised out of the routing table.

Filtering the networks that are advertised out of a routing process or accepted into the routing process helps to increase security because, if no route is advertised to a downstream or upstream neighbor, then no route apparently exists to the network. This will keep intruders from having logical connectivity to the target destination. It also increases the network stability to a certain degree. Misconfiguration is determined to be the largest contributor of network instability; however, an intruder could introduce into routing updates false information that could result in routing problems.

Suppressing Routing Advertisements

To prevent routers on a local network from learning about routes that are dynamically advertised out on the interface, you can define the interface as passive. Defining an interface as passive keeps routing update messages from being sent through a router interface, preventing other systems on the interface from learning about routes dynamically from this router. You can configure a passive interface for all IP routing protocols except Border Gateway Protocol (BGP).

In networks with large numbers of interfaces, you can set all interfaces to passive using the **passive-interface default** command. This feature allows the administrator to selectively determine over which interfaces the protocol needs to run. After the determination is made to allow the protocol to run on the interface, the administrator can disable the passive-interface feature on an interface-by-interface basis with the **no passive-interface** *<interface>* command.

NOTE: *Making an interface passive for the Enhanced Interior Gateway Routing Protocol (EIGRP) disables route advertisements sent out the interface that was made passive, just as any other routing protocol; however, the interface will not listen for route advertisements either.*

HTTP Access

Cisco IOS software on routers is equipped with a Web browser user interface that allows you to issue commands into the router via the Web interface. The Web browser user interface can be customized and tailored to your business environment. The HTTP server is disabled by default; when it's enabled, it introduces some new security vulnerabilities into your network. The HTTP server function, when it's enabled, gives all client devices with logical connectivity to the router the ability to monitor or modify the configuration of the router. All that needs to reside on the client is a software package that interprets packets on port 80. This is obviously a major security issue. However, the router software allows you to change the default port that the HTTP server is running on. You can also configure an access list of specific hosts that are allowed Web access to the router and apply the access list to the HTTP server. Authentication of each user provides better security if you elect to use the router's HTTP server functions. Authentication can take place by one of four different methods:

- *AAA*—Indicates that the AAA function is used for authentication.

- *Enable*—Indicates that the configured enable password is used for authentication. This is the default authentication method.

- *Local*—Indicates that the locally configured security database is used for authentication.

- *TACACS+*—Indicates that the Terminal Access Controller Access system is used for authentication.

Immediate Solutions

Configuring Console Security

The console port is used to attach a terminal directly into the router. By default, no security is applied to the console port and the setup utility does not prompt you to configure security for console access. Cisco routers have many different modes of operation, one of which is *user mode*. When you first access the router via the console port, the router will prompt you for a password, if one has been configured. After successfully supplying the password, you are logged into user mode on the router. When a Cisco router is in user mode, the router will display its hostname followed by the greater than symbol. Here is an example of user mode access:

```
SecureRouter>
```

User mode has limited functionality. *Enable mode*, also called *privileged mode*, can be accessed by typing the **enable** command. If passwords have been configured to access this level of the IOS, the router prompts you for the correct password. When a Cisco router is in enable mode, the router will display its hostname followed by the pound sign. Here is an example of enable mode access:

```
SecureRouter#
```

Cisco passwords are case sensitive. The simplest and most direct way to connect to the network device is to use a direct connection to the console port of a router or switch. You can configure a console password to authenticate users for user mode access by entering the following commands:

```
SecureRouter#config t
Enter configuration commands, one per line.  End with CNTL/Z.
SecureRouter(config)#line con 0
SecureRouter(config-line)#password Coriolis
SecureRouter(config-line)#login
SecureRouter(config-line)#end
```

The preceding configuration sets the user mode password to **Coriolis**. Cisco routers also maintain a local user authentication database, which can be used to authenticate users who connect directly to the console port of a router. Here's an example of configuring the router to use the local user database for authentication of users who attempt to access the router via the console:

```
!
username Fred privilege 15 password 0 Flintstone
username Elroy privilege 12 password 0 Jetson
username Captain privilege 8 password 0 Kirk
!
line con 0
 login local
 transport input none
!
```

The preceding configuration defines three users: **Fred**, **Elroy**, and **Captain**. Each user has an associated privilege level defined for their respective login credentials and has a password that is associated with their username. This allows Fred to log into the router with a username of **Fred** and a password of **Flintstone**. Because **Fred**'s privilege level defines the maximum privilege level that can be configured on the router, **Fred** is considered to be the super-user. **Elroy** has a privilege level of 12 and the password **Jetson**.

NOTE: *Assignment of privilege levels is discussed in detail later in this chapter.*

By assigning **Elroy** a privilege of 12, the administrator can limit the functionality that **Elroy** may have on the router. That's also the case for **Captain**. When a user plugs into the console port of a router configured with local authentication, they are first prompted for their username; after successfully passing the correct username to the router, they are then prompted for the password that is associated with that username. The following example details these steps:

```
User Access Verification

Username: Fred
Password: Flintstone
SecureRouter#
```

Now, what do you think would happen if you were to attempt to log in with the username of **Fred** and the password that is associated with

Elroy? You would suspect that the router would deny you access. This example details this attempt:

```
User Access Verification

Username: Fred
Password: Jetson
% Login invalid

Username:
```

From this, you can see that you must supply the password that is associated with the username with which you are attempting to gain access.

WARNING! When using local authentication and assigning privilege levels, you must be careful to associate the correct username with the correct privilege level. Anyone who logs in with a privilege level that is equal to 2 or above is logged directly into privileged mode.

Configuring Telnet Security

Directly connecting to the console of a router is generally a relatively easy method for gaining access to the device; however, this method is inconvenient and not abundantly scalable. If console access is the only method available to gain access into the device, an administrator must always walk, drive, or fly to the physical location of the router and plug into the device's console port. Fortunately, there are methods for gaining access into the router from a remote location. The most common method of remote administration for a Cisco router is to use a Telnet session. Unlike with console access, there are four configuration requirements that must be met before you can use this method of access:

- An enable password must be supplied. This is discussed in the next section.
- The router must have an IP address assigned to a routable interface.
- The routing table of the router must contain a route for the source of the Telnet packet.
- Under line configuration mode, a vty password must be supplied.

The steps involved in defining Telnet security are similar to the steps used to configure console security. An example of configuring the fourth requirement (after the first three have been met) can be seen here:

```
SecureRouter#config t
Enter configuration commands, one per line.  End with CNTL/Z.
SecureRouter(config)#line vty 0 4
SecureRouter(config-line)#login
SecureRouter(config-line)#password letmein
SecureRouter(config-line)#end
SecureRouter#
```

As mentioned in the preceding section, "Configuring Console Security," Cisco routers also maintain a local user authentication database, which can be used to authenticate users who directly connect to the console port of a router. Here is an example of configuring the router to use the local user database for authentication of users who attempt to access the router via the console:

```
!
username Fred privilege 15 password 0 Flintstone
username Elroy privilege 12 password 0 Jetson
username Captain privilege 8 password 0 Kirk
!
line vty 0 4
 login local
```

The result is that, when a user telnets to the router with this configuration, they will be prompted to enter a username and password before being allowed to gain access into the router.

Routers can also restrict Telnet access to authorized users with the use of an access list. The access list is then applied to the virtual terminal ports of the router with the **access-class** command. This allows you to restrict Telnet access from a particular IP address or a subnet of IP addresses. Use the following steps to this method of security:

1. Use the **access-list** global configuration command to configure an access list that permits the specific hosts that are allowed Telnet access.

2. Use the **access-class** *access-list-number* {in|out} command to apply the access list to the virtual terminal ports.

In the following example, the router is configured to allow only three hosts Telnet access on each of the available virtual terminal ports:

```
Router-A#config t
Enter configuration commands, one per line.  End with CNTL/Z.
Router-A(config)#access-list 10 permit 10.10.10.19
Router-A(config)#access-list 10 permit 10.10.11.20
Router-A(config)#access-list 10 permit 10.10.12.130
Router-A(config)#line vty 0 4
Router-A(config-line)#access-class 10 in
Router-A(config-line)#end
Router-A#
```

NOTE: *Remember, console and Telnet security is not preconfigured for you by default. One of your first configuration steps when you initially set up your router should be to configure each of these interfaces.*

Configuring Enable Mode Security

To configure enable mode access, you can use one of two commands: **enable password** or **enable secret**. Both commands accomplish the same thing, allowing access to enable mode. However, the **enable secret** command is considered to be more secure because it uses a one-way encryption scheme based on the MD5 hashing function. Only use the **enable password** command with older IOS images and/or boot ROMs that have no knowledge of the newer **enable secret** command.

NOTE: *The MD5 encryption algorithm will be discussed in detail in Chapter 6. For now, just remember that this method is considered more secure.*

You configure an enable password by entering the **enable password** *<password>* command in global configuration mode:

```
SecureRouter#config t
Enter configuration commands, one per line.  End with CNTL/Z.
SecureRouter(config)#enable password Omni-Pass01
SecureRouter(config)#end
SecureRouter#
```

The preceding configuration sets the enable password to **Omni-Pass01**. The result of setting the enable password can be seen in the following output. From the user mode prompt, you must enter the **enable** command to gain access into privileged mode:

```
SecureRouter>enable
Password: Omni-Pass01
SecureRouter#
```

NOTE: *After you enter the* **enable** *command, the password you type at the password prompt will not be displayed. Be sure to type the password exactly as it is configured in the* **enable password** *command.*

You configure an enable secret password by entering the following command in global configuration mode:

```
SecureRouter#config t
Enter configuration commands, one per line.  End with CNTL/Z.
SecureRouter(config)#enable secret Long@Horn10
SecureRouter(config)#end
SecureRouter#
```

The preceding configuration sets the enable secret password to **Long@Horn10**. The result of setting the enable secret password can be seen in the following output. From the user mode prompt, you must enter the **enable** command to gain access into privileged mode, as follows:

```
SecureRouter>enable
Password: Long@Horn10
SecureRouter#
```

NOTE: *After you enter the* **enable** *command, the password you type at the password prompt will not be displayed. Be sure to type the password exactly as it is configured in the* **enable password** *command.*

Disabling Password Recovery

The first line of defense against intruders is to set passwords on routers. Sometimes passwords are forgotten and must be recovered. There are, however, some instances in which the widely known password recovery procedures should be disabled. When physical security is not possible or in a network emergency, password recovery can be disabled.

NOTE: *Password recovery on routers and switches is outside the scope of this book. However, if you need an index of password recovery procedures for Cisco network devices, see the following Cisco Web page:* ***www.cisco.com/warp/public/474***.

The key to recovering a password on a Cisco router is through manipulation of the configuration registers of the router. All router passwords are stored in the startup configuration, so if the configuration registers are changed properly, the startup configuration with the passwords stored within them can be bypassed. If you have disabled the password recovery mechanisms, you will not be able to perform password recovery on the router. Disabling the password recovery procedure of a Cisco router is a decision that must be thought out ahead of time because the command used to disable password recovery also disables *ROMMON*.

WARNING! *The command discussed in this section is not recommended for use on any production router and is explained here only for the benefit of learning within a lab environment.*

You can disable the Cisco password recovery procedure by issuing the **no service password-recovery** command in global configuration mode:

```
SecureRouter#config t
Enter configuration commands, one per line. End with CNTR/Z.
SecureRouter(config)#no service password-recovery
WARNING:
Executing this command will disable password recovery mechanism.
 Do not execute this command without another plan for
password recovery.

Are you sure you want to continue? [yes/no]: yes
```

As you can see, the IOS reminds you of how serious disabling the password recovery procedures are with a warning message and a prompt allowing you to change your mind. To see the results of changing the password recovery feature, issue the **show running-config** command. The effects of issuing the command can be seen in the following configuration:

```
SecureRouter#show run
Building configuration...
```

```
Current configuration:
!
version 12.0
service password-encryption
no service password-recovery
!
hostname SecureRouter
```

After password recovery has been disabled and the configuration has been saved, the widely available password recovery procedure will not be available on the router. The following output verifies that password recovery is indeed disabled:

```
SecureRouter#reload
Proceed with reload? [confirm]

00:14:34: %SYS-5-RELOAD: Reload requested
System Bootstrap, Version 11.3(2)XA4, RELEASE SOFTWARE (fc1)
Copyright (c) 1999 by cisco Systems, Inc.
TAC:Home:SW:IOS:Specials for info
PC = 0xfff14ee8, Vector = 0x500, SP = 0x680127b0
C2600 platform with 49152 Kbytes of main memory

PASSWORD RECOVERY FUNCTIONALITY IS DISABLED
program load complete, entry point: 0x80008000, size: 0x928024
Self decompressing the image : #######################....
```

WARNING! *The use of the command discussed in this section is not recommended for a production router. It should be used only in extreme circumstances or in a lab environment!*

If the **no service password-recovery** command has been issued on a Cisco router and the passwords have been forgotten, you must contact your Cisco Technical Support Engineer to obtain help in gaining access into the router and enabling the password recovery process again.

Configuring Privilege Levels for Users

As mentioned earlier, the Cisco IOS software has two modes of operation. You can configure up to 16 levels of commands for each mode, which allows you to selectively assign authority on a per-user basis.

Commands entered into the IOS can be associated with each privilege level. You configure the privilege level for a command using the global configuration command **privilege** *<mode>* **level** *<level>* *<command>*. The exact syntax of this command is as follows:

```
privilege mode level level command | reset command
```

Figure 1.1 displays three users, **Cindy**, **Marsha**, and **Jan**, connected to a local segment. Cindy is the network engineer; she has full control over Router A. **Marsha** and **Jan** are system administrators; they need only limited functionality on Router A. Here is an example of the configuration that meets this requirement:

```
enable secret Cindy
enable secret level 3 Marsha
enable secret level 2 Jan
privilege exec level 3 debug
privilege exec level 3 show running-config
privilege exec level 3 telnet
privilege exec level 2 ping
privilege exec level 2 sh int ser0
privilege exec level 2 sh ip route
line con 0
login
```

This configuration provides **Cindy** with the default full administrative rights to the router. **Marsha** is given access to all features that are allowed with administrative **level 3** and can perform the com-

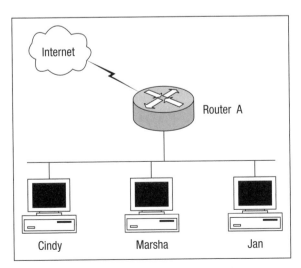

Figure 1.1   Using privilege levels to create administrative levels.

mands that are listed with a privilege level of 3. **Jan** is assigned a privilege level of 2 and is given access to all features and allowed to perform the commands listed with a privilege level of 2. The key is that each user must use the **enable** *<level>* command from the user mode prompt and log in with the password assigned for that level. An example is provided here:

```
SecureRouter>
SecureRouter>enable 3
Password: Marsha
SecureRouter#
```

Configuring Password Encryption

It's relatively simple to configure password encryption on Cisco routers. When password encryption is configured, all passwords that are configured on the router are converted to an unsophisticated reversible cipher. Although the algorithm that is used to convert the passwords is somewhat unsophisticated, it still serves a very good purpose. Intruders cannot simply view the password in plain text and know what the password is. To enable the use of password encryption, use the command **service password-encryption**.

The following example shows a router configuration prior to enabling password encryption. An enable password, a console password, and a Telnet password is configured:

```
SecureRouter#show running-config
!
enable password Cisco
!
line con 0
 password Networking
!
line vty 0 4
 password Security
!
```

The following example shows the command you would use to enable password encryption on the router:

```
SecureRouter#config t
Enter configuration commands, one per line.  End with CNTL/Z.
```

```
SecureRouter(config)#service password-encryption
SecureRouter(config)#end
SecureRouter#
```

The results of enabling password encryption can be seen in the following example. Notice that each password is now represented by a string of letters and numbers, which represents the encrypted format of the password:

```
SecureRouter#show running-config
!
enable password 7 05280F1C2243
!
line con 0
 password 7 04750E12182E5E45001702
!
line vty 0 4
 password 7 122A00140719051033
!
```

WARNING! *Password encryption does not provide a very high level of security. There are widely available passwords crackers that can reverse the encryption. I do, however, recommend using the password **encryption** command on all routers. I also recommend that you take additional security measures to protect your passwords.*

Configuring Banner Messages

As mentioned in the section "In Brief" at the beginning of this chapter, you can display banner messages to users who are attempting to gain access to the router. There are four types of banner messages:

- *Message of the Day (MOTD)*—Displayed at login. Useful for sending messages that affect all network users.

- *Login*—Displayed after the Message of the Day banner appears and before the login prompts.

- *EXEC*—Displayed whenever an EXEC process is initiated.

- *Incoming*—Displayed on terminals connected to reverse Telnet lines.

The process for configuring banner messages is fairly simple. Enter the following command in global configuration mode:

```
banner {exec|motd|login|incoming} [delimited character] -
   <message> [delimited character]
```

Here is a sample MOTD banner:

```
SecureRouter#config t
Enter configuration commands, one per line.  End with CNTL/Z.
SecureRouter(config)#banner motd #
Enter TEXT message.  End with the character '#'.

**************************************************************
*           WARNING...WARNING...WARNING...WARNING            *
*           YOU HAVE ACCESSED A RESTRICTED DEVICE            *
*      USE OF THIS DEVICE WITHOUT PRIOR AUTHORIZATION        *
*     OR FOR PURPOSES WHICH AUTHORIZATION HAS NOT BEEN       *
*            GRANTED IS STRICTLY PROHIBITED!!!               *
**************************************************************

#
SecureRouter(config)#end
SecureRouter#
```

The results of setting the MOTD banner message can be seen by using the **show running-config** command or by logging into the router. The following is an example of logging into the router from the console port:

```
SecureRouter con0 is now available
......
Press RETURN to get started.
......
**************************************************************
*           WARNING...WARNING...WARNING...WARNING            *
*           YOU HAVE ACCESSED A RESTRICTED DEVICE            *
*      USE OF THIS DEVICE WITHOUT PRIOR AUTHORIZATION        *
*     OR FOR PURPOSES WHICH AUTHORIZATION HAS NOT BEEN       *
*            GRANTED IS STRICTLY PROHIBITED!!!               *
**************************************************************
SecureRouter>
```

EXEC banner messages, as mentioned earlier, are invoked when a user attempts to gain access into privileged mode. (Accessing privileged mode was explained in "Configuring Enable Mode Security" earlier in this chapter.) Industry-standard best practices recommend configuring a MOTD banner message as well as an EXEC banner message. Working still on the same router, here's how to configure an EXEC banner to complement the MOTD banner. This can be accomplished using the following configuration:

```
SecureRouter#config t
Enter configuration commands, one per line.  End with CNTL/Z.
```

```
SecureRouter(config)#banner exec #
Enter TEXT message.  End with the character '#'.
*********************************************************
*          WARNING...WARNING...WARNING...WARNING         *
*                                                        *
*          THIS IS A REMINDER...THIS IS A REMINDER       *
*                                                        *
*          YOU HAVE ACCESSED A RESTRICTED DEVICE         *
*      USE OF THIS DEVICE WITHOUT PRIOR AUTHORIZATION    *
*      OR FOR PURPOSES WHICH AUTHORIZATION HAS NOT BEEN  *
*          GRANTED IS STRICTLY PROHIBITED!!!             *
*********************************************************

#
SecureRouter(config)#end
SecureRouter#
```

The results of setting the EXEC message can be seen by using the
show running-config command or by using the **telnet** command to
remotely connect to a router with the EXEC banner enabled. The results of configuring both the MOTD banner and the EXEC banner can
be seen here:

```
R1#telnet 192.168.10.1
Trying 192.168.10.1 ... Open

*********************************************************
*          WARNING...WARNING...WARNING...WARNING         *
*          YOU HAVE ACCESSED A RESTRICTED DEVICE         *
*      USE OF THIS DEVICE WITHOUT PRIOR AUTHORIZATION    *
*      OR FOR PURPOSES WHICH AUTHORIZATION HAS NOT BEEN  *
*          GRANTED IS STRICTLY PROHIBITED!!!             *
*********************************************************

User Access Verification

Username: Fred
Password:
*********************************************************
*          WARNING...WARNING...WARNING...WARNING         *
*                                                        *
*          THIS IS A REMINDER...THIS IS A REMINDER       *
*                                                        *
*          YOU HAVE ACCESSED A RESTRICTED DEVICE         *
*      USE OF THIS DEVICE WITHOUT PRIOR AUTHORIZATION    *
*      OR FOR PURPOSES WHICH AUTHORIZATION HAS NOT BEEN  *
*          GRANTED IS STRICTLY PROHIBITED!!!             *
*********************************************************
```

```
SecureRouter>en
Password:
SecureRouter#
```

Notice that the EXEC banner is displayed after the user has passed the local authentication phase on the router.

Configuring SNMP Security

There is no specific command that you use to enable SNMP. To configure SNMP support, perform the tasks described in the following steps, only the first two steps are mandatory:

1. Enable the SNMP community string to define the relationship between the network management station and the agent with the following command:

   ```
   snmp-server community <string> {ro|rw} {number}
   ```

   The *number* value references an optional access-list.

2. Use this command to configure the router to send traps to an NMS host:

   ```
   snmp-server host host [version {1|2c}] <community string> -
       <notification type>
   ```

3. Configure the type of traps for which a notification is sent to the NMS. You do so with the following command:

   ```
   snmp-server enable traps [notification type] -
       [notification option]
   ```

4. Set the system contact, location, and serial number. You can set the systems contact with the **snmp-server contact [*text*]** command. You set the location with the **snmp-server location [*text*]** command, and you set the serial number with the **snmp-server chassis-id [*text*]** command.

5. Use the **access-list** command to specify a list of hosts that are allowed read-, read/write, or write-only access to the router.

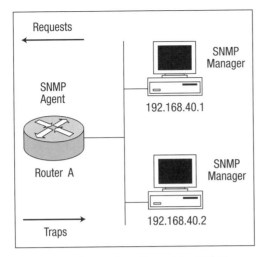

Figure 1.2   Router A configured for SNMP.

Figure 1.2 shows Router A, which is configured to allow SNMP read-only access and read/write access from two separate hosts. Router A is also configured to send SNMP trap information to the same two hosts. The following lines show how Router A should be configured so SNMP access from both host 192.168.40.1 and 192.168.40.2 is allowed and SNMP trap information is sent to both hosts:

```
access-list 12 permit 192.168.40.1
access-list 13 permit 192.168.40.2
snmp-server contact Harris
snmp-server location Network Engineering
snmp-server chassis-id 100000333
snmp-server community observe RO 12
snmp-server community adjust RW 13
snmp-server host 192.168.40.1 observe snmp
snmp-server host 192.168.40.2 adjust snmp
```

Configuring RIP Authentication

There are two versions of Routing Information Protocol (RIP): version 1 and version 2. RIP version 1 does not support authentication of routing updates; however, RIP version 2 supports both plain text and MD5 authentication. Figure 1.3 shows two routers, Router A and Router B, that exchange RIP version 2 MD5 authentication updates.

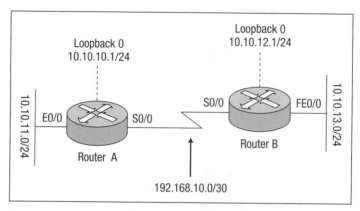

Figure 1.3   Router A and Router B configured for RIP authentication.

Configuring authentication of RIP version 2 updates is fairly easy and very uniform. The basic configuration includes the following steps:

1. Define the key chain using the command **key-chain** *<name>* in global configuration mode. This command transfers you to the key chain configuration mode.

2. Specify the key number with the **key** *<number>* command in key chain configuration mode. You can configure multiple keys.

3. For each key, identify the key string with the **key-string** *<string>* command.

4. Configure the period for which the key can be sent and received. Use the following commands:

```
accept-lifetime <starttime> {infinite|end-time|duration -
   seconds}
send-lifetime <starttime> {infinite|end-time|duration seconds}
```

5. Exit key chain configuration mode with the **exit** command.

6. Under interface configuration mode, enable the authentication of RIP updates with this command:

```
ip rip authentication key-chain <key chain name>
```

This command is all that is needed to use plain text authentication.

7. Optionally, under interface configuration mode, enable MD5 authentication of RIP updates using the **ip rip authentication mode md5** command.

The listings that follow show how Router A and Router B in Figure 1.3 should be configured to authenticate updates from one another using RIP MD5 authentication. Listing 1.1 shows the configuration of Router A, and Listing 1.2 shows the configuration of Router B.

Listing 1.1   Router A's configuration with MD5 authentication.

```
key chain systems
 key 1
  key-string router
!
interface Loopback0
 ip address 10.10.10.1 255.255.255.0
!
interface Ethernet0/0
 ip address 10.10.11.1 255.255.255.0
!
interface Serial0/0
 ip address 192.168.10.1 255.255.255.252
 ip rip authentication mode md5
 ip rip authentication key-chain systems
 clockrate 64000
!
router rip
 version 2
 network 10.0.0.0
 network 192.168.10.0
 no auto-summary
```

Listing 1.2   Router B's configuration with MD5 authentication.

```
key chain cisco
 key 1
  key-string router
!
interface Loopback0
 ip address 10.10.12.1 255.255.255.0
!
interface FastEthernet0/0
 ip address 10.10.13.1 255.255.255.0
!
interface Serial0/0
 ip address 192.168.10.2 255.255.255.252
 ip rip authentication mode md5
 ip rip authentication key-chain cisco
!
```

```
router rip
version 2
network 10.0.0.0
network 192.168.10.0
no auto-summary
```

The configuration in Listing 1.1 displays Router A's MD5 configuration. Router A is configured with a key chain value of **systems**, a key value of **1**, and a key-string value of **router**. Listing 1.2 displays Router B's MD5 configuration. Router B is configured with a key chain value of **cisco**, a key value of **1**, and a key-string value of **router**.

NOTE: *Notice that the **key-chain** <name> command of each router can have a different value; however, the **key-string** <string> command must match for each **key** <number> that is configured on each neighbor.*

You can use the command **debug ip rip** to examine how RIP receives the encrypted routing updates. Entering this command on Router A and Router B displays the output shown in Listing 1.3 and Listing 1.4, respectively.

Listing 1.3   The output of the command **debug ip rip** displays how Router A receives RIP routing updates from Router B.

```
Router-A#debug ip rip
RIP protocol debugging is on
Router-A#
RIP: received packet with MD5 authentication
RIP: received v2 update from 192.168.10.2 on Serial0/0
     10.10.12.0/24 -> 0.0.0.0 in 1 hops
     10.10.13.0/24 -> 0.0.0.0 in 1 hops
```

Listing 1.4   The output of the command **debug ip rip** displays how Router B receives RIP routing updates from Router A.

```
Router-B#debug ip rip
RIP protocol debugging is on
Router-B#
RIP: received packet with MD5 authentication
RIP: received v2 update from 192.168.10.1 on Serial0/0
     10.10.10.0/24 via 0.0.0.0 in 1 hops
     10.10.11.0/24 via 0.0.0.0 in 1 hops
```

Configuring EIGRP Authentication

EIGRP authentication of packets has been supported since IOS version 11.3. EIGRP route authentication is similar to RIP version 2, but EIGRP authentication supports only the MD5 version of packet encryption.

EIGRP's authentication support may at first seem limited, but plain text authentication should be configured only when neighboring routers do not support MD5. Because EIGRP is a proprietary routing protocol developed by Cisco, it can be spoken only between two Cisco devices, so the issue of another neighboring router not supporting the MD5 cryptographic checksum of packets should never arise.

The steps for configuring authentication of EIGRP updates are similar to the steps for configuring RIP version 2 authentication:

1. Define the key chain using the command **key-chain** *<name>* in global configuration mode. This command transfers you to the key chain configuration mode.

2. Specify the key number with the **key** *<number>* command in key chain configuration mode. You can configure multiple keys.

3. For each key, identify the key string with the **key-string** *<string>* command.

4. Optionally, you can configure the period for which the key can be sent and received. Use the following commands:

```
accept-lifetime <starttime> {infinite|end-time|duration -
    seconds}
send-lifetime <starttime> {infinite|end-time|duration seconds}
```

5. Exit key chain configuration mode with the **exit** command.

6. Under interface configuration mode, enable the authentication of EIGRP updates with this command:

```
ip authentication key-chain eigrp <autonomous system> -
    <key chain name>
```

7. Enable MD5 authentication of EIGRP updates using the following command:

```
ip authentication mode eigrp <autonomous system> md5
```

Listing 1.5 shows how Router A should be configured to authenticate updates from Router B using EIGRP MD5 authentication, and Listing 1.6 shows the configuration for Router B.

Listing 1.5   Router A's configuration with MD5 authentication.

```
key chain router-a
 key 1
  key-string eigrp
!
interface Loopback0
 ip address 10.10.10.1 255.255.255.0
!
interface Ethernet0/0
 ip address 10.10.11.1 255.255.255.0
!
interface Serial0/0
 ip address 192.168.10.1 255.255.255.252
 ip authentication mode eigrp 2 md5
 ip authentication key-chain eigrp 2 router-a
 clockrate 64000
!
router eigrp 2
 network 10.0.0.0
 network 192.168.10.0
 no auto-summary
 eigrp log-neighbor-changes
```

Listing 1.6   Router B's configuration with MD5 authentication.

```
key chain router-b
 key 1
  key-string eigrp
!
interface Loopback0
 ip address 10.10.12.1 255.255.255.0
!
interface Ethernet0/0
 ip address 10.10.13.1 255.255.255.0
!
interface Serial0/0
 ip address 192.168.10.2 255.255.255.252
 ip authentication mode eigrp 2 md5
 ip authentication key-chain eigrp 2 router-b
 clockrate 64000
!
router eigrp 2
 network 10.0.0.0
 network 192.168.10.0
```

```
no auto-summary
eigrp log-neighbor-changes
```

Listing 1.5 configures Router A with a key chain value of **router-a**, a key value of **1**, and a key-string value of **eigrp**. Listing 1.6 configures Router B with a key chain value of **router-b**, a key value of **1**, and a key-string value of **eigrp**. Notice again that the key chain need not match between routers; however, the key number and the key string associated with the key value must match between routers configured to use that key value.

Although debugging of encrypted EIGRP packets is somewhat limited, a few commands can be used to verify that packet encryption is taking place correctly. Two of those commands are **debug eigrp packet** and **show ip route**. The **debug eigrp packet** command informs you if the router has received a packet with the correct key value and key string. The output of issuing this command can be seen here:

```
Router-A#debug eigrp packet
EIGRP Packets debugging is on
(UPDATE, REQUEST, QUERY, REPLY, HELLO, IPXSAP, PROBE, ACK)
Router-A#
EIGRP: received packet with MD5 authentication
EIGRP: received packet with MD5 authentication
```

Router A is receiving MD5-authenticated packets from it neighbor, Router B. However, we cannot fully determine whether or not the authentication is taking place correctly without issuing the **show ip route** command on Router A. This allows us to look at the route table and determine that packet authentication is taking place correctly because the routes that Router B has sent to Router A are installed into the route table. Listing 1.7 displays the output of the **show ip route** command.

Listing 1.7   Route table of Router A with correct authentication configured.

```
Router-A#sh ip route
...
C  192.168.10.0/24 is directly connected, Ethernet0/0
C  10.10.10.0 is directly connected, Loopback0
C  10.10.11.0 is directly connected, Ethernet0/0
D  10.10.12.0 [90/409600] via 192.168.10.2, 00:18:36, Serial0/0
D  10.10.13.0 [90/409600] via 192.168.10.2, 00:18:36, Serial0/0
Router-A#
```

You can change Router A's key-string value for key 1 to see what kind of an effect this will have. The following lines will change the key-string value for key 1 on Router A to **ospf**:

```
Router-A#config t
Enter configuration commands, one per line.  End with CNTL/Z.
Router-A(config)#key chain router-a
Router-A(config-keychain)#key 1
Router-A(config-keychain-key)#key-string ospf
Router-A(config-keychain-key)#end
Router-A#
```

Now that Router A has a different key string associated with key 1, you would assume that packet authentication is not taking place correctly. By issuing the **debug eigrp packet** command, you can see that there is indeed a problem with authentication:

```
Router-A#debug eigrp packet
EIGRP Packets debugging is on
(UPDATE, REQUEST, QUERY, REPLY, HELLO, IPXSAP, PROBE, ACK)
Router-A#
EIGRP: received packet with MD5 authentication
EIGRP: ignored packet from 192.168.10.2 opcode = 5 (invalid
authentication)
```

Taking a quick look at the route table confirms that the authentication is incorrectly configured. Now that the key strings are different, no routes from Router B are installed into the route table of Router A. Listing 1.8 displays the routing table of Router A.

Listing 1.8   Route table of Router A with incorrect authentication configured.

```
Router-A#sh ip route
...
C    192.168.10.0/24 is directly connected, Ethernet0/0
     10.0.0.0/24 is subnetted, 2 subnets
C       10.10.10.0 is directly connected, Loopback0
C       10.10.11.0 is directly connected, Loopback1
Router-A#
```

TIP: You can also issue the **show ip eigrp neighbor** command to determine if authentication is configured correctly. If authentication is correctly configured, the neighboring router will be displayed in the output of the command. If authentication is incorrectly configured, the neighbor will not be displayed in the output.

Configuring OSPF Authentication

Open Shortest Path First (OSPF) supports two forms of authentication: plain text and MD5. Plain text authentication should be used only when neighboring devices do not support the more secure MD5 authentication. To configure plain text authentication of OSPF packets, follow these steps:

1. In interface configuration mode, use the **ip ospf authentication-key** <*key*> command. The key that is specified is the plain text password that will be used for authentication.

2. Enter OSPF configuration mode using the **router ospf** <*process id*> command. Then use the **area** <*area-id*> **authentication** command to configure plain text authentication of OSPF packets for an area.

Referring to Figure 1.4, we will configure Router A and Router B for plain text authentication of OSPF packets. Listing 1.9 and Listing 1.10 display each router's configuration.

Listing 1.9 Router A configured to authenticate OSPF packets using plain text authentication.

```
interface Loopback0
 ip address 10.10.10.1 255.255.255.0
!
interface Ethernet0/0
 ip address 10.10.11.1 255.255.255.0
!
interface Serial0/0
 ip address 192.168.10.1 255.255.255.252
 ip ospf authentication-key security
 clockrate 64000
```

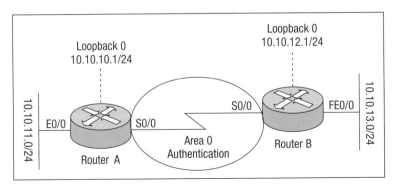

Figure 1.4 Router A and Router B configured for OSPF authentication.

```
router ospf 60
  area 0 authentication
  network 10.10.10.0 0.0.0.255 area 10
  network 10.10.11.0 0.0.0.255 area 11
  network 192.168.10.0 0.0.0.255 area 0
```

Listing 1.10   Router B configured to authenticate OSPF packets using plain text authentication.

```
interface Loopback0
  ip address 10.10.12.1 255.255.255.0
!
interface Ethernet0/0
  ip address 10.10.13.1 255.255.255.0
!
interface Serial0/0
  ip address 192.168.10.2 255.255.255.252
  ip ospf authentication-key security

router ospf 50
  area 0 authentication
  network 10.10.12.0 0.0.0.255 area 12
  network 10.10.13.0 0.0.0.255 area 13
  network 192.168.10.0 0.0.0.255 area 0
```

In Listing 1.9 and Listing 1.10, plain text authentication is configured to authenticate updates across area 0. By issuing the **show ip ospf** *<process-id>* command, you can determine if plain text authentication is properly configured for each area. Here is an example of the output for the **show ip ospf** command:

```
Router-B#show ip ospf 50
  Routing Process "ospf 50" with ID 10.10.13.1
  ......
      Area BACKBONE(0)
          Number of interfaces in this area is 1
          Area has simple password authentication
          SPF algorithm executed 7 times
```

To configure MD5 authentication of OSPF packets, follow the steps outlined here:

1. From interface configuration mode, enable the authentication of OSPF packets using MD5 with the following command:

```
ip ospf message-digest-key <key-id> md5 <key>
```

The value of the key-id allows passwords to be changed without having to disable authentication.

2. Enter OSPF configuration mode using the **router ospf** *<process id>* command. Then configure MD5 authentication of OSPF packets for an area using this command:

```
area <area-id> authentication message-digest
```

This time, Routers A and B will be configured to authenticate packets across the backbone using the MD5 version of authentication. Listing 1.11 shows the configuration for Router A, and Listing 1.12 shows Router B's configuration.

Listing 1.11 Router A configured for MD5 authentication.

```
interface Loopback0
 ip address 10.10.10.1 255.255.255.0
!
interface Ethernet0/0
 ip address 10.10.11.1 255.255.255.0
!
interface Serial0/0
 ip address 192.168.10.1 255.255.255.252
 ip ospf message-digest-key 15 md5 miller
 clockrate 64000

router ospf 60
 area 0 authentication message-digest
 network 10.10.10.0 0.0.0.255 area 10
 network 10.10.11.0 0.0.0.255 area 11
 network 192.168.10.0 0.0.0.255 area 0
```

Listing 1.12 Router B configured for MD5 authentication.

```
interface Loopback0
 ip address 10.10.12.1 255.255.255.0
!
interface Ethernet0/0
 ip address 10.10.13.1 255.255.255.0
!
interface Serial0/0
 ip address 192.168.10.2 255.255.255.252
 ip ospf message-digest-key 15 md5 miller

router ospf 50
 area 0 authentication message-digest
```

1. Securing the Infrastructure

```
network 10.10.12.0 0.0.0.255 area 12
network 10.10.13.0 0.0.0.255 area 13
network 192.168.10.0 0.0.0.255 area 0
```

When you use the **ip ospf message-digest-key** command, the key value allows the password to be changed without having to disable authentication.

NOTE: For OSPF, authentication passwords do not have to be the same throughout the area, but the key id value and the password must be the same between neighbors.

Using the **show ip ospf** *<process-id>* command again, you can see that it now states that MD5 authentication is being used across area 0:

```
Router-A#sh ip ospf 60
 Routing Process "ospf 60" with ID 10.10.11.1
......
    Area BACKBONE(0)
        Number of interfaces in this area is 1
        Area has message digest authentication
        SPF algorithm executed 4 times
```

As noted earlier, the key id value and the passwords must be the same between neighbors. If you change the key id value to a number other than 15 on Router A, authentication should not take place and OSPF should get mad. Here is the changed configuration:

```
interface Serial0/0
 ip address 192.168.10.1 255.255.255.252
 ip ospf message-digest-key 30 md5 miller
 clockrate 64000

router ospf 60
 area 0 authentication message-digest
 network 10.10.10.0 0.0.0.255 area 10
 network 10.10.11.0 0.0.0.255 area 11
 network 192.168.10.0 0.0.0.255 area 0
```

Notice that it has been changed to a value of **30**. The following lines show what OSPF has to say about this:

```
Router-A#debug ip ospf events
OSPF events debugging is on
Router-A#
00:03:58: OSPF: Send with youngest Key 30
```

```
00:04:04: OSPF: Rcv pkt from 192.168.10.2, Ethernet0/0 :
Mismatch Authentication Key - No message digest key 15 on
Interface
```

OSPF is obviously not happy. If you change the key value back, every-thing should again be all right. As mentioned earlier, the key id value allows passwords to be changed without having to disable authenti-cation. Listing 1.13 and Listing 1.14 display the configuration of Router A and Router B with multiple keys and passwords configured.

Listing 1.13   Router A configured with multiple keys and passwords.

```
interface Loopback0
 ip address 10.10.10.1 255.255.255.0
!
interface Ethernet0/0
 ip address 10.10.11.1 255.255.255.0
!
interface Serial0/0
 ip address 192.168.10.1 255.255.255.252
 ip ospf message-digest-key 15 md5 miller
 ip ospf message-digest-key 20 md5 ampaq
 clockrate 64000

router ospf 60
 area 0 authentication message-digest
 network 10.10.10.0 0.0.0.255 area 10
 network 10.10.11.0 0.0.0.255 area 11
 network 192.168.10.0 0.0.0.255 area 0
```

Listing 1.14   Router B configured with multiple keys and passwords.

```
interface Loopback0
 ip address 10.10.12.1 255.255.255.0
!
interface Ethernet0/0
 ip address 10.10.13.1 255.255.255.0
!
interface Serial0/0
 ip address 192.168.10.2 255.255.255.252
 ip ospf message-digest-key 15 md5 miller
 ip ospf message-digest-key 20 md5 ampaq

router ospf 50
 area 0 authentication message-digest
 network 10.10.12.0 0.0.0.255 area 12
 network 10.10.13.0 0.0.0.255 area 13
 network 192.168.10.0 0.0.0.255 area 0
```

As a result of this configuration, Routers A and B will send duplicate copies of each OSPF packet out of their serial interfaces; one will be authenticated using key number **15**, and the other will be authenticated using key number **20**. After the routers each receive from each other OSPF packets authenticated with key **20**, they will stop sending packets with the key number **15** and use only key number **20**. At this point, you can delete key number **15**, thus allowing you to change passwords without disabling authentication.

Configuring Route Filters

Route filters work by regulating what networks a router will advertise out of an interface to another router or what networks a router will accept on an interface from another router. Route filtering can be used by administrators to manually assure that only certain routes are announced from a specific routing process or interface. This feature allows administrators to configure their routers to prevent malicious routing attempts by intruders.

You can configure route filtering in one of two ways:

- *Inbound route filtering*—The router can be configured to permit or deny routes advertised by a neighbor from being installed to the routing process.

- *Outbound route filtering*—The route filter can be configured to permit or deny routes from being advertised from the local routing process, preventing neighboring routers from learning the routes.

Configuring Inbound Route Filters

The steps for configuring inbound route filters are as follows:

1. Use the **access list** global configuration command to configure an access-list that permits or denies the specific routes that are being filtered.

2. Under the routing protocol process, use the following command:

```
distribute-list <access-list-number> in [interface-name]
```

In this example, an inbound route filter will be configured on Router B to deny routes from being installed into its routing process (refer to Figure 1.5). Listing 1.15 displays Router A's configuration prior to applying the route filter, and Listing 1.16 displays Router B's.

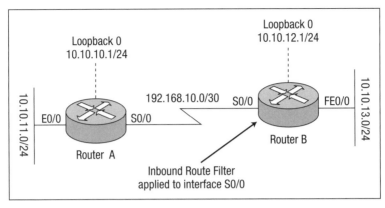

Figure 1.5   Router B configured with an inbound route filter.

Listing 1.15   Router A configuration.

```
interface Loopback0
 ip address 10.10.10.1 255.255.255.0
!
interface Loopback1
 ip address 10.10.11.1 255.255.255.0
!
interface Ethernet0/0
 ip address 10.10.12.1 255.255.255.0
!
interface Serial0/0
 ip address 192.168.10.1 255.255.255.252
 clockrate 64000
!
router rip
 version 2
 network 10.0.0.0
 network 192.168.10.0
 no auto-summary
```

Listing 1.16   Router B configuration.

```
interface Loopback0
 ip address 10.10.13.1 255.255.255.0
!
interface Loopback1
 ip address 10.10.14.1 255.255.255.0
!
interface FastEthernet0/0
 ip address 10.10.15.1 255.255.255.0
```

```
!
interface Serial0/0
 ip address 192.168.10.2 255.255.255.252
 !
router rip
 version 2
 network 10.0.0.0
 network 192.168.10.0
 no auto-summary
```

Taking a look at the route table of Router B, notice that it has learned of three networks from Router A: 10.10.10.0, 10.10.11.0, and 10.10.12.0. Listing 1.17 displays Router B's route table.

Listing 1.17   Router B's route table.

```
Router-B#show ip route
......

C        10.10.13.0 is directly connected, Loopback0
C        10.10.14.0 is directly connected, Loopback1
C        10.10.15.0 is directly connected, FastEthernet0/0
R        10.10.10.0 [120/1] via 192.168.10.1, 00:00:16, Serial0/0
R        10.10.11.0 [120/1] via 192.168.10.1, 00:00:16, Serial0/0
R        10.10.12.0 [120/1] via 192.168.10.1, 00:00:16, Serial0/0

Router-B#
```

Now, a route filter will be configured on Router B to deny the 10.10.10.0 and 10.10.11.0 networks from being installed into the route table. This will allow only the 10.10.12.0 network to be installed into the route table from Router A. Use the **access-list** *<number>* command to configure the router with a standard access list and use the **distrib-ute-list** *<list number>* in *<interface>* command to apply the access list under the routing process. Listing 1.18 displays Router B's new configuration.

Listing 1.18   Router B configured with an inbound route filter.

```
!
interface Serial0/0
 ip address 192.168.10.2 255.255.255.252
 !
router rip
 version 2
 network 10.0.0.0
 network 192.168.10.0
```

```
distribute-list 1 in Serial0/0
no auto-summary
!
access-list 1 permit 10.10.12.0
```

Looking back again at Router B's route table after applying the route filter, you can see that the 10.10.12.0 network is the only network that Router B is allowing to be installed into its route table. Listing 1.19 displays Router B's route table.

NOTE: *Access lists have an implicit* **deny any** *as the last configuration line that is not displayed in the output of the configuration. Therefore, there is no need to manually configure the access list to deny the .10 and .11 networks.*

Listing 1.19   Router B's route table with inbound route filter permitting only one network.

```
Router-B#show ip route
......

C       10.10.13.0 is directly connected, Loopback0
C       10.10.14.0 is directly connected, Loopback1
C       10.10.15.0 is directly connected, FastEthernet0/0
R       10.10.12.0 [120/1] via 192.168.10.1, 00:00:16, Serial0/0

Router-B#
```

Now, suppose Router A needs to learn only the 10.10.15.0 network from Router B and not the 10.10.13.0 and 10.10.14.0 networks. You can configure an inbound router filter on Router A to permit the installation of only the 10.10.15.0 network into the route table. Listing 1.15 displays Router A's configuration prior to the configuration change. Listing 1.20 displays the route table on Router A prior to the configuration change.

Listing 1.20   Route table of Router A.

```
Router-A#show  ip route
......
C       10.10.10.0 is directly connected, Loopback0
C       10.10.11.0 is directly connected, Loopback1
C       10.10.12.0 is directly connected, Ethernet0/0
R       10.10.13.0 [120/1] via 192.168.10.2, 00:00:17, Serial0/0
R       10.10.14.0 [120/1] via 192.168.10.2, 00:00:17, Serial0/0
R       10.10.15.0 [120/1] via 192.168.10.2, 00:00:17, Serial0/0
Router-A#
```

Listing 1.21 displays the configuration change needed on Router A.

Listing 1.21   Router A configured with an inbound route filter.

```
interface Serial0/0
 ip address 192.168.10.1 255.255.255.252
 !
router rip
 version 2
 network 10.0.0.0
 network 192.168.10.0
 distribute-list 1 in Serial0/0
 no auto-summary
!
access-list 1 permit 10.10.15.0
```

Taking another look at Router A's route table, you can see that the only network that is permitted into the route table is the 10.10.15.0 network. Listing 1.22 displays Router A's route table after the inbound route filter had been applied.

Listing 1.22   Router A's route table with inbound route filter permitting only one network.

```
Router-A#show  ip route
......
C       10.10.10.0 is directly connected, Loopback0
C       10.10.11.0 is directly connected, Loopback1
C       10.10.12.0 is directly connected, Ethernet0/0
R       10.10.15.0 [120/1] via 192.168.10.2, 00:00:17, Serial0/0
Router-A#
```

Configuring Outbound Route Filters

In the preceding section, you learned how to configure a router to accept only routes that the administrator deems necessary. However, Router A advertised the 10.10.10.0 and 10.10.11.0 networks all the way across the network only to have them dropped upon reaching Router B. Router B did the same with networks 10.10.13.0 and 10.10.14.0. The same results can be accomplished by configuring an outbound route filter. This filter will not allow the route to advertised across the network and gives the administrator finer granularity of control for advertising networks to external partners. The steps to configure outbound route filters are described here:

1. Use the **access-list** global configuration command to configure an access list that permits or denies the specific routes that are being filtered.

2. Under the routing protocol process, use the following command:

```
distribute-list access-list-number out [interface-name|-
routing - process|autonomous-system-number]
```

Continuing with the example, in the last section, you can configure Router A and Router B to accomplish the same results, using the reverse logic of inbound route filters and configure an outbound route filter. Router A, in listing 1.22, was configured to accept only the 10.10.15.0 network into its routing process, and Router B was configured to accept only the 10.10.12.0 network into its routing process. This was accomplished by configuring an inbound route filter on each respective router. However, a kind of reverse logic will be used in this next example to achieve the exact same result. Listing 1.23 and Listing 1.24 display Router A's and Router B's configuration prior to making the necessary changes.

Listing 1.23 Router A's configuration.

```
interface Loopback0
 ip address 10.10.10.1 255.255.255.0
!
interface Loopback1
 ip address 10.10.11.1 255.255.255.0
!
interface Ethernet0/0
 ip address 10.10.12.1 255.255.255.0
!
interface Serial0/0
 ip address 192.168.10.1 255.255.255.252
 clockrate 64000
!
router eigrp 50
 network 10.0.0.0
 network 192.168.10.0
 no auto-summary
 eigrp log-neighbor-changes
```

Listing 1.24 Router B's configuration.

```
interface Loopback0
 ip address 10.10.13.1 255.255.255.0
!
interface Loopback1
 ip address 10.10.14.1 255.255.255.0
!
interface FastEthernet0/0
 ip address 10.10.15.1 255.255.255.0
```

```
!
interface Serial0/0
 ip address 192.168.10.2 255.255.255.252
 !
router eigrp 50
 network 10.0.0.0
 network 192.168.10.0
 no auto-summary
 eigrp log-neighbor-changes
```

Notice that both routers are now using a different routing protocol. This was done to demonstrate that route filters work with any routing protocol. First, Router A will be configured such that it will advertise only the 10.10.12.0 network to Router B. This can be accomplished using the commands in Listing 1.25.

Listing 1.25   Router A configured with an outbound route filter.

```
interface Serial0/0
 ip address 192.168.10.1 255.255.255.252
 !
router eigrp 50
 network 10.0.0.0
 network 192.168.10.0
 distribute-list 3 out Serial0/0
 no auto-summary
 !
access-list 3 permit 10.10.12.0
```

Router A is configured with access list 3, which permits only the 10.10.12.0 network and has an outbound distribute-list applied to the EIGRP routing process. This should achieve the necessary results. You can check to see if the results have been met by looking at the route table of Router B, which is displayed in Listing 1.26.

Listing 1.26   Route table of Router B after applying an outbound route filter on Router A.

```
Router-B#show ip route
......
D       10.10.12.0 [90/409600] via 192.168.10.1, Serial0/0
C       10.10.13.0 is directly connected, Loopback0
C       10.10.14.0 is directly connected, Loopback1
C       10.10.15.0 is directly connected, FastEthernet0/0
Router-B#
```

Router A is only advertising the 10.10.12.0 network to Router B; thus, Router B only knows about the 10.10.12.0 network. Now Router B must be configured such that Router A only learns the 10.10.15.0 network. Listing 1.27 displays the configuration that is needed on Router B.

Listing 1.27   Router B configured with an outbound route filter.

```
interface Serial0/0
 ip address 192.168.10.2 255.255.255.252
 !
router eigrp 50
 network 10.0.0.0
 network 192.168.10.0
 distribute-list 3 out Serial0/0
 no auto-summary
!
access-list 4 permit 10.10.15.0
```

Router B is configured with access list 4, which permits only the 10.10.15.0 network and has an outbound distribute-list applied to the EIGRP routing process. The next step is to check the route table of Router A to determine if the required results have been met. Listing 1.28 displays the route table of Router A.

Listing 1.28   Route table of Router A after applying an outbound route filter on Router B.

```
Router-A#sh ip route
......
C     10.10.10.0 is directly connected, Loopback0
C     10.10.11.0 is directly connected, Loopback1
C     10.10.12.0 is directly connected, Ethernet0/0
D     10.10.15.0 [90/409600] via 192.168.10.2, Serial0/0
Router-A#
```

After viewing the route table of Router A, you can determine that Router B is advertising only the 10.10.15.0 network to Router A; thus, Router A only knows about the 10.10.15.0 network.

Suppressing Route Advertisements

To prevent other routers on a network from learning about routes dynamically, you can prevent routing update messages from being sent out a router interface. To accomplish this, use the **passive-interface** *<interface>* routing process configuration command. This command can be used on all IP-based routing protocols except for the Exterior Gateway Protocol (EGP) and Border Gateway Protocol (BGP). When an interface is configured to be in a passive state, the router disables the passing of routing protocol advertisements out of the interface; however, the interface still listens and accepts any route advertisement that is received into the interface. Configuring this on a router essentially makes the router a silent host over the interfaces that were specified. To configure an interface as passive, use the **passive-interface** *<interface>* command under routing protocol configuration mode; this command is all that is needed to make an interface no longer advertise networks.

Here is an example of configuring an interface as passive:

```
interface FastEthernet0/0
 ip address 10.10.15.1 255.255.255.0
 !
interface Serial0/0
 ip address 192.168.10.2 255.255.255.252
!
router eigrp 50
 passive-interface FastEthernet0/0
 passive-interface Serial0/0
 !
```

Configuring HTTP Access

Cisco routers include an HTTP server, which makes configuration and administration easier, especially for someone who does not have a lot of experience with the command-line interface. The HTTP server function is disabled by default and must be manually enabled. Follow these steps to enable the HTTP server functionality (only the first step is mandatory):

1. To enable the HTTP server, use the **ip http server** global configuration command.

2. You can specify the authentication method the router should use to authenticate users who attempt a connection to the server with the following global configuration command:

   ```
   ip http authentication {aaa|enable|local|tacacs}
   ```

3. You can control which hosts can access the HTTP server using this global configuration command:

   ```
   ip http access-class {access list number|access list name}
   ```

4. By default, the HTTP server listens for connection attempts on port 80. This can be changed using the **ip http port** *<number>* global configuration command.

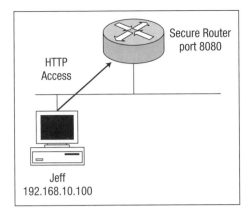

Figure 1.6   User Jeff needs HTTP access to the router.

Figure 1.6 displays a host named **Jeff** at IP address 192.168.10.100 who uses his Web browser to administer the router. Jeff accesses the HTTP server on the router on port 8080 and uses the local method of authentication. The following example configuration displays the HTTP server configuration that is needed so that Jeff can access the router.

```
SecureRouter#show running-config
......
username Jeff privilege 10 password 0 NewUser
!
interface FastEthernet0/0
 ip address 192.168.10.1 255.255.255.0
!
ip http server
ip http port 8080
ip http access-class 20
ip http authentication local
!
access-list 20 permit 192.168.10.100
!
```

WARNING! *If the HTTP server is enabled and local authentication is used, it is possible, under some circumstances, to bypass the authentication and execute any command on the device. For further information, please see the following Web page: www.cisco.com/warp/public/707/IOS-httplevel-pub.html.*

Chapter 2

AAA Security Technologies

In Brief

Chapter 1 covered security issues that are common to the infrastructure of a network and the counter measures that are needed to mitigate the effects of these issues. This chapter addresses the issues of unauthorized access and repudiation for enterprise environments, which both create a potential for intruders to gain access to sensitive network equipment.

I'll begin with a detailed examination of Cisco's authentication, authorization, and accounting (AAA) architecture and the technologies that not only use these features but also provide them. I'll discuss both of the major protocols used to provide the AAA architecture: TACACS+ and RADIUS. The focus will then shift to configuring network access servers and networking equipment to provide the security features of the AAA architectures. Then, I'll also examine the Cisco Secure Access Control Server (ACS) software. Cisco Secure Access Control Server is designed to ensure the security of networks and maintain detailed records of the people connecting to your networking devices.

Access Control Security

Access control has long been an issue that has frustrated both administrators and users alike. As networks continue to evolve into a state of convergence, administrators increasingly need flexibility to determine and control access to resources under their care. Administrators are being faced with new situations pertaining to remote access combined with strong security. For example, remote users and telecommuters need to access their corporate networks; they need to be able to work in the same network environment they would be working in if they were sitting at their desks at the office. This creates a significant need for an administrator to effectively give those users flexible and seamless access, yet at the same time, the administrator must have the ability to provide security and resource accountability. Also, within most networks, different administrators have varying responsibilities that require varying levels of access privileges.

There are three components to access control:

- Determining who is allowed access to a network
- Determining what services they are allowed to access
- Providing detailed accounting records of the services that were accessed

Access control is based on a modular architecture known as authentication, authorization, and accounting (AAA). The AAA network security services provide the framework through which you set up access control on your router. As mentioned earlier, AAA is based on a modular architecture; as such, each module will be discussed separately.

Authentication

Authentication is the process of determining whether someone or something is, in fact, who or what it is declaring to be. In private and public computer networks, authentication is commonly accomplished through the use of logon passwords. The assumption is that knowledge of the password guarantees the authenticity of the user. Each user registers initially using an assigned or self-declared password. On each subsequent use, the user must know and use the previously declared password.

Authentication provides a way of identifying a user, typically by having the user enter a valid username and valid password before access is granted. The process of authentication is based on each user having a unique set of criteria for gaining access. The AAA server compares a user's authentication credentials with other user credentials stored in a database. If the supplied credentials match, the user is granted access to the network. If the supplied credentials don't match, authentication fails and network access is denied. The authentication database may be configured either in a local security database, using the **username** *<username>* **password** *<password>* command discussed in Chapter 1, or with a remote security database, such as a Cisco Secure ACS server.

Authentication Methods

There are many forms of authentication; the most common is of course the use of usernames and passwords. Username and password combinations can range from very weak to somewhat strong. Other authentication methods provide far stronger security at an increased cost financially and increased complexity from a manageability standpoint. The trade-off is that weaker methods of authentication are often much easier to administer, whereas the stronger methods of authentication involve a greater degree of difficulty to administer. The following list includes the advantages and disadvantages of some of the popular current authentication methods:

- *Usernames and passwords*—This method has been the predominant method of authentication in the client/server environment. This is the least scalable method of authentication because usernames and passwords need to be assigned for each user and cannot be managed on a groupwide basis. Usernames and passwords may be assigned in a static manner so that they do not change unless they are changed manually by the administrator or user. Or they can be assigned so that after a certain period of time they age out and must be changed by the administrator or user.

Advantages:

- Inexpensive and easy to implement.
- Can be implemented entirely within software, avoiding the need for extra hardware.
- Username and password carried over hashed encryption.

Disadvantages:

- Increasingly prone to "eavesdropping" as username and password travel over the network.
- Subject to replay attacks.
- Subject to password guessing.
- Ineffective password management and controls.
- Can be captured by Trojan horses under false pretences.
- Susceptible to "Social Engineering."

- *Token Cards/Smart Cards*—These are typically small credit-card-sized devices that use a hardware-based challenge-response authentication scheme in which the server challenges the user to demonstrate that he possesses a specific hardware token and knows a PIN or passphrase by combining them to generate a response that is valid. This method of authentication has become very popular in recent years.

Advantages:

- Ease of use for users; they only need to remember a single PIN to access the token.
- Ease of management; there is only one token instead of multiple passwords.
- Enhanced security; the attacker requires both the PIN and the token to masquerade as the user.
- Better accountability.
- Mobility; security is not machine specific.
- No client-side software needed.

Disadvantages:

- Client is required to carry a token card to use facilities.
- Limited life span; tokens must be replaced about every four years.
- Ongoing operations cost associated with keeping track of token cards.
- Longer time to authenticate the identity of the user because numerous steps are required to authenticate the client.
- *Digital Certificates*—Digital certificates are electronic documents that are generally issued by a trusted third party called a Certificate Authority. The certificates contain information about the user that the Certificate Authority has verified to be true. They consist of a *public key* denoted by a series of characters, which reside on the user's computer. When an electronic message is sent from the mobile client to the enterprise, it is signed using the digital certificate. Digital certificates are an essential part of the public key infrastructure (PKI) because PKI manages the process of issuing and verifying the certificates used to grant people and systems access to other systems.

NOTE: *Digital certificates will be discussed in detail in Chapter 6, "Internet Security Protocol (IPSec)."*

Advantages that Digital certificates provide are as follows:

- Validation of file's creator. Recipients need to know that the sender created the file.
- Nonrepudiation.
- Confidentiality ensured.
- Guaranteed integrity.
- Personalization scalability features.
- Industry momentum is growing for digital certificates.

Disadvantages:

- Complicated for most users to install.
- Must be installed on every computer.
- Not feasible where users share machines.
- Extensive integration.

PAP and CHAP Authentication

Remote access is an integral part of any corporate mission. Traveling salespeople, executives, and telecommuters all need to communicate by connecting to the main office local area network. To make these remote connections, remote users should have appropriate software, protocol stacks, and link-layer drivers installed on their remote access device. Point-to-point links between local area networks can provide sufficient physical connectivity in many application environments. Most corporations provide access to the Internet over point-to-point links, thus providing an efficient way to access their service provider locally. The Internet community has adopted the Point-to-Point Protocol (PPP) scheme for the transmission of IP datagrams over serial point-to-point lines. PPP is a Data Link layer protocol that provides router-to-router and host-to-network connections over synchronous and asynchronous circuits. PPP has the following three main components:

- It has a method for encapsulating datagrams over serial links.

- *Link Control Protocols (LCPs)* establish, configure, authenticate, and test datalink connections.

- *Network Control Protocols (NCPs)* establish and configure different Network-layer protocols.

Link Control Protocols are used as a security measure for authentication with PPP and PPP callback. This method of authentication allows the dial-up destination to determine if the dial-up client is correctly authenticated based on a preassigned username and password combination. Point-to-Point Protocol (PPP) currently supports two authentication protocols: Password Authentication Protocol (PAP) and Challenge Handshake Authentication Protocol (CHAP). Both PAP and CHAP are specified in RFC 1334. The dial-up destination uses either PAP or CHAP to determine if the dial-up client is authenticated.

PAP provides a simple method for the remote client to establish its identity using a one-way authentication handshake when communication is taking place between a host and an access server; this is detailed in Figure 2.1.

The PAP authentication process occurs as follows:

1. Incoming client establishes PPP negotiation on the interface configured with PPP encapsulation and informs the access server to use PPP.

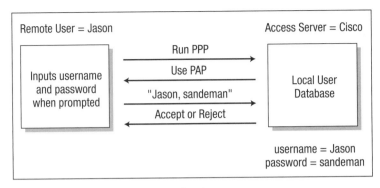

Figure 2.1   One-way PAP authentication.

2. The network access server determines which authentication method to use. In this case, the network access server tells the remote client to use PAP.

3. The client sends the username and password in cleartext PAP format to the network access server.

4. The network access server compares the values passed to it from the remote client against the values configured within its local database or queries a security server to accept or reject the remote client.

When communication is taking place between two routers, PAP uses a two-way authentication handshake; a username/password pair is repeatedly sent by the peer to the authenticator until the authentication is acknowledged or the connection is terminated. For PAP, this process proves to be an insecure authentication method because the password is passed over the link in cleartext. With PAP, there is no protection from playback.

With CHAP authentication, the access server sends a challenge message to the remote node after the PPP link is established. The access server checks the response against its own calculation of the expected hash value. If the values match, the authentication is accepted. This is detailed in Figure 2.2.

The following list explains the CHAP authentication process:

1. The incoming client establishes PPP negotiation on the interface configured with PPP encapsulation.

2. LCP negotiates CHAP and Message Digest 5 (MD5), and the network access informs the remote client to use CHAP.

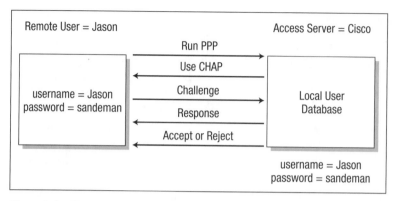

Figure 2.2   Three-way CHAP authentication.

3. The remote client acknowledges the request.

4. A CHAP packet is built and sent to the remote client. The CHAP packet contains the following items:

   • Packet type identifier

   • Sequential identification number

   • Random number

   • Authentication name

5. The remote client processes the CHAP challenge packet as follows:

   • Sequential id is run through a MD5 hash generator.

   • Random number is run through a MD5 hash generator.

   • Authentication name is used to determine the password.

   • Password is run through the MD5 hash generator.

   The result is a one-way hash CHAP challenge that will be sent back to the network access server in a CHAP response packet.

6. The CHAP response packet is received by the network access server and the following occurs:

   • The sequential id number identifies the original challenge.

   • The sequential id number is run through a MD5 hash generator.

   • The original random number is run through a MD5 hash generator.

   • The authentication name is used to look up a password.

   • The password is run through the MD5 hash generator.

   • The hash value that was received is then compared against the value the network access server calculated.

7. If authentication was successful, a CHAP success packet is built and sent to the remote client. Likewise, if authentication is unsuccessful, a CHAP failure packet is built and sent to the remote client.

CHAP provides protection against playback attacks through the use of a variable challenge value that is unique and unpredictable. The use of repeated challenges every two minutes during any CHAP session is intended to limit the time of exposure of any single attack. The access server controls the frequency and timing of the challenges.

Authorization

After authentication, a user must be authorized to do certain tasks. Simply put, *authorization* is the process of enforcing policies (or giving someone permission to do or have something)—determining what types or qualities of activities, resources, or services a user is permitted. After authenticating into a system, for instance, the user may try to issue commands. The authorization process determines whether the user has the authority to do so. Sometimes, authorization can occur within the context of authentication. After you have authenticated a user, she needs to be authorized for different types of access or activity. You configure the network device to control user access to the network so that users can perform only functions that are deemed to be within the context of their authentication credentials.

When authorization takes place, a set of attributes describing what actions a user is authorized to perform is compiled. After a user attempts to gain access to a system, the network device determines and enforces the permissions of the user based on the authorization information contained within the database and the user's authentication credentials. The assembled attributes may be configured in either a local security database or a remote security database, such as a Cisco Secure ACS server.

Accounting

Accounting, which is the third major requirement in the AAA security system, is the process of recording what the user does in addition to what the user accesses and for how long. You can also use accounting to measure the resources users consume during their sessions. This can include the amount of system time or the amount of data a user has sent and/or received during a session. Accounting is accomplished through logging of session statistics and usage information, and it's used for authorization control, billing, trend analysis, resource utilization, and capacity planning activities, which form an audit trail when combined. All of the information that is gathered during the accounting phase can be used to provide audit documentation to customers or clients.

An accounting record typically contains the following information:

- Username
- Network address
- Service accessed
- Start time, stop time, and date
- Log origination date and time

AAA Protocols

Many protocols require authentication verification before providing authorization and access rights to the user or device. Each of the protocols that will be discussed in detail in the following sections is an example of such protocols. TACACS+ and RADIUS are the two predominant protocols implemented with security servers and used by networking devices. A third protocol, Kerberos, is used in some enterprise environments to first verify that users and the network services they use are really who and what they claim to be before granting access privileges. These protocols forward information between the network device and the security server.

TACACS+

Terminal Access Controller Access Control Plus (TACACS+) is a security server protocol that enables central control of users attempting to gain access into networking devices. TACACS+ is the latest generation of the TACACS protocol, which was developed by the BBN for MILNET. At that time, TACACS was primarily a User Datagram Protocol (UDP) access-based protocol that orchestrated user access. There are three versions of TACACS:

- *TACACS*—An industry-standard protocol that forwards usernames and passwords to a central security server. TACACS is specified in RFC 1492. The original version of TACACS combined authentication and authorization and was based on the UDP protocol.

- *XTACACS*—An enhanced version of TACACS with extensions that Cisco added (thus, the "X" for "extension") to support advanced features. The most notable advanced feature is the added functionality for multiprotocol support and authorization of multifunction connections with syslog exporting. XTACACS separated authentication, authorization, and accounting. It has been superseded by TACACS+.

- *TACACS+*—Supported by the Cisco family of routers and access servers beginning in Cisco IOS release 10.3. TACACS+ is the third generation of Terminal Access Control, which is a Cisco proprietary client/server protocol. TACACS+ uses TCP as its transport protocol, and the server daemon usually listens on port 49. Its use originates from the need to manage and control terminal access. Its functions are based on the classic server/client relationship, using request and response to determine, in an algorithm format, whether or not users are authenticated, authorized, and accounted for. This protocol is a completely new version of the TACACS protocol referenced by RFC 1492.

TACACS+ surpasses TACACS and XTACACS, and furthermore, it's not compatible with its predecessors, which are considered end of life (EOL) by Cisco and should probably not be considered for implementation.

TACACS+ Benefits

TACACS+ uses TCP as the communication protocol to communicate between the network device and the security server on reserved port number 49. TCP, as opposed to UDP, was chosen in part because of its inherent capability to reliably retransmit data packets. Using MD5, TACACS+ also encrypts the data payload of the packet. However, the 12-byte header of a TACACS+ packet is sent in cleartext. Figure 2.3 shows the header of a TACACS+ packet.

TACACS+ Authentication Process

The TACACS+ protocol forwards many types of username/password information. The information is encrypted over the network with the MD5 encryption algorithm. TACACS+ authentication also supports multiple challenge and response demands from the TACACS+ server.

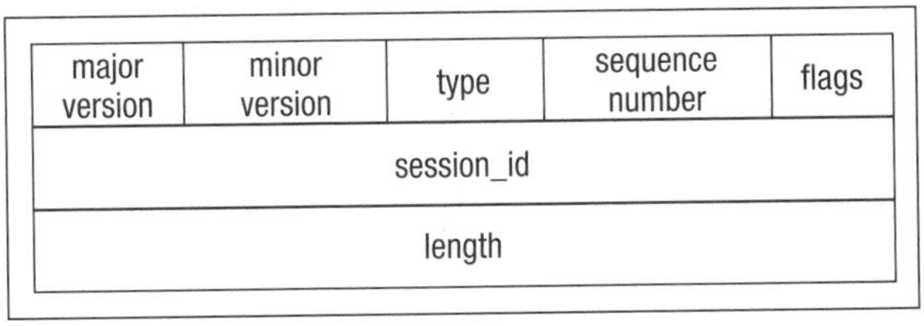

major version	minor version	type	sequence number	flags
session_id				
length				

Figure 2.3   TACACS+ packet header.

A TACACS+ server can authenticate a user based on its own internal username and password database, or it can act as a client to authenticate the user based on various other authentication systems, such as a Windows NT domain controller. The TACACS+ authentication process typically begins with the network access server sending a START message to the TACACS+ server. The START packet is always sent only as the first packet in the authentication process or following a reset.

Upon receipt of the START packet from the network access server, the TACACS+ server sends a REPLY packet with the value set to **GET USER**. This will present the client with a username prompt. The access server gets the requested information and returns it to the TACACS+ server in a CONTINUE packet. If the username is found either in the local database on the TACACS+ server or in an external database, the server sends another REPLY packet with the value set to **GET PASS**. This will present the client with a password prompt. The access server again gets the requested information and returns it to the TACACS+ server in a CONTINUE packet. If the password is found either in the local database on the TACACS+ server or in an external database and it creates a match with the corresponding username, the server sends another REPLY message with the value set to **ACCEPT** or **REJECT**. The authentication process is detailed in Figure 2.4.

NOTE: *One other TACACS+ packet can be returned to the network access server from the security server. The ERROR packet is sent in the event of an error due to a failed daemon or network congestion problem during the authentication phase. If the network access server receives an ERROR packet from the security server, it will attempt to authenticate the client using the next configured method in the method list.*

TACACS+ Authorization Process

Unlike the authentication process, the TACACS+ authorization process defines only two types of messages, REQUEST and RESPONSE. The authorization process begins with the network access server sending to the TACACS+ server a REQUEST packet requesting authorization. The REQUEST packet contains certain values that it sends to the TACACS+ server to distinguish the user. These values include the following:

- Authentication method
- Privilege level
- Authentication type
- Authentication service

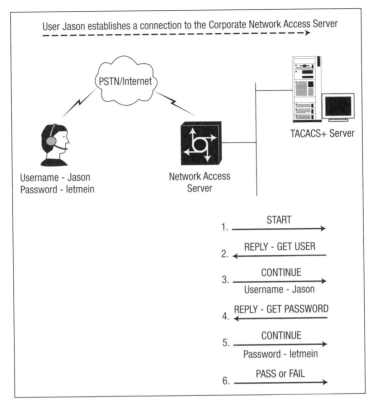

Figure 2.4   TACACS+ authentication.

After receipt of the REQUEST packet from the network access server, the TACACS+ server determines the permissions the user has and sends back a RESPONSE packet with bundled attributes to the network access server. The TACACS+ authorization process can be seen in Figure 2.5.

TACACS+ Accounting Process

Accounting is usually the final phase of the AAA architecture. The TACACS+ accounting phase and authorization phase are similar. The accounting process begins with the network access server sending an accounting REQUEST packet to the TACACS+ server. The REQUEST packet contains many of the same values that the authorization packet contained. After receiving the REQUEST packet, the TACACS+ server acknowledges the request with a RESPONSE packet indicating that all accounting took place correctly.

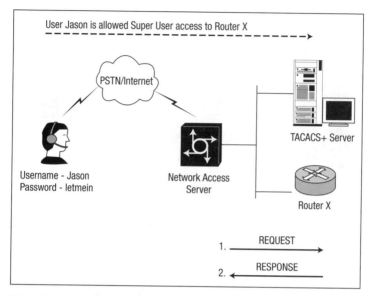

Figure 2.5   TACACS+ authorization.

RADIUS

RADIUS (Remote Access Dial In User Service) is an Internet security protocol originally developed by Livingston Enterprises. It is defined in RFC 2138 and RFC 2139. RADIUS uses UDP as its transport protocol and is generally considered to be a connectionless service. RADIUS clients run on routers and send authentication requests to a central RADIUS server, which contains all the user authentication credentials. The following list includes some key aspects of RADIUS that have led to its success:

- Open protocol
- Based on client/server architecture
- Support for many authentication mechanisms
- Encrypted transactions between client and server
- Centralized authentication
- Interoperability with other protocols

RADIUS is a fully open protocol, which means that the source code is freely available and can be modified to work with any security system on the market. This allows RADIUS to be tailored to suit the particular needs of a particular environment. RADIUS is based on a client/server model. The remote machine acts as the client, and the security RADIUS server at the other end handles authentication.

RADIUS supports the AAA model just as TACACS+ does; however, RADIUS combines authentication and authorization and separates only accounting. RADIUS is able to interact with other authentication protocols, such as TACACS, XTACACS, and TACACS+.

RADIUS Authentication Process

RADIUS supports a variety of methods for authenticating users, in part, because it is an open protocol. A RADIUS server can authenticate a user based on its own internal username or password list, or it can act as a client to authenticate the user based on various other authentication systems, such as a Windows NT domain controller. The method used, of course, depends on a specific vendor's implementation of RADIUS. Typically, a user login is queried from the network access server to the RADIUS server and a response is sent from the RADIUS server. The user login consists of what is commonly referred to as an Access-Request, and the server response is commonly referred to as an Access-Accept or an Access-Reject. The Access-Request packet contains the username, encrypted password, IP address, and port. After the RADIUS server receives the Access-Request packet, it begins to query its database for a matching username and password pair. If it cannot find a match, the server sends an Access-Reject packet back to the network access server. If it finds a match, the server sends an Access-Accept packet back to the network access server. This is detailed in Figure 2.6.

NOTE: *There is a third response a RADIUS server can use: Access-Challenge. A challenge packet sent from the RADIUS server simply asks the network access server to gather additional data from the client. Challenge packets are typically sent during an established session.*

RADIUS Authorization Process

As mentioned earlier, RADIUS combines authentication and authorization. But to a small degree, they are separate. The RADIUS authentication process must be complete before the authorization process can begin. After the RADIUS server has found within its database a matching pair for the credentials that were supplied to it from the network access server during the authentication phase, the RADIUS server returns an Access-Accept response to the network access server. It is at this point that the RADIUS server bundles within the Access-Accept packet a list of attribute-value pairs that determine the parameters to be used for this session. (Refer to Figure 2.6 earlier in this chapter.)

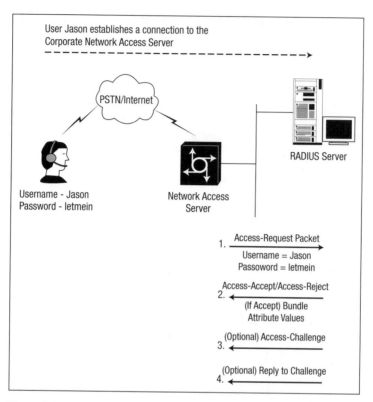

Figure 2.6   RADIUS authentication process.

RADIUS Accounting Process

The network access server and RADIUS server communicate accounting information between one another on UDP port 1646. It is the network access server's responsibility to send accounting information to
the RADIUS server after initial authentication and authorization is complete, and it does so by sending an Accounting-Request packet to the
server. This is considered the Accounting-Start packet. Because RADIUS
implements services using the UDP protocol (which is connectionless
oriented), the RADIUS server has the responsibility of acknowledging
the Accounting-Request packet with an Accounting-Response packet.
When the session is complete, the network access server sends another
Accounting-Request packet to the RADIUS security server, detailing the
delivered service. This is considered the Accounting-Stop packet. Finally,
the RADIUS security server sends an Accounting-Response packet back
to the network access server, acknowledging the receipt of the stop
packet. This is detailed in Figure 2.7.

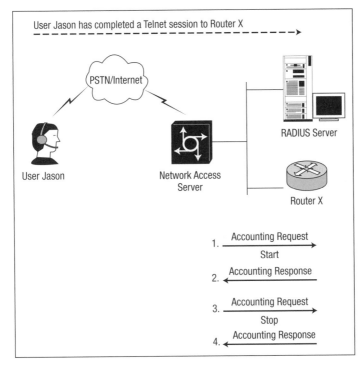

User Jason has completed a Telnet session to Router X

PSTN/Internet

User Jason

Network Access Server

RADIUS Server

Router X

1. Accounting Request Start
2. Accounting Response
3. Accounting Request Stop
4. Accounting Response

Figure 2.7   RADIUS accounting process.

Cisco Secure Access Control Server

Cisco Secure Access Control Server (ACS) is a scalable, centralized user access control software package for both Unix and Windows NT. Cisco Secure ACS offers centralized command and control of all user authentication, authorization, and accounting services via a Web-based, graphical interface. With Cisco Secure ACS, an enterprise can quickly administer accounts and globally change levels of security for entire groups of users. The Cisco Secure security server is designed to ensure the security of your network by providing authentication and authorization services and to track the activity of the people who connect to the network by providing feature-rich accounting services. The Cisco Secure security server software supports these features by using either the TACACS+ or RADIUS protocols. As mentioned, the Cisco Secure ACS software can run on either a Windows NT server or a Unix server; I'll discuss the Windows NT version.

Cisco Secure ACS for Windows

Cisco Secure ACS supports any network access servers that can be configured with the TACACS+ or RADIUS protocol. Cisco Secure ACS helps to centralize access control and accounting for dial-up access servers and firewalls and makes it easier to manage access to routers and switches. Cisco Secure ACS uses the TACACS+ and RADIUS protocols to provide AAA services to ensure a secure environment.

Cisco Secure ACS can authenticate users against any of the following user databases:

- Windows NT
- Windows 2000 Active Directory
- Cisco Secure ACS
- Novell NetWare Directory Services (NDS), version 4.6 or greater
- Generic Lightweight Directory Access Protocol (LDAP)
- Microsoft Commercial Internet System (MCIS)
- Relational databases fully compliant with Microsoft Open Database Connectivity (ODBC)

Cisco Secure ACS Requirements

To install Cisco Secure ACS, you must ensure that the system on which you are installing the software package meets the minimum system requirements, which are as follows:

- Pentium II, 300MHz processor or faster
- Windows NT Server 4 (with service pack 6a) or Windows 2000 Server
- 128MB RAM; recommended 256MB
- At least 250MB of free disk space; more if you're using the Cisco Secure local database
- Minimum resolution of 256 colors for 800×600
- Microsoft Internet Explorer 4.*x* or higher or Netscape Communicator 4.*x* or higher
- JavaScript enabled
- Microsoft Internet Information Server for User Changeable Passwords utility (optional)

Cisco Secure ACS Architecture

Cisco Secure ACS is designed to be both flexible and modular. Within the context of Cisco Secure ACS, *modular* refers to the seven modules that make up the architecture of the AAA server. These modules are installed as services within Windows NT and can be stopped and started by using the settings accessed by clicking the Services icon within Control Panel in Windows NT Server. The modules are described in the following list:

- *CSAdmin*—Cisco Secure is equipped with its own internal Web server and, as such, does not require the presence of a third-party Web server. CSAdmin is the service that controls the operation of the internal Web server, allowing users to remotely manage the server via the Web interface.

- *CSAuth*—CSAuth is the database manager that acts as the authentication and authorization service. The primary purpose of the CSAuth service is to authenticate and authorize requests to permit or deny access to users. CSAuth determines if access should be granted and, if access is granted, defines the privileges for a particular user.

- *CSTacacs and CSRadius*—The CSTacacs and CSRadius services communicate with the CSAuth module and the network access device that is requesting authentication and authorization services. CSTacacs is used to communicate with TACACS+ devices and CSRadius is used to communicate with RADIUS devices. The CSTacacs and CSRadius services can run at the same time. When only one protocol is used, only the corresponding service needs to be running; however, the other service will not interfere with normal operation and does not need to be disabled.

- *CSLog*—CSLog is the service used to capture logging information. It gathers data from the TACACS+ or RADIUS packet and the CSAuth service and then manipulates the data to be placed into the comma-separated value (CSV) files for exporting.

- *CSMon*—CSMon is a service that provides monitoring, recording, notification, and response for both TACACS+ and RADIUS protocols. The monitoring function monitors the general health of the machine the application is running on, as well as the application and the resources that Cisco Secure ACS is using on the server. Recording records all exception events within the server logs. Notification can be configured to send an email in the event of an error state on the server, and Response responds to the error by logging the event, sending notifications, and, if the event is a failure, carrying out a pre-defined or user-configured response.

- *CSDBSync*—CSDBSync is the service used to synchronize the Cisco Secure ACS database with third-party relational database management system (RDBMS) system.

Cisco Secure ACS Database

You can configure the Cisco Secure ACS server to use a user-defined database that is local to the server or you can configure an external user database, such as a Windows NT Server. There are advantages and disadvantages to each.

When the Cisco Secure ACS server is configured to use the local database for authentication of usernames and passwords and it receives a request from the network access server, it searches its local database for the credentials that were supplied in the REPLY packet of the GETUSER packet. If it finds a match for the GETUSER packet, it compares the values that it receives from the REPLY packet of the GETPASS packet to the locally configured password for the account. The Cisco Secure ACS server then returns a pass or fail response to the network access server. After the user has been authenticated, the Cisco Secure ACS server sends the attributes of authorization to the network access server. The advantage to using the locally configured database is ease of administration and speed. The disadvantage is that manual configuration is needed to populate the database.

You can also configure the Cisco Secure ACS server to authenticate usernames and passwords credentials against those already defined within a Windows NT or 2000 user database. If the Cisco Secure ACS server receives a request from the network access server, it searches its local database to find a match. If it does not find a match and the server is configured to forward requests to an external user database, the username and password are forwarded to the external database for authentication. The external database forwards back to the Cisco Secure ACS server a pass or fail response. If a match is confirmed, the username is stored in the Cisco Secure user database for future authentication requests; however, the password is not stored. This allows the user to authenticate much faster for subsequent requests.

In enterprises that have a substantial Windows NT network already installed, Cisco Secure ACS can leverage the work already invested in building the database without any additional input. This eliminates the need for separate databases. An added benefit of using an external user database is that the username and password used for authentication are also used to log into the network. This allows you to configure the Cisco Secure ACS so that users need to enter their usernames and passwords only once, thus providing a single login. One of the major disadvantages of using an external database for authentication is that the Cisco Secure server cannot store any third-party passwords such as PAP and CHAP passwords. Also, in the event of a network issue that prevents the Cisco Secure ACS server from receiving a response from the external database for an authentication request, you could potentially lock yourself out of the network access server because the user never gets authenticated.

2. AAA Security Technologies

Immediate Solutions

Configuring TACACS+ Globally

The process for configuring a Cisco router to support the TACACS+ protocol is fairly uniform. The basic configuration to enable the TACACS+ protocol always includes the following steps; however, the steps can be accomplished using two different methods. The first method configures TACACS+ globally on the network access server. This method is generally used in environments that use only one TACACS+ server or in environments in which all TACACS+ servers within the network are configured to use the same security values. This configuration method is outlined in the following steps:

1. Use the **aaa new-model** global configuration command to enable AAA. This command establishes a new AAA configuration. The command must be configured if you plan to support the TACACS+ protocol.

2. Use the **tacacs-server host** <*ip address*> command to specify the IP address of one or more TACACS+ servers.

3. Set the global TACACS+ authentication key and encryption key using the **tacacs-server key** <*key*> command. The key string configured on the network access server must match the key string configured on the TACACS+ server or all communication between the devices will fail.

The preceding steps include the basic configuration commands needed to enable TACACS+ globally on the network access server. Figure 2.8 illustrates how to configure the network access server named Seminole to provide TACACS+ services for user James. James is an administrator who must access the network access server Seminole remotely and perform administrative functions. The access server Seminole is configured to communicate with the Cisco Secure ACS server at IP address 192.168.10.4.

The following configuration commands are needed to configure the router based on the requirements:

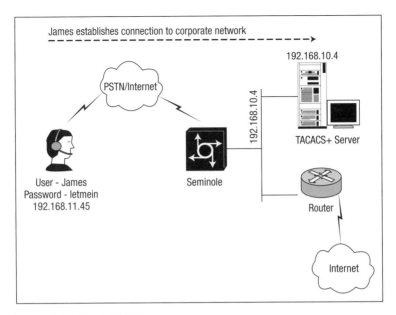

Figure 2.8   Single TACACS+ server.

```
Seminole#config t
Enter configuration commands, one per line.  End with CNTL/Z.
Seminole(config)#aaa new-model
Seminole(config)#tacacs-server host 192.168.10.4
Seminole(config)#tacacs-server key 1Cisco9
```

In this configuration, the key **1Cisco9** is the encryption key that is shared between router Seminole and the Cisco Secure server at IP address 192.168.10.4. The encryption key should be kept secret for privacy reasons because it is encrypted only after it is sent across the network to the Cisco Secure server but it's not stored in encrypted format on the local device. Issuing the **show running-config** command allows you see the results of the preceding configuration:

```
Seminole#show running-config
!
hostname Seminole
!
aaa new-model
tacacs-server host 192.168.10.4
tacacs-server key 1Cisco9
!
```

Issuing the **show running-config** command allows you to review the configuration changes that were made to the local device; however, a few more commands are needed to verify that the network access server and TACACS+ server are communicating properly. After you verify that the configuration changes are correct, the next command you should issue is the **show tacacs** command. The output of this command verifies that the network access server and the TACACS+ server are communicating properly. Issuing the **show tacacs** command will verify that network access server **Seminole** in Figure 2.8 is communicating with the TACACS+ server.

```
Seminole#sh tacacs

Server: 192.168.10.4/49: opens=215 closes=214 aborts=79 errors=4
        packets in=1637 packets out=1930 expected replies=0
        connection 62524500 state=ESTAB
```

The output of the **show tacacs** command first lists the TACACS+ server's IP address and the port number that the router and the TACACS+ server are communicating on; port 49 is the default port number. The port number may be changed in instances in which the TACACS+ server has been configured to communicate on a different port number. The values for **opens** and **closes** are the number of times the router opened or closed a session with the TACACS+ server. The most important output that is displayed by the **show tacacs** command is the state of the connection. In the preceding example, the state equals Established. If, for instance, the router and TACACS+ server could not communicate, the following output listed would be seen:

```
Server: 192.168.10.4/49: opens=0 closes=0 aborts=0 errors=227
        packets in=0 packets out=0 expected replies=0
        no connection
```

Notice the high number of errors. The number is high because there is no connection between the router and the TACACS+ server after a determination has been made that the router and the TACACS+ server are communicating. The command **debug tacacs events** is needed to make sure the session communication is functioning properly. The **debug tacacs events** command displays the opening and closing of TCP connections to the TACACS+ server and also displays the bytes written and read during the connection. This output can be seen in Listing 2.1.

Listing 2.1 Debugging TACACS+ events output.

```
Seminole#debug tacacs events
TACACS+ events debugging is on
Seminole#
: TAC+: Opening TCP/IP to 192.168.10.4/49 timeout=5
: TAC+: Opened TCP/IP handle 0x47B76A to 192.168.10.4/49
: TAC+: req=6257CD64 Qd id=3392702625 ver=192 handle=0x0 -
  : TAC+: (NONE) expire=4
  AUTHEN/START/LOGIN/ASCII processed
: TAC+: periodic timer stopped (queue empty)
: TAC+: periodic timer started
: TAC+: 192.168.10.4 req=6257CD64 Qd id=3392702625 ver=192 -
  : TAC+: handle=0x0 (NONE) expire=5
  AUTHEN/START/LOGIN/ASCII queued
: TAC+: 192.168.10.4 ESTAB id=3392702625 wrote 37 of 37 bytes
: TAC+: 192.168.10.4 req=6257CD64 Qd id=3392702625 ver=192 -
  : TAC+: handle=0x0 (NONE)expire=4
  AUTHEN/START/LOGIN/ASCII sent
: TAC+: 192.168.10.4 ESTAB read=12 wanted=12 alloc=55 got=12
: TAC+: 192.168.10.4 ESTAB read=28 wanted=28 alloc=55 got=16
: TAC+: 192.168.10.4 received 28 byte reply for 6257CD64 -
  : TAC+: id=3392702625
: TAC+: req=6257CD64 Tx id=3392702625 ver=192 handle=0x0 -
  : TAC+: (NONE) expire=4
  AUTHEN/START/LOGIN/ASCII processed
: TAC+: periodic timer stopped (queue empty)
: TAC+: periodic timer started
: TAC+: 192.168.10.4 req=6252CD78 Qd id=3392702625 ver=192 -
  : TAC+: handle=0x0 (NONE)expire=5AUTHEN/CONT queued
: TAC+: 192.168.10.4 ESTAB id=3392702625 wrote 24 of 24 bytes
: TAC+: 192.168.10.4 req=6252CD78 Qd id=3392702625 ver=192 -
  : TAC+: handle=0x0 (NONE)expire=4
  AUTHEN/CONT sent
: TAC+: 192.168.10.4 ESTAB read=12 wanted=12 alloc=55 got=12
: TAC+: 192.168.10.4 ESTAB read=28 wanted=28 alloc=55 got=16
: TAC+: 192.168.10.4 received 28 byte reply for 6252CD78 -
  : TAC+: id=3392702625
: TAC+: req=6252CD78 Tx id=3392702625 ver=192 handle=0x0 -
  : TAC+: (NONE) expire=4
  AUTHEN/CONT processed
: TAC+: periodic timer stopped (queue empty)
: TAC+: periodic timer started
: TAC+: 192.168.10.4 req=6257CD64 Qd id=3392702625 ver=192 -
  : TAC+: handle=0x0 (NONE)expire=5
```

```
        AUTHEN/CONT queued
      : TAC+: 192.168.10.4 ESTAB id=3392702625 wrote 27 of 27 bytes
      : TAC+: 192.168.10.4 req=6257CD64 Qd id=3392702625 ver=192 -
      : TAC+: handle=0x0 (NONE)expire=4
        AUTHEN/CONT sent
      : TAC+: 192.168.10.4 ESTAB read=12 wanted=12 alloc=55 got=12
      : TAC+: 192.168.10.4 ESTAB read=18 wanted=18 alloc=55 got=6
      : TAC+: 192.168.10.4 received 18 byte reply for 6257CD64 -
      : TAC+: id=3392702625
      : TAC+: req=6257CD64 Tx id=3392702625 ver=192 -
      : TAC+: handle=0x0 (NONE) expire=3
        AUTHEN/CONT processed
      : TAC+: periodic timer stopped (queue empty)
```

Configuring TACACS+ Individually

The second method used to enable TACACS+ allows a finer granularity of control in specifying features on a per-security-server basis. This method is generally used in environments that use multiple TACACS+ servers, and each server is configured to use separate values. Use the following steps to enable this method of TACACS+ configuration:

1. Use the **aaa new-model** global configuration command to enable AAA. This command establishes a new AAA configuration. The command must be configured if you plan to support the TACACS+ protocol.

2. Use the following command to specify the IP address of one or more TACACS+ servers:

   ```
   tacacs-server host hostname <single-connection> <port integer>
   <timeout <integer> <key string>
   ```

   The network access server searches for the hosts in the order specified; this feature allows you to set up a list of preferred servers.

The optional **single-connection** argument specifies that the network access server should maintain a single connection to the TACACS+ server as opposed to having the network access server open and close a TCP connection to the daemon process on the TACACS+ server each time it needs to communicate with the server. This allows the daemon process on the TACACS+ server to handle a higher number of TACACS+ operations. The default TCP port the network access server uses to communicate with the TACACS+ server may be changed using the **port** *integer* argument. If this argument is not specified, the default TCP port 49 is used. The **timeout integer** argument allows the network access server to specify the period of time it will wait for a response from the TACACS+ server daemon before it times out and declares an error; the default is set to 5 seconds. The **key string** argument allows for specification of an encryption key for encrypting and decrypting all traffic between the network access server and the TACACS+ daemon. The key string configured on the network access server must match the key string configured on the TACACS+ server or all communication between the devices will fail.

As mentioned, there are two different methods used to enable the TACACS+ process on a Cisco router. The Cisco IOS allows you to configure many values at a global level, which affects all other related values configured on the router. The method detailed in this section allows you to enhance security on your network by uniquely configuring individual TACACS+ connections for multiple servers and applying separate values for each server. Use the preceding configuration in instances in which your network has many independent TACACS+ servers and each server has different values configured.

NOTE: *Some of the parameters of the **tacacs-server host** command override other globally configured TACACS+ commands.*

Figure 2.9 shows another TACACS+ server added to the local network. The new TACACS+ server has an IP address of 192.168.10.5. This server is configured to use a different key value and timeout value than the server located at IP address 192.168.10.4:

```
config t

aaa new-model
tacacs-server host 192.168.10.4 single-connection key 1Cisco9
tacacs-server host 192.168.10.5 single-connection timeout 15 -
  key 2Systems8
```

This configuration names two TACACS+ servers: 192.168.10.4 and 192.168.10.5. TACACS+ server 192.168.10.4 is configured as it was in the global configuration; only the **single-connection** option has been added to the configuration. However, the 192.168.10.5 server has been added to the network and the values that the network access server needs to have configured are different for this server. Notice the timeout

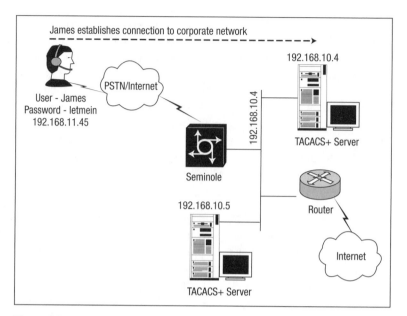

James establishes connection to corporate network

User - James
Password - letmein
192.168.11.45

PSTN/Internet

192.168.10.4

192.168.10.4

TACACS+ Server

Seminole

192.168.10.5

Router

Internet

TACACS+ Server

Figure 2.9   Multiple TACACS+ servers.

value—the network access waits for a response from the security server according to the timeout value, which has been changed from the default value of 5 seconds to a value of 15 seconds. The encryption key and authentication that is used to communicate with this server has been changed as well. Issuing the **show running-config** command allows you to view the results of the configuration:

```
Seminole#show running-config
!
hostname Seminole
!
aaa new-model
tacacs-server host 192.168.10.4 single-connection key 1Cisco9
tacacs-server host 192.168.10.5 single-connection timeout -
  15 key 2Systems8
!
```

After you verify that the configuration changes are correct, the next command you should issue is the **show tacacs** command. The output of this command verifies that the network access server and the TACACS+ server are communicating properly. Here is the output of the **sh tacacs** command:

```
Seminole#sh tacacs

Server: 192.168.10.4/49: opens=127 closes=126 aborts=24 errors=1
        packets in=1083 packets out=1233 expected replies=0
        connection 623F8098 state=ESTAB

Server: 192.168.10.5/49: opens=1 closes=0 aborts=0 errors=0
        packets in=14 packets out=14 expected replies=0
        connection 623FFC28 state=CLOSEWAIT
```

Configuring RADIUS Globally

The configuration of RADIUS is almost identical to the configuration of TACACS+. RADIUS can be configured on a global basis, which is generally used in environments that use one RADIUS server or in environments in which all RADIUS servers within the network are configured to use the same security values. To configure RADIUS on the network access server, you must perform the following steps (note Steps 4 through 6 are optional):

1. Use the **aaa new-model** global configuration command to enable AAA. This command establishes a new AAA configuration. The command must be configured if you plan to support the RADIUS protocol.

2. Use the *following* command to configure the IP address or hostname of the RADIUS server:

   ```
   radius-server host <hostname|ip-address>
   ```

3. Use this command to define the secret encryption key that is shared between the network access server and the RADIUS server:

   ```
   radius-server key <0 string|7 string|string>
   ```

4. Use the **radius-server retransmit** *<retries>* command to specify how many times the router transmits each RADIUS request to the server before giving up.

5. Use the **radius-server timeout** *<second>* command to specify how many seconds a router waits for a reply to a RADIUS request before retransmitting the request.

6. Use the **radius-server deadtime** *<minutes>* command to specify how many minutes should pass before a RADIUS server that is not responding to authentication requests is passed over by requests for RADIUS authentication.

The preceding steps include the basic configuration commands needed to enable RADIUS globally on the network access server. Continuing with the example in Figure 2.8, the network access server named Seminole should now be configured to provide RADIUS services for user James. The access server Seminole is configured to communicate with the Cisco Secure ACS server at IP address 192.168.10.4.

The following configuration commands are needed to configure the router based on the requirements:

```
Seminole#config t
Enter configuration commands, one per line.  End with CNTL/Z.
Seminole(config)#aaa new-model
Seminole(config)#radius-server host 192.168.10.4
Seminole(config)#radius-server key 1Cisco9
```

Notice the similarities between the global configuration of TACACS+ and the global configuration of RADIUS. In the preceding configuration, the key **1Cisco9** is the encryption key that is shared between router Seminole and the Cisco Secure server at IP address 192.168.10.4. Issuing the **show running-config** command allows you to see the results of the preceding configuration:

```
Seminole#show running-config
!
hostname Seminole
!
aaa new-model
radius-server host 192.168.10.4
radius-server key 1Cisco9
!
```

By issuing the **show running-config** command, you can review the configuration changes that were made to the local device; however, a few more commands are needed to verify that the network access server and the RADIUS server are communicating properly. After you verify that the configuration changes are correct, the next command you should issue is the **debug radius** command. The output of this command verifies that the network access server and the RADIUS server are communicating properly. The output of the **debug radius** command verifies that the network access server and the RADIUS server are communicating properly; the following lines show that the network access server Seminole in Figure 2.8 is communicating with the RADIUS server:

```
Seminole#debug radius
: Radius:  IPC send 0.0.0.0/1645, Access-Request, id 0xB, len 52
: Attribute 4 6 AB187D5B
: Attribute 5 6 0000000B
: Attribute 2 6 0212D3C2
: Attribute 2 18 D21512AC
: Radius:  Received from 192.168.10.4:1645, Access-Accept, -
  : id 0xB, len 24
```

The output of the **debug radius** command displays the attribute values that are carried in the RADIUS Access-Request packet and the length of the packet. The last line in the output displays the packet that is received from the RADIUS server and the Access-Accept value being returned to the network access server. If, however, the RADIUS server and the network access server could not communicate properly, the output from the **debug radius** would resemble this output:

```
: Radius: IPC Send 0.0.0.0:1645, Access-Request, id 0xA, len 57
: Attribute 4 6 AC150E5A
: Attribute 5 6 0000000A
: Attribute 1 7 62696C6C
: Attribute 2 18 49C28F6C
: Radius: Received from 192.168.10.4:1645, Access-Reject, -
  : id 0xA, len 20
: Radius: Reply for 4 fails decrypt
```

Configuring RADIUS Individually

As with TACACS+, RADIUS allows a finer granularity of control in specifying features on a per-security-server basis. This method of RADIUS configuration is generally used in environments that utilize multiple RADIUS servers and each server is configured to use separate values. Follow these steps to enable this method of RADIUS configuration:

1. Use the **aaa new-model** global configuration command to enable AAA. This command establishes a new AAA configuration. The command must be configured if you plan to support the RADIUS protocol.

2. Use the following command to specify the IP address of one or more RADIUS servers:

```
radius-server host {hostname|ip-address} <auth-port -
    port-number> <acct-port port-number> <timeout seconds> -
    <retransmit retries> <key string> <alias -
    {hostname|ip address}>
```

The network access server searches for the hosts in the order specified; this feature allows you to set up a list of preferred servers.

The IP address parameter above specifies the IP address or hostname of the remote RADIUS server host and assigns authentication and accounting destination port numbers. The **auth-port** *port-number* option allows the administrator to configure on this RADIUS server a specific UDP port to be used solely for authentication. This port number defaults to 1645 if it is not explicitly configured. The **acct-port** *port-number* option allows the administrator to configure on this RADIUS server a specific UDP port to be used solely for accounting. This port number defaults to 1646 if it is not explicitly configured. Use the **alias** keyword to configure up to eight multiple IP addresses for use when referring to RADIUS servers. Set the timeout, retransmit, and encryption key values to use with the specific RADIUS host.

The Cisco IOS allows you to configure many values at a global level; these values affect all other related values configured on the router. The method detailed in the preceding steps allows you to enhance security on your network by uniquely configuring individual RADIUS connections for multiple servers and applying separate values for each server. Use the preceding configuration steps in instances in which your network has many independent RADIUS servers and each server has different values configured.

The following example configures two servers with separate values (refer back to Figure 2.9); the servers should now be configured to support RADIUS as opposed to TACACS+:

```
#config t
#aaa new-model
#radius-server host 192.168.10.4 timeout 20 key 1Cisco9
#radius-server host 192.168.10.5 timeout 45 key 2Systems8
```

The server with the IP address 192.168.10.4 is configured with a timeout value of **20** and a key value of **1Cisco9**. However, the server with the IP address 192.168.10.5 is configured with different values. It is configured with a higher timeout value of **45** and a separate key value of **2Systems8**. Issuing the **show running-config** command allows you to view the results of the preceding configuration:

```
Seminole#show running-config
!
hostname Seminole
!
aaa new-model
radius-server host 192.168.10.4 auth-port 1645 acct-port 1646 -
   timeout 20 key 1Cisco9
!
radius-server host 192.168.10.5 auth-port 1645 acct-port 1646 -
   timeout 45 key 2Systems8
!
```

After verifying that the configuration changes are correct, you should issue the **debug radius** command. The output of this command verifies that the network access server and the TACACS+ server are communicating properly:

NOTE: *Use **debug** commands with great care. In general, it is recommended that these commands only be used under the direction of a technical support representative when troubleshooting specific problems. Enabling debugging can disrupt operation of the router when networks are experiencing high load conditions.*

```
Seminole#debug radius
: Radius:  IPC send 0.0.0.0/1645, Access-Request, id 0xB, len 52
: Attribute 4 6 AB187D5B
: Attribute 5 6 0000000B
: Attribute 2 6 0212D3C2
: Attribute 2 18 D21512AC
: Radius:  Received from 192.168.10.4:1645, Access-Accept, -
  : id 0xB, len 24
!
: Radius: IPC Send 0.0.0.0:1645, Access-Request, id 0xB, len 56
: Attribute 4 6 AB246E4C
: Attribute 5 6 0000000A
: Attribute 1 6 62696C6C
: Attribute 2 18 C22631BD
: Radius: Received from 192.168.10.5:1645, Access-Accept, -
  : id 0xB, len 26
!
```

Configuring Authentication

After you enable TACACS+ or RADIUS globally on the network device, you must define the authentication methods used to verify users before they are allowed access to the network and network services. To configure AAA authentication, first define a named list of authentication methods and then apply that list to the correct interfaces. The method list defines the types of authentication to be performed and the sequence in which they will be performed; it must be applied to a specific interface before any of the defined authentication methods will be performed. The default method list, however, is an exception; it is automatically applied to all interfaces except those that have a named method list explicitly defined on them. A defined method list overrides the default method list.

A method list is a sequential list that describes the authentication methods to be used to authenticate a user. Cisco IOS software uses the first configured method listed to authenticate users. If that method fails to respond or returns an error, it selects the next authentication method listed in the method list. This process continues until there is successful communication with a listed authentication method or until all methods defined in the method list are exhausted.

NOTE: *The Cisco IOS software attempts authentication with the next configured authentication method only when there is no response from the preceding method or the method returns an error.*

To configure AAA authentication, perform the following steps:

1. Enable AAA by using the **aaa new-model** global configuration command and configuring any security protocol parameters, such as the key value. This step was outlined earlier in the sections on configuring TACACS+ and RADIUS.

2. Define the method lists for authentication by using the following command:

   ```
   aaa authentication <arap|login|enable|ppp|nasi> <default| -
      list-name> group <method1> <method2> <method3> -
      <method4>
   ```

3. Apply the method lists to a particular interface or line, using the following command:

   ```
   login authentication {default|list name}
   ```

The **aaa authentication** command authenticates arap, login, enable, ppp, and nasi connections. As an example of how to configure these connections, router Seminole in Figure 2.8 will be configured to authenticate user James for Telnet access via the security server at IP address 192.168.10.4. All other lines will use the default list. Listing 2.2 displays the configuration commands needed to enable Seminole to authenticate James for Telnet access via the TACACS+ server.

Listing 2.2   Router Seminole authentication configuration.

```
#aaa new-model
#tacacs-server host 192.168.10.4
#tacacs-server key 1Cisco9
#aaa authentication login TELNET group tacacs -
   local enable none
#aaa authentication login ADMIN none
#line con 0
#login authentication ADMIN
#line vty 0 4
#login authentication TELNET
#end
```

The configuration in Listing 2.2 creates a list named **TELNET** and defines four methods that should be used to authenticate the virtual terminal lines that are configured to use the list. The console port will use the method list named **ADMIN**, which specifies that no authentication is to take place. Listing 2.3 is part of the output from the command **debug aaa authentication**, which is used to verify whether the login attempt from user James was successful. This output also indicates that TACACS+ is the authentication method used by the router.

Listing 2.3   Successful login authentication output.

```
Seminole#debug aaa authen
AAA Authentication debugging is on
Seminole#
: AAA: parse name=tty2 idb type=-1 tty=-1
: AAA: name=tty2 flags=0x11 type=5 shelf=0 slot=0 adapter=0 -
: port=2 channel=0
: AAA/MEMORY: create_user (0x62527B28) user='' ruser='' -
    port='tty2' rem_addr='192.168.11.45' authen_type=ASCII -
    service=LOGIN priv=1

: AAA/AUTHEN/START (3898654566): port='tty2' list='TELNET' -
    action=LOGINservice=LOGIN: AAA/AUTHEN/START : found list -
    TELNET
```

```
: AAA/AUTHEN/START (3898654566): Method=tacacs+ (tacacs+)
: TAC+: send AUTHEN/START packet ver=192 id=3898654566
: TAC+: ver=192 id=3898654566 received AUTHEN status = GETUSER
: AAA/AUTHEN (3898654566): status = GETUSER
: AAA/AUTHEN/CONT (3898654566): continue_login (user='(undef)')
: AAA/AUTHEN (3898654566): status = GETUSER
: AAA/AUTHEN (3898654566): Method=tacacs+ (tacacs+)
: TAC+: send AUTHEN/CONT packet id=3898654566
: TAC+: ver=192 id=3898654566 received AUTHEN status = GETPASS
: AAA/AUTHEN (3898654566): status = GETPASS
: AAA/AUTHEN/CONT (3898654566): continue_login (user='James')
: AAA/AUTHEN (3898654566): status = GETPASS
: AAA/AUTHEN (3898654566): Method=tacacs+ (tacacs+)
: TAC+: send AUTHEN/CONT packet id=3898654566
: TAC+: ver=192 id=3898654566 received AUTHEN status = PASS
: AAA/AUTHEN (3898654566): status = PASS
: TAC+: (4047621580): received author response status = PASS_ADD
```

Notice that the first few lines of the output determine that a connection has been requested on port tty2 and the authentication list named **TELNET** is defined on the line for LOGIN services. The router then begins to read through its configured lists to find a match for **TELNET**. Upon finding the list named **TELNET**, the router determines that the authentication method that should be used to authenticate the user is method TACACS+. The router then receives a request from the security server to retrieve the username from the user requesting access with the **GETUSER** request. The process continues with the security server, and then the router is asked to supply a password for the user. After verifying the supplied credentials, the security server responds with a **PASS** status packet and the user has been authenticated.

If, for instance, user James fails the authentication process, the response that is generated by the router would resemble the output in Listing 2.4.

Listing 2.4   Failed login authentication output.

```
: AAA: parse name=tty2 idb type=-1 tty=-1
: AAA: name=tty2 flags=0x11 type=5 shelf=0 slot=0 adapter=0 -
  port=2 channel=0
: AAA/MEMORY: create_user (0x6257E6A8) user='' ruser='' -
  port='tty2'
  rem_addr='192.168.11.45' authen_type=ASCII service=LOGIN -
  priv=1
: AAA/AUTHEN/START (2841923342): port='tty2' list='TELNET' -
  action=LOGINservice=LOGIN: AAA/AUTHEN/START : found list -
  TELNET
```

```
: AAA/AUTHEN/START (2841923342): Method=tacacs+ (tacacs+)
: TAC+: send AUTHEN/START packet ver=192 id=2841923342
: TAC+: ver=192 id=2841923342 received AUTHEN status = GETUSER
: AAA/AUTHEN (2841923342): status = GETUSER
: AAA/AUTHEN/CONT (2841923342): continue_login (user='(undef)')
: AAA/AUTHEN (2841923342): status = GETUSER
: AAA/AUTHEN (2841923342): Method=tacacs+ (tacacs+)
: TAC+: send AUTHEN/CONT packet id=2841923342
: TAC+: ver=192 id=2841923342 received AUTHEN status = GETPASS
: AAA/AUTHEN (2841923342): status = GETPASS
: AAA/AUTHEN/CONT (2841923342): continue_login (user='James')
: AAA/AUTHEN (2841923342): status = GETPASS
: AAA/AUTHEN (2841923342): Method=tacacs+ (tacacs+)
: TAC+: send AUTHEN/CONT packet id=2841923342
: TAC+: ver=192 id=2841923342 received AUTHEN status = FAIL
: AAA/AUTHEN (2841923342): status = FAIL
: AAA/MEMORY: free_user (0x6257E6A8) user='James' ruser='' -
  port='tty2' rem_addr='192.168.11.45' authen_type=ASCII -
  service=LOGIN priv=1
```

As explained in Chapter 1, Cisco routers have different modes of operation. These modes are generally protected with passwords so that certain users cannot just walk up and gain access to the router. The enable password and enable secret password are frequently configured to secure privileged mode access into a Cisco router. Although it's a good start, there are some limitations to using this method alone. This method of security is burdensome to administer in enterprises that contain hundreds of routers. For instance, if the password needs to be changed for any reason, someone either has to physically go to each router and plug into it to change the password or has to telnet to each router. The point is that this could become an administrative nightmare. Another drawback to using this method is that the password must be known by all users who need access into the router. Fortunately, Cisco routers can be configured to authenticate a user via a security server for privileged mode access. This allows administrators to change the password in one place, giving them centralized control. In environments that use an external Windows NT/2000 database for authentication, each user has control of his or her own enable password.

Continuing with the authentication example, the router Seminole should be configured to authenticate users via the security server for privileged mode access. This can be accomplished using the following configuration commands:

```
#config t
#aaa authentication enable default group tacacs+ enable none
#end
#
```

The configuration commands in Listing 2.4 configure the router to authenticate privileged mode access using the TACACS+ method; if the security server returns an error, then authenticate the user using the configured enable password. After initiating a Telnet session to the router, James now must enter enable mode. Listing 2.5 shows the output when James accesses privileged mode is shown in.

Listing 2.5   Authentication debug output.

```
Seminole>en
Password:
Seminole#
: AAA/MEMORY: dup_user (0x6255EA00) user='James' ruser='' -
  port='tty2' rem_addr='192.168.11.45' authen_type=ASCII -
  service=ENABLE priv=15 source='AAA dup enable'
: AAA/AUTHEN/START (757557072): port='tty2' list='' -
  action=LOGIN service=ENABLE
: AAA/AUTHEN/START (757557072): using "default" list
: AAA/AUTHEN/START (757557072): Method=tacacs+ (tacacs+)
: TAC+: send AUTHEN/START packet ver=192 id=757557072
: TAC+: ver=192 id=757557072 received AUTHEN status = GETPASS
: AAA/AUTHEN (757557072): status = GETPASS
: AAA/AUTHEN/CONT (757557072): continue_login (user='James')
: AAA/AUTHEN (757557072): status = GETPASS
: AAA/AUTHEN (757557072): Method=tacacs+ (tacacs+)
: TAC+: send AUTHEN/CONT packet id=757557072
: TAC+: ver=192 id=757557072 received AUTHEN status = PASS
: AAA/AUTHEN (757557072): status = PASS
: AAA/MEMORY: free_user (0x6255EA00) user='James' ruser='' -
  port='tty2' rem_addr='10.191.150.45' authen_type=ASCII -
  service=ENABLE priv=15
```

In the first line, the router determines that the user logging in is a duplicate user who is requesting enable mode access. The router knows that the user is a duplicate user because after the user is successfully authenticated, the router caches the supplied username credential. After receiving the **GETPASS** from the security server, the router prompts James to enter his password and passes the value back to the security server. The security server then sends the Pass or Fail status to the router.

Prior to Cisco IOS 12.0, there were instances when an administrator could accidentally lock himself out of his network access server with an incorrect AAA configuration. In order to remedy this problem, Cisco developed the **aaa authentication local-override** command. This command proved to be very useful when you wanted to configure an override to the normal authentication method list processing the network access server performed for certain personnel, such as system administrators. With the override command configured, the user was always prompted for his username. The system then checked to see if the username that was entered corresponded to a local account configured with the following command:

```
username name privilege level password password
```

If the username does not correspond to one in the local database, login proceeds with the methods configured with other **aaa** commands (such as **aaa authentication login**). An example of configuring the local-override feature is shown here:

```
Seminole# config t
Enter configuration commands, one per line.  End with CNTL/Z.
Seminole(config)#aaa authentication local-override
Seminole(config)#end
Seminole#
```

The result of configuring the **local-override** command can be viewed by using the **show running-config** command:

```
Seminole#show running-config
Building configuration...
!
Current configuration:
!
version 11.2
aaa new-model
aaa authentication local-override
!
```

However, with newer 12.0+ code, the **aaa authentication local-override** is no longer a configuration option. This can be verified using the following method.

```
Seminole#config t
Enter configuration commands, one per line.  End with CNTL/Z.
Seminole(config)#aaa authen
Seminole(config)#aaa authentication ?
  arap             Set authentication lists for arap.
  banner           Message to use when starting login.
  enable           Set authentication list for enable.
  fail-message     Message to use for failed authentication.
  login            Set authentication lists for logins.
  nasi             Set authentication lists for NASI.
  password-prompt  Text to use when prompting for a password.
  ppp              Set authentication lists for ppp.
  username-prompt  Text to use when prompting for a username.
```

With 12.0+ code, when access to the network access devices is critical at all times and administrators need the same functionality they get when they use the **local-override** command, you can configure a default method of access into the network access device. This can be accomplished using the following command:

```
#config t
#aaa authentication login default local group tacacs enable line
Seminole#
```

This example provides the same features that the **aaa authentication local-override** command provided. For login authentication, the network access server will first check the default method that is configured to authenticate the remote user (in this case, it's the local database). Then, if the username is not found in the local database, the network access server will attempt to authenticate the user using the first method configured in the method list—in this case, TACACS+. If the TACACS+ server returns an error to the network access server, the network access server will then try the next method configured—in this case, the enable password—in an attempt to authenticate the user.

Configuring PAP and CHAP Authentication

The CHAP and PAP protocols are supported on synchronous and asynchronous serial interfaces. When using CHAP or PAP authentication, each router or access server uses a name to identify itself. This identification process prevents a router from placing another call to a router it's already connected to, and it also prevents unauthorized access. Access control using CHAP or PAP is available on all serial interfaces that use PPP encapsulation. To use the features of PAP and CHAP, perform the following steps:

1. Enable PPP encapsulation on an interface using the interface configuration mode **encapsulation ppp** command.

2. Enable CHAP or PAP authentication on the interface configured for PPP encapsulation by using the following command in interface configuration mode:

```
ppp authentication {chap|chap pap|pap chap|pap} [if-needed] -
    [list-name|default] [callin]
```

3. Configure the appropriate usernames and passwords using this command:

```
username name <user-maxlinks link-number> password <secret>
```

The passwords are case sensitive and must be identical at both ends.

Figure 2.10 lists three users who need secure remote access to the corporate office. The users remotely connect to the corporate network and are authenticated via CHAP. The configuration of the network access server is shown in Listing 2.6.

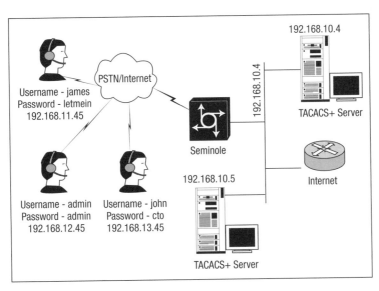

Figure 2.10   Remote client PPP connection.

Listing 2.6   PPP network access server.

```
!
hostname Seminole
!
username james password letmein
username admin password admin
username john password cto
!
interface Ethernet0
 ip address 192.168.10.1 255.255.255.0
!
interface Group-Async1
 encapsulation ppp
 async mode interactive
 peer default ip address pool remote-users
 ppp authentication pap
 group-range 1 16
!
ip local pool remote-users 192.168.39.239 192.168.39.254

!
line 1 16
 login local
 autoselect during-login
 autoselect ppp
 modem InOut
 transport input all
```

The configuration in Listing 2.6 defines three users with separate pass-words. **Interface group-assync1** is configured for PPP as the encap-sulation protocol, and the method of authentication is PAP. The **group-range** command under **interface group-async1** defines the lines that are part of the **group-async1** interface. Notice that PAP was chosen as the authentication protocol; CHAP could have been speci-fied instead using the **ppp authentication chap** command. In envi-ronments that support both PAP and CHAP, the access server attempts to authenticate a user with the first configured authentication method; if that method fails or if the client device does not support the first authentication method, the access server will attempt to use the next configured method. This is accomplished using the following command:

```
ppp authentication chap pap
```

However, the example in Listing 2.6 can sometimes become a burden because of the overhead of maintaining a local security database on the network access server. In environments in which there is the potential to have hundreds, maybe even thousands of remote clients connecting to the access server, the local security database method is not feasible because of scalability issues. Fortunately, in environments that use the services of a central security database, like the Cisco Secure ACS server, the authentication process can be offloaded to the Cisco Secure ACS server. As an example, the network access server in Figure 2.10 will be configured to authenticate the users via the AAA security server. Listing 2.7 details the configuration needed to enable authentication via the AAA security server.

Listing 2.7 Remote authentication using TACACS+.

```
!
hostname Seminole
!
aaa new-model
aaa authentication login default group tacacs+ enable local none
aaa authentication login ADMIN none
aaa authentication ppp default if-needed group tacacs+ -
  local enable
!
username admin password admin
!
interface Ethernet0
ip address 192.168.10.1 255.255.255.0
!
interface Serial0:23
no ip address
encapsulation ppp
!
interface Group-Async1
ip unnumbered Ethernet0
encapsulation ppp
ip tcp header-compression passive
async mode interactive
peer default ip address pool IP
ppp callback accept
ppp authentication chap
group-range 1 16
!
ip local pool IP 192.168.10.239 192.168.10.254
!

tacacs-server host 192.168.10.4 single-connection timeout 10 -
key 1Cisco9
!
```

```
line con 0
login authentication ADMIN
line 1 16
modem InOut
autoselect during-login
autoselect ppp
```

This configuration authenticates the remote clients via the TACACS+ server prior to authorizing and accounting the users.

Related solution:	*Found on page:*
Configuring Console Security	13

Configuring Authorization

AAA authorization provides administrators with the power to limit the services that are available to users. After authorization is enabled, the network access server uses the authorization information that was supplied to it by the security server based on the user's profile. This allows the network access server to limit the access granted to the user based on the information in the user's profile.

Just as with authentication method lists are used to define the ways and the sequence in which authorization will be performed. Method lists enable you to designate one or more security protocols to be used for authorization, thus ensuring a backup system in case the initial method fails. Cisco IOS software uses the first method listed to authorize users for specific network services; if that method fails to respond, the Cisco IOS software selects the next method listed in the method list. This process continues until there is successful communication with a listed authorization method or until all methods defined are exhausted.

Use the **aaa authorization** global configuration command to define the parameters that determine what clients are allowed to do. To configure authorization, perform the following steps (Steps 4 and 5 are optional):

1. Enable AAA by using the **aaa new-model** global configuration command and configuring any security protocol parameters, such as the key value. This step and the steps used to configure the key value were outlined in the sections on configuring TACACS+ and RADIUS.

2. Configure AAA authentication as described in the "Configuring Authentication" section. Authorization generally takes place after authentication and relies on authentication to work properly.

3. Use the following command to enable authorization:

```
aaa authorization <auth-proxy|network|exec|commands> -
   <level|reverse-access|configuration|ipmobile>-
   <default|list-name> group <if-
   authen|none|local|tacacs+|radius>
```

4. Define the rights associated with specific users by using the **username** command if you are using local authorization.

5. Use the **no aaa authorization config-commands** command to stop the network access server from attempting configuration command authorization. There are some configuration commands that are identical to some **EXEC**-level commands; this can cause some confusion in the authorization process because the **aaa authorization** command with the keyword **commands** attempts authorization for all **EXEC**-level commands; this includes global configuration commands associated with a specific privilege level.

The command parameters listed in Step 3 are described in Table 2.1.

Table 2.1   Authorization command parameters.

Command	Description
Author-proxy	Used to apply policies to specific users
Network	Used for network services, such as PPP
Exec	Used for starting the **EXEC** process
Commands	Used for **EXEC** mode commands
Reverse-access	Used for reverse Telnet sessions, such as on a terminal server
Configuration	Used for downloading configurations from the security server
Ipmobile	Used for IP mobile services
If-authenticated	Allows user to access function if the user is already authenticated
None	No authorization performed
Local	Uses the local database for authorization
tacacs+	Uses the TACACS+ database for authorization
radius	Uses the RADIUS database for authorization

2. AAA Security Technologies

Figure 2.10 displays a network in which multiple users are connected to the corporate office via dial-up and the Internet. After the initial authentication phase, limitations must be placed on each user's session for security purposes. Some users should be allowed full access to the network and networking devices; such is the case with administrators. Other remote users need to be provided with the services that are deemed necessary to perform their job functions. This is done through the use of authorization. Continuing with the examples that were discussed in the section on configuring authentication, the network access server should be configured so that all users connecting to the network are authorized for the proper services via the security server. This can be accomplished using the configuration in Listing 2.8.

Listing 2.8   Authorization configuration.

```
#config t
#username James privilege 15 password letmein
#username admin privilege 15 password adim
#username John privilege 15 password cto
#aaa authorization exec default if-authenticated tacacs+ local
#aaa authorization exec ADMIN_ONLY none
#aaa authorization commands 15 ADMIN if-authenticated tacacs+
#aaa authorization commands 8 Associate tacacs+ local none
#aaa authorization network default tacacs+ local none
# line con 0
#authorization exec ADMIN_ONLY
#end
```

The configuration in Listing 2.8 defines three users within the local security database of the network access server. The first authorization command uses the default method list to authorize the **EXEC** process for all interfaces and lines if the user has already been authenticated during the authentication phase. The second authorization command is applied to the console port of the network access server and overrides the default method list. It creates a named method list called **ADMIN_ONLY** and specifies that no authorization is to take place. The third authorization command creates a method list named **ADMIN** and authorizes all level 15 commands if the remote client has already authenticated. If the remote client has not already authenticated, the access server will attempt to authorize the remote client via the TACACS+ security server. If the access server does not receive a response from the security server, it will attempt to authorize the remote client using the locally configured database. The fourth authorization command is similar to the second, only it is authorizing all commands associated with level 8 privileges. The final authorization command that is configured uses the default method list to authorize all network services the remote client attempts to use. It accomplishes this by authorizing the remote client using the configured TACACS+ security server, and if there is no response from the security server, it will attempt to authorize the client by looking into its locally configured security database.

Consider this scenario: James is at home one night watching a really close football game on the television (it's a two-point game in the fourth quarter with two minutes to go), and all at once, the phone rings—it is someone from his network operations center calling to inform him that she is having an issue with a couple of devices on the network. James dials into the network to have a look around. After he connects to the network access server and it uses the configured methods of authentication to authenticate him, James enters privileged mode on the network access server. The process the network access server used to authorize James can be seen in the output of Listing 2.9, using the **debug aaa authorization** command.

Listing 2.9   Authorization process.

```
Seminole#debug aaa authorization
AAA Authorization debugging is on
Seminole#
: AAA: parse name=tty2 idb type=-1 tty=-1
: AAA: name=tty2 flags=0x11 type=5 shelf=0 slot=0 adapter=0 -
  port=2 channel=0
: AAA/MEMORY: create_user (0x6251D064) user='' ruser='' -
  port='tty2' rem_addr='192.168.11.45' authen_type=ASCII -
  service=LOGIN priv=1
: tty2 AAA/AUTHOR/EXEC (2897440801): Port='tty2' list='' -
  service=EXEC
: AAA/AUTHOR/EXEC: tty2 (2897440801) user='James'
: tty2 AAA/AUTHOR/EXEC (2897440801): send AV service=shell
: tty2 AAA/AUTHOR/EXEC (2897440801): send AV cmd*
: tty2 AAA/AUTHOR/EXEC (2897440801): found list "default"
: tty2 AAA/AUTHOR/EXEC (2897440801): Method=tacacs+ (tacacs+)
: AAA/AUTHOR/TAC+: (2897440801): user=James
: AAA/AUTHOR/TAC+: (2897440801): send AV service=shell
: AAA/AUTHOR/TAC+: (2897440801): send AV cmd*
: AAA/AUTHOR (2897440801): Post authorization status = PASS_ADD
: AAA/AUTHOR/EXEC: Authorization successful
: AAA/MEMORY: free_user (0x62558A94) user='James' ruser='' -
  port='tty2' rem_addr='192.168.11.45' authen_type=ASCII -
  service=ENABLE priv=15
```

Notice that the access server first allocates a portion of memory in order to create the user. The network access server then determines that the user is attempting to access privileged exec mode. This can be determined by the output **service=EXEC**. The access server then determines that the user has a name that equals James. At this point, the network access server determines that method list default is configured and the first configured viable authorization method is to authorize James using the method TACACS+. The network access server passes the TACACS+ security server all of James's information, and the security server sends back a response of **PASS**.

Configuring Accounting

The accounting portion of the AAA security architecture enables you to track the services users are accessing as well as the amount of network resources they are consuming. When accounting is enabled, the network access server reports user activity to the TACACS+ or RADIUS security server. The accounting service reports to the security server using accounting records. Each accounting record contains accounting attribute-value (AV) pairs and is stored on the security server. This combined data can be analyzed for network management, client billing, and auditing purposes.

Just as authentication and authorization support method lists, accounting uses method lists to define the ways that authorization will be performed and the order in which the methods will be used. Method lists enable you to designate one or more security protocols to be used for accounting, thus ensuring a backup system in case the initial method fails. Cisco IOS software uses the first method listed to account for the network services a client accesses; if that method fails to respond, the Cisco IOS software selects the next method listed in the method list. This process continues until there is successful communication with a listed accounting method or until all methods defined are exhausted.

Use the **aaa accounting** global configuration command to define the parameters that record what services clients have accessed. To configure accounting, perform the following steps:

1. Enable AAA by using the **aaa new-model** global configuration command and configuring any security protocol parameters, such as the key value. This step and the steps used to configure the key value were outlined in the sections on configuring TACACS+ and RADIUS.

2. Configure AAA authentication and authorization as described in the "Configuring Authentication" and "Configuring Authorization" sections. Accounting generally takes place during and after authentication and authorization.

3. Use the following command to enable the accounting process:

```
aaa accounting <system|network|exec|connection|commands> level
<default|list-name> <start-stop|stop-only|wait-start|none>
<tacacs+|radius>
```

The command parameters listed in Step 3 are described in Table 2.2.

Table 2.2   Accounting command parameters.

Command	Description
system	Audits all system-level events
network	Audits network service requests, such as PPP
exec	Audits **EXEC** process
connection	Audits outbound connections
commands *level*	Audits all commands for the specified privilege level
default	Default method list that is applied to all lines
list name	Creates a named method list
start-stop	Sends start notice at start of the process and stop notice at the end of the process
wait-start	Specifies accounting process does not begin until the start accounting notice is acknowledged
stop-only	Sends accounting notice at the end of the process
none	Specifies no accounting service takes place
tacacs+	Accounts the client services using the TACACS+ protocol
radius	Accounts the client services using the RADIUS protocol

Continuing with the example in Figure 2.10, the network access server should be configured to account for all activity that takes place on the access server. This requirement can be met using the configuration in Listing 2.10.

Listing 2.10   Accounting configuration.

```
!
aaa accounting exec default start-stop group tacacs+
aaa accounting commands 15 default start-stop group tacacs+
aaa accounting system default wait-start group tacacs+
aaa accounting network default stop-only group tacacs+
!
username admin password admin
```

99

```
!
interface Ethernet0
ip address 192.168.10.1 255.255.255.0
!
interface Serial0:23
no ip address
encapsulation ppp
!
interface Group-Async1
ip unnumbered Ethernet0
encapsulation ppp
ip tcp header-compression passive
async mode interactive
peer default ip address pool IP
ppp callback accept
ppp authentication chap
group-range 1 16
!
ip local pool IP 192.168.10.239 192.168.10.254
!
tacacs-server host 192.168.10.4 single-connection timeout 10 -
  key 1Cisco9
!
line con 0
login authentication ADMIN
line 1 16
modem InOut
autoselect during-login
autoselect ppp
```

The configuration in Listing 2.10 sets up accounting on the network access server. Each method list defined uses the default method list, which applies the configured method to all interfaces and lines. Each method list is also configured to use the TACACS+ protocol to perform the accounting function. After James dials into the network and begins his troubleshooting efforts, the accounting process on the network access server starts. The details of the accounting process can be seen in Listing 2.11.

Listing 2.11   Accounting process.

```
Seminole#debug aaa account
AAA Accounting debugging is on
Seminole#
: AAA/ACCT/ACCT_DISC: Found list "default"
: tty2 AAA/DISC: 1/"User Request"
: AAA/ACCT/EXEC/STOP User James, Port tty2: -
  task_id=273 start_time=1004308320 timezone=CST -
  service=shell disc-cause=1 disc-cause-ext=1020
```

```
      elapsed_time=40
      nas-rx-speed=0 nas-tx-speed=0
  !
  : AAA/ACCT: user James, acct type 0 (3132070800):
      Method=tacacs+ (tacacs+)
  : TAC+: (3132070800): received acct response status = SUCCESS
  : AAA/MEMORY: free_user (0x62527B28) user='James' ruser='' -
      port='tty2' rem_addr='192.168.11.45'
      authen_type=ASC II service=LOGIN priv=1
  : AAA: parse name=tty2 idb type=-1 tty=-1
  : AAA: name=tty2 flags=0x11 type=5 shelf=0 slot=0 adapter=0
      port=2 channel=0
  : AAA/MEMORY: create_user (0x625249DC) user='' ruser='' -
      port='tty2' rem_addr='192.168.11.45' authen_type=ASCII -
      service=LOGIN priv=1
  !
  : AAA/ACCT/EXEC/START User James, port tty2
  : AAA/ACCT/EXEC: Found list "default"
  : AAA/ACCT/EXEC/START User James, Port tty2,task_id=276
   start_time=1004308382
    timezone=CST service=shell
  !
  : AAA/ACCT: user James, acct type 0 (2103966373):
      Method=tacacs+ (tacacs+)
  : TAC+: (2103966373): received acct response status = SUCCESS
  : AAA/MEMORY: free_user (0x62527B28) user='James' ruser='' -
      port='tty2' rem_addr='192.168.11.45' -
      authen_type=ASCII service=ENABLE priv=15
  !
  : AAA/ACCT/CMD: User James, Port tty2, Priv 15:"show run-config"
  : AAA/ACCT/CMD: Found list "default"
  : AAA/ACCT: user James, acct type 3 (3950182121): Method=tacacs+
  : TAC+: (3950182121): received acct response status = SUCCESS
  : AAA/ACCT/ACCT_DISC: Found list "default"
  : tty2 AAA/DISC: 1/"User Request"
  : AAA/ACCT/EXEC/STOP User James, Port tty2:task_id=276 -
    start_time=1004308382 timezone=CST service=shell -
   disc-cause=1 disc-cause-ext=1020 elapsed_time=29

  !
  : AAA/ACCT: user James, acct type 0 (1600314757): -
      Method=tacacs+ (tacacs+)
  : TAC+: (1600314757): received acct response status = SUCCESS
  : AAA/MEMORY: free_user (0x625249DC) user='James' ruser='' -
      port='tty2' rem_addr='192.168.11.45' authen_type=ASCII -
      service=LOGIN priv=1
  : AAA/ACCT/CMD: User James, Port tty1, Priv 15: "sh ip route"
  : AAA/ACCT/CMD: Found list "default"
```

```
: AAA/ACCT: user James, acct type 3 (668218192): Method=tacacs+
: TAC+: (668218192): received acct response status = SUCCESS
```

Notice that the access server first determines that method list **"default"** is configured to provide accounting services for user **James**. The access server then determines that in order to account for the users' actions, it should use the **tacacs+** method. You should notice the following key aspects of the accounting feature:

```
: AAA/ACCT/CMD: User James, Port tty2, Priv 15:"show run-config"
: AAA/ACCT/CMD: User James, Port tty1, Priv 15: "sh ip route"
```

The access server will account for every command that is entered during the session in which **James** is connected. This feature provides the nonrepudiation aspect of the **AAA** architecture.

Installing and Configuring Cisco Secure NT

It's somewhat easy to install and configure the Cisco Secure ACS server. This section presents a brief overview of the installation steps.

For the AAA security architecture to function as designed, there are a few requirements that must be met prior to configuring the Cisco Secure ACS software on the server. First, the administrator must ensure that the following items are configured:

- Make sure your network access server is running IOS 11.2 or higher or you are using a third-party device that can be configured with TACACS+ and/or RADIUS.

- Make sure remote clients can successfully connect to your network access server.

- Use the **ping** command to ensure that the network access server can successfully establish logical communication to the server that the Cisco Secure ACS software will be installed on.

- Ensure that the server has a compatible Internet Web browser installed and that Java and JavaScript are enabled.

- Identify the security that will be used, identify the network access server's name and IP address, and validate the encryption and authentication key.

Cisco Secure ACS server installs from a CD-ROM, and the process is similar to any other Windows-based application. Although the installation steps are somewhat detailed, the installation process is quite easy. You should be aware that there are some major decisions that should be made during the installation process, and they will be mentioned.

During the installation process, the first major decision is to determine if Cisco Secure ACS software is already installed on the system. If it is, you are asked if you would like to remove the previous version and save the existing database information. If you want to keep the existing data, select the Yes, Keep Existing Database checkbox. If you want to create a new database, click to clear the checkbox and click the Next button. You're then asked to choose a destination location folder in which to install the software. If you choose to install the software into the default location, click the Next button to proceed to the next section. To use a different directory, click the Browse button and enter the name of the directory to use. If the directory does not exist, Setup asks if you want to create it. Click the Yes button to proceed. At this point, the Authentication Database Configuration window opens.

In the Authentication Database Configuration window, you will choose the database that is to be used to verify all authentication requests. The choices are as follows:

- *Cisco Secure ACS Database*—Choosing this option configures the Cisco Secure ACS to use only the locally populated Cisco Secure ACS database for authentication. Using the Cisco Secure ACS database is the default method.

- *Windows NT User Database*—Choosing this option configures the Cisco Secure ACS to authenticate clients using the Windows NT/2000 user database.

This step requires some planning ahead because, in order for the Cisco Secure ACS server to use the local database on the server, the database must first be populated. To populate the database, you must manually enter the information for each and every client. The advantage of using the Cisco Secure ACS database is speed of response time to the network access server. Also, note that if the administrator chooses to use the Windows NT/2000 database option, the Cisco Secure ACS server will still attempt to authenticate the client using the local Cisco Secure ACS database. However, most enterprises do not configure the local database if they elect to use the external Windows NT/2000 database. When you've chosen the database, click the Next button.

The next few abbreviated configuration windows are very critical for ensuring communication between the Cisco Secure ACS server and the network access server:

2. AAA Security Technologies

- *Authenticate Users*—This window determines the security protocol to be used for communication between the Cisco Secure ACS server and the access server. The TACACS+ protocol is the default choice.

- *Access Server Name*—This window allows the administrator to configure the name of the network access server that will use the services of the Cisco Secure ACS server.

- *Access Server IP Address*—This window allows the administrator to configure the IP address of the network access server that was defined in the preceding step.

- *Windows NT Server IP Address*—This window defines the IP address of this Windows NT/2000 server.

- *TACACS+ or RADIUS Key*—This is one of the most important configuration windows in the configuration process. It allows the administrator to configure the shared secret encryption key exchanged between the network access server and the Cisco Secure ACS. These passwords must be identical to ensure proper function and communication between the NAS and Cisco Secure ACS. Shared secrets are case sensitive.

After you successfully install the Cisco Secure ACS software and re-load the server, an icon will be displayed on the desktop of the server. You can double-click this icon to continue configuring the Cisco Secure ACS server. Because the Cisco Secure ACS server is an HTML-only software package, you will need a Web browser to continue. Double-clicking the icon will open the default Web browser, and the screen in Figure 2.11 will appear. The Cisco Secure ACS server is also accessible from any workstation with a functioning Web browser and logical connectivity to the server by entering the following URL: **http://<ip address of the server>:2002** or **http://<hostname of the server>:2002**. Figure 2.11 is the interface that is displayed after the server is accessed.

Upon initially accessing the Cisco Secure ACS server, the administrator will be prompted to enter a username and password. By default, the username and password are set to admin and admin. After the correct username and password pair is entered, the server logs the user into the console and the interface displays the output screen shown in Figure 2.12.

Notice the navigation bar (the column of buttons) on the left side of the screen in Figure 2.12. Each button represents a particular area that you can configure. Depending on your requirements, you might not need to configure all areas. Click one of the buttons on the navigation bar to begin configuring the ACS server:

Figure 2.11   Cisco Secure ACS server interface.

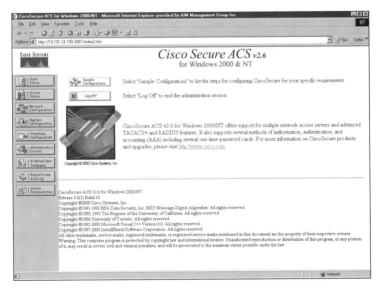

Figure 2.12   Console of the Cisco Secure ACS server.

- *User Setup*—View a list of all users contained within the Cisco Secure ACS database, find or add a user, assign a user to a group, edit a user's account, and disable or delete a user account.

- *Group Setup*—Create, rename, edit, and assign users to a group.

- *Network Configuration*—Edit network access server parameters. You can also add or delete network access servers from the Cisco Secure ACS server.

- *System Configuration*—Configure service control parameters that stop or restart the Cisco Secure ACS services, configure logging, set password validation, and control database replication.

- *Interface Configuration*—Configure TACACS+ and RADIUS options and control what options are displayed in the user interface.

- *Administration Control*—Configure the parameters that pertain to the administration of the Cisco Secure ACS server.

- *External User Databases*—Configure the unknown user policy, database group mappings, and the external user database, such as Windows NT/2000 Server database.

- *Reports and Activities*—View or export the reports that the ACS server generates.

The Cisco Secure ACS server comes with a Command-line Database Utility that lets administrators use the CSUtil.exe utility to import or export usernames, passwords, and group information all at once from a standard text file, allowing for backup and maintenance of the database. The utility can be run while the server is online or offline; the only disadvantage to running the utility while the server is online is a degradation of performance. To import the text file database into the Cisco Secure ACS server user database, add new users into the database, or modify users' authentication information, you must first open a DOS window and change the directory as follows:

```
C:\Program Files\CiscoSecure ACS v2.6\Utils
```

This is the location of the utility directory if you elected to install the Cisco Secure ACS software to the default location. The CSUtil.exe uses text files to perform the import and export functions. To configure the text file to add, update, or delete users, enter the following information of each field listed below on a single line and separate the fields with a colon:

Username field:

- *add*—Add user information to the Cisco Secure user database. If the username already exists, no information is changed.

- *update*—Update the information associated with the existing username in the Cisco Secure user database.

- *delete*—Remove the user information from the Cisco Secure user database.

Authentication field:

- *csdb*—Authenticate the username against the Cisco Secure user database.

- *ext_ldap*—Authenticate the username against a generic LDAP database.

- *ext_nt*—Authenticate the username against a Windows NT/2000 database.

- *ext_nds*—Authenticate the username against a Novell NDS database.

- *ext_sdi*—Authenticate the username against an SDI database.

- *ext_anpi*—Authenticate the username against an AXENT database.

- *ext_eniga*—Authenticate the username against a SafeWord database.

- *chap*—Use a CHAP password for authentication.

User Group:

- *profile*—Group number between 0 and 99 that the user is assigned.

The following is a sample import text file:

```
ADD:James:CSDB:letmein:PROFILE:1
ADD:admin:CSDB:admin:PROFILE:1
ADD:John:CSDB:cto:PROFILE:
ADD:joe:EXT_NT:CHAP:dialuppassword
ADD:jeff:CSDB:iloveunix
ADD:steve:EXT_NT:unixpassword
```

The CSUtil.exe utility supports the following arguments for importing and exporting the database files. Use the following arguments to import and/or export the database information:

```
CSUtil <-q> <-c> <-d> <-g> <-i filename> <-l filename> -
   <-e errornumber> <-b filename> <-r filename> <-f> <-n> -
   <-s> <-y> <-u> <-x>
```

Each argument has the following meaning:

- *q*—Runs the import or export in quiet mode and does not prompt for other options.

- *b*—Runs a complete system backup.

- *c*—Recalculates the database CRC values.

- *d*—Exports the complete database to a dump.txt file.

- *e*—Decodes error numbers to an ASCII message.

2. AAA Security Technologies

- *f*—Fixes group assignments.
- *g*—Exports all group information to the group.txt file.
- *i*—Imports or merges a named user file.
- *n*—Creates a new database.
- *r*—Restores a database from a named file.
- *s*—Removes deleted users from the database.
- *x*—Displays the help options.
- *y*—Dumps the server Registry information to a named file.
- *u*—Creates a file of all users within each group.

To create the backup of user information for each group, you will need to run a command like the following example from the DOS prompt of the Cisco Secure ACS server:

```
C:\Program Files\CiscoSecure ACS v2.6\Utils>CSUtil -u users.txt
```

This command creates a text file with the names of the group's members displayed under the group name. The output of this file is shown in Listing 2.12.

Listing 2.12   Output of the Users.txt file.
```
#Users listed on TACACS-SERVER01 at 08:50 November 01 2001
#SW version 2.6(1.10)
Group 'Network Engineers' (20 users):
nsa
nsanat
cw2000
TAC
<clipped>
Group 'Cable Engineers' (3 users):
testuser
CableGuy
FlukeMan
```

The file first lists the name of the Cisco Secure ACS server and the date on which the file was generated. The second line displays the current software version of the Cisco Secure ACS server. The lines following the first two display all the users in the Cisco Secure ACS server database and each group's members. This command is a useful backup command you can run quite often to maintain a current list of all users contained within the database. The preceding file only exported the users and the groups the users that are associated with. In many instances, the information contained in the file is not sufficient. Using the **CSUtil** command with the **–d** option, you can create a complete database backup that is exported to a file named dump.txt. The abridged output the dump.txt file creates is displayed in Listing 2.13.

Listing 2.13 Output of the dump.txt file.

```
#DB dumped on TACACS-SERVER01 at 08:51 November 01 2001
#DB version 8.0
#SW version 2.6(1.10)
#-------------------------
Name           :nsa
Password       :       0x0020 ca 64 ad 2c c0 13 8d 21 85 7f 0b -
  a5 75 63 11 9e 1f a5 f6 15 e3 96 2c d8 39 86 9c 4a 5f 53 e0 6c
Chap password :       0x0020 23 a6 08 39 d4 88 db 10 8e f7 ba -
  5d cf 5f 8d 21 ff c4 e4 63 86 c3 d6 27 c4 be 24 4a b1 ae 9a fe
State          :       0
S_flags        :       1
Aging policy   :       group0
Good count     :       0
Warning count :       0
Change count   :       0
Last change Lo:        334080752
Last change Hi:        29445163
Last auth Lo   :       0
Last auth Hi   :       0
Rights         :       1
Type           :       4
EnableType     :       4
Status         :       1
Reset          :       1
Expiry         :       209    100    4294937589    638    0    5
MaxSession     :       0
MaxSess2       :       0
Profile        :       0
LogonHrs       :       0x0016 00 ff ff ff ff ff ff ff ff ff ff ff
ff ff ff ff ff ff ff ff ff
Alias          :       0
Value Flags    :       524324
CounterVals_00:        161    161    689    1888
CounterRst_00 :        2667b8401c16164
CounterVals_01:        1      3      60      137
CounterRst_01 :        49391a60      1c161f7
##- User End
App00  EXTRN_PASSWD  ESTRING  0x0020 ca 64 2c c0 13 8d 21 58 73
f3 9c c0 5c bf 8d 12 d9 9a d8 b5 2e 61 3f b1 d8 91 f3 df d7 18
App00  USER_DEFINED_FIELD_0  STRING   Cisco NSA
App00  USER_DEFINED_FIELD_1  STRING   National Service
App00  IP_ACS_POOLS_LENGTH   INTEGER  2
```

```
App00   IP_ACS_POOLS            STRING
App00   IP_ALLOCATION_METHOD    INTEGER   5
App00   IP_STATIC_ADDR_LENGTH   INTEGER   1
App00   IP_STATIC_ADDR          STRING
App00   IP_NAS_POOL_LENGTH      INTEGER   1
App00   IP_NAS_POOL             STRING
App00   user_callback_type      INTEGER   0
App00   user_callback           STRING
App00   disp_callback           STRING
App01   Filters\NAS\records     MSTRING
App01   Filters\NAS\enabled     STRING    0
App01   Filters\NAS\option      STRING    PERMIT
App01   Filters\Dialup\records  MSTRING
App01   Filters\Dialup\enabled  STRING    0
App01   Filters\Dialup\option   STRING    PERMIT
App01   max_priv                STRING    15,1
App01   max_priv_LENGTH         INTEGER   4
App01   enable_passwd  ESTRING  0x0020 ca 64 ad 2c 13 8d 21 0c -
   13 ab e0 2d e1 60 ab 1f c1 c5 c7 33 07 ce ee c2 13 b2 22 a9 3a
ba
----------------------------
#End Of Dump
```

The most useful function of the CSUtil.exe utility is that it gives you the ability to back up the entire system, export it to secure location, and restore the server from the backup in the event of a catastrophic failure. To create the backup of the Cisco Secure ACS server, perform the following step:

1. From the command prompt of the Utility directory, use the **csutil –b** *filename* command. This command will create four compressed files in the Utils\SysBackup*directory*\: folder:

   - Registry.dat
   - User.dat
   - User.idx
   - Varsdb.mdb

   A fifth file is also created and stored in the Utils\dbcheckpoint directory. This file is stored in *yyyymmddhhmm*.zip format.

   Each time a backup is initiated, separate files are created, meaning the server does not overwrite the existing files in the directory. Performing the backup procedure on a regular basis is always recommended.

Perimeter Router Security

In Brief

To say that the Internet is the single-most amazing technological achievement of the "Information Age" is a gross understatement. This massive network has changed the way the world conducts business and approaches education, and it has even changed the way in which people spend their leisure time. At the same time, the Internet has presented a new, complex set of challenges that not even the most sophisticated technical experts have been able to adequately solve. The Internet is only in its infancy, and its growth is measured exponentially on a yearly basis.

With the rapid growth of the Internet, network security has become a major concern for companies throughout the world, and although protecting an enterprise's informational assets may be the security administrator's highest priority, protecting the integrity of the enterprise's network is critical to protecting the information it contains. A breach in the integrity of an enterprise's network can be extremely costly in time and effort, and it can open multiple avenues for continued attacks.

When you connect your enterprise network to the Internet, you are connecting your network to thousands of unknown networks, thus giving millions of people the opportunity to access your enterprise's assets. Although such connections open the door to many useful applications and provide great opportunities for information sharing, most enterprises contain some information that should not be shared with outside users on the Internet.

This chapter describes many of the security issues that arise when connecting an enterprise network to the Internet and details the technologies that can be used to minimize the threat of potential intruders to the enterprise and its assets. In this chapter, I'll discuss the Unicast Reverse Path Forwarding (Unicast RPF) feature, which helps to mitigate problems that are caused by forged IP source addresses that the perimeter router receives. I'll also discuss Committed Access Rate (CAR) and the features it provides to rate-limit traffic, thus providing mitigation services for DoS attacks. In addition, I'll discuss TCP SYN-flooding attacks and the features of TCP Intercept, which protect your network from this method of attack. This chapter covers Network Address Translation (NAT) and Port Address Translation (PAT), which were developed to address the depletion of global IP addresses and the security features that each provide. Finally, there is a discussion on logging of events that take place on the perimeter routers.

Defining Networks

This chapter classifies three different types of networks:

- Trusted
- Untrusted
- Unknown

Trusted Networks

Trusted networks are the networks inside your network's security perimeter. These are the networks you are trying to protect. Often, someone in your organization's IT department administers the computers that these networks comprise, and your enterprise's security policy determines their security controls. Usually, trusted networks are within the security perimeter.

Untrusted Networks

Untrusted networks are the networks that are known to be outside your security perimeter. They are untrusted because they are outside of your control. You have no control over the administration or security policies for these networks. They are the private, shared networks from which you are trying to protect your network. However, you still need and want to communicate with these networks even though they are untrusted. Untrusted networks are outside the security perimeter and external to the security perimeter.

Unknown Networks

Unknown networks are networks that are neither trusted nor untrusted. They are unknown to the security router because you cannot explicitly tell the router that the network is a trusted or an untrusted network. Unknown networks exist outside your security perimeter.

Cisco Express Forwarding

Cisco Express Forwarding (CEF) is an advanced layer 3 topology-based forwarding mechanism that optimizes network performance and accommodates the traffic characteristics of the Internet for the IP protocol. The topology-based forwarding method builds a forwarding table that exactly matches the topology of the routing table; thus, there is a one-to-one correlation between the entries in the CEF table and the prefixes in the route table. CEF offers improved performance over other router switching mechanisms by avoiding the overhead associated with other cache-driven switching mechanisms. CEF uses a *Forwarding Information Base (FIB)* to make destination prefix-based switching decisions. The FIB is very similar to the routing table. It maintains an identical copy of the forwarding information contained in the routing table. When topology changes occur in the network, the IP routing table will be updated, and the updated changes are reflected in the FIB. The FIB maintains next-hop address information based on the information in the routing table. Because there is a correlation between FIB entries and the routing table entries, the FIB contains all known routes.

CEF also builds an adjacency table, which maintains layer 2 next-hop addresses for all Forwarding Information Base entries, is kept separate from the CEF table, and can be populated by any protocol that can discover an adjacency. The adjacency table is built by first discovering the adjacency. Each time an adjacency entry is created through a dynamic process, the adjacent node's link-layer header is precomputed and stored in the adjacency table. After a route is resolved, its CEF entry points to a next-hop and corresponding adjacency entry. The entry is subsequently used for encapsulation during CEF switching of packets.

CEF can operate in two different modes: central and distributed. In *central mode*, the FIB and adjacency tables reside on the route processor and the route processor performs the forwarding.

CEF can act in a *distributed mode* on routers that support interface line cards, which have their own built-in processors, allowing CEF to take advantage of distributed architecture routers. When CEF is operating in distributed mode, the CEF table is copied down to the router line cards so that switching decisions can be made on the line cards instead of being made by the router processor. Distributed CEF uses a reliable Inter Process Communication mechanism that guarantees a synchronized FIB.

Unicast Reverse Path Forwarding

Unicast Reverse Path Forwarding (Unicast RPF) is a feature used to prevent problems caused by packets with forged IP sources addresses passing through a router. Unicast RPF helps to prevent denial-of-service (DoS) attacks based on source IP address spoofing. Unicast RPF requires the CEF switching mechanism to be enabled globally on the router. The router does not have to have each input interface config-ured for CEF switching because Unicast RPF searches through the FIB using the packet's source IP address. As long as CEF is running glo-bally on the router, each individual interface can be configured to use other switching modes. The effect of Unicast RPF is that packets with forged source IP addresses will be dropped by the router and will not be forwarded beyond the router's ingress interface.

NOTE: *Cisco Express Forwarding must be enabled for Unicast Reverse Path Forwarding to operate.*

When Unicast RPF is enabled on an interface, the router will verify that all packets received from that interface have a verifiable source address, which is reachable via that same interface or the best return path to the source of the packet via the ingress interface. The back-ward lookup ability used by Unicast RPF is available only when CEF is enabled on the router because the lookup relies on the presence of the FIB. If there is a reverse path route in the FIB, the packet is for-warded as normal. If there is no reverse path route via the interface from which the packet was received, the router may interpret that packet as being forged, meaning that the source address was modi-fied. If Unicast RPF does not find a reverse path for the packet, the packet is dropped or forwarded, depending on whether an access control list is specified in the configuration. If an access list is speci-fied in the command, then when a packet fails the Unicast RPF check, the access list is checked to see if the packet should be dropped or forwarded. The decision is made based on the presence of a permit or deny statement within the access list. Unicast RPF events can also be logged by specifying the logging option within the ACL entries used by the Unicast RPF command. The log information can be used to gather information about an attack.

Unicast RPF can be used in any enterprise environment that is single-homed to the Internet service provider (ISP), where there is only one access point out of the network; that is, one upstream connection. This would provide ingress filtering to protect the enterprise from receiving forged packets from the Internet. Networks having one en-trance and exit point provide symmetric routing, which means that the interface where a packet enters the network is also the interface the return packet takes to the source of the packet. Unicast RPF is best used at the network perimeter for Internet connections. It will also work in environments in which customers are multihomed to separate ISPs, where the enterprise has multiple access points out of the network. With Unicast RPF configured on the enterprise's perimeter router, all equal-cost return paths are considered valid.

Unicast RPF's advantage, when used for IP address spoof prevention, is that it dynamically adapts to changes in the routing tables, including static routes. Unicast RPF has minimal CPU overhead and has a far lower performance impact as an antispoofing tool compared to the traditional access list configuration approach. Unicast RPF should not be used on interfaces that are internal to the network because these interfaces are likely to have routing asymmetry.

TCP Intercept

Management's major misconception is that the firewall is the first, and in many cases the last, line of defense for security-related issues. In fact the external perimeter router should provide the first line of defense for external security-related issues from the enterprises perspective.

NOTE: *The enterprise should develop a positive working relationship with its ISP. If this relationship is established, the enterprise can request that the ISP provide many of the first-line defense mechanisms.*

TCP Intercept is a software feature designed to combat the denial-of-service (DoS) attack known as SYN flooding. The TCP protocol uses a three-way handshake to set up an end-to-end connection before data is allowed to flow. This handshake is detailed in Figure 3.1.

Referring to Figure 3.1, assume that Host B would like to open a connection to Host A. The connection must take place via Router C. Host B sends a SYN packet (a TCP packet with the SYN bit set) to Host A, requesting a connection. Host A then replies with a SYN/ACK packet

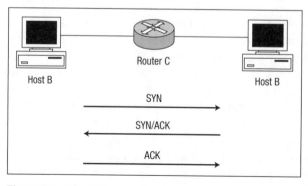

Figure 3.1   ICP three-way handshake.

with both the SYN and ACK bits set, allowing Host B to complete the three-way handshake with a TCP ACK packet. At this point, a connection is established and data is permitted to flow.

A TCP SYN attack occurs when an attacker exploits the buffer space a networked device uses during a TCP session initialization handshake. The attacker sends a large amount of packets with the SYN bit set to the target host, and the target host's in-process queue buffers the request and responds to it with a packet that has the SYN and ACK bits set within it. However, because these packets have an invalid return address, the connections can never be established and remain in a state known as *half-open*. As these half-open requests begin to build, buffer space is exhausted, which causes the machine to deny service for valid requests because all resources are exhausted waiting for a response. The target host eventually times out while waiting for the proper response.

Many TCP implementations are able to handle only a small number of outstanding connections per port; therefore, the ports become unavailable until the half-open connections time out. Additionally, this attack may also cause the server to exhaust its memory or waste processor cycles in maintaining state information for these connections.

TCP Intercept is designed to prevent a SYN flooding DoS attack by tracking, intercepting, and validating TCP connection requests. Intercept can run in one of two configurable modes: intercept mode and watch mode. In intercept mode, the software actively intercepts each incoming (SYN) request, responds on behalf of the server with a SYN/ACK, and then waits for an ACK from the client. When that ACK is received, the original SYN is sent to the server and the software performs a three-way handshake with the server. When this is complete, the two connections are joined by the router in a source-destination session.

In watch mode, connection requests are allowed to pass through the router to the server but are watched passively until they become established. If they fail to become established within 30 seconds or a software configurable timeout, the software sends a reset packet to the server to clear the in-process buffer, allowing the server to reallocate the buffer to legitimate requests.

After a device comes under attack from SYN floods, TCP Intercept will transition to a mode known as aggressive mode. Aggressive mode is triggered if the number of incomplete connections exceeds 1,100 or the number of connections arriving in one minute exceeds 1,100; after aggressive mode has triggered, each new arriving connection causes the oldest half-open connection to be deleted. TCP Intercept will also lower its initial retransmission timeout of 1 second by half, to 0.5 seconds. This allows the router to cut in half the time allotted to establish a connection.

When TCP Intercept is in aggressive mode, the following occurs:

- Each newest connection request causes the oldest half-open connection to be deleted.

- The initial retransmission timeout is reduced by half, to 0.5 seconds.

- If TCP Intercept is configured for watch mode, the watch timeout is reduced by half.

Network Address Translation

IP address depletion is one of the key problems that faces the Internet today. To address the IP address depletion problem Cisco has implemented a feature known as *Network Address Translation (NAT)*. NAT, described in RFC 1631, provides a way to use IP addresses in multiple Internetworks by replacing the original source or destination IP address in an IP packet. The functionality of NAT allows privately addressed networks to connect to public networks such as the Internet. When the host on the private inside network sends a packet through the NAT router, the private addresses are converted to registered globally routable IP addresses.

NAT helps to solve other problems aside from the rapid depletion of global network address space and provides an enterprise with many advantages, some of which are listed here:

- NAT reduces the instances in which addressing schemes overlap. If an IP scheme was originally set up within a private network and the network was connected to the public network, such as the Internet, or merges with another company that may use the same address, space communication could not take place because of overlapping IP address schemes. Without NAT, overlapping of address schemes could potentially take place on a global scale.

- Implementing NAT automatically creates a makeshift firewall between the internal trusted network and the outside untrusted networks or the Internet. NAT allows only connections that originate inside the trusted network. Essentially, this means that a computer on an external untrusted network cannot connect to a computer on the inside trusted network unless the inside computer has initiated the contact.

- NAT increases the flexibility of connecting to a public network and provides network designers with greater flexibility when designing an organization's addressing plan. This flexibility allows for multiple pools and loadsharing/balancing features. NAT also saves on the cost of renumbering a private network address space with a unique global address space.

Although most networking devices support NAT because of its many beneficial features, NAT does have a few disadvantages that should be weighed against the benefits when determining if it is a viable solution for the enterprise:

- NAT increases the overall switching delay of the packet, which is caused by the translation that must take place, but also because NAT is performed using process switching. The router must examine every packet to determine if a header rewrite is required.

- NAT causes the loss of end-to-end traceability and forces some applications that use IP addressing to stop functioning because of NAT's inherent functionality of hiding IP addresses.

At a high level, NAT has two types of networks: internal and external. Internal networks, also referred to as stub domains, are networks that have been assigned IP addresses that are considered to be private or not routable. Likewise, external networks are networks that are considered to be public and routable. NAT also has its own terminology for types of IP addresses:

- *Inside local IP address*—The IP address assigned to a host on the inside trusted network. These addresses are typically allocated from the private IP address ranges.

- *Inside global IP address*—A legitimate IP address that represents one or more inside local addresses to the outside network(s). These are the IP addresses that the inside local IP addresses are translated to. They are advertised outside the inside local address space.

- *Outside global IP address*—The IP address that is assigned to a host on the outside network by its owner. These addresses are allocated from legitimate globally routable address space.

- *Outside local IP address*—The IP address of an outside host as it appears to the inside network. This address is allocated from IP address space that is routable on the inside network.

NAT creates two types of address translations: simple and extended. A simple translation entry is an entry that simply maps one IP address to another IP address. An extended translation entry is a translation entry that maps one IP address and port pair information to another IP address and port pair.

Port Address Translation (PAT) is a variant of Network Address Translation (NAT). NAT creates a one-to-one address translation at the network layer and does not maintain port parameters per translation. PAT, on the other hand, creates a many-to-one address translation and maintains port parameters per translation. PAT allows many inside local IP address packets to be translated to one outside global address. It allows enterprises to conserve public IP addresses by translating the source of all inside addresses or all inside addresses matched by an access list to one global public IP address. When PAT is enabled on a perimeter router, the translation process chooses a unique source port number for each outbound connection request.

PAT can allow for translation of one IP address for up to 64,000 hosts. However, in most cases, a more realistic number of translations is in the vicinity of 4,000 hosts. PAT does not use well-known port numbers in its address translation, nor are any destination fields translated—only source information is translated.

Committed Access Rate

Committed Access Rate (CAR) is a software feature that implements both classification of services and policing of traffic through rate-limiting, which, in effect, limits the input or output transmission rate of an interface based on a configurable set of criteria. Network administrators can use CAR to designate traffic-handling policies when traffic either conforms to or exceeds a specified rate limit. CAR's rate-limiting feature manages the bandwidth policy for a network by ensuring that traffic falling within the specified rate parameters is sent while dropping packets that exceed the acceptable amount of traffic. CAR also specifies an exceed action, which can be set to drop packets.

CAR uses a token bucket measuring system. Tokens are inserted into the bucket at the committed rate, and the number of tokens in the bucket is limited by the configured burst size. Traffic arriving at the bucket when tokens are available is traffic that matches a configured conform action. If tokens are available when the traffic arrives, the appropriate number of tokens are removed from the bucket and the specified conform action is executed. If there is not an adequate number of tokens available, the traffic matches a configured exceed action. The token bucket is a culmination of three components: a Mean Rate (CIR), a Burst Size (Bc), and a Time Interval (Tc). Each of these components is further detailed in the following list:

- *Mean Rate (CIR)*—The average rate at which you would like to transmit. The rate is averaged over an increment of time (Tc), and traffic that is under this rate will always conform. This is measured in bits/second.
- *Burst Size (Bc)*—The amount of data sent per time interval (Tc). When used with CAR, this is measured in bytes per burst interval.
- *Time Interval (Tc)*—A measurement of Bc/CIR.

The token bucket formula for determining the Mean Rate of transfer is as follows:

```
Mean Rate (CIR) = Burst Size (Bc) / Time Interval (Tc)
```

The equation solves for Mean Rate (CIR) by dividing the Time Interval (Tc) by the Burst Size (Bc). One other formula that relates to the token bucket measuring system solves for the Time Interval (Tc):

```
Time Interval (Tc) = Burst Size (Bc) / Mean Rate (Cir)
```

Each action, conform and exceed, can be configured to provide another action based on the available tokens:

- *Transmit*—The packet is forwarded accordingly.
- *Drop*—The packet is dropped and no further processing takes place on it.
- *Set precedence then transmit*—The IP Precedence bit in the packet is rewritten. The packet is then transmitted.
- *Continue*—The packet is compared to the next policy that is configured in the list of rate limits. If no other policy is configured, the packet is sent.
- *Set precedence and continue*—The IP Precedence bits are rewritten to a specified value, and the packet is then compared to the next policy configured in the list of rate limits.

3. Perimeter Router Security

A security administrator can use CAR's rate-limiting feature to control the maximum rate at which traffic is sent or received during times the router is receiving a stream of DoS attack packets. To define a rate limit, three values must be specified:

- *Average rate*—The average rate at which you want to transmit. All traffic that is transmitted at or below the average rate meets the conform action. Traffic that is transmitted above the average rate meets the exceed action, depending on the values configured for normal burst and excess burst. This value is specified in bits per second.

- *Normal burst*—The amount of traffic, specified in bytes per second, that is allowed to burst before partial amounts of traffic are subjected to the excess burst action.

- *Excess burst*—The amount of traffic, specified in bytes per second, that is allowed in a burst before all traffic is subjected to the excess burst action. Setting this value to zero disables bursting.

When CAR rate-limiting is applied to a packet, CAR removes from the bucket tokens that are equivalent in number to the byte size of the packet. If a packet arrives and its byte size is greater than the number of tokens available in the standard token bucket, extended burst capability is engaged if it is configured. Extended burst is configured by setting the extended burst so it's greater than the normal burst value. Setting the extended burst value equal to the normal burst value, in effect, disables extended burst.

Logging

Routers are a mainstay of most network-connected organizations. Over the past few years, they have become increasingly sophisticated and moved beyond the realm of simply connecting different subnets. Although routers provide a high degree of network security, it can sometimes be challenging to security administrators to answer questions such as the following:

- Who's on my network and where are they spending their time?

- Are my network security and usage policies being adhered to?

- Is my router secure?

- Have there been any attempts to breach it?

- Are there any system failures or configuration issues to attend to?

Logging of events that take place on the perimeter routers provides a security administrator with a clear audit trail of each and every bit of information that traverses the router. This information is needed in order to assess network activity and find out if security and network usage policies are functioning as designed. Accomplishing complete network security is an investigative process that requires ongoing analysis of network device activity. Because of this investigative process, security administrators should log every event that takes place on the perimeter router to a syslog server daemon to aid in analyzing attacks that take place from a trusted or untrusted network.

Cisco routers define certain levels of message logging, and each level is based upon the severity of the event. Table 3.1 lists each event error message and its corresponding severity level.

Table 3.1 Logging messages and severity level.

Level keyword	Level	Description
debugging	7	Debug message
informational	6	Informational message
notifications	5	Significant informational message
warnings	4	Warning condition message
errors	3	Error condition message
critical	2	Critical condition error message
alerts	1	Action needed message
emergency	0	System down message

3. Perimeter Router Security

Immediate Solutions

Configuring Cisco Express Forwarding

On most platforms, CEF is not enabled by default, so security administrators must remember to enable the feature.

NOTE: Cisco Express Forwarding (CEF) is not a security feature; therefore, CEF will not be covered in detail. However, the majority of the security features discussed in this chapter must have CEF enabled to function.

Use the **ip cef** global configuration command to enable CEF switching or enable the use of distributed CEF by using the **ip cef distributed** global configuration command. Distributed CEF functions only on platforms that support a distributed architecture.

To give you an idea about how CEF works, Figure 3.2 shows Router C with multiple connections to other networks. The configuration of Router C to support CEF switching is shown here:

```
#config t
#ip cef distributed
#end
#
```

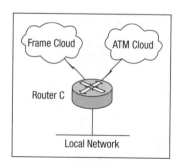

Figure 3.2   Example of CEF network.

The **ip cef distributed** global configuration command was used to enable CEF on Router C. After it is enabled on Router C, CEF should create an adjacency table listing each connected device. CEF can create an adjacency by using Address Resolution Protocol (ARP); if Router B is using a routing protocol, an adjacency can be created by using the routing protocol B, and an adjacency can be can be created from a static mapping, using a layer 2 protocol. To verify that CEF created the table, use the **show adjacency detail** command. Listing 3.1 shows the output of the **show adjacency detail** command issued on Router B after enabling CEF.

Listing 3.1 The adjacency table of Router B.

```
Router-B#show adjacency detail
Protocol     Interface          Address
IP           Serial5/0/0        point2point(5)
                                61528 packets,  5684464 bytes
                                0F000800
                                CEF     expires: 00:02:17
                                        refresh: 00:00:17
IP           GigEthernet1/0/0   192.168.15.73(2425)
                                1281569464 packets,
                                310581090467 bytes
                                0030962EB2E800307B6AC0200800
                                ARP         02:04:24
IP           ATM8/0/0           192.168.14.253(73)
                                6276628796 packets,
                                6720323814548 bytes
                                00010000AAAA030000000800
                                ATM-PVC     never
Router-B#
```

In Listing 3.1, you can see that Router B has created an adjacency with each of the routers it is connected to. Each of the fields details specifics related to the CEF adjacency. The protocol field lists the routed protocol with which the adjacency is related. The interface field lists the outgoing interface used to reach the adjacency neighbor. The address field is the address of the adjacency and can contain either the adjacency's next-hop address or a point-to-point address. The numbers that are in parentheses in the address field are used only by the local router and as a reference to the adjacency. The next field is an encapsulation string, which is prepended to each packet. And the last field is a timer, which is periodically refreshed for each neighbor. The adjacency table will periodically refresh each of these neighbors with the exception of the neighbor connected via the ATM interface. Because this entry is a permanent circuit, CEF will not refresh the neighbor.

As mentioned in the section "In Brief" earlier in this chapter, CEF builds its table based on information within the route table, and as such, a one-to-one correlation between the CEF table and the route table is maintained. The CEF table is stable as long as the topology of the route table is stable. The CEF table of Router B can be viewed using the **show ip cef** command. Listing 3.2 shows the output of the command **show ip cef** entered on Router B.

Listing 3.2   An example CEF table for Router B.

```
Router-B#show ip cef
Prefix                 Next Hop            Interface
0.0.0.0/0              192.168.15.73       GigabitEthernet1/0/0
0.0.0.0/32             receive
4.18.103.0/24          192.168.15.73       GigabitEthernet1/0/0
4.24.104.92/30         192.168.14.253      ATM8/0/0
192.168.200.0/24       192.168.15.73       GigabitEthernet1/0/0
192.168.200.1/32       192.168.15.73       GigabitEthernet1/0/0
192.168.200.2/32       192.168.15.73       GigabitEthernet1/0/0
192.168.200.3/32       192.168.15.73       GigabitEthernet1/0/0
192.168.1.40/30        attached            Serial5/0/0
192.168.1.40/32        receive
192.168.1.42/32        receive
192.168.1.43/32        receive
192.168.15.73/32       192.168.15.73       GigabitEthernet1/0/0
192.168.15.75/32       receive
192.168.15.79/32       receive
192.168.15.80/29       192.168.15.73       GigabitEthernet1/0/0
192.168.14.252/30      attached            ATM8/0/0
192.168.14.253/32      receive
192.168.14.254/32      receive
```

Further information for each CEF table entry can be seen by issuing the **sh ip cef** *network* command. The following information is returned:

```
Router-B#sh ip cef 4.24.104.92
4.24.104.92/30, version 1046593, cached adjacency 10.191.150.242
0 packets, 0 bytes
  via 192.168.241.2, ATM8/0/0, 0 dependencies
    next hop 192.168.14.253, ATM8/0/0
    valid cached adjacency
```

The routing table entry for 4.24.104.92 has a next-hop address of 192.168.241.2, which is not directly connected. This entry requires a recursive lookup for the next hop for 192.168.241.2 to determine that 192.168.241.2 can be reached using the next hop of 192.168.14.253, which is reachable sending the packet out interface ATM8/0/0.

Configuring Unicast Reverse Path Forwarding

Enterprise networks should use Unicast RPF as an ingress filter to protect themselves from untrusted networks. Although most enterprises use access lists for ingress filtering, Unicast RPF provides many advantages over the traditional access list approach. The following section will provide some examples of how Unicast RPF can provide valuable protection options for networks connected to the Internet.

NOTE: *Unicast RPF should not be configured on any internal network device where asymmetric routing is taking place. This will cause Unicast RPF to drop legitimate return traffic.*

When Unicast RPF is enabled on an interface, the router examines all packets received on that interface. The router checks to make sure that the source address appears in the routing table and matches the interface on which the packet was received. To configure Unicast RPF for ingress filtering, follow these steps:

1. Use the **ip cef** or **ip cef distributed** command to enable CEF switching or distributed CEF switching.

2. Use the following command to select the input interface on which to apply Unicast RPF:

```
interface <interface name> <interface number>
```

The input interface is the receiving interface, which allows Unicast RPF to verify the best return path before forwarding the packet to the destination.

3. Use the following command to enable Unicast RPF on the interface:

```
ip verify unicast reverse-path <access list number>
```

The **access list number** option identifies an optional access list. If the access list denies network access, packets with changed headers are dropped at the interface. If the access list permits network access, packets with changed headers are forwarded to the destination address.

4. Use the following command to define an extended access list and its parameters:

```
access-list <access-list-number> {deny|permit} <protocol> -
    <source> <source-wildcard> <destination> <destination -
    wildcard>
```

A **deny** statement configures the router to drop the packet and a **permit** statement allows the packet to forward out the egress interface toward its destination.

Figure 3.3 displays a network in which Unicast RPF is enabled on both interfaces of Router 1.

The objective is to use Unicast RPF for filtering traffic at the ingress interfaces of Router 1 to provide protection from malformed packets arriving from the Internet or from the internal network. The following commands configure Router 1 for Unicast RPF:

```
Router-1
!
ip cef distributed
!
interface Serial1/0
ip verify unicast reverse-path
!
interface Ethernet0/0
ip verify unicast reverse-path
!
```

The preceding configuration is all that is needed to have Unicast RPF running on the router. It is very important to remember that CEF must be enabled on the router prior to configuring Unicast RPF. In fact, the router will not allow Unicast RPF to be configured until CEF is enabled, as shown in the following display:

```
Router-1(config-if)#ip verify unicast reverse-path
% CEF not enabled. Enable first
```

As you can see, the router will display a prompt that demands that you enable CEF on the router prior to configuring Unicast RPF. To verify that Unicast is operational, use the **show cef interface** *<interface name>* *<interface number>* command. The output should verify that Unicast RPF is in fact operational. Listing 3.3 displays the output.

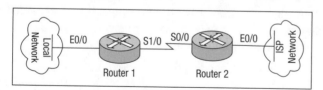

Figure 3.3   Unicast RPF.

Listing 3.3   An example of the **show cef interface** command.

```
Router-1#sh cef interface serial1/0 detail
Serial1/0 is up (if_number 3)
  Internet address is 172.16.10.1/24
  ICMP redirects are always sent
  Per packet loadbalancing is disabled
  IP unicast RPF check is enabled
  Inbound access list is not set
  Outbound access list is not set
  IP policy routing is disabled
  Hardware idb is serial1/0
  Fast switching type 1, interface type 18
  IP CEF switching enabled
  IP CEF Feature Fast switching turbo vector
  Input fast flags 0x4000, Output fast flags 0x0
  ifindex 2(2)
  Slot 1 Slot unit 0 VC -1
  Transmit limit accumulator 0x0 (0x0)
  IP MTU 1500
Router-1#
```

Unicast RPF also allows for the configuration of an optional access list to control the exact behavior when the received packet fails the source IP address check. The access list can be defined as a standard access list or as an extended access list. If an access list is defined, then after a packet fails a Unicast RPF check, the access list is checked to see if the packet should be dropped or forwarded. Unicast RPF events can also be logged by specifying the logging option for the access list entries used by Unicast RPF.

The following example configures Router 1 in Figure 3.3 to use access lists and logging with Unicast RPF. In the example in Listing 3.4, the extended access list 114 contains entries that should permit or deny network traffic for specific address ranges received on **interface serial1/0**. Unicast RPF is configured on interface **serial1/0** to check packets arriving at that interface.

Listing 3.4   An example Unicast RPF logging configuration.

```
ip cef distributed
!
int serial1/0
ip verify unicast reverse-path 114
!
int ethernet0/0
ip verify unicast reverse-path
!
```

```
access-list 114 deny ip 192.168.10.0 0.0.0.255 any log-input
access-list 114 deny ip 192.168.20.0 0.0.0.255 any log-input
access-list 114 deny ip 192.168.30.0 0.0.0.255 any log-input
access-list 114 permit ip 192.168.9.0 0.0.0.255 any log-input
```

The configuration in Listing 3.4 denies packets with a source address of 192.168.10.0, 192.168.20.0, or 192.168.30.0 from arriving at interface serial1/0 because of the deny statement in access list 114. The access lists also logs any packet that is matched by the access list. Packets with a source address within the 192.168.9.0 subnet arriving at interface serial1/0 are forwarded if the source cannot be verified against interface serial1/0 because of the permit statement in access list 114. To verify that logging of the access list entries are taking place, use the **show access-lists** command:

```
Router-1# show access-lists
Extended IP access list 114
deny ip 192.168.10.0 0.0.0.255 any log-input (87 match)
deny ip 192.168.20.0 0.0.0.255 any log-input (32 match)
deny ip 192.168.30.0 0.0.0.255 any log-input (76 match)
permit ip 192.168.9.0 0.0.0.255 any log-input (63 match)
```

Each time a packet is dropped at an interface, information is not only logging globally on the router but also at each interface configured for Unicast RPF. Global statistics about packets that have been dropped provide information about potential attacks. To view the global drop statistics, use the **show ip traffic** command. Here is the output:

```
Router-1#show ip traffic
IP statistics:
  Rcvd:  1290449399 total, 75488293 local destination
         0 format errors, 183 checksum errors, 8684 bad hop count
         62 unknown protocol, 0 not a gateway
         0 security failures, 0 bad options, 1147 with options
  .....
  Drop:  1468583 encap failed, 325 unresolved, 0 no adjacency
         7805049 no route, 41 unicast RPF, 1428682 forced drop
Router-1#
```

Interface statistics help to provide information about which interface is the source of the attack. Statistics for each interface can be viewed using the **show ip interface** command. Interface statistics display two separate types of RPF drops: Unicast RPF drops and Unicast RPF suppressed drops. The display for Unicast RPF drops shows the number of drops at the interface, and the display for Unicast suppressed drops shows the number of packets that failed the Unicast RPF reverse lookup check but were forwarded because of a permit statement configured within the access list that is applied to Unicast RPF. The following output is from the **show ip interface** command:

```
Router-1#show ip interface serial1/0
...
Unicast RPF ACL 114
37 unicast RPF drops
12 unicast RPF suppressed drops
Router-1#
```

Configuring TCP Intercept

The configuration of TCP Intercept is based on access lists, which are bound within TCP Intercept commands. Thus, access lists bound within TCP Intercept are not bound to an interface, as in most access list configurations.

Use the following steps to configure TCP Intercept (Steps 4, 5 and 6 are optional):

1. Use the following global configuration command to define an extended IP access list:

   ```
   access-list access-list number [deny|permit] tcp any -
      <destination> <destination-wildcard mask>
   ```

   The access list can be configured to intercept either all TCP requests or only those coming from specific networks or destined for specific servers. The access list should define the source as any and define specific destination networks or servers; do not attempt to filter on the source addresses because you may not know which source address to intercept packets from. Identify the destination to protect destination servers.

2. Use the following command to enable TCP Intercept:

   ```
   ip tcp intercept list access-list number
   ```

3. Use this command to configure the mode in which TCP Intercept should operate:

   ```
   ip tcp intercept mode <watch|intercept>
   ```

4. If Intercept is configured to run in watch mode, configure the amount of time it will wait for a watched connection to an established state before terminating the connection. Use this command to do so:

```
ip tcp intercept watch-timeout <seconds>
```

5. Configure the mode that Intercept should use to drop connections when under attack and running in aggressive mode by using this command:

```
ip tcp intercept drop-mode <random|oldest>
```

6. Configure the amount of time that a connection will be managed by Intercept by using the following command:

```
ip tcp intercept connection-timeout <seconds>
```

TCP Intercept has a number of other command arguments, which will be discussed in detail throughout this section. It should be noted that only the first three steps in the preceding list are required to take advantage of the features that TCP Intercept provides. The other steps, as well as the commands that will be discussed later, are considered commands that are used to fine-tune the operation of TCP Intercept.

NOTE: Do not configure TCP Intercept on the perimeter router if the router is configured for Context-Based Access Control (CBAC).

In Figure 3.4, Router B is the perimeter router for the enterprise and is configured for TCP Intercept. Router B has been configured to intercept requests to a Web server that has an IP address of 192.168.20.20 and to intercept requests to an FTP server with an IP address of 192.168.20.21.

Listing 3.5 details the configuration commands needed to configure Router B to intercept requests to the Web server and FTP server. Router B is configured for TCP Intercept in watch mode.

Listing 3.5   TCP Intercept configuration of Router B.

```
#config t
#access-list 100 permit tcp any host 192.168.20.20
#access-list 100 permit tcp any host 192.168.20.21
#ip tcp intercept list 100
#ip tcp intercept mode intercept
#end
#
```

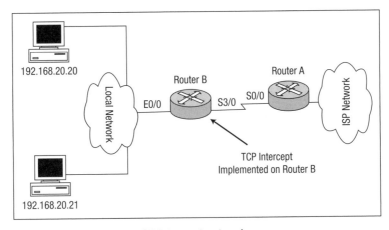

Figure 3.4   An example TCP Intercept network.

The configuration in Listing 3.5 defines access list 100 and permits any TCP traffic with a destination of 192.168.20.20 and 192.168.20.21 to be intercepted by Router B. TCP Intercept is configured on Router B and access list 100 is bound to the TCP Intercept configuration and the mode is configured for watch mode. TCP Intercept has a limited number of verification and debugging tools. One of the most useful verification commands is the **show tcp intercept statistics** command. Listing 3.6 lists the output of this command.

Listing 3.6   The output of show tcp intercept statistics.

```
Router-B#show tcp intercept statistics
Intercepting new connections using access-list 100
148 incomplete, 851 established connections (total 999)
1 minute connection request rate 49 requests/sec
Router-B#
```

The output of the **show tcp intercept statistics** command demonstrates that TCP Intercept is using access list 100 to compare against all new connections. The output of the command displays the number of incomplete connections and established connections.

The connection requests for each server can be monitored in realtime using the **sh tcp intercept connections** command. Issuing the command on Router B displays the output shown in Listing 3.7.

Listing 3.7   Example of show TCP intercept connections output.

```
Router-B# show tcp intercept connections
Incomplete:
Client                 Server             State   Create    Timeout M
208.19.121.12:58190 192.168.20.20:80 SYNRCVD 00:00:06 00:00:02 I
```

```
208.19.121.12:57934  192.168.20.20:80  SYNRCVD 00:00:06 00:00:02 I
168.41.18.4:59274    192.168.20.21:23  SYNRCVD 00:00:06 00:00:02 I
168.41.18.4:56196    192.168.20.21:23  SYNRCVD 00:00:06 00:00:02 I
...
Established:
Client                Server            State  Create   Timeout   M
17.96.23.23:1045  192.168.20.20:80      ESTAB  00:01:10 23:58:52  I
...
```

NOTE: *The "M" in the 3rd and 10th lines in Listing 3.7 represents the word "Mode."*

In Listing 3.7, the Incomplete section displays information related to connections that are not yet established. The Client field displays the source IP address of the client requesting service from the server and also lists the randomly generated source port number the source is using to communicate on. The Server field displays the destination server IP address and port number that is being protected by TCP Intercept. As discussed earlier, TCP Intercept will intercept each incoming connection request from the source and respond to the source on behalf of the server. After the source responds back to the router, the router will send the original SYN request packet to the server and merge the connections. The state of each of the connection requests is listed in the State field. The State field can contain one of three values:

- *SYNRCVD*—When the connection is in this state, the router is attempting to establish a connection with the source of the connection request. It is during this phase that the router sends a SYN-ACK to the source and is awaiting an ACK from the source.

- *SYNSENT*—When the connection is in this state, the router is attempting to establish a connection with the destination of the connection request. It is during this phase that the router has received an ACK from the source and is sending the original SYN request to the server in an attempt to perform the three-way handshake.

- *ESTAB*—In order for the connection to reach this state, the two separate connections have been joined and communication between the source and destination is established.

The Create field details the amount of time since the connection was created. The Timeout field lists the amount of time remaining until the retransmission timeout is reached. The Mode field displays the mode under which TCP Intercept is running; the values can be either **I** (for intercept mode) or **W** (for watch mode). The Established section displays information related to connections that have become established. All fields in the Established section maintain the same values they have in the Incomplete section with the exception of the Timeout field, which displays the time remaining until the connection timeout is reached and the connection is dropped.

In Listing 3.5, Router B was configured to operate in intercept mode in the earlier configuration; however, this can be changed using the **ip tcp intercept mode** command. Below, Router B is configured to operate in watch mode, and the **ip tcp intercept watch-timeout** command is used to lower the watch timeout from the default 30 seconds to a value of 16 seconds. Changing the watch timeout will define how long Intercept will wait for a watched TCP connection to reach an established state before it sends a reset to the server. The following configuration reflects the changes:

```
#config t
#ip tcp intercept mode watch
#ip tcp intercept watch-timeout 16
#end
```

The default timeout value for an established session with no activity is 24 hours, or one day. Notice in Listing 3.7 that there is one established session between the client and server. The timeout value for the connection still has 23 hours, 58 minutes, and 52 seconds left before it times out. This means the connection will still be managed by the router for that amount of time, even if there is no activity between the client and server. In some environments, such as those with a large amount of connection requests, the default connection timeout value should be lowered so that the router does not have to use resources managing connections that are not being used. The connection timeout value can be changed using the **ip tcp intercept connection-timeout** command. Router B will now be configured to lower the default connection timeout value to 6 hours:

```
#config t
#ip tcp intercept connection-timeout 21600
#end
```

The **connection-timeout** command accepts the timeout value in seconds. The timeout value can be configured as low as 1 second and as high as 2147483 seconds.

3. Perimeter Router Security

Another method of viewing TCP Intercept statistics is to use the **debug ip tcp intercept** command. Using the debug command allows administrators to view a connections request in realtime. Using Listing 3.7 as a reference, the **debug ip tcp intercept** command was issued to monitor each connection request. Listing 3.8 details the output of the debug command; only the first and second connection requests are recorded in the output.

Listing 3.8   Example output from debug ip tcp intercept.

```
!1st connection attempt
: new connection (208.19.121.12:58190) => (192.168.20.20:80)
: (208.19.121.12:58190) <- ACK+SYN (192.168.20.20:58190)

!2nd connection attempt
: new connection (168.41.18.4:59274) => (192.168.20.21:23)
: (168.41.18.4:59274) <- ACK+SYN (192.168.20.21:59274)

!Router B retransmits to the 1st client
: retransmit 4 (208.19.121.12:58190) <- (192.168.20.20:80)
: SYNRCVD

!Router B establishes a connection to the second client
: 1st half of conn is established
: (168.41.18.4:59274)=>(192.168.20.21:23)
: (168.41.18.4:59274) SYN -> (192.168.20.21:23) SYNSENT

!Server responds and the connection is established
: 2nd half of conn established
: (168.41.18.4:59274)=>(192.168.20.21:23)
: (168.41.18.4:59274) ACK -> (192.168.20.21:23)

!The router tries to establish a connection to the 1st client,
!then times the connection out and sends a reset to the server.
: retransmit 16 (208.19.121.12:58190)<-(192.168.20.20:80)
: SYNRCVD
: retransmit  expire
: (208.19.121.12:58190)=>(192.168.20.20:80) SYNRCVD
: (208.19.121.12:58190) <- RST (192.168.20.20:80)
```

The debug output in Listing 3.8 details the steps that TCP Intercept takes after it's configured, and a new connection request to a device that is matched by the configured access list is initiated.

After a device comes under attack from SYN floods, TCP Intercept will transition to a mode known as aggressive mode. Whether or not Intercept transitions to aggressive mode is determined by two values: the total number of incomplete connections and the total number of connection requests during Intercept's last 60-second sampling period. If either of these values is exceeded, TCP Intercept assumes that the device is under attack and transitions to aggressive mode. After both of the values fall below the configured minimum, the aggressive behavior ends.

When TCP Intercept is in aggressive mode, it will begin to drop the oldest partial connection request for each new connection that is requested when under attack; however, this action can be changed using the **ip tcp intercept drop-mode** global configuration command. The drop mode can be changed, so that TCP Intercept will drop any connection request regardless of age, instead of dropping the oldest partial connection request. TCP Intercept will also change the watch timeout if it is configured to run in watch mode. If Intercept is running in watch mode, the watch mode timeout value is reduced by half when TCP Intercept transitions to aggressive mode. The threshold for triggering aggressive mode is based on the total number of incomplete connections and can be configured using the following commands:

```
ip tcp intercept max-incomplete low number
ip tcp intercept max-incomplete high number
```

The default for the low value is 900 incomplete connections, and the default for the high value is 1100 incomplete connections. The threshold for triggering aggressive mode based on the number of connection requests received in the last 60-second sample period can be configured using the following commands:

```
ip tcp intercept one-minute low number
ip tcp intercept one-minute high number
```

The default for the 60-second low value is the same as the **max-incomplete low** value, 900. The default value for the 60-second high value is the same as the **max-incomplete high** value, 1100.

Router B should be configured to trigger TCP Intercept aggressive mode sooner than normal, and the drop mode should be configured such that it will randomly drop partial connections regardless of the age time for each connection request. This can be accomplished using the configuration in Listing 3.9.

Listing 3.9   Example Intercept aggressive mode configuration.

```
#config t
#ip tcp intercept drop-mode random
#ip tcp intercept max-incomplete low 400
#ip tcp intercept max-incomplete high 600
#ip tcp intercept one-minute low 400
#ip tcp intercept one-minute high 600
#end
```

The drop mode for router B has been changed from the default of dropping the oldest partial connection to dropping any connection regardless of the age value. The configuration also lowered the values that TCP Intercept uses to trigger aggressive mode behavior. The final TCP configuration of Router B can be seen in Listing 3.10.

Listing 3.10   Final TCP Intercept configuration.

```
#ip tcp intercept list 100
#ip tcp intercept mode watch
#ip tcp intercept watch-timeout 16
#ip tcp intercept connection-timeout 21600
#ip tcp intercept drop-mode random
#ip tcp intercept max-incomplete low 400
#ip tcp intercept max-incomplete high 600
#ip tcp intercept one-minute low 400
#ip tcp intercept one-minute high 600
#access-list 100 permit tcp any host 192.168.20.20
#access-list 100 permit tcp any host 192.168.20.21
```

Configuring Network Address Translation (NAT)

Perimeter routers help enterprises to solve IP address space depletion problems; they can also hide internal IP addresses from outside networks. To provide these functions as well as many others, perimeter routers use Network Address Translation (NAT) and Port Address Translation (PAT). The following sections provide guidelines for configuring the various types of NAT and PAT on Cisco routers.

Configuring Static NAT Translations

Static Network Address Translation (NAT) allows security administrators to configure their routers such that individual inside local IP addresses can be translated to individual global inside IP addresses.

Static NAT is particularly useful when hosts on the outside network need the capability to access a host or hosts on the inside network. NAT compares the packets that are destined to a global outside address against the inside local address that is configured on the NAT translation entries. If the source of the packet has a valid entry in the translation table, the packet source address is rewritten with the matching inside global IP address.

NAT maintains a table of translated IP addresses. To the outside network, the inside network appears to have a certain range of IP addresses. These addresses are mapped to the actual IP addresses that are used inside the enterprise. Static NAT is referred to as a *simple translation entry*.

Use the following steps to configure static NAT translation for inside IP addresses:

1. Use the following command to establish a static translation between an inside local address and an inside global address:

```
ip nat inside source static <inside local address> <inside
global address>
```

   The inside local address is the address that is to be translated, and the inside global address is the address that the inside local address is to be translated to.

2. Use this command to move into interface configuration mode:

```
interface <interface type> <interface number>
```

3. Use the **ip nat inside** interface configuration command to apply NAT to the interface that is connected to the networks with the local addresses.

4. Use this command to move into interface configuration mode:

```
interface <interface type> <interface number>
```

5. Use the **ip nat outside** interface configuration command to apply NAT to the interface that is connected to the networks with the inside global addresses.

The preceding steps included the minimum commands needed to configure static NAT translation. Figure 3.5 displays a network that must use NAT to communicate with outside networks.

3. Perimeter Router Security

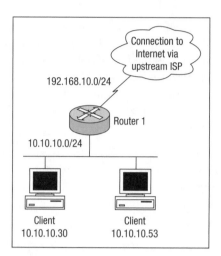

Figure 3.5   Static NAT.

The networks that are behind Router 1 are all allocated from RFC 1918 nonroutable address space. The Web server has an inside local address of 10.10.10.30 and must be accessible to outside networks via the address 192.168.10.30. The other server is an email server that has an IP address of 10.10.10.53 and must be accessible to outside networks via the address 192.168.10.53. The commands used to configure static NAT translations on Router 1 are shown in Listing 3.11.

Listing 3.11   Static NAT configuration.

```
#config t
#ip nat inside source static 10.10.10.30 192.168.10.30
#ip nat inside source static 10.10.10.53 192.168.10.53
!
#interface FastEthernet0/0
#ip address 10.10.10.2 255.255.255.0
#ip nat inside
!
#interface Serial1/0
#ip address 192.168.10.2 255.255.255.0
#ip nat outside
```

In Listing 3.11, Router 1 has been configured with two static translation entries.

NOTE: *Although the 192.168.0.0 range is allocated from RFC 1918 private address space, it is being used in these examples as a registered IP address block.*

The Fast Ethernet interface is designated as the inside interface with the **ip nat inside** command, and interface Serial1/0 is designated as the outside interface with the **ip nat outside** command. To verify that the configuration is correct, issue the **sh ip nat translation** command. The following output lists the information related to the simple translation entry:

```
Router-1#sh ip nat trans
Pro Inside global   Inside local   Outside local   Outside global
-  192.168.10.30   10.10.10.30   -              -
-  192.168.10.53   10.10.10.53   -              -
```

The **show ip nat translations** command lists the protocol field, the inside global address, the inside local address, the outside local address, and the outside global address. The outside local and outside global fields will be discussed later in this chapter when you learn more about extended entries. Another command that can be used to monitor and verify the operation of NAT is the **show ip nat translations verbose** command. Issuing this command on Router 1 displays the following output:

```
Router-1#sh ip nat trans ver
Pro Inside global   Inside local   Outside local   Outside global
-  192.168.10.30   10.10.10.30       -              -
      create 00:49:01, use 00:00:01,
      flags: static, use_count: 74
-  192.168.10.53       10.10.10.53   -              -
      create 00:49:12, use 00:00:7,
      flags: static, use_count: 50
Router-1#
```

The **verbose** argument of the **show ip nat translations** command produces more detailed information regarding the status of the NAT translations. As you can see in the preceding output, the fields that are listed with the **verbose** argument are the same as the fields that were listed without it. The output when the **verbose** argument is used includes a create field that lists how long ago the entry was created. The use field lists how long ago the translation entry was last used. The times in the create and use fields are listed in the *hours:minutes:seconds* format. The flag field indicates the type of translation entry, and there are a total of five possible flags:

- *static*—States that the entry was created by a static translation entry

- *extended*—States that the entry was created by an extended translation entry

- *outside*—States that the entry was created by an outside translation entry

- *destination*—States that the entry was created by an outside translation entry

- *time out*—States that the entry will no longer be used and is being torn down

The use count field lists the total number of times the entry has been used. One last command used to monitor and verify the operation of NAT is the **show ip nat statistics** command. The following output is displayed when the **show ip nat statistics** command is issued on Router 1:

```
Router-1#sh ip nat stat
Total active translations: 2 (2 static, 0 dynamic; 0 extended)
Outside interfaces:
  Serial1/0
Inside interfaces:
  FastEthernet0/0
Hits: 124  Misses: 0
Expired translations: 0
Dynamic mappings:
Router-1#
```

The total active translations field lists the total number of active NAT translations on the router. This field is populated in realtime; each time a translation entry is created, the field is incremented accordingly, and each time a translation entry is dropped or times out, the field is decremented accordingly. The outside interface is then listed and is determined based on the **ip nat outside** command. The inside interface is listed next and is determined based on the **ip nat inside** command. The hits field lists the total number of times NAT does a translation table lookup and finds a match. The misses field list the total number of times NAT does a translation table lookup, fails to find an entry, and attempts to create one. The expired translations field lists the total number of entries that have expired. The dynamic mapping field lists information that pertains to a NAT entry that was created by a dynamic translation entry. This field will be discussed later in this chapter.

Configuring Static NAT Translations Using Route Maps

Static NAT supports the use of route maps, which give enterprises the opportunity to take advantage of multihoming without having to lose the features that static NAT provides. To configure static NAT with route maps, use the following steps:

1. Use this command to enable static NAT with route maps configured on the inside interface:

```
ip nat inside source list {acl-number|acl-name} pool pool-name
[overload]|static local-ip global-ip route-map map-name}
```

2. Use the following command to define an extended access list and the parameters of the access list:

```
access-list <acl-number> {deny|permit} <protocol> -
  <source> <source-wildcard> <destination> <destination-
  wildcard>
```

The access list should specify which traffic arriving at the inside interface and destined to the outside interface is eligible to create a translation entry.

3. Use this command to move into interface configuration mode:

```
interface <interface type> <interface number>
```

4. Use the **ip nat inside** interface configuration command to apply NAT to the interface that is connected to the networks with the local addresses.

5. Use the following command to move into interface configuration mode:

```
interface <interface type> <interface number>
```

6. Use the **ip nat outside** interface configuration command to apply NAT to the interface that is connected to the networks with the inside global addresses.

7. Use this command to enter route map configuration mode and define the parameters of the route map:

```
route-map <name> {permit|deny} <sequence number>}
```

Figure 3.6 shows a network in which the use of static NAT and route maps would be beneficial. Router 1 has a connection to Router 2 and another connection to Router 3. The hosts behind Router 1 have varying requirements: When a connection is established to hosts within Network 2 behind Router 2, their IP address should appear to be

3. Perimeter Router Security

sourced from one subnet. Yet, when connections are established to hosts within Network 3 behind Router 3, their IP address should appear to be sourced from a different subnet. To meet the requirements, the configuration in Listing 3.12 can be used.

Listing 3.12   Router 1 static NAT with route map configuration.

```
hostname Router-1
!
interface Serial2/0
 ip address 192.168.20.1 255.255.255.0
 ip nat outside
!
interface Serial3/0
 ip address 192.168.30.1 255.255.255.0
 ip nat outside
!
interface Ethernet1/0
 ip address 10.10.10.1 255.255.255.0
 ip nat inside
 duplex full
 speed 100
!
ip route 20.20.20.0 255.255.255.0 192.168.20.2
```

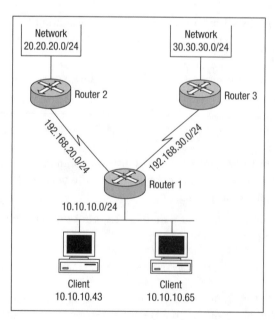

Figure 3.6   Example static NAT and route map network.

```
ip route 30.30.30.0 255.255.255.0 192.168.30.2
!
ip nat inside source static 10.10.10.43 192.168.20.2 -
  route-map network2
!
ip nat inside source static 10.10.10.43 192.168.30.2 -
  route-map network3
!
ip nat inside source static 10.10.10.65 192.168.20.3 -
  route-map network2
!
ip nat inside source static 10.10.10.65 192.168.30.3 -
  route-map network3
!
access-list 101 permit ip 10.10.10.0 0.0.0.255 -
  20.20.20.0 0.0.0.255
!
access-list 102 permit ip 10.10.10.0 0.0.0.255 -
  30.30.30.0 0.0.0.255
!
route-map network2 permit 10
 match ip address 101
 set ip next-hop 192.168.20.2
!
route-map network3 permit 10
 match ip address 102
 set ip next-hop 192.168.30.2
```

NOTE: *Because of the format limitations of this book, some lines of code listed above have been broken with a hyphen.*

The configurations in Listing 3.11 and Listing 3.12 are very similar; in Listing 3.12 the **route-map** option is at the end of the **ip nat inside source** command. The inside and outside NAT interfaces are defined for Router 1. Each of the **ip nat inside source static** commands creates a static NAT translation entry and defines a route map that should be applied for each of the entries. The route map is configured to match addresses sourced from an inside subnet and destined for an outside subnet. The next hop to send the packet to is then defined.

Configuring Dynamic NAT Translations

Dynamic NAT translation of addresses is one of many types of NAT configurations. The difference in the configuration of dynamic NAT translations and static NAT translations is minimal. However, the manner in which the translation table is populated is vastly different. With static NAT, you need to manually enter the pairs of translation addresses. Using dynamic NAT, the table is populated dynamically after a packet is received on the inside interface and the packet matches parameters defined within an access list. Packets that are to be translated by NAT should match a permit statement within the access list. A deny statement in the access list tells NAT not to perform translation on the packet.

To perform translation on packets moving between interfaces labeled as "inside" and interfaces labeled as "outside," NAT must be told what address to change the packet to. With static NAT, the address is manually entered so NAT doesn't have to decide which address to allocate to a certain flow. With dynamic NAT, a pool of inside global addresses is configured, and NAT chooses the next available address to allocate to every new flow. NAT chooses addresses from the configured pool, starting with the lowest IP address first and then continuing to translate each new flow with the next available address. After all of the addresses in the pool are in use and allocated, NAT translates a new flow until a translation times out or is cleared and released back into the pool. To configure basic dynamic NAT, use the following steps:

1. Use the following global configuration command to define a pool of inside global addresses to be allocated as needed:

   ```
   ip nat pool <name> <start-ip address> <end-ip address> -
   {netmask netmask|prefix-length prefix-length}
   ```

   The **start IP address** is the address that NAT will begin with when creating a dynamic translation entry. The **end IP address** is the last IP address that NAT will be able to use when creating a dynamic translation entry.

2. Use this command to define an extended access list and its parameters:

   ```
   access-list <access-list-number> {deny|permit} <protocol> -
   <source> <source-wildcard> <destination> <destination-
   wildcard>
   ```

   The access list should specify which traffic arriving at the inside interface and destined to the outside interface is eligible to create a translation entry.

3. Use the following command to establish an association between the local inside addresses and the pool of global addresses:

```
ip nat inside source list <access-list-number> pool <name>
```

4. Use the following command to move into interface configuration mode:

```
interface <interface type> <interface number>
```

5. Use the **ip nat inside** interface configuration command to apply NAT to the interface that is connected to the networks with the local addresses.

6. Use this command to move into interface configuration mode:

```
interface <interface type> <interface number>
```

7. Use the **ip nat outside** interface configuration command to apply NAT to the interface that is connected to the networks with the inside global addresses.

The preceding steps contain all the commands needed to configure dynamic NAT translation. Figure 3.7 displays a network that must use NAT to communicate with outside networks. The networks that are behind Router 1 are all allocated from RFC 1918 nonroutable address space. The clients located behind Router 1 have inside local addresses allocated from the 10.10.10.0 subnet. The configuration of Router 1 is shown in Listing 3.13.

Listing 3.13   Dynamic NAT configuration.

```
ip subnet-zero
!
ip nat pool INTERNET 192.168.10.129 192.168.10.254 -
```

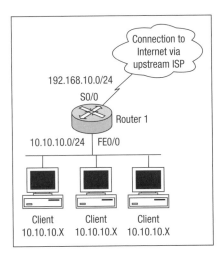

Figure 3.7   Dynamic NAT network example.

```
netmask 255.255.255.128
!
ip nat inside source list 1 pool INTERNET
!
interface Serial0/0
 ip address 192.168.10.1 255.255.255.128
 ip nat outside
!
int FastEthernet0/0
ip address 10.10.10.1 255.255.255.0
 ip nat inside
!
access-list 1 permit 10.10.10.0 0.0.0.255
```

The configuration in Listing 3.13 defines an inside global pool of addresses named **INTERNET** with 126 inside global addresses. The access list command is used to tell NAT which inside local addresses are eligible for translation. The **ip nat inside source** command is used to bound the access list and the pool of addresses together. Interface serial0/0 is defined as the *outside* interface, and interface fastethernet0/0 is defined as the *inside* interface.

When hosts on the 10.10.10.0 network need to connect to networks outside of their local network, NAT will perform a translation table lookup and determine if a translation entry already exists. If a translation is present in the translation table, the router performs no other function. If no translation exists in the translation table, NAT performs a translation and allocates the next lowest available IP address for the packet. To view the translation table of Router 1, use the **sh ip nat translations** command. Listing 3.14 displays the output when the command is issued on Router 1.

Listing 3.14   Display of NAT translations.

```
Router-1#show ip nat translations
Pro  Inside global   Inside local  Outside local  Outside global
-    192.168.10.129  10.10.10.1    -              -
-    192.168.10.130  10.10.10.35   -              -
-    192.168.10.131  10.10.10.47   -              -
-    192.168.10.132  10.10.10.68   -              -
...
Router-1#
```

The output from Listing 3.14 confirms that NAT is allocating IP addresses from the inside global pool of addresses and translating the inside local address to an inside global address. After an entry is created, all connections from hosts on the inside network to hosts on the outside network should be successful.

Another command used to monitor and verify the operation of NAT is the **show ip nat statistics** command. This command was used earlier to monitor and verify the operation of static NAT; however, when it was used with static NAT, no information regarding the dynamic mappings was listed. When the command is issued on Router 1, information specific to the dynamic mappings is included. Listing 3.15 displays the output of issuing the command on Router 1 with dynamic mapping.

Listing 3.15   Display of NAT statistics.

```
Router-1#sh ip nat stat
Total active translations: 11 (0 static, 11 dynamic; 0 extended)
Outside interfaces:
  Serial0/0
Inside interfaces:
  FastEthernet0/0
Hits: 63  Misses: 5
Expired translations: 0
Dynamic mappings:
-- Inside Source
access-list 1 pool INTERNET refcount 11
 pool INTERNET: netmask 255.255.255.128
 start 192.168.10.129 end 192.168.10.254
 type generic, total addresses 126, allocated 11 (8%), misses 0
Router-1#
```

Configuring Dynamic NAT Translations Using Route Maps

As discussed earlier, NAT supports the use of static translations using route maps; it also supports the use of dynamic translation using route maps. To configure dynamic NAT translations using route maps, use the following steps:

1. Use the following command to establish an association between the configured route map and the pool of global addresses:

    ip nat inside source route-map <route map name> pool <pool-
      name>

2. Use this command to define a pool of addresses to be allocated for translation as needed:

    ip nat pool <pool name> <start-ip address> <end-ip address> -
      {netmask netmask | prefix-length prefix-length}

    The ***start IP address*** is the address that NAT will begin with when creating a dynamic translation entry. The ***end IP address*** is the last IP address that NAT will be able to use when creating a dynamic translation entry.

3. Use the following command to define an extended access list and its parameters:

```
access-list <access-list-number> {deny|permit} <protocol> -
    <source> <source-wildcard> <destination> <destination -
    wildcard>
```

The access list should specify which traffic arriving at the inside interface and destined to the outside interface is eligible to create a translation entry.

4. Use this command to enter route map configuration mode and define the parameters of the route map:

```
route-map <name> {permit|deny} <sequence number>}
```

5. Use the following command to move into interface configuration mode:

```
interface <interface type> <interface number>
```

6. Use the **ip nat inside** interface configuration command to apply NAT to the interface that is connected to the networks with the local addresses.

7. Use the following command to move into interface configuration mode:

```
interface <interface type> <interface number>
```

8. Use the **ip nat outside** interface configuration command to apply NAT to the interface that is connected to the networks with the inside global addresses.

Referring to Figure 3.8, you can see that Router 1 is multihomed to two different routers. It has a connection to Router 2 and another to Router 3. When the hosts behind Router 1 in network 10.10.10.0 establish a connection to hosts within Network 2 behind Router 2 with IP addresses of 20.20.20.0, their IP addresses should appear to be sourced from one subnet; yet, when establishing connections to hosts within Network 3 behind Router 3 with a network of 30.30.30.0, their IP addresses should appear to be sourced from a different subnet. To meet the requirements using dynamic NAT and route maps, the configuration in Listing 3.16 can be used.

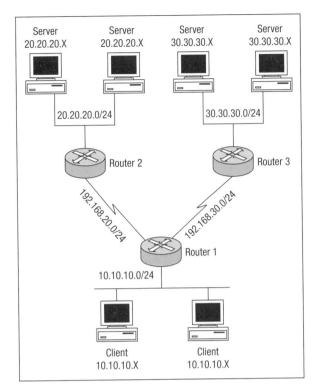

Figure 3.8   Router 1 Dynamic NAT with route map.

Listing 3.16   Router 1 Dynamic NAT with route map configuration.

```
hostname Router-1
!
interface Serial2/0
 ip address 192.168.20.1 255.255.255.0
 ip nat outside
!
interface Serial3/0
 ip address 192.168.30.1 255.255.255.0
 ip nat outside
!
interface Ethernet1/0
 ip address 10.10.10.1 255.255.255.0
 ip nat inside
 duplex full
 speed 100
!
ip route 20.20.20.0 255.255.255.0 192.168.20.2
```

```
ip route 30.30.30.0 255.255.255.0 192.168.30.2
!
ip nat pool network-20 192.168.20.20 192.168.20.254 -
  prefix-length 24
!
ip nat pool network-30 192.168.30.20 192.168.30.254 -
  prefix-length 24
!
ip nat inside source route-map network2 pool network-20
ip nat inside source route-map network3 pool network-30
!
access-list 101 permit ip 10.10.10.0 0.0.0.255 -
  20.20.20.0 0.0.0.255
!
access-list 102 permit ip 10.10.10.0 0.0.0.255 -
  30.30.30.0 0.0.0.255
!
route-map network2 permit 10
 match ip address 101
 set ip next-hop 192.168.20.2
!
route-map network3 permit 10
 match ip address 102
 set ip next-hop 192.168.30.2
```

NOTE: Because of the format limitations of this book, some lines of code in Listing 3.16 have been broken with a hyphen.

If you compare the configurations in Listing 3.12 and Listing 3.16, you'll notice that there are slight differences between the two. The configuration in Listing 3.16 does not include any static mappings and the **ip nat pool** command has been added. When a route map is used by NAT to match the inside traffic to be translated, NAT will create a fully extended translation entry that can be viewed using the **show ip nat translations** command. The translation entry created by NAT will contain both the inside and outside local and global address entries and also contain any TCP or UDP port information. Issuing the **show ip nat translations** command on Router 1 displays the following output:

```
Router-1#show ip nat translations
...

Pro  Inside global      Inside local    ...
TCP  192.168.20.20:1134 10.10.10.43:1134 ...
```

```
TCP  192.168.30.20:1135   10.10.10.43:1135 ...
TCP  192.168.20.21:1026   10.10.10.65:1026 ...
TCP  192.168.30.21:1027   10.10.10.65:1027 ...
                          ... Outside local    Outside global
                          ... 20.20.20.20:21   20.20.20.20:21
                          ... 30.30.30.30:23   30.30.30.30:23
                          ... 20.20.20.21:23   20.20.20.21:23
                          ... 30.30.30.31:21   30.30.30.31:21
```

NOTE: *Because of the format limitations of this book, lines of code have been broken with ellipsis points.*

Configuring Port Address Translation (PAT)

Because of the rapid depletion of public IP version 4 address space and the limited number of public IP addresses that can be used on the Internet, enterprises may not be able to purchase blocks of public addresses that contain the number of private addresses being used on the inside network to perform Network Address Translation. A solution to working with the limited number of addresses being allocated to enterprises is the use Port Address Translation (PAT). PAT allows multiple hosts on the inside local network to access hosts located on outside networks using a single inside global address. PAT utilizes a NAT feature known as *overloading*. When overloading is configured on the router, the router maintains enough information from the higher-layer protocols like TCP or UDP port numbers, which allows the router to translate the global address back to the originating local address. More than one inside local address can be mapped to an inside global address, and when multiple inside local addresses map to one global address, the TCP or UDP port numbers of each inside host distinguish between the local addresses.

To configure PAT, perform the following steps (these steps are similar to the steps for configuring dynamic NAT translations):

1. Use the following global configuration command to define a pool of inside global addresses to be allocated as needed:

```
ip nat pool <name> <start-ip address> <end-ip address> -
  {netmask netmask|prefix-length prefix-length}
```

   The **start IP address** is the address that NAT will begin with when creating a dynamic translation entry. The **end IP address** is the same IP address used for the **start** IP address.

2. Use this command to define an extended access list and its parameters:

```
access-list <access-list-number> {deny|permit} <protocol> -
   <source> <source-wildcard> <destination> <destination-
   wildcard>
```

The access list should specify which traffic arriving at the inside interface and destined to the outside interface is eligible to create a translation entry.

3. Use this command to establish an association between the local inside addresses and the pool of global addresses (notice the use of the **overload** keyword):

```
ip nat inside source list <access-list-number> pool <name> -
   overload
```

4. Use the following command to move into interface configuration mode:

```
interface <interface type> <interface number>
```

5. Use the **ip nat inside** interface configuration command to apply NAT to the interface that is connected to the networks with the local addresses.

6. Use this command to move into interface configuration mode:

```
interface <interface type> <interface number>
```

7. Use the **ip nat outside** interface configuration command to apply NAT to the interface that is connected to the networks with the inside global addresses.

Using Figure 3.7 as a reference, you can see that Router 1 must now be configured to support PAT. The figure displays a network that must use PAT to communicate with outside networks. The networks that are behind Router 1 are all allocated from RFC 1918 nonroutable address space. The clients located behind Router 1 have inside local addresses allocated from the 10.10.10.0 subnet; however, the enterprise has been allocated only one public IP address. Listing 3.17 shows the configuration needed to configure Router 1 for PAT.

Listing 3.17   PAT configuration example.

```
ip subnet-zero
!
```

```
ip nat pool INTERNET 192.168.10.254 192.168.10.254 -
  netmask 255.255.255.128
!
ip nat inside source list 1 pool INTERNET overload
!
interface Serial0/0
 ip address 192.168.10.1 255.255.255.128
 ip nat outside
!
int FastEthernet0/0
ip address 10.10.10.1 255.255.255.0
 ip nat inside
!
access-list 1 permit 10.10.10.0 0.0.0.255
```

Here is the NAT table of Router 1; notice that PAT creates an extended entry and all fields of the output are populated:

```
Router-1#show ip nat translations
...

Pro   Inside global         Inside local      ...
TCP   192.168.10.254:1036   10.10.10.3:1036    ...
TCP   192.168.10.254:1037   10.10.10.162:1037 ...
TCP   192.168.10.254:1056   10.10.10.15:1056  ...
                            ... Outside local     Outside global
                            ... 20.20.20.184:23

20.20.20.184:23
                            ... 20.20.20.200:23  20.20.20.20:23
                            ... 20.20.20.21:23   20.20.20.21:23
```

NOTE: *Because of the format limitations of this book, lines of code have been broken with ellipses points.*

Configuring Committed Access Rate (CAR)

The process for configuring CAR to rate-limit traffic is fairly straight-forward. To configure a CAR policy for IP traffic, use the following steps beginning in global configuration mode:

1. Enter interface configuration using the following command:

```
interface interface-type interface-number
```

2. Use this command to specify a CAR policy:

```
rate-limit {input|output} [access-group [rate-limit] -
  access-list-number] <bps><burst-normal><burst-max> -
  conform-action action exceed-action action
```

3. Use this command to define a CAR policy based on the contents of the access list:

```
access-list access-list-number {deny|permit} [protocol] -
  [source] [source-wildcard] [destination] [destination-
  wildcard] -
  [precedence precedence][tos tos] [log]
```

The preceding commands are all that are needed to define a policy to rate-limit traffic. Cisco Express Forwarding (CEF) must also be enabled for CAR to operate. Figure 3.9 shows a network in which Router A and Router B are neighbors. Router A is the customer edge perimeter router for Company A and provides Internet access for the company. Router B is the provider edge router for ISP B, which provides Internet access to Company A. Company A would like to configure Router A such that it will rate-limit DoS packets during an attack. Listing 3.18 details the configuration commands needed to enable CAR on each router.

Listing 3.18   Router A configured for rate-limiting.

```
#config t
#ip cef
#access-list 110 permit icmp any any echo
#access-list 110 permit icmp any any echo-reply
#interface serial3/0
#rate-limit input access-group 110 32000 8000 8000 -
  conform-action transmit exceed-action drop
```

The steps shown earlier include the basic configuration commands

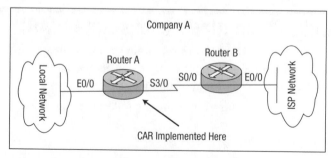

Figure 3.9   Rate-limiting Denial of Service.

needed to enable CAR for rate-limiting traffic. The configuration shown in Listing 3.18, enables CEF on a global basis for the router. CEF must be enabled for CAR to provide rate-limiting services. Access list 110 matches ICMP traffic. The access list is applied to CAR under the serial interface for inbound traffic. Notice that the rate-limit command defines the extended burst limit as being the same as the normal limit, which effectively disables the extended burst capability. Use the **show running-config** command to see the output of the configuration, which is shown in Listing 3.19.

Listing 3.19   Rate limit configuration of Router A.

```
Router-A#sh ru
Building configuration...
!
ip cef
!
interface Serial3/0
 ip address 192.168.10.9 255.255.255.252
 rate-limit input access-group 110 32000 8000 8000 -
   conform-action transmit exceed-action drop

!
access-list 110 permit icmp any any echo
access-list 110 permit icmp any any echo-reply
!
```

When you issue the **show running-config** command, you can review the configuration changes that were made to the local device; however, a few more commands are needed in order to verify the operation of CAR. After you verify that the configuration changes are correct, you should issue the **show interface rate-limit** command. The output of this command verifies the configuration of CAR and allows you to monitor CAR statistics. The output of the command is shown in Listing 3.20.

Listing 3.20   Verifying the operation of CAR.

```
Router-A# sh int ser3/0 rate-limit
Serial3/0 Internet Connection (Network Engineering)
  Input
    matches: access-group 110
      params:  32000 bps, 8000 limit, 8000 extended limit
      conformed 445884 packets, 128442746 bytes; action: transmit
      exceeded 22272 packets, 15068096 bytes; action: drop
      last packet: 3176ms ago, current burst: 0 bytes
      last cleared 1w5d ago, conformed 0 bps, exceeded 0 bps
  Router-A#
```

The output of the **show interface rate-limit** command first lists the direction that rate-limiting is applied, inbound or outbound. The next line defines the access list for traffic that CAR is using to apply its policy. And the next line defines the parameters that CAR applies to traffic matching the defined access list. The output then shows the number of packets that CAR defined as conforming to or exceeding the defined limits.

In the configuration in Listing 3.20, Company A defined its rate-limiting policy for ICMP traffic. The configuration effectively polices the traffic; however, the traffic is policed after traveling across Company A's upstream connection from ISP B. Enterprises traditionally connect to their ISP via smaller links, and their ISP connects to neighboring peers on the Internet via much larger links. In situations in which the attack takes on a distributed form that uses hundreds or thousands of zombie machines running preconfigured bots, the traffic that is generated can consume the enterprise's link to its service provider. The example in Figure 3.9 depicted Company A connected to ISP B via one single T1 connection running at 1.544 megabits. With the configuration in Listing 3.18, ICMP travels across the T1 only to be dropped at Router A. Although Router A performs the rate-limiting function, the configuration in Listing 3.20 does nothing to deny traffic from traveling across the link.

In these instances, ISP B should configure Router B to deny ICMP traffic from traveling across the T1, thus allowing legitimate traffic while denying nonlegitimate traffic. The configuration for Router B is shown in Listing 3.21; the configuration for Router B is similar to the configuration for Router A except that the rate-limiting feature is applied in an outbound direction.

Listing 3.21   Router B configuration.

```
#config t                                          .
#ip cef
#access-list 110 permit icmp any any echo
#access-list 110 permit icmp any any echo-reply
#interface serial2/1
#rate-limit output access-group 110 32000 8000 8000 -
  conform-action transmit exceed-action drop
```

In both configurations, Listing 3.20 and Listing 3.21, each router has been configured to rate-limit ICMP traffic, or what is commonly referred to as the Ping of Death and Smurf attacks.

NOTE: *Smurf attacks use a combination of IP spoofing and ICMP traffic to saturate a target network by sending a spoofed Ping packet to the broadcast address of a large network. The packet contains the source address of the actual target machine.*

There are other forms of DoS attacks. Another common attack is the SYN attack, in which an attacker exploits the use of buffer space used during the TCP session initialization handshake. CAR can be used to rate-limit this type of traffic. Refer again to Figure 3.9; Router A should be configured to rate-limit all ICMP traffic and traffic that contains characteristics of a SYN attack. This configuration defines multiple rate-limiting policies and is detailed in Listing 3.22.

Listing 3.22 Multiple rate-limiting policies configuration.

```
#config t
#ip cef
#access-list 110 permit icmp any any echo
#access-list 110 permit icmp any any echo-reply
#access-list 111 deny tcp any any established
#access-list 111 permit tcp any any
#interface serial3/0
#rate-limit input access-group 110 32000 8000 8000 -
   conform-action transmit exceed-action drop
!
# rate-limit input access-group 111 64000 4000 4000 -
   conform-action transmit exceed-action drop
```

In this example, two access lists, as well as two rate-limiting policies, have been defined. Access list 110 rate-limits ICMP traffic to defend against Ping attacks, and access list 111 defends against SYN floods. When you issue the following command, established sessions won't be considered in the rate-limiting policy:

```
access-list 111 deny tcp any any established
```

This command rate-limits all initial SYN packets the router receives; the remaining packets in the flow will conform to the deny statement in access list 111 and not be rate-limited:

```
access-list 111 permit tcp any any
```

Configuring Logging

The process for configuring a router to log events is fairly straightforward and simple, yet it's one of the most important security configuration changes that security administrators will make on their routers. To enable logging, follow these steps:

1. Use the **logging on** global configuration command to enable logging of messages. This command is enabled by default and will be needed only if message logging has been disabled.

2. Use the following command to configure all logging messages to contain the same IP address:

   ```
   logging source-interface <interface type interface number>
   ```

   By default the logging message contains the IP address of the interface it uses to leave the router.

3. Use this command to define a logging server that should receive the logging messages (more than one host may be defined):

   ```
   logging <buffered|monitor|console|ip address>
   ```

4. Use the **logging trap** *<level>* command to define the level of detail for logged messages. Table 3.1 earlier in this chapter lists event error messages and their corresponding severity levels.

5. Use the following command to enable time stamping of log messages:

   ```
   service timestamps log <datetime|uptime> [msec] [localtime] -
   [show timezone]
   ```

The **logging buffered** command copies logging messages to an internal buffer within the router. This buffer is circular in nature, meaning newer messages overwrite older messages when the buffer becomes full. The **logging ip address** command identifies a server to receive logging messages. The **logging monitor** command logs messages to the nonconsole terminal. The **logging console** command copies logging messages to the console port of the router.

Router B in Figure 3.10 is configured to send warning level logging messages to the syslog server at IP address 192.168.10.250. Router B is configured with a loopback interface that has an IP address of

192.168.11.1, and this interface is to be the source of all logging messages that Router B sends. Listing 3.23 details the configuration commands needed to enable Router B for message logging to host 192.168.10.250.

Listing 3.23   Router B's logging configuration.

```
#config t
#service timestamps log uptime
#service timestamps log datetime msec
#no logging console
#logging 192.168.11.1
#logging source-interface loopback1
#logging trap 4
#end
#
```

In Listing 3.23, Router B has been configured to log warning level messages to the system logging server with an IP address of 192.168.11.1. To verify that logging has been properly configured, issue the **show logging** command. Listing 3.24 displays the output.

Listing 3.24   Show logging output.

```
Router-B#show logging
Syslog logging: enabled (0 messages dropped,
0 flushes, 0 overruns)
    Console logging: disabled
    Monitor logging: level debugging, 0 messages logged
    Buffer logging: level debugging, 146 messages logged
    Trap logging: level warning, 151 message lines logged
        Logging to 192.168.11.1, 151 message lines logged
```

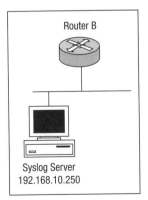

Figure 3.10   A network design with logging defined.

```
Log Buffer (8192 bytes):
: %SONET-4-ALARM:  POS0/1/0: B3 BER exceeds threshold
: %SONET-4-ALARM:  POS0/1/0: B3 BER below threshold
: %WCCP-5-CACHEFOUND: Web Cache 192.168.31.32 acquired
: %WCCP-5-CACHEFOUND: Web Cache 192.168.31.31 acquired
: %STANDBY-6-STATECHANGE: Standby: 1: Vlan1 state Standby
: %STANDBY-6-STATECHANGE: Standby: 1: Vlan1 state Active
: %STANDBY-6-STATECHANGE: Standby: 1: Vlan1 state Speak
```

The output in Listing 3.24 shows that console logging has been disabled. Monitor and buffer logging are logged at the default debugging level. Notice that the trap logging has been changed from the default informational logging level to the warning level and the server the trap messages are sent to is displayed as well. The **show logging** command also displays the number of messages logged by each method.

Another command that can be used to view logging information is the **show logging history** command. The output of the **show logging history** command displays information in the system logging history table, such as the table size, the status of messages, and the text of the messages stored in the table. If the logging of message traps to a Simple Network Management Protocol (SNMP) management station, be sure network management station traps has been enabled with the **snmp-server enable trap** command.

The level of messages sent and stored in a history table on the router can be changed. The number of messages that get stored in the history table can be changed as well. Messages are stored in the history table because SNMP traps are not guaranteed to reach their destination. By default, one message of the level warning is stored in the history table even if log traps are not enabled. The output of the **show logging history** command is shown in Listing 3.25.

Listing 3.25   **Show logging history** output.

```
Router-B#sh logging history
Syslog History Table:1 maximum table entries,
saving level warnings or higher
 73 messages ignored, 0 dropped, 0 recursion drops
 72 table entries flushed
SNMP notifications not enabled
 entry number 73 : SYS-4-SNMP_WRITENET
SNMP WriteNet request. Writing current config to 192.168.11.1
    timestamp: 313923920
Router-B#
```

As mentioned earlier, the logging history level can be changed; notice in Listing 3.25 that the logging history table lists 1 maximum table entry. The table history size can be changed as well. You can change the history level as well as the size of the history table by using the following commands:

1. Use the **logging history** *<level>* command, where the *level* equals the values detailed in Table 3.1, to change the default level of log messages stored in the history file and sent to the SNMP server.

2. Use the **logging history size** *<size>* command, where the *size* is a number between 0 and 500, to change the number of log messages that can be stored in the history table.

The following commands add the **logging history** and **logging history size** commands to the configuration of Router B. The arguments of these commands should be reflected in the **show logging history** command:

```
#config t
#logging history 3
#logging history size 400
#end
#
```

The configuration changes that were made can be seen in the output of the **show logging history** command. Listing 3.26 reflects the changes that were made.

Listing 3.26   Show logging history.

```
Router-B#sh logging history
Syslog History Table:400 maximum table entries,
saving level errors or higher
 73 messages ignored, 0 dropped, 0 recursion drops
 72 table entries flushed
 SNMP notifications not enabled
 entry number 74 : SYS-5-CONFIG_I
 SNMP WriteNet request. Writing current config to 192.168.11.1
    timestamp: 176910958
```

Related solution:	Found on page:
Configuring SNMP Security	26

Chapter 4

IOS Firewall Feature Set

In Brief

The *IOS Firewall feature set* available for Cisco routers is an add-on component to the Cisco IOS that provides routers with many of the features available to the PIX firewall, thus extending to routers functionality similar to the functionality a separate firewall device provides. When a Cisco router is configured with the Cisco IOS Firewall feature set, it is transformed into an effective, robust featured firewall. The IOS Firewall feature set software has been designed with security services that include access controls, strong authentication, and encryption services, and it maintains all fundamental routing features. It is a value-added option for Cisco IOS software that enforces security policies while maintaining vital traffic flow requirements within the enterprise. The Firewall feature set is currently available for the Cisco 1600, 1720, 2500, 2600, 3600, and 7200 series router platforms.

Some of the key features of the IOS Firewall feature set are listed here:

- Context-Based Access Control (CBAC) provides secure IP traffic filtering for each unique session for many applications.

- Java blocking protects against malicious Java applets, allowing only applets from identified and trusted sources.

- Denial-of-service (DoS) detection and prevention protects resources against common attacks.

- Realtime alerts notify administrators during DoS attacks and certain other conditions.

- Audit trail mechanisms track sessions by time, source and destination address, ports, and total number of bytes transmitted.

- Intrusion detection provides realtime monitoring, interception, and response to network misuse with a set of common attack and probing intrusion detection signatures.

- Provides multiservice integration, advanced security for dialup connections, and integrated routing and security at the Internet gateway.

As you can see, the IOS Firewall feature set has an extensive set of features that are designed to help secure an enterprise's network with robust firewall functionality. This chapter aims to discuss many of the enhanced features the IOS Firewall feature set encompasses. I'll discuss Context-Based Access Control (CBAC), which examines not only Network layer and Transport layer information, but also the Application layer protocol information to learn about the state of TCP and UDP connections. CBAC maintains connection state information for individual connections. This state information is used to make intelligent decisions about whether packets should be permitted or denied and dynamically creates and deletes temporary openings in the firewall. I'll discuss Port Application Mapping (PAM), which allows enterprises to customize TCP or UDP port numbers to support network environments that run services using ports that are different from the registered or well-known ports associated with an application. The information in the PAM table enables CBAC-supported services to run on nonstandard ports. I'll also discuss the IOS Firewall Intrusion Detection System (IDS), which acts as an inline intrusion detection sensor, watching packets and sessions as they flow through the router and scanning each to match any of the IDS signatures.

Context-Based Access Control

Context-Based Access Control was designed for use with multiple protocols that are unable to be processed with access lists. During many types of network attacks, packets that are not part of an existing session are sent to a target machine, or there may be an attempt to inject packets within an existing session. Additionally, devices that are not properly configured can cause interruptions in service by sending inappropriate packets. The CBAC process will stop these types of attacks and problems by inspecting the TCP and UDP sessions. Only packets within sessions that meet certain criteria will be allowed to pass. Packets that are not within recognized sessions or that do not meet the security policy will be dropped.

More often than not, a router will make every attempt to forward a packet toward its destination in the most efficient manner. CBAC changes the forwarding nature by investigating aspects of each packet within the context of its session to determine if the packet or session meets the policy. If the packet or session meets the policy, it will be forwarded. If it does not, it will be discarded, and in some cases, the session will be terminated. To determine this, CBAC adds processes to a router so it will be able to perform the following:

- Watch for the start of new sessions and ensure they meet the policy.

- Maintain the state information of each session flowing through it by watching flags, sequence numbers, and acknowledgment numbers.

- Set up and install dynamic access control lists for permitted sessions.

- Close out sessions and remove temporary access control lists that have been terminated.

- Closely examine SMTP sessions to allow only a minimum set of permitted commands.

- Watch the permitted control sessions (such as FTPcontrol) and allow associated data sessions (such as FTPdata) to pass.

- Watch for Java applets within HTTP sessions and block them if the router is configured to do so.

- Examine each packet within each session to ensure that it conforms to the current session state.

- Maintain a timer after each session's packet is forwarded and terminate any sessions that have exceeded the session timeout policy.

- Watch for signs that a SYN attack is in progress, and if so, reset excessive session requests.

- Send out alerts of unexpected events and packets that have been dropped because they don't meet the policy.

- Optionally record time, source, and destination addresses; ports; and the total number of bytes transmitted by each participant at the end of the session.

Each of these security elements uses memory and processing cycles that will decrease normal packet forwarding efficiency of the Cisco IOS software on the router. CBAC uses 600 bytes of memory per connection and CPU resources during the access list inspection process.

Context-Based Access Control Protocol Support

CBAC can be configured to inspect the following protocols:

- TCP sessions
- UDP sessions

CBAC can also be configured to specifically inspect certain Application layer protocols. The following Application layer protocols can all be configured for CBAC:

- CU-SeeMe
- FTP
- H.323

- HTTP
- Java
- Microsoft NetShow
- Unix R-commands
- RealAudio
- RPC, specifically Sun RPC and Microsoft RPC
- SMTP
- SQLNet
- StreamWorks
- TFTP
- VDOLive

When a protocol is configured for CBAC that protocol's traffic is inspected and all state information is updated and maintained in the state table. Return traffic will be permitted back only through the firewall if the state table contains information indicating that the packet belongs to a permissible session. CBAC controls the traffic that belongs to a valid session. When return traffic is inspected, the state table information is updated as necessary.

4. IOS Firewall Feature Set

NOTE: *UDP is a connectionless protocol; therefore, there are no actual "sessions," so the CBAC process examines particular information within the UDP packet and keeps track of that information. To determine if the packet is part of UDP "session," the CBAC process compares the information gathered against similar packets received within the idle timeout.*

Operation of Context-Based Access Control

CBAC inspects traffic traveling through a router to discover and manage information about the state of the TCP or UDP sessions. This state information is used to create a temporary opening in access lists, which allows the returning traffic from the same session to enter the internal network through the firewall. To illustrate the operation of CBAC, Figure 4.1 shows an example CBAC network. When the router in Figure 4.1 initializes after a power-up or reload, it begins with an empty table to maintain state information for every session. When the host on the inside network of the router initiates a connection to a host on the outside network of the router, the router receives the first packet and will match the packet against any inbound access lists on the interface. If the packet is permitted by the inbound access list, CBAC will set up a table entry to record information about the session. CBAC will also set up temporary access lists to permit returning packets that are part of the same session. This setup is handled through process-switching the first packet, and the information gathered is used as a reference so that all subsequent packets in the session may be fast-switched. The TCP and UDP sessions are identified through the IP addresses and the port numbers. To protect the session, the firewall feature set will inspect the TCP sequence and acknowledgment values as well as the flags, which must correspond to the transmitted data. For UDP and TCP, the subsequent packets must arrive within a timeout period. After the session has completed, the opened session entry is torn down and the connection is closed.

When using CBAC, the protocols that are to be inspected must be specified, and the interface and interface direction where inspection originates should be configured. Only protocols that have been specified will be inspected by CBAC. Packets that enter the IOS firewall are inspected by CBAC only if they first pass the inbound access list at the input interface, and the outbound access list at the output interface will be serviced by the router. If a packet is denied by the access list, the packet is simply dropped and not inspected by CBAC. CBAC inspection tracks sequence numbers in all TCP packets and drops those packets with sequence numbers that are not within expected ranges.

There are some protocols, such as Telnet or SMTP, that will have only one connection between client and server. These are called single-channel sessions. All packets are identified as conforming to the session by acknowledging the receipt of bytes from the other device. After the session ends, one side or the other can start the termination

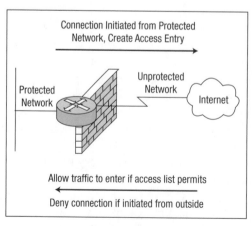

Figure 4.1   Basic operation of CBAC.

process by setting the FIN flag. CBAC monitors this, and when the returning ACK is seen, CBAC will remove the temporary access control list. Removing the temporary access list will deny packets from the outside network from entering the inside network after the two devices in the session have agreed to terminate. During a session, CBAC will drop packets that violate its policy, such as packets with sequence/acknowledgment values outside of the acceptable window or with incorrectly set flags.

In addition to the single-channel sessions, several applications also use a control channel and create one or more additional data channels to carry information. These are called multichannel sessions, such as FTP and H.323. When the control channel forms, CBAC watches for an indication that a subsequent data channel will be needed. When this occurs, CBAC will add the access control list elements to accommodate the data channels. When the data channels are terminated, CBAC will remove the temporary access control list elements.

Two special cases also need to be mentioned: SMTP and Java processing. If SMTP inspection is enabled, only a set of the SMTP commands will be permitted through the firewall feature set. If some other command is seen coming from the untrusted network, CBAC will send a TCP/IP packet within the session to each participant with the RST flag set. This will terminate the session.

A Web browser request may return an HTML document that will initiate more than one TCP session from the client to the server to retrieve additional parts of the page. These can include text and graphics and may also include Java applets. If HTTP inspection is enabled and Java applets are being filtered, CBAC will inspect the leading parts of each HTTP session to match the Java applet signature. If CBAC finds this signature, it will terminate the session with a TCP packet, with the RST flag set sent to both client and server. When CBAC terminates a session like this, the temporary access control list is also removed, but the remainder of the page, text, and graphics will continue to load through each TCP session as they normally would.

These data channels are inspected for properly incrementing sequence and acknowledgment numbers as well as proper flag use. They will also be terminated in the way described earlier if they exceed the idle timeout values. However, to speed processing, the contents of the data channel packets are not inspected for commands as the control channel packets are.

4. IOS Firewall Feature Set

Context-Based Access Control and IPSec

Because CBAC is configured on perimeter devices that protect internal devices, one question always arises: Is CBAC compatible with IPSec? And the answer is, in a limited fashion. If the router is running both CBAC and IPSec, it must be configured as an IPSec endpoint. For CBAC to function properly, the data within the packets must be examined, and if this data is encrypted, CBAC cannot examine the payload, which causes CBAC to cease functioning.

As mentioned in the preceding paragraph, when CBAC and IPSec are enabled on the same router, that router must be an IPSec end point. CBAC cannot accurately inspect the payload of packets that have been encrypted with IPSec because the protocol number in the IP header of the packet is not TCP or UDP and CBAC inspects only TCP and UDP packets. This should, however, be expected; the purpose of encryption is to prevent unauthorized deciphering of the packets in the first place.

Port Application Mapping

Port Application Mapping (PAM) allows security administrators to customize or change TCP and UDP port numbers for services or applications used with CBAC. This gives networks the flexibility to support services that use ports that are different from the registered and well-known port numbers commonly associated with certain applications. Port Application Mapping should be used under these conditions:

• To apply a nonstandard port number to a service or application

• When host or subnets use a port number for an application that is different from the default port number associated with the application in the PAM table

• When different hosts or subnets use the same port number for different applications

Port Application Mapping creates and maintains a table of default port-to-application mapping information on the router. The table that is created is populated with system-defined maps by default at boot time; however, the table can be modified to include host-defined mappings as well as user-defined mappings. PAM supports host- or subnet-based port mapping, which allows you to apply PAM to a single host or subnet using standard access control lists. The PAM table information enables Context-Based Access Control services to run on non-standard ports. Previously, CBAC was limited to inspecting traffic that was using only the well-known ports associated with an application.

PAM entries can consist of three different types of mappings: system-defined mapping entries, user-defined mapping entries, and host-specific mapping entries. Each of these mapping entries will be discussed in greater detail in the following sections.

System-Defined Mapping

After the router loads, PAM populates a table of system-defined mapping entries with the well-known or registered port mapping information. The PAM table entries contain all the services that are supported by CBAC and needed to function properly. The system-defined mapping information cannot be deleted or changed, but you can create host-defined mappings, which in effect would override the system-defined parameters. Table 4.1 details each of the system-defined services.

User-Defined Mapping

When the network includes applications that use nonstandard ports, the security administrator must configure user-defined mapping entries into the PAM table. Each user-defined mapping entry requires a table entry for the application. User-defined mapping entries can also specify a range of ports for an application to use by configuring a

Table 4.1 System-defined port application services.

Application	Port Number	Protocol
http	80	Hypertext Transfer Protocol
ftp	21	File Transfer Protocol
exec	512	Remote Process Execution
cuseeme	7648	Cu-SeeMe Protocol
h.323	1720	H.323 Protocol
msrpc	135	Microsoft Remote Procedure Call
netshow	1755	Microsoft NetShow
real audio	7070	RealAudio
real video	707	RealVideo
sqlnet	1521	SQLNet
smtp	25	Simple Mail Transport Protocol
streamworks	1558	StreamWorks Protocol
sunrpc	111	Sun Remote Procedure Call
tftp	69	Trivial File Transfer Protocol
vdolive	7000	VDOLive

4. IOS Firewall Feature Set

separate entry in the PAM table for each port number of the range in succession. If a user-defined mapping entry is entered multiple times, it overwrites the previous entry in the table. An example of a user-defined mapping entry would be if HTTP services ran on the non-standard port of 4010 instead of the system-defined port 80. In this case, PAM would be used to map port 4010 with HTTP services. You are not allowed to map a user-defined entry over a system-defined entry, and the router will complain with an error message.

Host-Specific Mapping

Host-specific port mapping entries create port application mapping on a per-host or per-subnet basis. User-defined mapping entries cannot overwrite system-defined mapping entries in the PAM table; however, host-specific port mapping allows you to override a system-defined entry in the PAM table. Using host-specific port mapping, you can use the same port number for different services on different hosts. For example, a security administrator can assign port 1717 to FTP for one host while assigning port 1717 to Telnet for another host. Host-specific port mapping also lets you configure mapping entries on a per-subnet basis. This allows security administrators to apply PAM to a specific subnet when that subnet runs a service that uses a port number that is different from the port number defined in the default mapping information. This is similar to host-specific port mapping, but it works on a per-subnet basis and not a per-host basis.

IOS Firewall Intrusion Detection

The *IOS Firewall Intrusion Detection System (IDS)* feature extends the features of intrusion detection to Cisco routers and provides a cost-effective method for extending security services across network boundaries. Intrusion detection systems provide a level of protection beyond the firewall by protecting the network from internal and external attacks and threats caused by routers forwarding traffic from one network to another network. By leveraging the features of intrusion detection, the router can act as an inline probe examining packets and flows to match against current IDS signatures, thus providing the same features that a dedicated probe or sensor device can provide without adding additional hardware onto the network. Intrusion detection should be deployed within all parts of the network with the exception of the core layer elements in the network design; it should especially be deployed within the perimeter of the enterprise network and distribution layer of the network or in locations where a router is being deployed and additional security between different network segments is required.

Typically, intrusion detection consists of three components:

- *Sensor*—A network device—in this case, a router with the IDS Firewall feature set loaded—that uses a rules-based engine to interpret large volumes of IP network traffic into meaningful security events. The Sensor can also log security data and close TCP sessions. The Sensor reports the events to an IDS Director or a syslog server.

- *Director*—A device that provides centralized management and reporting for security issues. Sensors are managed through a graphical user interface, and the Director can provide a multitude of other services outside of centralized reporting.

- *Post Office*—A protocol that provides the backbone by which all IDS devices communicate among one another.

The IOS Firewall IDS uses realtime monitoring of network packets to detect intrusions or malicious network activity through the use of attack signatures. The IOS Firewall IDS searches for patterns of misuse by examining either the data portion or the header portion of network packets. Currently, the IOS Firewall IDS identifies 59 attack signatures.

4. IOS Firewall Feature Set

A signature detects patterns of misuse in network traffic. In the Cisco IOS Firewall IDS, signatures are categorized into four types:

- *Info Atomic*—Info signatures detect information-gathering activity, such as a port probe. These attacks can be classified as either atomic or compound signatures.

- *Info Compound*—Attack signatures detect attacks attempted with the protected network as the intended target. These attacks can be classified as either atomic or compound signatures.

- *Attack Atomic*—Can detect simple patterns of misuse.

- *Attack Compound*—Can detect complex patterns of misuse.

When the IOS Firewall IDS detects suspicious network traffic, and before the traffic causes a breech in the security policy of the network, the IDS responds and logs all activity to a syslog server or to an IDS Director using the Post Office Protocol (POP).

Security administrators have the ability with the IOS Firewall IDS software to configure the method of response to packets that match one of the attack signatures just mentioned. The IOS Firewall IDS software can be configured to use four different methods to respond to an attack when it matches a signature:

- *Generate alarms*—Alarms are generated by the Sensor and sent to one or more Directors. The Director displays the alarm and logs the event.

- *Generate logs*—Event logs can be sent to separate syslog server in order analyze the event.

- *Reset TCP connections*—The Sensor will reset individual TCP connection requests during and after an attack to minimize the threat yet will allow all other valid requests to continue.

- *Shun the attack*—Upon matching a signature the Sensor can be configured to deny request attempts to a host or subnet by dropping the packets. Shunning should be carefully thought out before being deployed in the production network.

If there are multiple signature matches in a session, only the first match triggers an action from the IOS Firewall IDS. Other matches in other modules trigger additional alarms, but only one per session. This process is different than on the dedicated IDS Sensor device, which identifies all signature matches for each packet. The IOS Firewall IDS capabilities provide additional security visibility at the enterprise network perimeters. Security administrators enjoy more robust protection against attacks on the network and can automatically respond to threats from internal or external hosts.

The only significant disadvantage to using the features of the IOS Firewall IDS is that the overall performance of the router will be slightly degraded and end-to-end propagation delay will be added.

Immediate Solutions

Configuring Context-Based Access Control

Many steps must be followed to configure CBAC to function properly. The first major step is to decide whether to configure CBAC on the inside or outside interface of your firewall router. The inside interface is the interface that originates the sessions and allows traffic back through the firewall. The outside interface refers to the interface where sessions cannot originate. This step is a mental step and requires no configuration command at this point. To configure CBAC, perform the tasks described in the following steps:

1. Use the following command to define an extended access list and the parameters that CBAC will use to inspect traffic or deny traffic:

   ```
   access-list <access-list-number> <deny | permit> <protocol> -
     <source source-wildcard> <destination destination-wildcard>
   ```

2. Use the following command to configure CBAC for generic TCP or UDP packet inspection:

   ```
   ip inspect name <inspection-name> <tcp | udp> <alert on | off> -
     <audit-trail on | off> <timeout seconds>
   ```

3. Use the following command to define an inspection rule on a per-Application-layer-traffic basis:

   ```
   ip inspect name <inspection-name> <protocol> <alert on | off> -
     <audit-trail <on | off> <timeout seconds>
   ```

   This command can be used for all CBAC inspection protocols except for RPC and Java. Per-protocol inspection takes precedence over generic TCP or UDP inspection.

4. Use the following command to enable CBAC for RPC inspection:

```
ip inspect name <inspection-name> <rpc program-number number> -
   <wait-time minutes> <alert on | off> <audit-trail on |
   off> <timeout seconds>
```

Use of this command is optional, but it must be used to support blocking of RPC protocols.

5. Use the following command to enable CBAC for Java applet blocking:

```
ip inspect name <inspection-name> http <java-list access-
   list> -
   <alert on | off> <audit-trail on | off> <timeout seconds>
```

This command specifies the use of the HTTP protocol and a standard numbered access list to use to determine if a site's Java applets should be allowed. Use of this command is optional; however, it must be used to support blocking of Java applets.

6. Use the following command to configure the router for inspection of fragmented packets:

```
ip inspect name <inspection-name> <fragment -
   max number> <timeout seconds>
```

Use of this command is optional, but it is always recommended because it specifies the maximum number of packets that can arrive at the router interface before the initial packet for a session, for which state information is allocated.

7. Use the **ip inspect audit-trail** command to turn on audit trail logging for CBAC messages. Use of this command is optional.

The next few steps configure the timeouts and thresholds that CBAC uses to determine how long to manage the state information for each session and to determine when to drop a session if the session does not become established. The timeouts and thresholds apply globally to all sessions, and the default timeout and threshold values may be used or you can change them to the values that are determined by the enterprise's security policy. To configure specific CBAC timeout and threshold values, use the commands in the following steps:

8. Use this command to determine the length of time the software waits for a TCP session to reach the established state before dropping the session:

```
ip inspect tcp synwait-time seconds
```

The session has reached the established state after the session's first SYN bit is detected.

9. Use this command to determine the length of time a TCP session will still be managed after the firewall detects a FIN-exchange, which determines that a session is about to close:

```
ip inspect tcp finwait-time seconds
```

10. Use the following command to determine the length of time a TCP session will still be managed after no activity:

```
ip inspect tcp idle-time seconds
```

CBAC will not continue to maintain state information for a session that violates the idle time.

11. Use this command to determine the length of time a UDP session will still be managed after no activity:

```
ip inspect udp idle-time seconds
```

Because UDP is a connectionless service, there are no actual sessions, so CBAC will approximate sessions by examining the information in the packet and determining if the packet is similar to other UDP packets and if the packet was detected soon after another similar UDP packet. CBAC will not continue to maintain state information for a session that violates the idle time.

12. Use this command to determine the length of time a DNS name lookup session will still be managed after no activity:

```
ip inspect dns-timeout seconds
```

CBAC applies the DNS timeout to all DNS name lookup sessions, and the DNS timeout overrides the timeout value specified by the UDP timeout.

4. IOS Firewall Feature Set

13. Because CBAC measures both the total number of existing half-open sessions and the rate of session establishment attempts for both TDP and UDP, use this command to determine the number of existing half-open sessions that will cause the software to start deleting them:

```
ip inspect max-incomplete high number
```

A high number of half-open sessions could indicate a denial-of-service attack.

14. If the total max-incomplete high session threshold is reached, CBAC will begin dropping half-open sessions and continue to do so until the total number of half-open sessions falls below the value configured using this command:

```
ip inspect max-incomplete low number
```

15. Use this command to set the rate of thresholds that are measured as the number of new session connection attempts are detected in the last one-minute sample period:

```
ip inspect one-minute high number
```

When new connection attempts rise above the configured threshold within the sample period, CBAC will begin to drop new connection requests.

16. If the total one-minute high session threshold is reached, CBAC will begin dropping half-open sessions and continue to do so until the total number of half-open sessions fall below the value configured using this command:

```
ip inspect one-minute low number
```

17. Use the following command to set the number of existing half-open TCP sessions with the same destination host address that will cause the software to start dropping half-open sessions to the same destination host address:

```
ip inspect tcp max-incomplete host number block-time minutes
```

Some very important rules relate to Step 1, configuring the access lists for CBAC operation on the internal and external interfaces. These rules will be referred to over and over again within this section, and it is highly recommended that you refer back to these rules for clarity if you are planning to implement CBAC within your organization, and you are having trouble implementing CBAC within your network. If you are configuring CBAC on the internal interface, follow these rules:

- If an inbound IP access list is configured on the internal interface, the access list can be either a standard or extended access list. The access lists should permit traffic that should be inspected by CBAC. If traffic is not permitted, it will not be inspected by CBAC and will be dropped.

- An outbound IP access list at the internal interface must be an extended access list. The outbound access list should deny traffic that you want to be inspected by CBAC. CBAC will create temporary openings in the outbound access list as needed to permit only return traffic that is part of an existing session.

If you are configuring CBAC on the external interface, follow these rules:

- If an outbound IP access list is configured on the external interface, the access list can be a standard or extended access list. The access list should permit traffic that should be inspected by CBAC. If traffic is not permitted, it will not be inspected by CBAC and will be dropped.

- If an inbound IP access list is configured on the external interface, the access list must be an extended access list. The inbound access list should deny traffic that should be inspected by CBAC. CBAC will create temporary openings in the inbound access list as needed to permit only return traffic that is part of an existing session.

NOTE: *If you are planning to implement CBAC within your organization, refer to the access list rules listed above for help in understanding how to configure your access lists to define your rules of inspection.*

Well, think about it; are there enough commands for CBAC? At first glance the configuration for CBAC may seem overwhelming, but I shall take a slow approach into explaining the configuration power that CBAC provides. I will start with a simple network that is shown in Figure 4.2. In this network, Router 3 has two interfaces and is the router that provides CBAC functionality for the inside trusted network. Router 3's inside trusted network uses address space within the private 192.168.10.0 address space. Router 3 is also connected to the outside untrusted network using its Serial interface and using the public address space 192.168.20.0.

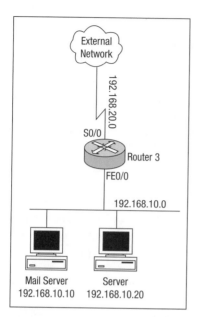

Figure 4.2   Sample CBAC network.

NOTE: *The 192.168.20.0 network is actually private address space as allocated from RFC 1918, which can be found at* **www.ietf.org/rfc/rfc1918.txt?number=1918**. *It is only used here for the benefit of protecting the innocent.*

In Figure 4.2, you can see that Router 3 is connected to an inside and outside network. The security administrators for Router 3 want to provide CBAC security for the hosts displayed in Figure 4.2. The first host is a mail server, at IP address 192.168.10.10, which needs to have the Simple Mail Transport Protocol opened for its use. The other host is a host on the network, at IP address 192.168.10.20; the security administrators have decided it would also benefit from the security functionality that CBAC provides.

CBAC actively inspects the activity behind a firewall. CBAC specifies what traffic should be let in and what traffic should be let out by using access lists. However, CBAC access lists include **ip inspect** statements that allow the inspection of the protocol to make sure that it has not been tampered with before the protocol goes to the systems behind the firewall. Listing 4.1 displays Router 3's configuration for CBAC, which meets the security requirements of the network displayed in Figure 4.2.

Listing 4.1   Example configuration of Router 3 for CBAC.

```
access-list 110 permit tcp 192.168.10.0 0.0.0.255 any
access-list 110 permit udp 192.168.10.0 0.0.0.255 any
access-list 110 permit icmp 192.168.10.0 0.0.0.255 any
access-list 110 deny ip any any
access-list 120 permit icmp any 192.168.10.0 0.0.0.255 -
  echo-reply
access-list 120 permit icmp any 192.168.10.0 0.0.0.255 -
  unreachable
access-list 120 permit icmp any 192.168.10.0 0.0.0.255 -
  admin-prohibited
access-list 120 permit icmp any 192.168.10.0 0.0.0.255 -
  packet-too-big
access-list 120 permit icmp any 192.168.10.0 0.0.0.255 -
  echo
access-list 120 permit icmp any 192.168.10.0 0.0.0.255 -
  time-exceeded
access-list 120 deny ip any any
!
ip inspect name samplecbac ftp
ip inspect name samplecbac smtp
ip inspect name samplecbac tcp
ip inspect name samplecbac fragment max 6000 timeout 8
!
interface FastEthernet0/0
ip address 192.168.10.1 255.255.255.0
ip access-group 110 in
ip inspect samplecbac in
ip inspect samplecbac out
!
interface Serial0/0
ip address 192.168.20.1 255.255.255.0
ip access-group 120 in
!
ip route 0.0.0.0 0.0.0.0 192.168.20.2
```

Notice that CBAC is performing a more generic TCP and UDP inspection. The access list that permits ICMP traffic, access list 110, is there to permit outbound ICMP traffic that arrives inbound on interface FastEthernet0/0. CBAC does not inspect ICMP traffic but it has to be listed in order to permit the outbound ICMP traffic because of the **deny any any** statement at the end of the access list. The **ip inspect name** command configures Router 3 to perform CBAC inspection. At first glance, the CBAC configuration combined with the access lists that are configured on each interface may not seem correct, but remember that CBAC creates temporary access list openings. Referring back to the rules for creating an inbound access list on an interface, the rule states that the access lists should permit traffic that should be inspected by CBAC. If traffic is not permitted, it will not be inspected by CBAC and will be dropped. The temporary openings will be created in access list 120, which is applied to the outside Serial interface.

Looking now at access list 120, you can see that the access list is applied as an inbound access list on interface Serial0/0. Still doesn't look correct though, does it? Look again at the rules for creating an inbound access list on the external interface. The rule states that an inbound access list applied to the external interface should deny traffic that should be inspected by CBAC. CBAC will create temporary openings in the inbound access list as needed to permit only return traffic that is part of an existing session. Notice that access list 120 permits only ICMP traffic inbound on the Serial interface and denies all other traffic; all traffic that is denied by an access list will be inspected by CBAC, and an opening was created within this access list by the originating traffic.

To view the complete CBAC inspection configuration, you must issue the **sh ip inspect config** command. The output of this command displays the protocols that should be inspected by CBAC and the associated timeout values for each protocol. Issuing the **show ip inspect config** command on Router 3 lists the output displayed in Listing 4.2.

Listing 4.2   Output of the show ip inspect command.

```
Router-3#sh ip inspect config
Session audit trail is disabled
Session alert is enabled
one-minute (sampling period) thresholds are [400:500] -
  connections
max-incomplete sessions thresholds are [400:500]
max-incomplete tcp connections per host is 50. Block-time 0 -
  minute.
tcp synwait-time is 30 sec — tcp finwait-time is 5 sec
tcp idle-time is 3600 sec — udp idle-time is 30 sec
dns-timeout is 5 sec
Inspection Rule Configuration
Inspection name samplecbac
ftp alert is on audit-trail is off timeout 3600
smtp alert is on audit-trail is off timeout 3600
tcp alert is on audit-trail is off timeout 3600
```

```
fragment Max 6000 In Use 0 alert is on audit-trail is off timeout -
8
Router-3#
```

The output of the **show ip inspect config** command displays many of the configured timeout and threshold values for the CBAC configuration. The first line of the output tells you that CBAC audit trail messages are disabled. The second line shows that session alerting is enabled; use of the **show ip inspect config** command displays alert messages to the console port of the router. The next six lines display output that pertain to timeout values for CBAC. The inspection rules section is the major output section within the **show ip inspect config** command and details the inspection name and the protocols that are configured for CBAC operation, the audit trail information, and the configured timeout values for each inspection rule.

You can use the **ip inspect audit-trail** global configuration command to configure CBAC audit trail messages and display them on the console after each session closes. Audit trail messages help in analyzing problems that are occurring during CBAC operation. The following shows the command issued on Router 3:

```
Router-3#config t
Router-3(config)#ip inspect audit-trail
Router-3(config)#end
Router-3#
```

Immediately after the command is issued on Router 3, audit trail information begins to appear on the console. The output of the audit trail messages is shown in Listing 4.3.

Listing 4.3   Audit trail messages on Router 3.

```
: tcp session initiator (192.168.10.13:38992)sent 22 bytes -
  responder (192.168.40.11:25) sent 198 bytes
: ftp session initiator 192.168.10.18:32294) sent 336 bytes -
  responder (192.168.129.11:21) sent 495 bytes
```

After enabling audit trail output and taking a quick glance back at the inspection configuration, you can see that audit trail messages are now enabled. Listing 4.4 shows the updated listing.

Listing 4.4   Updated output from the show ip inspect command.

```
Router-3#show ip inspect config
Session audit trail is enabled
Session alert is enabled
```

```
one-minute (sampling period) thresholds are [400:500] -
  connections
max-incomplete sessions thresholds are [400:500]
max-incomplete tcp connections per host is 50. Block-time 0 -
  minute.
tcp synwait-time is 30 sec - tcp finwait-time is 5 sec
tcp idle-time is 3600 sec - udp idle-time is 30 sec
dns-timeout is 5 sec
Inspection Rule Configuration
Inspection name samplecbac
ftp alert is on audit-trail is on timeout 3600
smtp alert is on audit-trail is on timeout 3600
tcp alert is on audit-trail is on timeout 3600
fragment Maximum 6000  In Use 0 alert is on audit-trail is off -
  timeout 8
Router-3#
```

Changes to any of the global timeout and threshold values described earlier can be made to the configuration, and the change will be reflected in the output of the **show ip inspect config**.

CBAC can also be configured to perform Java blocking, which will allow into the network Java applets from specified sites on the Internet and deny all others. This type of blocking denies access to Java applets that are not embedded in an archived or compressed file. Referring to Figure 4.3, I will continue with the example from above and configure Router 3 for Java blocking. In Figure 4.3, you can see that three different Web servers have been added to the outside network of Router 3. The IP addresses of the Web servers are 192.168.100.100,

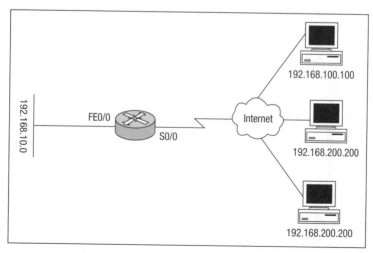

Figure 4.3   Network configured for Java blocking.

192.168.200.200, and 192.168.300.300. The security policy of the company is to configure Router 3 such that any Java applet from the Web servers at IP addresses 192.168.100.100 and 192.168.200.200 are permitted and inspected by CBAC, yet the Java applets from the server at IP address 192.168.300.300 are denied. Listing 4.5 shows the configuration needed to configure Router 3 for Java blocking.

Listing 4.5   Configuring Router 3 for Java blocking.

```
access-list 30 permit 192.168.100.100
access-list 30 permit 192.168.200.200
access-list 110 permit tcp 192.168.10.0 0.0.0.255 any
access-list 110 permit udp 192.168.10.0 0.0.0.255 any
access-list 110 permit icmp 192.168.10.0 0.0.0.255 any
access-list 150 permit icmp any 192.168.10.0 0.0.0.255 -
  echo-reply
access-list 150 permit icmp any 192.168.10.0 0.0.0.255 -
  unreachable
access-list 150 permit icmp any 192.168.10.0 0.0.0.255 -
  admin-prohibited
access-list 150 permit icmp any 192.168.10.0 0.0.0.255 -
  packet-too-big
access-list 150 permit icmp any 192.168.10.0 0.0.0.255 -
  echo
access-list 150 permit icmp any 192.168.10.0 0.0.0.255 -
  time-exceeded
access-list 150 deny ip any any
!
ip inspect name mytest tcp
ip inspect name mytest udp
ip inspect name mytest http java-list 30
ip inspect name mytest fragment max 6000 timeout 8
ip inspect audit-trial
!
interface FastEthernet0/0
ip address 192.168.10.1 255.255.255.0
ip access-group 110 in
!
interface Serial0/0
ip address 192.168.20.1 255.255.255.0
ip access-group 150 in
ip inspect mytest out
ip inspect mytest in
```

In this example, access-list 30 allows Java from friendly sites at IP addresses 192.168.100.100 and 192.168.200.200 while implicitly denying Java from other sites. The output displayed in Listing 4.6 is sample debug output from the **debug ip inspect detail** command after attempting to connect to the Web servers on 192.168.100.100, 192.168.200.200, and 192.168.300.300. The **debug ip inspect detail** displays the output of connection requests from friendly Java Web servers, and it also shows Java being blocked from a nonfriendly Web server. Friendly Web servers are servers that are listed with a permit statement within the access list configuration.

Listing 4.6   Debug output of Java blocking.

```
Router-3#debug ip inspect detail
...
: http session initiator (192.168.10.37:3271) sent 215 bytes -
  responder (192.168.100.100:80) sent 3162 bytes
: http session initiator (192.168.10.28:4972) sent 143 bytes -
  responder (192.168.200.200:80) sent 254 bytes
: http session initiator (192.168.10.37:3272) sent 324 bytes -
  responder (192.168.100.10:80) sent 234 bytes
: http session initiator (192.168.10.28:4973) sent 343 bytes -
  responder (192.168.200.200:80) sent 314 bytes
: http session initiator (192.168.10.37:3274) sent 344 bytes -
  responder (192.168.100.100:80) sent 8 bytes
: http session initiator (192.168.10.28:4974) sent 360 bytes -
  responder (192.168.200.200:80) sent 206 bytes
: http session initiator (192.168.10.37:3275) sent 345 bytes -
  responder (192.168.100.100:80) sent 12276 bytes
: http session initiator (192.168.10.28:4975) sent 369 bytes -
  responder (192.168.200.200:80) sent 206 bytes
: http session initiator (192.168.10.37:3276) sent 354 bytes -
  responder (192.168.100.100:80) sent 278 bytes
: JAVA applet is blocked from (192.168.300.300:80) to -
  (192.168.10.28:8394).
: JAVA applet is blocked from (192.168.300.300:80) to -
```

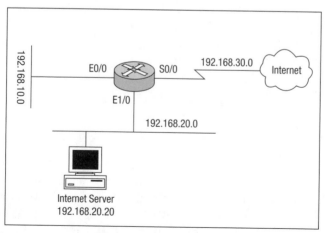

Figure 4.4   Router 3 configured for CBAC with three interfaces.

```
(192.168.10.28:8395).
: http session initiator (192.168.10.37:1298) sent 215 bytes -
  responder (192.168.100.100:80) sent 302 bytes
: JAVA applet is blocked from (192.168.300.300:80) to -
  (192.168.10.37:1422).
: http session initiator (192.168.10.28:1203) sent 362 bytes -
  responder (192.168.100.100:80) sent 162 bytes
: JAVA applet is blocked from (192.168.300.300:80) to -
  (192.168.10.37:1723).
```

The CBAC configurations have been fairly basic so far. In the next example, Router 3 will be configured for CBAC, but this time, another interface has been added to the Router (see Figure 4.4). This interface, interface Ethernet1/0, will be used for providing Web, FTP, and mail services to the outside external Internet. Ethernet1/0 is connected to the "DMZ" network and has a single host within the network used to provide the services mentioned earlier to the outside world. Ethernet0/0 is connected to the internal local network. Router 3's configuration is shown in Listing 4.7.

4. IOS Firewall Feature Set

Listing 4.7   CBAC configuration of Router 3 with three interfaces.

```
ip inspect audit-trail
ip inspect tcp idle-time 14400
ip inspect udp idle-time 1800
ip inspect dns-timeout 7
!
ip inspect name cbactest cuseeme
ip inspect name cbactest ftp
ip inspect name cbactest h323
ip inspect name cbactest http
ip inspect name cbactest rcmd
ip inspect name cbactest realaudio
ip inspect name cbactest smtp
ip inspect name cbactest sqlnet
ip inspect name cbactest streamworks
ip inspect name cbactest tcp
ip inspect name cbactest tftp
ip inspect name cbactest udp
ip inspect name cbactest vdolive
ip inspect name cbactest fragment max 6000 timeout 8

!
interface ethernet0/0
ip address 192.168.10.1 255.255.255.0
ip access-group 100 in
ip access-group 101 out
ip inspect cbactest in
!
```

```
interface ethernet1/0
ip address 192.168.20.1 255.255.255.0
ip access-group 102 in
ip access-group 103 out
!
interface serial0/0
ip address 192.168.30.1 255.255.255.0
ip access-group 104 in
ip access-group 105 out
ip inspect cbactest in
!
access-list 100 permit ip 192.168.10.0 0.0.0.255 any
access-list 100 deny ip any any
!
access-list 101 permit icmp any 192.168.10.0 0.0.0.255 -
  admin-prohibited
access-list 101 permit icmp any 192.168.10.0 0.0.0.255 -
  echo
access-list 101 permit icmp any 192.168.10.0 0.0.0.255 -
  echo-reply
access-list 101 permit icmp any 192.168.10.0 0.0.0.255 -
  packet-too-big
access-list 101 permit icmp any 192.168.10.0 0.0.0.255 -
  time-exceeded
access-list 101 permit icmp any 192.168.10.0 0.0.0.255 -
  traceroute
access-list 101 permit icmp any 192.168.10.0 0.0.0.255 -
  unreachable
access-list 101 deny ip any any
!
access-list 102 permit ip 192.168.20.0 0.0.0.255 any
access-list 102 deny ip any any
!
access-list 103 permit udp any host 192.168.20.20 eq domain
access-list 103 permit tcp any host 192.168.20.20 eq domain
access-list 103 permit tcp any host 192.168.20.20 eq www
access-list 103 permit tcp any host 192.168.20.20 eq ftp
access-list 103 permit tcp any host 192.168.20.20 eq smtp
access-list 103 permit tcp 192.168.10.0 0.0.0.255 host -
  192.168.20.20 eq pop3
access-list 103 permit tcp 192.168.10.0 0.0.0.255 any eq telnet
access-list 103 permit icmp any 192.168.20.0 0.0.0.255 -
  admin-prohibited
access-list 103 permit icmp any 192.168.20.0 0.0.0.255 echo
access-list 103 permit icmp any 192.168.20.0 0.0.0.255 echo-reply
access-list 103 permit icmp any 192.168.20.0 0.0.0.255 -
  packet-too-big
```

```
access-list 103 permit icmp any 192.169.20.0 0.0.0.255 -
time-exceeded
access-list 103 permit icmp any 192.168.20.0 0.0.0.255 traceroute
access-list 103 permit icmp any 192.168.20.0 0.0.0.255 unreachable
access-list 103 deny ip any any
!
access-list 104 deny ip 192.168.10.0 0.0.0.255 any
access-list 104 deny ip 192.168.20.0 0.0.0.255 any
access-list 104 permit ip any any
!
access-list 105 permit icmp 192.168.10.0 0.0.0.255 any echo-reply
access-list 105 permit icmp 192.168.20.0 0.0.0.255 any echo-reply
access-list 105 permit icmp 192.168.10.0 0.0.0.255 any -
time-exceeded
access-list 105 permit icmp 192.168.20.0 0.0.0.255 any -
time-exceeded
access-list 105 deny ip 192.168.20.0 0.0.0.255 any
access-list 105 permit ip 192.168.10.0 0.0.0.255 any
```

In the configuration in Listing 4.7, the first command line enables audit trail logging of session information, the second and third lines set the length of time a TCP and UDP session is managed after no activity is received, and the fourth line sets the length of time a DNS name lookup session is still managed after no activity is received. The next set of configuration lines sets up an inspection list that is named **cbactest**; this CBAC inspection list will be used for inspection of inbound traffic on Ethernet0/0 and inbound return traffic on Serial0/0. Under interface Ethernet0/0, access list 100 is applied to allow all legitimate traffic from the inside network. Access list 101 is also applied to allow some ICMP traffic and deny everything else. The inspection list **cbactest** will add entries to this list to permit return traffic for connections established from the inside. Finally, under interface Ethernet0/0, the inspection list **cbactest** is applied to inspect inbound traffic on Ethernet0/0.

Under interface Ethernet1/0, access list 102 is applied to permit inbound traffic initiated from hosts within the DMZ. Access list 103 is also applied, which allows only certain services to establish a connection with the hosts within the DMZ network. The inspection rules that are configured on other interfaces will add temporary entries to this list. Under interface Serial0/0, access list 104 is applied; it is configured to prevent any spoofing of packets that are inbound on Serial0/0 and contain a source address in the header of the packet such that the packet appears to have originated from within the "inside" network. Access list 105 is also configured; it allows Ping replies from the inside network or the DMZ network and permits inside traffic back out.

4. IOS Firewall Feature Set

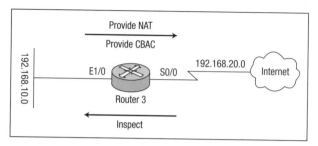

Figure 4.5   CBAC and NAT network design.

CBAC can also function on a router that also has Network Address Translation (NAT) or Port Address Translation (PAT) configured. The configuration in the next example works well for any office connected directly to the Internet and utilizing the functionality of NAT.

In the sample network shown in Figure 4.5, no services are run on the inside network behind Router 3. Ethernet1/0 is the "inside" network. Serial0/0 is the outside interface. Users on the inside local network of 192.168.10.0 must have their IP addresses translated to public routable addresses within the 192.168.20.0 address space. Also, CBAC services must be provided for users on the inside network. The configuration for Router 3 that is shown in Listing 4.8 meets these requirements.

NOTE: *The 192.168.20.0 network is actually private address space as allocated from RFC 1918, which can be found at* **www.ietf.org/rfc/rfc1918.txt?number=1918**. *It is only used here for the benefit of protecting the innocent.*

Listing 4.8   Router 3 configured for CBAC and NAT.

```
ip inspect name cbacnat cuseeme timeout 3600
ip inspect name cbacnat ftp audit-trail on timeout 3600
ip inspect name cbacnat h323 timeout 3600
ip inspect name cbacnat http timeout 3600
ip inspect name cbacnat realaudio timeout 3600
ip inspect name cbacnat smtp timeout 3600
ip inspect name cbacnat sqlnet timeout 3600
ip inspect name cbacnat streamworks timeout 3600
ip inspect name cbacnat tcp timeout 3600
ip inspect name cbacnat tftp timeout 30
ip inspect name cbacnat udp timeout 15
!
ip inspect tcp synwait-time 15
ip inspect tcp idle-time 1800
ip inspect udp idle-time 60
ip inspect max-incomplete high 250
ip inspect max-incomplete low 150
```

```
ip inspect one-minute high 250
ip inspect one-minute low 150
!
interface Ethernet0
ip address 192.168.10.1 255.255.255.0
ip access-group 101 in
no ip directed-broadcast
ip nat inside
ip inspect cbacnat in
!
interface Serial0
ip address 192.168.20.1.1 255.255.255.0
ip access-group 112 in
no ip directed-broadcast
ip nat outside
!
ip nat pool natpool 192.168.20.3 192.168.20.254 -
 netmask 255.255.255.0
ip nat inside source list 1 pool natpool
ip classless
ip route 0.0.0.0 0.0.0.0 192.168.20.2
ip route 192.168.10.0 255.255.255.0 192.168.10.2
!
access-list 1   permit 192.168.10.0 0.0.0.255
access-list 101 permit tcp 192.168.10.0 0.0.0.255 any
access-list 101 permit udp 192.168.10.0 0.0.0.255 any
access-list 101 permit icmp 192.168.10.0 0.0.0.255 any
access-list 112 permit icmp any 192.168.20.0 0.0.0.255 -
 unreachable
access-list 112 permit icmp any 192.168.20.0 0.0.0.255 -
 echo-reply
access-list 112 permit icmp any 192.168.20.0 0.0.0.255 -
 packet-too-big
access-list 112 permit icmp any 192.168.20.0 0.0.0.255 -
 time-exceeded
access-list 112 permit icmp any 192.168.20.0 0.0.0.255 -
 traceroute
access-list 112 permit icmp any 192.168.20.0 0.0.0.255 -
 admin-prohibited
access-list 112 permit icmp any 192.168.20.0 0.0.0.255 echo
access-list 112 deny   ip 127.0.0.0 0.255.255.255 any
access-list 112 deny   ip any any
```

4. IOS Firewall Feature Set

Related solution:	Found on page:
Configuring Dynamic NAT Translations	145

Configuring Port Application Mapping

The configuration of Port Application Mapping (PAM) is relatively straightforward and simple, but the power of PAM is really the way in which CBAC uses the information in the PAM table to identify a service or application from traffic flowing through the firewall. With PAM, CBAC can associate nonstandard port numbers with specific protocols. To configure PAM, use the commands in the following steps:

1. Use this global configuration command to establish a port mapping entry using TCP or UDP port number and application name:

    ```
    ip port-map <application-name> port <port-number> -
       list <list-number>
    ```

    The list argument is optional and is used to specify a standard access list that matches specific hosts or subnets that have an application that uses a specific port number.

2. Optionally, configure a standard access list that specifies the specific hosts or subnets that should be configured for host-specific port application mapping.

Looking at the network detailed in Figure 4.6, you can see that Router 3 is the perimeter router, which provides Internet access for Company A. Router 3 has a connection to its ISP via its Serial1/1/0 outside interface. Router 3 also has a connection to its local inside network with FastEthernet0/1/0 interface. Router 3 is configured for PAM. Users on the local inside network use their Web browsers to access Web servers on the outside network using the nonstandard HTTP ports of 6100 through 6105. For Router 3 to map HTTP traffic to port 6100 through 6105, use the configuration shown in Listing 4.9.

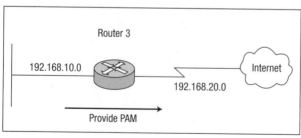

Figure 4.6   Network layout for PAM.

Listing 4.9   PAM configuration for Router 3.

```
#ip port-map http port 6100
#ip port-map http port 6101
#ip port-map http port 6102
#ip port-map http port 6103
#ip port-map http port 6104
#ip port-map http port 6105
#end
```

Notice in Listing 4.9 that Router 3 has been configured to map six sequential port numbers to HTTP traffic. You can view port map table information on the router by issuing the following command:

```
show ip port-map {application-name | port port-number}
```

To view the port mapping table of Router 3, issue the **show ip port-map http** command. The port mapping of Router 3 is displayed in Listing 4.10.

Listing 4.10   Port mapping table on Router 3.

```
Router-3#show ip port-map http
Default mapping: http        port 6100    user defined
Default mapping: http        port 6101    user defined
Default mapping: http        port 6102    user defined
Default mapping: http        port 6103    user defined
Default mapping: http        port 6104    user defined
Default mapping: http        port 6105    user defined
Default mapping: http        port 80      system defined
Router-3#
```

I issued the **show ip port-map** command above in Listing 4.10 with the **application-name** argument to specify that I wanted to display only information related to HTTP traffic. Each of the ports that were configured earlier is displayed in Listing 4.10; notice that they are configured as a user-defined table entry. Also, note that the final line specifies a system-defined entry for HTTP. Table 4.1 earlier in this chapter stated that HTTP was a system-defined entry on the default port 80.

While on the subject of system-defined entries, I'll remove the configuration that created the user-defined entries and display the default PAM table. First I'll remove the prior configuration:

```
Router-3#config t
Router-3(config)#no ip port-map http port 6100
Router-3(config)#no ip port-map http port 6101
```

```
Router-#(config)#no ip port-map http port 6102
Router-3(config)#no ip port-map http port 6103
Router-3(config)#no ip port-map http port 6104
Router-3(config)#no ip port-map http port 6105
Router-3(config)#end
Router-3#
```

I can now issue the **show ip port-map** command without using any argument to display the entire PAM table. Issuing the command on Router 3 should now display the default PAM table. Listing 4.11 displays Router 3's default PAM table.

Listing 4.11   Default PAM table of Router 3.

```
Router-3#show ip port-map
...
Default mapping: vdolive      port 7000    system defined
Default mapping: sunrpc       port 111     system defined
Default mapping: netshow      port 1755    system defined
Default mapping: cuseeme      port 7648    system defined
Default mapping: tftp         port 69      system defined
Default mapping: rtsp         port 8554    system defined
Default mapping: realmedia    port 7070    system defined
Default mapping: streamworks  port 1558    system defined
Default mapping: ftp          port 21      system defined
Default mapping: telnet       port 23      system defined
Default mapping: rtsp         port 554     system defined
Default mapping: h323         port 1720    system defined
Default mapping: sip          port 5060    system defined
Default mapping: smtp         port 25      system defined
Default mapping: http         port 80      system defined
Default mapping: msrpc        port 135     system defined
Default mapping: exec         port 512     system defined
Default mapping: login        port 513     system defined
Default mapping: sql-net      port 1521    system defined
Default mapping: shell        port 514     system defined
Default mapping: mgcp         port 2427    system defined
Router-3#
```

System-defined table entries are important to the port application process, and as mentioned earlier, any attempt to map a user-defined entry over a system-defined entry is not permitted. Attempting to configure HTTP to run on the system-defined port of 21, which maps to FTP, is not allowed. An example of this type of attempt is shown in Listing 4.12.

Listing 4.12   Attempt to map over a system-defined entry.

```
Router-3#config t
Router-3(config)#ip port-map http port 21
Command fail: the port 21 has already been defined for ftp by -
              the system.
              No change can be made to the system defined port -
              mappings.
Router-3(config)#end
Router-3#
```

Host-defined entries are actually user-defined entries that have a finer granularity of configuration on a per-host or per-subnet basis. In Figure 4.7, three hosts on the internal inside network need FTP access to a host on the external outside network of Router 3. The host on the external outside network of Router 3 only uses FTP on port 7142. To configure Router 3 to map the host-defined entries for FTP on Router 3, you must configure an access list to specify which hosts need the mapping created. Listing 4.13 shows the configuration needed to accomplish this.

Listing 4.13   Creating host-defined entries on Router 3.

```
Router-3#config t
Router-3(config)#access-list 1 permit 192.168.10.240
Router-3(config)#access-list 1 permit 192.168.11.16
Router-3(config)#access-list 1 permit 192.168.11.112
Router-3(config)#ip port-map ftp port 7142 list 1
Router-3(config)#end
```

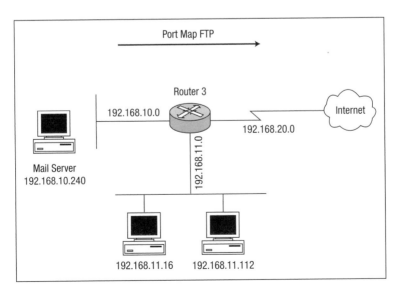

Figure 4.7   Host that needs PAM configuration.

If you examine the output of the **show ip port-map** command, you can see that Router 3 has created the host-defined entry and bound it to access list 1. Listing 4.14 shows the output from the **show ip port-map** command with the newly created host-defined entries in the PAM table.

Listing 4.14   Display of the host-defined PAM table entries.

```
Router-3#show ip port-map
...
Default mapping: http      port 80                    system
Host specific:   ftp       port 7142    in list 1     user
Default mapping: ftp       port 21                    system
Default mapping: msrpc     port 135                   system
Default mapping: exec      port 512                   system
Default mapping: login     port 513                   system
Default mapping: sql-net   port 1521                  system
Default mapping: shell     port 514                   system
Default mapping: mgcp      port 2427                  system
Router-3#
```

Just as host-specific entries can populate the PAM table (which was demonstrated in the configuration above), so can subnets. The three hosts on the internal network in the configuration in Listing 4.13 all need FTP access to a host on the external network using port 7142; however, all hosts on each of the 192.168.10.0 and 192.168.11.0 subnets need to access a RealVideo server on the outside network using port number 5050 as opposed to the default 7070. To configure subnet-defined entries, I will create a new access list and bind it to the **ip port-map** command. Listing 4.15 shows the configuration.

Listing 4.15   Subnet-defined PAM configuration.

```
Router-3#config t
...
Router-3(config)#access-list 2 permit 192.168.10.0
Router-3(config)#access-list 2 permit 192.168.11.0
Router-3(config)#ip port-map realmedia port 5050 list 2
Router-3(config)#end
Router-3#
```

Pay particular attention to the last octet of the IP addresses configured in Listing 4.15; this octet allows the router to determine whether the access list is a host-specific entry or a subnet-specific entry. Notice that the number 0 is specified and not a number between 1 and 254 for the class C subnet. Issuing the **show ip port-map** command again displays the PAM table for Router 3. Listing 4.16 shows the output of the PAM table.

Listing 4.16   Output of the PAM table on Router 3.

```
Router-3#sh ip port-map
Default mapping: netshow      port 1755                  system
Host specific:   realmedia    port 5050    in list 2     userDefault -
   mapping:      realmedia    port 7070                   system
Default mapping: ftp          port 21                     system
Host specific:   ftp          port 7142    in list 1      user
Default mapping: mgcp         port 2427                   system
Router-3#
```

Listing 4.12 showed that a system-defined entry could not be over-written; however, a host-specific entry or a subnet-specific entry can change the default system entry on a per-host or per-subnet basis for any or all system entries. Referring again to Listing 4.13, Router 3 was configured to create a port table mapping for each of the three hosts listed so that the hosts could access an FTP server on the outside network using port 7142. The three hosts now have a requirement to access a Web server on the outside network, and they need to access the Web server using the port that is normally used by FTP, port 21. So Router 3 needs to create a PAM table entry such that HTTP traffic maps to port 21, FTP's standard port. To configure Router 3 to meet the new requirements of the three hosts and override the system-defined entries, use the configuration shown in Listing 4.17.

Listing 4.17   Router 3 configured to override system-defined entries.

```
Router-3#config t
Router-3(config)#access-list 1 permit 192.168.10.240
Router-3(config)#access-list 1 permit 192.168.11.16
Router-3(config)#access-list 1 permit 192.168.11.112
Router-3(config)#ip port-map http port 21 list 1
Router-3(config)#end
```

First, notice that the router did not prompt with any error message as a result of the configuration change. If you examine the output of the **show ip port-map** command, you can see that HTTP is indeed a user-defined map that is mapped to port 21. Listing 4.18 displays the output.

Listing 4.18   Display of PAM table on Router 3.

```
Router-3#sh ip port-map
...
Default mapping: vdolive      port 7000                  system
Host specific:   realmedia    port 5050    in list 2     user
Default mapping: realmedia    port 7070                  system
Default mapping: ftp          port 21                     system
Host specific:   http         port 21      in list 1      user
```

```
Default mapping: http        port 80                 system
Default mapping: exec        port 512                system
Default mapping: login       port 513                system
Default mapping: sql-net     port 1521               system
Default mapping: shell       port 514                system
Host specific:   ftp         port 7142   in list 1   user
Default mapping: mgcp        port 2427               system
Router-3#
```

Finally, two new inside hosts need to access two different outside hosts using different services; however, both hosts need to use the same port number. The host with the IP address of 192.168.10.118 needs the Telnet service to be an external host and the Telnet service needs to run over port 6200. The host with the IP address of 192.168.11.205 needs to access the Microsoft NetShow service of a host on the external network and also needs the Microsoft NetShow service to run over port 6200. The configuration for Router 3 in Listing 4.19 accomplishes the hosts' requirements.

Listing 4.19   Configuration of mapping different hosts to the same port.

```
Router-3#config t
Router-3(config)#access-list 12 permit 192.168.10.118
Router-3(config)#access-list 13 permit 192.168.11.205
Router-3(config)#ip port-map telnet port 6200 list 12
Router-3(config)#ip port-map netshow port 6200 list 13
Router-3(config)#end
```

The final configuration of Router 3 can be displayed using the **show running-config** command (see Listing 4.20).

Listing 4.20   Final configuration of Router 3.

```
Router-3#sh ru
Building configuration...
!
ip port-map http port 6100
ip port-map http port 6101
ip port-map http port 6102
ip port-map http port 6103
ip port-map http port 6104
ip port-map http port 6105
ip port-map realmedia port 5050 list 2
ip port-map http port 21 list 1
ip port-map ftp port 7142 list 1
ip port-map netshow port 6200 list 13
ip port-map telnet port 6200 list 12
!
access-list 1 permit 192.168.11.112
```

```
access-list 1 permit 192.168.11.16
access-list 1 permit 192.168.10.240
access-list 2 permit 192.168.10.0
access-list 2 permit 192.168.11.0
access-list 12 permit 192.168.10.118
access-list 13 permit 192.168.11.205
!
```

After viewing the final PAM configuration, you can view the final PAM table on Router 3 by issuing the **show ip port-map** command. Listing 4.21 displays the complete PAM table for Router 3, including the system-defined entries, user-defined entries, and host-defined entries.

Listing 4.21   Complete PAM table for Router 3.

```
Router-3#sh ip port-map
Default mapping: vdolive       port 7000                 system
Default mapping: http          port 6100                 user
Default mapping: sunrpc        port 111                  system
Default mapping: http          port 6101                 user
Default mapping: netshow       port 1755                 system
Default mapping: http          port 6102                 user
Default mapping: http          port 6103                 user
Default mapping: http          port 6104                 user
Default mapping: http          port 6105                 user
Host specific:   realmedia     port 5050   in list 2     user
Default mapping: cuseeme       port 7648                 system
Default mapping: tftp          port 69                   system
Default mapping: rtsp          port 8554                 system
Default mapping: realmedia     port 7070                 system
Default mapping: streamworks   port 1558                 system
Default mapping: ftp           port 21                   system
Host specific:   http          port 21     in list 1     user
Default mapping: telnet        port 23                   system
Default mapping: rtsp          port 554                  system
Default mapping: h323          port 1720                 system
Default mapping: sip           port 5060                 system
Default mapping: smtp          port 25                   system
Default mapping: http          port 80                   system
Default mapping: msrpc         port 135                  system
Default mapping: exec          port 512                  system
Default mapping: login         port 513                  system
Default mapping: sql-net       port 1521                 system
Default mapping: shell         port 514                  system
Host specific:   ftp           port 7142   in list 1     user
Default mapping: mgcp          port 2427                 system
Host specific:   netshow       port 6200   in list 13    user
Host specific:   telnet        port 6200   in list 12    user
Router-3#
```

4. IOS Firewall Feature Set

Configuring IOS Firewall Intrusion Detection

The process used to configure the IOS Firewall IDS is far more detailed and complex than the process used to configure most technologies. However, if you take one step at a time, the task becomes a bit easier. If the router IDS is configured to log messages to a syslog server and not a CiscoSecure IDS Director, the configuration can be made even simpler. To enable the IOS Firewall IDS, follow these steps:

1. Use this **Director** command to send event notifications to a CiscoSecure IDS Director or to a syslog server:

   ```
   ip audit notify <nr-Director | log>
   ```

   The **nr-Director** argument specifies a CiscoSecure IDS Director and the **log** argument specifies a syslog server.

2. Use the following command to configure the Post Office parameters for the local router:

   ```
   ip audit po local <hostid host-id> <orgid org-id>
   ```

   The *host-id* is a unique number between 1 and 65535 that identifies the router, and *org-id* is a unique number between 1 and 65535 that identifies the organization to which the router and Director both belong. Use this command if events are being sent to a CiscoSecure IDS Director.

3. If alarms are being sent to a CiscoSecure IDS Director, the Post Office parameters for the CiscoSecure IDS Director must be configured on the router by using this command:

   ```
   ip audit <po> remote <hostid host-id> <orgid org-id> <rmtaddress -
      ip-address> <localaddress ip-address> <port port-number> -
      <preference preference-number> <timeout seconds> <application -
      application-type>
   ```

   The *host-id* is a unique number between 1 and 65535 that identifies the Director. The *org-id* is a unique number between 1 and 65535 that identifies the organization to which the router and Director both belong. The **rmtaddress** *ip-address* is the Director's IP address. The **localaddress** *ip-address* is the router's interface IP address. The *port-number* identifies the UDP port on which the Director is listening for alarms; port 45000 is the default. The *preference-number* is the priority of the route to the Director. The *seconds* is the number of seconds the Post Office will wait before it determines that a connection has timed out. The options for the *application-type* can be either **Director** or **logger**.

4. Use the following command to define the audit rules used by the IOS Firewall IDS:

```
ip audit name audit-name <info | attack> <list standard-acl> -
  <action alarm | drop | <reset>
```

5. Optionally, use the following command to specify the default action the IOS Firewall IDS should take for info and attack signatures (if this command is not used, the default action is to send an **alarm**):

```
ip audit <info | attack> action <alarm | drop | reset>
```

6. Optionally, use this command to configure a threshold that once reached, spamming in email messages is suspected:

```
ip audit smtp spam <recipients>
```

The *recipients* option is the maximum number of recipients in an email message; the default is 250 recipients.

7. Optionally, use this command to set the threshold that, once reached, will cause cued events that are to be sent to the CiscoSecure IDS Director to be dropped from the cue:

```
ip audit po max-events <events>
```

8. Use the following command to disable the signatures that should not be included in the audit rule:

```
ip audit signature signature-id <disable | list acl-list>
```

9. Use this command to apply the audit rule to an interface:

```
ip audit audit-name <in | out.
```

Other commands can be used with the IOS Firewall IDS and they will be addressed as needed throughout the explanations that follow. Figure 4.8 displays a simple network design with a router that will be used

4. IOS Firewall Feature Set

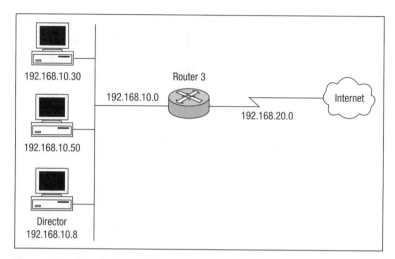

Figure 4.8   Simple firewall IDS network design.

to enable the IOS Firewall IDS. I will begin with a basic configuration of the IOS Firewall IDS. In this configuration, the audit rule **testrule** is created and is applied inbound on Router 3's Ethernet interface. Listing 4.22 outlines the configuration of Router 3.

Listing 4.22   IDS configuration of Router 3.

```
ip audit smtp spam 42
ip audit notify nr-Director
ip audit notify log
ip audit po local hostid 1 orgid 34
ip audit po remote hostid 5 orgid 34 rmtaddress 192.168.10.8 -
  localaddress 192.168.10.1
!
ip audit name testrule info action alarm
ip audit name testrule attack action alarm drop reset
!
interface FastEthernet0/0
ip address 192.168.10.1 255.255.255.0
ip audit testrule in
```

In Listing 4.22, Router 3 is configured to perform the IOS Firewall IDS functions. The first line of the configuration uses the **ip audit smtp** command to specify the number of recipients in a certain mail message the intrusion detection system considers a spam attack after the threshold is reached or exceeded. The next line configures the IOS Firewall IDS to send messages to a CiscoSecure IDS Director. The next line configures the IOS Firewall IDS to send messages to a syslog server, which can also be the local logging service of the router. The

ip audit po local command specifies the local Post Office parameters used when event notifications are sent to the CiscoSecure Director. A router can report to more than one CiscoSecure Director. In the event that two or more Directors are configured, you must give each Director a preference number that establishes its relative priority among the Directors. You can do this by using the hosted values. In Listing 4.22 above, only one remote Director has been configured, and it has been given a hosted value of 5; if you add another Director to the network and the router is supposed to prefer this Director over the previously configured Director, it would need to be configured with a lower hosted value. The router will always attempt to use the Director with the lowest number, switching automatically to Director with the next higher number when a Director fails and then switching back when the Director begins functioning again.

The next two lines configure audit rules for info and attack signature types using the name **testrule** and specifies that, for matched info signatures, the action the router should take is to send an alarm—the default action. For attack signatures, the action the router should take is to send an alarm and drop the packets and reset the session. The audit rule is then applied inbound on the Ethernet interface of Router 3. The IOS Firewall IDS software keeps detailed statistics that display the number of packets audited and the number of alarms sent. To view the statistics that the software has gathered, use the **show ip audit statistics** command. Listing 4.23 displays the output of this command.

Listing 4.23   Output of the show ip audit statistics command.

```
Router-3#show ip audit statistics
Signature audit statistics [process switch:fast switch]
  signature 2000 packets audited: [0:2]
  signature 2001 packets audited: [9:9]
  signature 2004 packets audited: [0:2]
  signature 6103 packets audited: [0:42]
  signature 6151 packets audited: [0:23]
  signature 6152 packets audited: [0:18]
  signature 6153 packets audited: [0:31]
  signature 6154 packets audited: [0:29]
  signature 6155 packets audited: [3:47]
  signature 6180 packets audited: [0:8]
Interfaces configured for audit 1
Session creations since subsystem startup or last reset 19
Current session counts (estab/half-open/terminating) [16:3:1]
Maxever session counts (estab/half-open/terminating) [52:8:0]
Last session created 09:12:29
Last statistic reset never
Router-3#
```

4. IOS Firewall Feature Set

Listing 4.23 displays the statistics for each signature matched and lists the switching method used for each. The output also provides other information related to the auditing process the router uses. One other useful command that can be issued to verify the operation of the auditing process is the **sh ip audit config** command. Listing 4.24 shows the output of the **show ip audit config** command.

Listing 4.24   Router 3 audit configuration.

```
Router-3#show ip audit config
Event notification through syslog is enabled
Event notification through Net Director is enabled
Default action(s) for info signatures is alarm
Default action(s) for attack signatures is alarm
Default threshold of recipients for spam signature is 42
PostOffice:HostID:5 OrgID:34 Msg dropped:0
              :Curr Event Buf Size:100  Configured:100
HID:13 OID:34 S:1 A:2 H:82 HA:49 DA:0 R:0 Q:0
 ID:1 Dest:192.168.10.8:45000 Loc:1192.168.10.1:45000 T:5 -
   S:ESTAB
Audit Rule Configuration
 Audit name testrule
    info actions alarm
    attack actions alarm drop reset
Router-3#
```

In the next configuration, the security administrator of a small business has a machine with many security software packages installed and preconfigured to automatically kick off at various times during the day. After software applications begin running, the IDS software begins to send alarms to the Director and the Director continuously sends email and page notifications to the security administrator. As a result, the security administrator would like to configure the IOS Firewall so that any packets originating from his machine and the owner's machine will not be subjected to inspection by the IDS software. Listing 4.25 details the configuration of Router 3 that is needed so that packets from the security administrator's machine and the owner's machine are not subject to auditing.

Listing 4.25   Denying devices from inspection.

```
ip audit smtp spam 42
ip audit notify nr-Director
ip audit notify log
ip audit po local hostid 1 orgid 34
ip audit po remote hostid 5 orgid 34 rmtaddress 192.168.10.8 -
   localaddress 192.168.10.1
!
```

```
ip audit name testrule info list 10 action alarm
ip audit name testrule attack list 10 action alarm drop reset
!
interface FastEthernet0/0
ip address 192.168.10.1 255.255.255.0
ip audit testrule in
!
access-list 10 deny 192.168.10.50
access-list 10 deny 192.168.10.30
access-list 10 permit any
```

The configuration in Listing 4.25 is very similar to the configuration that was displayed in Listing 4.22. The only significant changes to this configuration are the addition of the access list. The access list is bound to the audit rule named **testrule**. The access list in Listing 4.25 is not denying traffic from the hosts with IP addresses of 192.168.10.50 and 192.168.10.30. Instead, the two hosts are not filtered through the signatures because they are considered to be trusted hosts; all other hosts as defined by the **permit any** command are subjected to filtering through the signatures.

Viewing the output of the **show ip audit interface** command, you can see that access list 10 is bound to audit rule **testrule** for info signatures and attack signatures and the rule is bound to interface FastEthernet0/0. Listing 4.26 displays the output of the **show ip audit interface** command.

Listing 4.26   Access list configuration.

```
Router-3# show ip audit interface
Interface Configuration
 Interface FastEthernet0/0
  Inbound IDS audit rule is testrule
    info acl list 10 actions alarm
    attack acl list 10 actions alarm drop reset
  Outgoing IDS audit rule is not set
Router-3#
```

Attack signatures can also be disabled if a device is using a legitimate program on the network and generating false positive results to the IOS Firewall IDS. To disable attack signatures, use the **ip audit signature** command and specify the specific attack signature that needs to be disabled. Continuing with the example in Listing 4.26, the security administrator would like to disable attack signatures with values in the range of 1000 to 1004 and the signature with the value of 3040. To disable these signatures use the following commands:

```
ip audit signature 1000 disable
ip audit signature 1001 disable
ip audit signature 1002 disable
ip audit signature 1003 disable
ip audit signature 1004 disable
ip audit signature 3040 disable
```

To verify that the attack signatures listed above have indeed been disabled, you must issue the **show ip audit config** command. Listing 4.27 displays the output of issuing the command after disabling the signatures.

Listing 4.27   Verification of disabled attack signatures.

```
Router-3#show ip audit config
Event notification through syslog is enabled
Event notification through Net Director is enabled
Default action(s) for info signatures is alarm
Default action(s) for attack signatures is alarm
Default threshold of recipients for spam signature is 42
Signature 1000 disable
Signature 1001 disable
Signature 1002 disable
Signature 1003 disable
Signature 1004 disable
Signature 3040 disable
PostOffice:HostID:5 OrgID:34 Msg dropped:0
        :Curr Event Buf Size:100  Configured:100
HID:13 OID:34 S:1 A:2 H:82 HA:49 DA:0 R:0 Q:0
 ID:1 Dest:192.168.10.8:45000 Loc:1192.168.10.1:45000 T:5 -
   S:ESTAB
Audit Rule Configuration
 Audit name testrule
    info actions alarm
    attack actions alarm drop reset
Router-3#
```

It can be risky to disable the signature globally on the router because in the event another device begins to create traffic that is not legitimate and that matches the characteristics of the signature(s) that have been disabled, there will no way to detect the attack signature. So the IOS Firewall IDS gives you the power to disable attack signatures on a per-host basis with the use of a standard access list. To disable attack signatures, use the configuration displayed in Listing 4.28.

Listing 4.28   Disabling attack signatures on a per-host basis.

```
access-list 20 deny 192.168.10.51
access-list 20 deny 192.168.10.66
access-list 20 deny 192.168.10.212
```

```
access-list 20 permit any
!
ip audit signature 2150 list 20
ip audit signature 2151 list 20
ip audit signature 3150 list 20
```

Listing 4.28 configures an access list, which matches according to the source address listed within the access list. The access list is then bound to each attack signature. The access list logic for this configuration does not deny the host access as in a typical access list configuration, but the configuration states that the hosts that are in the access list configuration with a deny statement are not subject to filtering through the audit process for the attack signature in which the access list is applied. The complete intrusion detection configuration of Router 3 is shown in Listing 4.29.

Listing 4.29   Complete intrusion detection configuration.

```
ip audit smtp spam 42
ip audit notify nr-Director
ip audit notify log
ip audit po local hostid 1 orgid 34
ip audit po remote hostid 5 orgid 34 rmtaddress 192.168.10.8 -
  localaddress 192.168.10.1
!
ip audit name testrule info list 10 action alarm
ip audit name testrule attack list 10 action alarm drop reset
ip audit signature 1000 disable
ip audit signature 1001 disable
ip audit signature 1002 disable
ip audit signature 1003 disable
ip audit signature 1004 disable
ip audit signature 3040 disable
ip audit signature 2150 list 20
ip audit signature 2151 list 20
ip audit signature 3150 list 20
!
interface FastEthernet0/0
ip address 192.168.10.1 255.255.255.0
ip audit testrule in
!
access-list 10 deny 192.168.10.50
access-list 10 deny 192.168.10.30
access-list 10 permit any
access-list 20 deny 192.168.10.51
access-list 20 deny 192.168.10.66
access-list 20 deny 192.168.10.212
access-list 20 permit any
```

Related solution:	See page:
Attack Signatures	368

Chapter 5

Cisco Encryption Technology

In Brief

Many organizations are wary about transmitting sensitive data over networks. Hospitals transmit sensitive patient information to insurance companies. Banks and stock exchange companies transfer vital financial information over networks. There is a valid fear that the data could be viewed, altered in transit, or used by malicious people to harm patients, cause lawsuits, or defraud corporations. People want this kind of data communication to remain private. Almost every company has transactions that need to be protected from eavesdroppers. Companies want to ensure that when sensitive data passes over a medium susceptible to eavesdropping, it cannot be altered or observed. Data encryption is designed to protect sensitive data.

Cisco's implementation of Network-layer encryption allows security administrators to smoothly integrate the security of encryption into a network. The integration is transparent to end users and their applications. Encryption must happen only at the edge of the network on the LAN where the sensitive data originates, and decryption is not necessary until the data reaches the router on the far LAN where the destination host resides. Network managers retain the option of encrypting anywhere in the data path. By encrypting after the User Datagram Protocol (UDP) or TCP headers, so that only the IP payload is encrypted, Cisco IOS network-layer encryption allows all intermediate routers and switches to forward the traffic as they would any other IP packets. This payload-only encryption allows flow switching and all access list features to work with the encrypted traffic, just as they would with plain text traffic, thereby preserving desired Quality of Service (QoS) for all data. Users can send encrypted data over the Internet transparently.

This chapter examines Cisco's proprietary encryption solution known as Cisco Encryption Technology. I will present introductions to many of the components that are used to provide encryption services for Cisco Encryption Technology, as well as services for IPSec, which will be discussed in the next chapter. In this chapter, I will explain what encryption is, its history, how it works, and the security issues it solves. Symmetric and asymmetric keys will be discussed, and the Diffie-Hellman key algorithm and message-digest will be explained in detail. Finally, the Cisco proprietary encryption solution will be discussed, and I will present the methods that are used to configure it.

Cryptography

Cryptography, also known as encryption, is a method of transforming original data, called *plaintext* or *cleartext*, into a form that appears to be random and unreadable, which is called *ciphertext*. A simpler definition would be that cryptography is the method of storing and transmitting data in a form that only the intended recipient can read or process. Cryptography is the science of secure and secret communications. Security allows the sender to transform information into a coded message by using a secret key, a piece of information known only to the sender and the authorized receiver. The authorized receiver can decode the cipher to recover hidden information. If unauthorized individuals somehow receive the coded message, they should be unable to decode it without knowledge of the key. The key, which is usually a variable-length series of bits, works with the encryption algorithm to encrypt or decrypt messages. The algorithm, the set of mathematical rules, dictates how enciphering and deciphering take place. Many algorithms are publicly known and are not the secret part of the encryption process.

The way that encryption algorithms work can be kept secret from the public, but many of them are publicly known and well understood. If the internal mechanisms of the algorithm are not a secret, then something must be. The secret behind the use of a well-known encryption algorithm is the key. The key can be any value made up of a large sequence of random bits. Is it just any random number of bits crammed together? Not really. An algorithm contains a keyspace, which is a range of values that can be used to construct a key. The key is made up of random values within the keyspace range. The larger the keyspace, the more available values can be used to represent different keys, and the more random the keys are, the harder it is for intruders to figure them out. A large keyspace allows for more possible keys. The encryption algorithm should use the entire keyspace and choose the values to make up the keys as randomly as possible. If a smaller keyspace were used, there would be fewer values to choose from when forming a key. This would increase an attacker's chance of figuring out the key value and deciphering the protected information.

After a message is transformed into ciphertext, neither human nor machine should be able to properly process it until it is decrypted. This enables the transmission of confidential information over insecure channels without unauthorized disclosure. When data is stored on a computer, it is usually protected by logical and physical access controls. When this same sensitive information is sent over a network, you can no longer take these controls for granted, and the information is in a much more vulnerable state. If an eavesdropper captures a message as it passes between two people, the eavesdropper will be able to view the message, but it appears in its encrypted form and is therefore unusable. Even if the eavesdropper knows the algorithm that the two people are using to encrypt and decrypt the information, without the key, the information remains useless to the eavesdropper.

Modern day cryptography is a science that has one goal: to protect sensitive information by encoding it in a format that is unreadable. However, most modern cryptographic algorithms can be broken and the information can be revealed if the attacker is given enough time and resources to find the key.

History of Cryptography

Cryptography dates back as early as 4000 B.C. when hieroglyphics were used by the Egyptians to decorate tombs to tell the story of the life of the deceased person. This practice was not as much to hide the messages as it was to make them more majestic and ceremonial. Encryption methods began to evolve from ceremonial to more practical applications for war, crisis, and espionage. Throughout history, individuals and governments alike have worked to protect communication between trusted sources through the use of encryption. The first known use of encryption by a government for military purposes was around 400 B.C. It was used by the Spartans in the form of a thin strip of papyrus wrapped around a staff. Messages were written down or up the length of the staff and then the papyrus was unwrapped. For the message to be read, the papyrus had to be wrapped around a staff equal in diameter to the first staff. This system is called a skytale cipher, and it was used to send secret messages between Greek warriors. Without a staff of equal diameter (d) and minimum length (l), it would be difficult to decode the message because the message would appear to be random characters written on the unwrapped papyrus. The keys you need to decipher the skytale cipher are d and l. Figure 5.1 displays an example of the Scytale cipher, and the following versions of the alphabet demonstrate the technique. First you see the wrapped version:

```
ADGJMPSVY
BEHKNQTWZ
CFILORUX
```

Then you see the unwrapped version:

```
ADGJMPSVYBEHKNQTWZCFILORUX
```

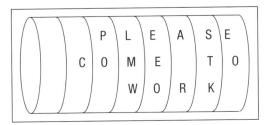

Figure 5.1   An Example of the Scytale cipher.

At or around 50 B.C., Julius Caesar used a system of cryptography known as the Caesar Cipher, or C3. It shifted each letter three places forward in the alphabet (for example, "A" shifts to "D," "K" shifts to "N," etc.). In the following example, the first row is plaintext and the second row is the equivalent ciphertext. The distance of the letter placement within the algorithm is not important to the scheme, and in fact, neither is the order of the letters that are chosen. Because only one alphabet is used with this sort of cipher, the Caesar Cipher is referred to as a *monoalphabetic substitution cipher*, wherein each letter is mapped into another letter in a one-to-one fashion.

```
ABCDEFGHIJKLMNOPQRSTUVWXYZ-Plaintext
DEFGHIJKLMNOPQRSTUVWXYZABC-Ciphertext
```

During the Middle Ages, cryptography started to progress. All of the governments of western Europe used cryptography in one form or another, and codes started to become more popular. Ciphers were commonly used to keep in touch with ambassadors. The first major advances in cryptography were made in Italy. In the middle of the 1400s, an elaborate organization was created in Venice with the sole purpose of dealing with cryptography. There were three cipher secretaries who solved and created ciphers used by the government.

Around the same time Leon Battista Alberti developed the polyalphabetic substitution. A *polyalphabetic substitution* is a technique in which different ciphertext symbols can represent the same plaintext symbol. This makes it more difficult to use frequency analysis to interpret ciphertext. To develop this technique, Alberti analyzed all of the available methods used for breaking ciphers and devised a cipher he hoped would render these techniques invalid. What he designed were two copper disks that fit into each other, and each had an alphabet inscribed upon it. To start the enciphering, a predetermined letter on the inner disk is lined up with any letter on the outer disk, which is written as the first character of the ciphertext. The disks are kept

5. Cisco Encryption Technology

stationary, with each plaintext letter on the inner disk aligned with a ciphertext letter on the outer disk. After a few words of ciphertext, the disks are rotated so that the index letter on the inner disk is aligned with a new letter on the outer disk, and in this manner, the message is enciphered. Because the disk was rotated every few words, this allowed the cipher to change enough to limit the effectiveness of frequency analysis. This technique is very weak; however, it was the ingenious idea of rotating the disks, which therefore changed the cipher many times within a message, that became a major breakthrough in cryptography.

Thomas Jefferson, around 1795, invented the wheel cipher. Although he never did much with it. The wheel cipher consists of a set of 26 wheels, each with the letters of the alphabet in random order. The key to the system is the order in which the wheels where placed on an axle. The message is encoded by aligning the letters along the rotational axis of the axle such that the desired message is formed. Any other row of aligned letters can then be used as the ciphertext for transmission. The decryption requires the recipient to align the letters of the ciphertext along the rotational axis and find a set of aligned letters that makes linguistic sense as plaintext. This is the message. There is a small probability that there will be two sensible messages from the decryption process, but this can be checked easily by the originator.

In 1844, the development of cryptography was dramatically altered by the invention of the telegraph. Communication with the telegraph was by no means secure, so ciphers were needed to transmit secret information. The public's interest in cryptography blossomed, and many individuals attempted to formulate their own cipher systems. The advent of the telegraph provided the first instance in which a base commander could be in instant communication with his field commanders during battle. Thus, a field cipher was needed. At first, the military used a Vigenere cipher with a short repeating keyword, but in 1863, a solution was discovered by Friedrich W. Kasiski for all periodic polyalphabetic ciphers, which until this time were considered unbreakable, so the military had to search for a new cipher to replace the Vigenere.

In the 1920s, Herbert Yardley, known as the "Father of American Cryptography," was in charge of the top-secret U.S. MI-8 organization. This organization has come to be known as the Black Chamber. MI-8 cracked the codes of a number of different countries. In 1929, the U.S. State Department, acting upon the orders of then President Herbert Hoover, closed MI-8, much to the disagreement of Yardley.

To feed his family, Yardley, hard-pressed to find work during the depression, wrote a book describing the secret workings of MI-8. It was called *The American Black Chamber* and became a best seller. Many people criticized him for divulging secrets and glorifying his own actions during the war.

Up to 1917, transmissions sent over telegraph wires were encoded in Baudot code for use with teletypes. The American Telephone and Telegraph company was very concerned about how easily the teletypes could be read, so Gilbert S. Vernam developed a system that added together the plaintext electronic pulses with a key to produce ciphertext pulses. It was difficult to use at times because keys were cumbersome. Vernam developed a machine to encipher messages, but the system was never widely used.

The use of cryptographic machines dramatically changed the nature of cryptography and cryptanalysis. Cryptography became intimately related to machine design, and security personnel became involved with the protection of these machines. The basic systems remained the same, but the method of encryption became reliable and electromechanical.

As computers came to be, the possibilities for encryption methods and devices advanced, and cryptography efforts expanded exponentially. This era brought unprecedented opportunity for cryptographic designers and encryption techniques. The most well-known and successful project was Lucifer, which was developed at IBM. *Lucifer* introduced complex mathematical equations and functions that were later adopted and modified by the U.S. National Security Agency (NSA) to come up with the U.S. Data Encryption Standard (DES). DES has been adopted as a federal government standard, is used worldwide for financial transactions, and is imbedded into numerous commercial applications. DES has had a rich history in computer-oriented encryption and has been in use for more than 20 years.

A majority of the protocols developed at the dawn of the computing age have been upgraded to include cryptography to add the necessary layers of protection. Encryption is used in hardware devices and software to protect data, banking transactions, corporate extranets, email, Web transactions, wireless communication, storing of confidential information, faxes, and phone calls.

5. Cisco Encryption Technology

NOTE: For more information on the history of cryptography, please visit the National Cryptologic Museum at ***www.nsa.gov/museum/index.html.***

Benefits of Encryption

Modern encryption can be accomplished through the use of software or hardware. Hardware encryption is usually the preferred method, in part because of specialized Application Specific Integrated Circuits (ASICs) and advanced signal processors that do not rely on the central processing unit (CPU) of the device, which is usually busy performing many other functions, to provide intensive encryption services. Encryption provides many services, four of which are included in the following list (however, encryption can never provide availability of data or systems):

* Confidentiality

* Authenticity

* Integrity

* Nonrepudiation

Confidentiality means that unauthorized parties cannot access information. *Authenticity* refers to validating the source of the message to ensure that the sender is properly identified; that is, that the peer device you are communicating with is legitimate and is not part of a hijacked session. *Integrity* means assurance that the message was not modified during transmission, accidentally or intentionally. *Nonrepudiation* means that a sender cannot deny sending the message at a later date, and the receiver cannot deny receiving it. With nonrepudiation, you are provided with proof that a message was sent and that it was received. A digital signature that provides proof of the identity of the sender is attached to the message that was sent, and in many instances, the time the message was sent is also included.

Different types of messages and transactions require a higher degree of one or all of the services that encryption methods can supply. Financial institutions care about confidentiality, but they care more about the integrity of the data being transmitted, so the encryption mechanism they would choose may differ from a professional sports coach's encryption methods. If messages that had a misplaced decimal point or zero were accepted, the ramifications could be far reaching to the financial institution. Legal agencies care more about the authenticity of messages they receive. If information that was received needed to be presented in a court of law, its authenticity would certainly be questioned; therefore, the encryption method used should ensure authenticity to confirm who sent the information.

Symmetric and Asymmetric Key Encryption

Encryption algorithms can use one of two different keying methods: symmetric keys, also known as private keys, or asymmetric keys, also known as public keys.

Symmetric Key Encryption

Symmetric key encryption is the most popular type of encryption and understood by most people. In symmetric key encryption, both the sender and receiver know a secret key and will use this key for both encryption and decryption. Obviously, the challenge with symmetric encryption is to make the secret key available to both the sender and receiver without compromise. Thus, is can be stated that the security of the symmetric encryption method is completely dependent on how well users protect the key.

Each pair of peers who want to exchange data in encrypted format using symmetric key encryption must posses their own identical set of keys. For example, in Figure 5.2, Host A needs to communicate to Host B using symmetric key encryption. Notice that both Host A and Host B have obtained a copy of the same private key.

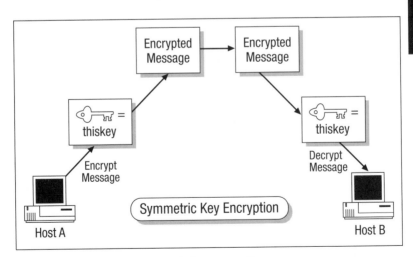

Figure 5.2   Example of symmetric key encryption.

If Host A wants to communicate with another host, say Host C, using symmetric key encryption, Host A will need to possess two keys, one for Host B and another for Host C. Now this does not sound like a big deal at this point, but if Host A has to begin communicating to hundreds of other hosts using symmetric key encryption, Host A must possess a separate key for each host that it must communicate with and use the correct key with the correct host, which can become a burdensome task.

Because both users use the same key to encrypt and decrypt messages, symmetric key encryption can provide confidentiality, but it cannot provide authentication or nonrepudiation. There is no way to prove who actually sent a message if two people are using the exact same key.

Symmetric key encryption has a few advantages over asymmetric key encryption. If a large key size is used (greater than 128 bits), symmetric key encryption is very difficult to break. When comparing symmetric key encryption to asymmetric key encryption, you'll find that symmetric key encryption is also extremely faster and can be used to encrypt large volumes of data.

Symmetric key encryption also has a few disadvantages. It provides no secure mechanisms to ensure proper delivery of keys and each pair of encryption peers must maintain a unique pair of keys. Symmetric key encryption also can only provide confidentiality and cannot provide authentication or nonrepudiation.

Symmetric key encryption can use several different types of symmetric key algorithms. Each uses a different method of providing encryption and decryption functionality, and two symmetric key algorithm will be discussed in detail in the following sections, "DES" and "Triple DES."

Data Encryption Standard (DES)

The *Data Encryption Standard* is a symmetric key algorithm that was devised in 1972 as a deviation of the Lucifer algorithm developed by IBM. DES is used for commercial and nonclassified purposes. DES defines a 64-bit block size and uses a 56-bit key. It begins with a 64-bit key and strips off 8 bits. Using a 56-bit key means that an attacker would have to try 2^{56}, or 70 quadrillion, possible keys in order to find the private key using a brute force attack. This may at first seem like a tremendous amount of possible combinations, but given today's distributed computing environments, DES can and has been broken. In fact, the Electronic Frontier Foundation built a distributed computer network system that broke DES in 22 hours and 15 minutes. The system contained a supercomputer known as Deep Crack and a distributed network of almost 100,000 worldwide PCs connected to the Internet. For further information on the breaking of DES, see **www.rsasecurity.com/news/pr/990119-1.html**. Because of vulnerabilities like these, the U.S. government has not used DES since November of 1998.

There are four defined modes of operation for DES: cipher block chaining (CBC), Electronic Code Book (ECB), cipher feedback (CFB), and Output Feedback (OFB). Electronic Code Book is the most commonly used.

Cipher block chaining (CBC) operates with plaintext blocks of 64 bits. It uses what is known as an initialization vector (IV) of 64 bits. In cipher block chaining, each plaintext block is **XOR**ed with the previous ciphertext block and the result is encrypted using the DES key. Identical ciphertext blocks can be the result, only if the same plaintext block is encrypted using both the same key and the initialization vector and if the ciphertext block order is not changed. Ideally, the initialization vector should be different for any two messages encrypted with the same key. One of the cipher block chaining major characteristics is that it uses a chaining mechanism that makes the decryption of a block of ciphertext dependant upon all the preceding ciphertext blocks. As a result, the entire validity of all preceding blocks is contained in the previous ciphertext block. A single bit error in a ciphertext block affects the decryption of all subsequent blocks. Rearrangement of the order of the ciphertext blocks causes decryption to become corrupted. It has the advantage over the ECB mode in that the **XOR**ing process hides plaintext patterns.

Electronic Code Book (ECB) is the default native mode of DES and is a block cipher. In other words, the same plaintext value will always result in the same ciphertext value. ECB is used when a volume of plaintext is separated into several blocks of data, each of which is then encrypted independently of other blocks. In fact, ECB has the capability to support a separate encryption key for each block type. ECB is applied to 64-bit blocks of plaintext, and it produces corresponding 64-bit blocks of ciphertext. It operates by dividing the 64-bit input vector into two 32-bit blocks that are referred to as the *right block* and the *left block*. The bits are then recopied to produce two 48-bit blocks. Then, each of these 48-bit blocks is **XOR**ed with a 48-bit encryption key.

ECB is not the preferred system to use with small block sizes and identical encryption modes. Some words and phrases may be reused often enough so that the same repetitive blocks of ciphertext can emerge, laying the groundwork for a codebook attack because the plaintext patterns would become fairly obvious. However, security may be improved if random pad bits are added to each block. On the other hand, 64-bit or larger blocks should contain enough unique characteristics to make a codebook attack unlikely to succeed. In terms of error correction, any bit errors in a ciphertext block affect decryption of that block only. Chaining dependency is not an issue in that reordering of the ciphertext blocks will only reorder the corresponding plaintext blocks but not affect them.

Cipher feedback (CFB) is a stream cipher in which the DES is used to generate pseudorandom bits, which are exclusively-**OR**ed with binary plain text to form cipher text. The cipher text is fed back to form the next DES input block. Identical messages that are encrypted using the CFB mode and different initialization vectors will have different cipher texts. Initialization vectors that are shorter than 64 bits should be put in the least significant bits of the first DES input block and the unused, most significant bits initialized to 0s. In the CFB mode, errors in any K-bit unit of cipher text will affect the decryption of the garbled cipher text and also the decryption of succeeding cipher text until the bits in error have been shifted out of the CFB input block. The first affected K-bit unit of plain text will be garbled in exactly those places where the cipher text is in error. Succeeding decrypted plain text will have an average error rate of 50 percent until all errors have been shifted out of the DES input block. Assuming no additional errors are encountered during this time, the correct plain text will then be obtained.

Output feedback (OFB) is a stream cipher and has some similarities to the ciphertext feedback mode in that it permits encryption of differing block sizes; the key difference is that the output of the encryption block function is the feedback. It functions by generating a stream of random binary bits to be combined with the plaintext to create ciphertext. The **XOR** value of each plaintext block is created independently of both the plaintext and ciphertext. Because there are no chaining dependencies, it is this mode that is used when there can be no tolerance for error propagation. Like the ciphertext feedback mode, it uses an initialization vector (IV). Changing the IV in the same plaintext block results in different ciphertext. In this mode, output feedback can tolerate ciphertext bit errors but is incapable of self-synchronization after losing ciphertext bits because it disturbs the synchronization of the aligning keystream.

Triple DES

Triple DES currently enjoys a much wider use than DES because DES is relatively easy to break with today's rapidly advancing technology. Triple DES was the answer to many of the shortcomings of DES. Because it is based on the DES algorithm, it is very easy to modify existing software to use Triple DES. It also has the advantage of proven reliability and a longer key length that eliminates many of the shortcut attacks that can be used to reduce the amount of time it takes to break DES. However, even this more powerful version of DES may not be strong enough to protect data for very much longer. The DES algorithm itself has become obsolete and is in need of replacement. The *Advanced Encryption Standard (AES)* is a replacement for DES. The AES will be at least as strong as Triple DES, and probably much faster. Many security systems will probably use both Triple DES and AES for at least the next five years. After that, AES may supplant Triple DES as the default algorithm on most systems if it lives up to its expectations. But Triple DES will be kept around for compatibility reasons for many years after that. So the useful lifetime of Triple DES is far from over, even with the AES near completion. For the foreseeable future, Triple DES is an excellent and reliable choice for the security needs of highly sensitive information.

Triple DES is simply another mode of DES operation. It takes three 64-bit keys for an overall key length of 192 bits. You simply type in the entire 192-bit (24-character) key rather than entering each of the three keys individually. Triple DES then breaks the user-provided key into three subkeys, padding the keys if necessary so they are each 64 bits long. The procedure for encryption is exactly the same as it is for regular DES, but it is repeated three times; hence the name Triple DES. The data is encrypted with the first key, decrypted with the second key, and finally encrypted again with the third key. Consequently, Triple DES runs much slower than standard DES because of the processing power needed to perform the multiple permutations, but it is much more secure if used properly. The procedure for decrypting something is the same as the procedure for encryption except it is executed in reverse. As with DES, data is encrypted and decrypted in 64-bit chunks. Unfortunately, there are some weak keys that one should be aware of: If all three keys, the first and second keys, or the second and third keys are the same, the encryption procedure is essentially the same as it is with standard DES. This situation should be avoided because it is the same as using a really slow version of regular DES.

Note again that, although the input key for DES is 64 bits long, the actual key used by DES is only 56 bits in length. The least significant (rightmost) bit in each byte is a parity bit and should be set so that there is always an odd number of 1s in every byte. These parity bits are ignored, so only the seven most significant bits of each byte are used, resulting in a key length of 56 bits. This means that the effective key strength for Triple DES is actually 168 bits because each of the three keys contains 8 parity bits that are not used during the encryption process.

Asymmetric Key Encryption

Whereas symmetric key encryption makes use of a single key that is known to a sender and a receiver, *asymmetric key encryption,* also known as public key encryption, makes use of two keys, a public key and a private key. If a message is encrypted by one key, the other key is required to decrypt the message. The public key can be known by anyone, but the private key must be known only by the owner.

Both the public and private keys are related from a mathematical point of view; however, if one of the keys is compromised, it is also mathematically infeasible to determine the contents of the other key based on the contents of the key that was compromised. In Figure 5.3, Host A needs to communicate to Host B using asymmetric key encryption. Notice that both Host A and Host B are using copies of different keys.

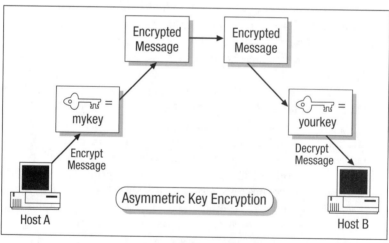

Figure 5.3   Example of asymmetric key encryption.

If Host A encrypts a message with its private key, Host B must have a copy of Host A's public key to decrypt it. Host B can decrypt Host A's message and decide to reply back to Host A in an encrypted form. All Host B needs to do is encrypt its reply with Host A's public key and then Host A can decrypt the message with its private key. It is not possible to encrypt and decrypt using the exact same key when using an asymmetric key encryption technology.

Host A can encrypt a message with its private key, and the receiver can then decrypt it with Host A's public key. By decrypting the message with Host A's public key, the receiver can be sure that the message really came from Host A. A message can only be decrypted with a public key if the message was encrypted with the corresponding private key. This provides authentication because Host A is the only one who is supposed to have his private key. When the receiver wants to make sure Host A is the only one that can read her reply, she will encrypt the response with her public key. Only Host A will be able to decrypt the message because it is the only one who has the necessary private key. Now the receiver can also encrypt her response with her private key instead of using Host A's public key. Why would she do that? She wants Host A to know that the message came from her and no one else. If she encrypted the response with Host A's public key, it does not provide authenticity because anyone can get a hold of Host A's public key. If she uses her private key to encrypt the message, then Host A can be sure that the message came from her and no one else.

Symmetric keys do not provide authenticity because the same key is used on both ends. Using one of the secret keys does not ensure that the message originated from a specific entity. If confidentiality is the most important aspect of security to a sender, the sender would encrypt the file with the receiver's public key. This is called a secure message format because it can be decrypted only by the person who has the corresponding private key. If authentication is the most important security service to the sender, the sender would encrypt the message with her private key. This provides assurance to the receiver that the only person who could have encrypted the message is the individual who has possession of that private key. If the sender encrypted the message with the receiver's public key, authentication is not provided because this public key is available to anyone. Encrypting a message with the sender's private key is called an open message format because anyone with a copy of the corresponding public key can decrypt the message; thus, confidentiality is not ensured. For a message to be in a secure and signed format, the sender would encrypt the message with his private key and then encrypt it again with the receiver's public key. The receiver would then need to decrypt the message with her own private key and then decrypt it again with the sender's public key. This provides confidentiality and authentication for that delivered message.

Each key type can be used to encrypt and decrypt, so do not get confused and think the public key is used only for encryption and the private key is used only for decryption. They both have the capability to encrypt and decrypt data. However, if data is encrypted with a private key, it cannot be decrypted with a private key. If data is encrypted with a private key, it must be decrypted with the corresponding public key. If data is encrypted with a public key, it must be decrypted with the corresponding private key.

Asymmetric key encryption has a few advantages over symmetric key encryption. Asymmetric key encryption enhances the ability to distribute keys between peers, which in turn, provides another advantage, which is increased scalability when compared to symmetric key encryption. Asymmetric key encryption also can provide confidentiality, authenticity, and nonrepudiation.

Asymmetric key encryption's major disadvantage when compared to symmetric key encryption is that it is slower than symmetric key encryption.

Asymmetric key encryption can use several different types of asymmetric key algorithms. Each has a different method of providing encryption and decryption functionality, and two will be discussed in detail in the following sections.

RSA

"RSA" stands for Rivest, Shamir, and Addleman, the names of its inventors. RSA is the asymmetric key algorithm that is easiest to implement, and it's the best understood. The *RSA cryptosystem* is a public-key cryptosystem that offers both encryption and digital signatures, which provides authentication. The RSA algorithm is based on the difficulty of factoring a number, x, that is the product of two large prime numbers. The two large prime numbers may include up to 200 digits each. Here is how it works:

1. Take two large primes numbers of equal length, p and q, and compute their product $x=pq$; x is called the modulus.

2. Choose a random public number, e, which is the public key that is less than x and relatively prime to $(p$-$1)(q$-$1)$. This will mean that e and $(p$-$1)(q$-$1)$ have no common factors except 1.

3. Then find another number, d, which is the private key and such that $(ed$-$1)$ is divisible by $(p$-$1)(q$-$1)$.

4. This equates to $d=e^{-1}$ modulus $(p$-$1)(q$-$1)$.

Given the preceding calculations, you can determine that (d,x) is the private key and (e,x) is the public key. So to calculate encryption for plaintext, P, such that it is generated into ciphertext, C, you use the following formula:

$C=P^e$ modulus x

And then, to calculate decryption for ciphertext, C, such that is generated into plaintext, P, you can use the following formula:

$P=C^d$ modulus x

It is extremely difficult to obtain the private key d from the public key (x,e). However, if someone or something could factor x into p and q, then they could obtain the private key d. The security of the RSA system is based on the assumption that factoring is difficult.

Using the network displayed in Figure 5.3, Host A would like to send a message to Host B using RSA encryption. The message will be denoted by m. Host A creates the ciphertext, c, by using the exponentiation of $c=m^e$ modulus x; both e and x are Host B's public key. Host A then sends ciphertext, c, to Host B. Host B then attempts decryption by using the exponentiation of $m=c^d$ modulus x. There is a one-to-one relationship between e and d that ensures that Host B can recover the message, m.

RSA encryption can also provide authentication services, something that symmetric key encryption cannot do. To provide authentication services between Host A and Host B, such that the message, m, can be verified to be authentic and not tampered with, Host A creates a digital signature, s, by using the exponentiation of $s=m^d$ modulus x. Both d and x in this example are Host A's private key. Host A then sends both the message, m, and the signature, s, to Host B. Host B then must verify the signature, s, by using the exponentiation of the message, $m=s^e$ modulus x. Both values of e and x at Host B are Host A's public key.

Using RSA encryption means that encryption and decryption take place between two hosts without the exchange of each host's private keys. Each host only uses the other host's public key, or it uses its own private key. This means that any host can send an encrypted message or verify the signature of an authenticated message, but only a host that has possession of the correct private key can decrypt or sign a message.

5. Cisco Encryption Technology

Diffie-Hellman Key Exchange

Diffie-Hellman was developed by Diffie and Hellman in 1976 and published in the paper "New Directions in Cryptography" (**citeseer. nj.nec.com/diffie76new.html**). The protocol allows two users to exchange a secret key over an insecure medium without any prior secrets.

Diffie-Hellman is primarily used to provide a secure mechanism for exchanging public keys so that shared secret keys can be securely generated for DES keys. It provides a means for two parties to agree upon a shared secret in such a way that the secret will be unavailable to eavesdroppers. Diffie-Hellman key agreement requires that both the sender and recipient of a message have key pairs. By combining one's private key and the other party's public key, both parties can compute the same shared secret number. This number can then be converted into cryptographic keying material.

NOTE: *The functional operation of the Diffie-Hellman key exchange is explained in detail in Chapter 6.*

Digital Signature Standard

Digital Signature Standard (DSS) is defined by the Federal Information Processing Standards Publication 186. Cisco implements DSS, which is used for peer router authentication and to protect data from undetected change. This standard specifies a *Digital Signature Algorithm (DSA)* for applications that require a digital signature as opposed to a written signature. The DSA signature is a pair of large numbers represented in a computer as strings of binary digits. The digital signature is computed using a set of rules and a set of parameters such that the identity of the signature and integrity of the data can be verified. The DSA provides the capability to generate and verify signatures. Signature generation makes use of a private key. Signature verification makes use of a public key that corresponds to, but is not the same as, the private key. Each user possesses a private and public key pair. Public keys can be known by anyone and shared with anyone, but private keys are never shared. Anyone can verify the signature of a user by employing that user's public key. Signature generation can be performed only by the possessor of the user's private key.

The algorithm relies on the MD5 hash function to verify the authenticity of the data sent. The hash function is equivalent to taking a "fingerprint" of the message. If two fingerprints match, the message has not been altered in transit, and if the two fingerprints do not match, the message has been altered in transit. The hash is run through a function that uses the private key to sign the message and is reversible only if you have the public key. The peer runs the same hash and verifies the signature to determine the identity and content of the message.

Cisco Encryption Technology Overview

Cisco Encryption Technology (CET) is a proprietary Network layer encryption process that encrypts the data payload of an IP packet. Special portions of the IP header, for instance the UDP and TCP portions, are not encrypted. This allows the packet to be successfully routed through the internetwork. Only IP packets can be encrypted. The actual encryption and decryption of IP packets occur only at routers that you configure for CET. Such routers are considered to be *peer routers*. Intermediate routers do not participate in the encryption or decryption process. CET features include the following:

- CET allows for granularity in the specification of which packets are encrypted. Packets needing to be encrypted can be defined with the configuration of an extended access list.
- DSS is used to provide authentication.
- Diffie-Hellman is used to manage each session's key.
- DES is used to provide confidentiality (encryption).

Peer router authentication occurs during the setup of each encrypted session. Prior to peer router authentication, DSS public and private keys must be generated for each peer and the DSS public keys must be exchanged with each peer. This allows peer routers to authenticate each other at the start of encrypted communication sessions. The generation and exchange of DSS keys occurs only once on a per-peer basis, and afterward, these DSS keys will be used each time an encrypted session occurs. To be successfully exchanged, DSS public keys must be verified via a trusted source at the location of each encryption peer. This usually occurs via a phone call and is called "voice authentication." During the exchange process, one peer is configured to be the "passive" and the other peer is configured to be the "active" peer.

Each peer router's DSS keys are unique: a unique DSS public key and a unique DSS private key. DSS private keys are stored in a private portion of the router's NVRAM, which cannot be viewed. If you have a router with an Encryption Service Adapter (ESA), DSS keys are stored in the tamper-resistant memory of the ESA. The DSS private key is not shared with any other device. However, the DSS public key is distributed to all other peer routers. You must cooperate with the peer router's administrator to exchange public keys between the two peer routers, and you and the other administrator must verbally verify to each other the public key of the other router. When an encrypted session is being established, each router uses the peer's DSS public key to authenticate the peer.

Prior to a router passing encrypted data to a remote peer, an encrypted session needs to be established. This is determined when the router receives a packet that matches a permit statement, which determines whether or not encryption should take place for this packet. To establish a session, peer encryption routers must exchange connection messages. This allows each router to authenticate each other. Authentication is accomplished by attaching "signatures" to the connection messages: A signature is a character string that is created by each local router using its own DSS private key and verified by the remote router using the local router's DSS public key. A signature is always unique to the sending router and cannot be forged by any other device. When a signature is verified, the router that sent the signature is authenticated. A temporary session key is also generated during the exchange of connection messages; it is the key that will be used to actually encrypt data during the encrypted session. To generate the session key, Diffie-Hellman numbers must be exchanged in the connection messages. Then, the Diffie-Hellman numbers are used to compute a common DES session key that is shared by both routers.

After both peer routers are authenticated and the session key has been generated, data can be encrypted and transmitted. The DES encryption algorithm is used with the DES key to encrypt and decrypt IP packets during the encrypted session. After the session times out, because no packets match a permit statement within the configured access list, the encrypted session is terminated. When the session terminates, both the DH numbers and the DES key are discarded. When another encrypted session is required, new DH numbers and DES keys will be generated.

The process for configuring Cisco's proprietary encryption technology on routers consists of four major tasks:

1. Prepare for Cisco Encryption by identifying the peer routers and choosing an encryption policy between both peers. The network topology should also be taken into consideration during this stage. The typical network topology used for encryption is a hub-and-spoke arrangement between an enterprise router and branch routers. Other things to consider during this stage are frequent route changes between pairs of peer encrypting routers and load-balancing, which will cause excessive numbers of connections to be set up and very few data packets to be delivered.

2. Each router involved in the process of encrypting packets between one another must be prepared to perform encryption. This is done through a series of configuration commands that will be discussed later.

3. After preparing each router to perform encryption, you much establish an encrypted session between each peer to pass encrypted packets.

4. The final task is to test and verify the configuration and operation of CET. This is done through the use of certain **show** and **debug** commands. These same commands are also used during troubleshooting of CET.

5. Cisco Encryption Technology

Immediate Solutions

Configuring Cisco Encryption Technology

Configuring CET involves prior coordination between the local security administrator and the remote encryption peer's security administrator. After that is accomplished, perform the following configuration tasks:

1. Use the following *command to* generate DSS keys for each crypto engine you will use:

```
crypto key generate dss key-name
```

The DSS key pair that is generated is used by peer routers to authenticate each other before each encrypted session. The same DSS key pair is used by a crypto engine with all its encrypted sessions.

2. Use this command to save the DSS keys that are generated to private NVRAM on the router (this command is only needed if the router is using a software-based crypto engine):

```
copy running-config startup-config
```

3. Next, the exchange of DSS public keys with all participating peer routers must be configured, which allows peer routers to authenticate each other at the start of encrypted communication sessions. Use this command to enable a DSS key exchange on the passive peer router:

```
crypto key exchange dss passive <tcp-port>
```

The passive router will wait to exchange keys until after the active router has exchanged keys with the passive router.

4. Use this command to define the active peer, which initiates a connection to the passive peer and exchanges keys:

```
crypto key exchange dss <ip-address> <key-name> <tcp-port>
```

Tasks 3 and 4 need a little further explanation. Prior to configuring a peer router for DSS key exchange in Step 3, "voice authentication" must take place between the security administrator of the local peer router and the security administrator of the remote peer router. You and the other administrator decide which of you will be what is referred to as the "passive" peer and which of you will be what is referred to as the "active" peer. The passive router enables a DSS exchange connection using the command listed in Step 3. The active router then initiates a DSS exchange connection with the passive peer router and sends a DSS public key to it. The serial number and fingerprint of the active router's DSS public key will then be displayed on screen of each security administrator's machine. The serial number and fingerprint that are displayed are numeric values that are generated from the active router's DSS public key. Each security administrator should verbally verify that the serial number and fingerprint are the same on both screens. If the displayed serial numbers and fingerprints match and the security administrators are in agreement that the serial numbers and fingerprints are valid, the administrator of the passive router should agree to accept the active router's DSS key by typing "yes" at the prompt. The passive router's security administrator then sends the active router's security administrator its DSS public key by pressing Return at the screen prompt and selecting a crypto engine at the next prompt. The passive router's DSS serial number and fingerprint are then displayed on each of the security administrators' screens. Each security administrator should verbally verify that the serial number and fingerprint are the same on both screens. If the displayed serial numbers and fingerprints match, and the security administrators are in agreement that the serial numbers and fingerprints are valid, the administrator of the active router should agree to accept the passive router's DSS key by typing "yes" at the prompt. At this point, both routers have been "verbally authenticated." This process can be seen in Figure 5.4.

5. Use the following command to enable 56-bit DES with 8-bit or 64-bit cipher feedback:

```
crypto cisco algorithm des <cfb-8 | cfb-64>
```

Or use this command to enable 40-bit DES with 8-bit or 64-bit cipher feedback to configure the global encryption policy of the router:

```
crypto cisco algorithm 40-bit-des <cfb-8 | cfb-64>
```

The 56-bit DES option is the default.

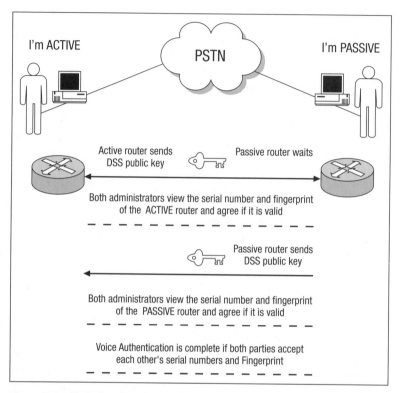

Figure 5.4   Verbal authentication process.

6. Use one of the following commands *to define an extended access list* that will signify which IP packets will be encrypted and which IP packets will not be encrypted:

```
access-list <access-list-number> <deny | permit><protocol> -
   <source - source-wildcard> <destination destination -
   wildcard><precedence - precedence>
```

When defined for encryption of traffic, access lists function differently than when they function when they're used as a packet filter. Using a **permit** keyword will cause the selected traffic that is passed between the specified source and destination addresses to be encrypted/decrypted by peer routers. Using a **deny** keyword prevents that traffic from being encrypted/decrypted by peer routers. The encryption access list you define at the local router must have a "mirror-image" encryption access list defined at the remote router so that traffic that is encrypted locally is decrypted at the remote peer.

7. Use this command to define a crypto map name:

    ```
    crypto map <map-name> <seq-num> {cisco}
    ```

    Use of this command moves you into the crypto map configuration mode.

8. Under crypto map configuration mode, use this command to define the remote peer with which an encrypted session will take place:

    ```
    set peer <key-name>
    ```

9. Under crypto map configuration mode, use the following command to assign the previously configured access list to the crypto map:

    ```
    match address <access-list-id | name>
    ```

10. Under crypto map configuration mode, use the command to define the encryption algorithms that the router can negotiate for the session:

    ```
    set algorithm des <cfb-8 | cfb-64> command or -
        the set algorithm - 40-bit-des <cfb-8 | cfb-64>
    ```

    Any encryption algorithms that have been previously defined at the global level can be defined in the crypto map. If an encryption algorithm has not been defined at the global level, it cannot be defined in the crypto map.

11. Use this command to move into interface configuration mode:

    ```
    interface <interface type> <interface number>
    ```

12. In interface configuration mode, use this command to apply the previously configured crypto map to an interface:

    ```
    crypto map <map-name>
    ```

    Only one crypto map set can be applied to each interface that will encrypt outbound data and decrypt inbound data. This interface provides the encrypted connection to a peer encrypting router.

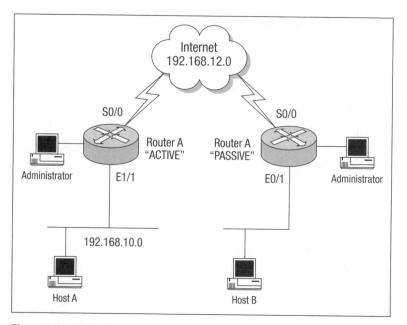

Figure 5.5   CET network topology.

Figure 5.5 illustrates the network topology and components of the fictitious company that will be used throughout the configuration example of CET. This network displays two routers; Router A is defined as the active router and Router B is defined as the passive router.

One key step that should always be performed prior to the configuration of encryption on any network device is to ensure that the network functions properly; this means that basic connectivity between peer routers has been tested and is functioning before encryption is configured on the routers. The **ping** command can be used to test basic connectivity between encrypting peer routers. Also, although a successful ping will verify basic connectivity between peers, you should ensure that the network operates with other protocols or ports you want to encrypt before beginning the CET configuration. After CET is configured and activated, basic troubleshooting can become difficult to perform because the security configuration could mask a more fundamental network problem.

NOTE: *This configuration example in this chapter will not follow the same structure as examples in other chapters have followed. In this example, I will present the beginning configuration of the routers involved, then walk you through each step of configuring Cisco Encryption Technology, and finally, present to you the final completed configuration.*

To verify that Router A and Router B in Figure 5.5 function properly prior to configuring CET on the routers, Listing 5.1 and Listing 5.2 display the basic configurations of the routers. Listing 5.3 and Listing 5.4 verify that basic connectivity between each peer functions properly without encryption configured. This will allow the routers to be baselined prior to the CET configuration.

Listing 5.1 Initial configuration of Router A.

```
version 12.1
service timestamps debug uptime
service timestamps log uptime
no service password-encryption
!
hostname Router-A
!
username routera privilege 15 password 0 routera
!
memory-size iomem 10
ip subnet-zero
no ip finger
ip tcp synwait-time 10
no ip domain-lookup
!
interface Ethernet1/1
ip address 192.168.10.1 255.255.255.0
no ip directed-broadcast
duplex auto
speed auto
!
interface Serial0/0
ip address 192.168.12.1 255.255.255.0
no ip directed-broadcast
no fair-queue
!
ip classless
no ip http server
!
ip route 0.0.0.0 0.0.0.0 serial0/0
!
line con 0
 session-timeout 30
 exec-timeout 30 0
 login local
 transport input none
line aux 0
line vty 0 4
```

```
 session-timeout 30
  exec-timeout 30 0
  login local
 !
 end
```

Listing 5.2   Initial configuration of Router B.

```
version 12.1
service timestamps debug uptime
service timestamps log uptime
no service password-encryption
!
hostname Router-B
!
username routerb privilege 15 password 0 routerb
!
memory-size iomem 10
ip subnet-zero
no ip finger
ip tcp synwait-time 10
no ip domain-lookup
!
interface Ethernet0/1
ip address 192.168.11.1 255.255.255.0
no ip directed-broadcast
duplex auto
speed auto
!
interface Serial0/0
ip address 192.168.12.2 255.255.255.0
no ip directed-broadcast
no fair-queue
!
ip classless
no ip http server
!
ip route 0.0.0.0 0.0.0.0 serial0/0
!
line con 0
 session-timeout 30
 exec-timeout 30 0
 login local
 transport input none
line aux 0
line vty 0 4
session-timeout 30
 exec-timeout 30 0
```

```
 login local
 !
 end
```

Both routers in Listing 5.1 and Listing 5.2 provide access to the Internet and act as the single entry and exit point from the local network to the outside world, which is why they each have a static default route pointing out their serial interface. Prior to configuring CET on your routers, you must ensure that each router that needs to perform encryption can communicate with each peer. For CET to function properly and for encryption to take place, Layer 3 communication must be established between each peer. In Listing 5.3 and Listing 5.4, the **ping** command will be used to verify Layer 3 connectivity between Router A and Router B.

Listing 5.3   Layer 3 connectivity verified on Router A.

```
Router-A#ping 192.168.12.2

Type escape sequence to abort.
Sending 5, 100-byte ICMP Echos to 192.168.12.2, timeout -
 is 2 seconds:
!!!!!
Success rate is 100 percent (5/5), round-trip -
 min/avg/max = 1/2/4 ms

Router-A#
```

Listing 5.4   Layer 3 communication verified on Router B.

```
Router-B#ping 192.168.12.1

Type escape sequence to abort.
Sending 5, 100-byte ICMP Echos to 192.168.12.1, timeout -
 is 2 seconds:
!!!!!
Success rate is 100 percent (5/5), round-trip -
 min/avg/max = 1/2/4 ms

Router-B#
```

The output in Listing 5.3 and Listing 5.4 confirms that communication between each peer is working properly because each peer can ping the serial interface of the other router.

The first task that must be performed to configure CET is to generate each peer router's public and private key and save them to NVRAM.

5. Cisco Encryption Technology

Listing 5.5 displays an example of generating Router A's public and private keys. Listing 5.6 displays an example of generating Router B's public and private keys.

Listing 5.5   Generating Router A's key.

```
Router-A(config)#crypto key generate dss routera
Generating DSS keys ....
  [OK]
```

Listing 5.6   Generating Router B's key.

```
Router-B(config)#crypto key generat dss routerb
Generating DSS keys ....
  [OK]
```

After each router's key pair is generated, the keys need to be saved into a private portion of NVRAM on the routers. To save the each router's key to NVRAM on the routers, the **copy running-config startup-config** command is used. Listing 5.7, shows Router A saving its private key to NVRAM. Listing 5.8 shows Router B saving its private key to NVRAM.

Listing 5.7   Router A saving private key to NVRAM.

```
Router-A#copy running-config startup-config
Destination filename [startup-config]?
Building configuration...
[OK]
Router-A#
```

Listing 5.8   Router B saving private key to NVRAM.

```
Router-B#copy running-config startup-config
Destination filename [startup-config]?
Building configuration...
[OK]
Router-B#
```

As mentioned previously, the command used in Listing 5.5 and Listing 5.6 generate a public key and a private key. The private keys that generated on each router are saved into NVRAM and are inaccessible for viewing because if anyone were to gain access to the private key, she could masquerade as the owner of the private key and all data secured using the private key could be compromised. Cisco routers have been designed so that the private keys that are generated and saved to NVRAM cannot be accessed or tampered with. The public key can be viewed, however, because it is shared with its encryption peers. To view the public keys that were generated as a result of issuing the **crypto key generate dss** command, issue the **show crypto**

key mypubkey dss command. Listing 5.9 shows an example of issuing the **show crypto key mypubkey dss** command on Router A. Listing 5.10 displays an example of issuing the **show crypto key mypubkey dss** command on Router B.

Listing 5.9   Viewing Router A's public key.

```
Router-A#show crypto key mypubkey dss
Key name: routera
 Serial number: 6B86ECF4
 Usage: Signature Key
 Key Data:
  CC0438CE 125C2C5E DAE47A2C B47B44EE 4737C1D9 9FDF3164
  69CAACA7 82D25416 8CA218AC 644BE782 36966277 BBF437DF
  1347FFAA F2E3C04E 94CE60E5 5485C539
Router-A#
```

Listing 5.10   Viewing Router B's public key.

```
Router-B#sh crypto key mypubkey dss
Key name: routerb
 Serial number: 0615EC60
 Usage: Signature Key
 Key Data:
  4B013A5D DB942F8F 556B6F67 13110723 A05F17F9 D7BA15BF
  74B1C17B D2E5C4A5 ABC0A7DE D1188289 A54C80EC 5BB3B9AE
  F4366FB1 D5DBB125 C44F904A 62209467
Router-B#
```

Now each router must exchange its public keys. According to Figure 5.5, Router B has been determined to be the passive router and Router A has been determined to be the active router. Router B must now be configured to initiate a key exchange connection; to do so, use the **crypto key exchange dss passive** command. Listing 5.11 displays an example of configuring Router B to be passive.

Listing 5.11   Router B enabling DSS key exchange.

```
Router-B(config)#crypto key exchange dss passive
Enter escape character to abort if connection does not complete.
Wait for connection from peer[confirm]
Waiting ....
```

Router B is now waiting for a connection from the active router, Router A. In order for the public keys to be exchanged, Router A must now be configured to initiate a key exchange connection; this is done by using the **cypto key exchange dss** command. Listing 5.12 displays an example of configuring Router A to be active and send its public DSS keys to Router B.

5. Cisco Encryption Technology

Listing 5.12   Router A enabling DSS key exchange.

```
Router-A(config)#crypto key exchange dss 192.168.12.2 routera
Public key for routera:
    Serial Number 6B86ECF4
    Fingerprint   6974 475B 3FB7 F64B B40A

Wait for peer to send a key[confirm]
Waiting ....
```

In Listing 5.12, Router A defines the IP address of Router B as the peer with which it would like to exchange public keys. After configuring the **crypto key exchange dss** command, Router A displays the public key that it intends to send to Router B and sends its public key to Router B. Notice that after sending its public key to Router B, Router A transitions to a state of waiting. It is now waiting for a public key in return from Router B. When Router B receives the key, it displays the output in Listing 5.13.

Listing 5.13   Router B asking to accept Router A's public key.

```
Public key for routera:
    Serial Number 6B86ECF4
    Fingerprint   6974 475B 3FB7 F64B B40A

Add this public key to the configuration? [yes/no]: yes
```

The public key that Router B receives from Router A in Listing 5.13 includes the serial number for the key and the fingerprint of the key. The serial number and the fingerprint of the key Router B receives should be verbally compared against the key that Router A generated and displayed in Listing 5.5 and 5.9 and displayed in Listing 5.12 as the key that it was to send to Router B. Router B at this point must send Router A its public key, and Router B prompts you to send Router A its public key. In the next line of code (following the last line in Listing 5.13), Router B asks to send to Router A its public key. This can be seen in Listing 5.14

Listing 5.14   Router B asks to send Router A its public key.

```
Send peer a key in return[confirm]
Which one?

routerb? [yes]:
Public key for routerb:
    Serial Number 0615EC60
    Fingerprint   9C98 0488 7058 AF43 D4FC
```

Router B now sends Router A it public key. Router A should receive the key and prompt you to accept it. This can be seen in Listing 5.15.

Listing 5.15 Router A receives Router B's public key.

```
Public key for routerb:
  Serial Number 0615EC60
  Fingerprint  9C98 0488 7058 AF43 D4FC

Add this public key to the configuration? [yes/no]: yes
```

The public key that Router A receives from Router B in Listing 5.15 includes the serial number for the key and the fingerprint of the key. The serial number and the fingerprint of the key Router A receives should be verbally compared against the key that Router B generated and displayed in Listings 5.6 and 5.10 and displayed in Listing 5.14 as the key that it was to send to Router B.

At this point, the key exchange process is complete. To view the key that each peer receives, issue the **show crypto key pubkey-chain dss** command. Listing 5.16 displays an example of viewing Router B's public key from Router A. Compare the output of Listing 5.16 on Router A with the output of Listing 5.10 on Router B. The value of the serial number and data fields should be equal.

Listing 5.16 Router A viewing Router B's public key.

```
Router-A#sh crypto key pubkey-chain dss serial 0615EC60
Key name:
 Serial number: 0615EC60
 Usage: Signature Key
 Source: Manually entered
 Data:
  4B013A5D DB942F8F 556B6F67 13110723 A05F17F9 D7BA15BF
  74B1C17B D2E5C4A5 ABC0A7DE D1188289 A54C80EC 5BB3B9AE
  F4366FB1 D5DBB125 C44F904A 62209467
Router-A#
```

Listing 5.17 displays an example of viewing Router A's public key from Router B. Compare the output of Listing 5.17 on Router B with the output of Listing 5.9 on Router A. The value of the serial number and data fields should be equal.

Listing 5.17 Router B viewing Router A's public key.

```
Router-B#sh crypto key pubkey-chain dss serial 6B86ECF4
Key name:
 Serial number: 6B86ECF4
 Usage: Signature Key
```

```
Source: Manually entered
Data:
 CC0438CE 125C2C5E DAE47A2C B47B44EE 4737C1D9 9FDF3164
 69CAACA7 82D25416 8CA218AC 644BE782 36966277 BBF437DF
 1347FFAA F2E3C04E 94CE60E5 5485C539
Router-B#
```

To summarize what has happened up to this point, each router has generated a public and a private key and successfully exchanged its public key with its encrypting peer router. Listing 5.18 displays a partial output of Router A's configuration after generating and exchanging keys. Listing 5.19 displays a partial output of Router B's configuration after generating and exchanging keys.

Listing 5.18   Router A's configuration after exchanging keys.

```
Building configuration...
!
version 12.1
service timestamps debug uptime
service timestamps log uptime
no service password-encryption
!
hostname Router-A
!
username routera privilege 15 password 0 routera
!
memory-size iomem 10
ip subnet-zero
no ip finger
ip tcp synwait-time 10
no ip domain-lookup
!
crypto key pubkey-chain dss
 named-key routerb signature
  serial-number 0615EC60
  key-string
   4B013A5D DB942F8F 556B6F67 13110723 A05F17F9 D7BA15BF -
   74B1C17B D2E5C4A5
   ABC0A7DE D1188289 A54C80EC 5BB3B9AE -
   F4366FB1 D5DBB125 C44F904A 62209467
  quit
 !
```

Listing 5.19   Router B's configuration after exchanging keys.

```
Building configuration...
!
version 12.1
```

```
service timestamps debug uptime
service timestamps log uptime
no service password-encryption
!
hostname Router-B
!
username routerb privilege 15 password 0 routerb
!
memory-size iomem 10
ip subnet-zero
no ip finger
ip tcp synwait-time 10
no ip domain-lookup
!
crypto key pubkey-chain dss
 named-key routera signature
  serial-number 6B86ECF4
  key-string
   CC0438CE 125C2C5E DAE47A2C B47B44EE 4737C1D9 9FDF3164 69CAACA7
-
    82D25416
   8CA218AC 644BE782 36966277 BBF437DF 1347FFAA F2E3C04E 94CE60E5
-
    5485C539
  quit
 !
```

Now that each router has generated a private and a public key pair and exchanged its public key with its peer router, the next step is to configure and enable a global encryption algorithm for use in encrypting traffic between each peer. Cisco Encryption Technology makes use of the DES algorithm for encrypted communication between peers. All encryption algorithms that your router will use during an encrypted session must be enabled globally on the router. To have an encrypted session, each peer router must have at least one DES algorithm enabled that is the same as the algorithm used by the peer router. Cisco routers support the following four types of DES encryption algorithms:

- 56-bit DES with 8-bit cipher feedback
- 56-bit DES with 64-bit cipher feedback
- 40-bit DES with 8-bit cipher feedback
- 40-bit DES with 64-bit cipher feedback

Listing 5.20 displays an example of configuring a global encryption policy on Router A, and Listing 5.21 displays an example of configuring a global encryption policy on Router B.

5. Cisco Encryption Technology

Listing 5.20   Configuring a global encryption policy on Router A.

```
Router-A#config t
Router-A(config)#crypto cisco algorithm des cfb-8
Router-A(config)#crypto cisco algorithm des cfb-64
Router-A(config)#crypto cisco algorithm 40-bit-des cfb-64
Router-A(config)#end
```

Listing 5.21   Configuring a global encryption policy on Router B.

```
Router-B#config t
Router-B(config)#crypto cisco algorithm des cfb-64
Router-B(config)#crypto cisco algorithm des cfb-8
Router-B(config)#crypto cisco algorithm 40-bit-des cfb-8
Router-B(config)#end
```

Notice in the configurations in Listing 5.20 and Listing 5.21 that each router encryption policy is configured to use the 56-bit DES algorithm with both cipher feedback 64 and 8. However, the third encryption policy on each router is configured differently. Router A is configured to use the 40-bit DES encryption algorithm using cipher feedback 64, and Router B is configured to use the 40-bit DES encryption algorithm using cipher feedback 8. Because the third encryption policy on each router is different, it will not be used to provide encryption services between each of these peer routers; however, it could be used with another router that has a similar encryption policy.

To display and verify the global encryption algorithms currently in use on each router, issue the **show crypto cisco algorithms** command. Listing 5.22 displays an example of issuing the **show crypto cisco algorithms** command on Router A, and Listing 5.23 displays an example of issuing the same command on Router B.

Listing 5.22   Viewing encryption algorithms in use on Router A.

```
Router-A#show crypto cisco algorithms
  des cfb-64
  des cfb-8
  40-bit-des cfb-64

Router-A#
```

Listing 5.23   Viewing encryption algorithms in use on Router B.

```
Router-B#show crypto cisco algorithms
  des cfb-64
  des cfb-8
  40-bit-des cfb-8

Router-B#
```

The next task to configuring Cisco Encryption Technology is to configure access lists to define which packets are to be protected by encryption and which packets should not be. Access lists that are used for encryption function a little differently than normal access lists used for packet filtering. When an access list is defined for encryption and the rule specifies a permit statement, if a packet matches the permit rule, the router performs encryption on the packet. If a packet matches a deny statement within an access list, the packet is not encrypted and is forwarded as normal via the routing process. IP extended access lists are used to define which packets are encrypted. Listing 5.24 displays an example of configuring Router A to provide encryption on packets with a source address within the range of 192.168.10.0 and a destination address of 192.168.11.0. Listing 5.25 displays an example of configuring Router B to provide encryption on packets with a source address within the range of 192.168.11.0 and a destination address of 192.168.10.0. It is recommended that each encrypting peer router maintain mirror copies of each other's access lists.

Listing 5.24   Encryption access list configuration on Router A.

```
Router-A#config t
access-list 100 permit ip 192.168.10.0 0.0.0.255 -
 192.168.11.0 0.0.0.255
access-list 100 permit icmp 192.168.10.0 0.0.0.255 -
 192.168.11.0 0.0.0.255
access-list 100 deny ip 192.168.10.0 0.0.0.255 any
!
```

Listing 5.25   Encryption access list configuration on Router B.

```
Router-B#config t
access-list 100 permit ip 192.168.11.0 0.0.0.255 -
 192.168.10.0 0.0.0.255
access-list 100 permit icmp 192.168.11.0 0.0.0.255 -
 192.168.10.0 0.0.0.255
access-list 100 deny ip 192.168.11.0 0.0.0.255 any
!
```

The configurations in Listing 5.24 and Listing 5.25 define on each router an access list in which the rules state that any IP or ICMP traffic between the router with a source address local to the router and a destination address of behind the peer encrypting router should be protected by encryption. The third match rule of each access list is a **deny** statement, and it can be interpreted as any packet with a source address local to the router that as a destination address of any address, does not provide encryption for the packet and forward the packet as usual. At first, the access list rules might not seem correct because a packet with a source address local to the router and with any destination could be a packet that is local to the router with a destination address that is local to the peer encrypting router. However, access list rules are read in sequential order by the router, and once a packet matches a rule within the access list, the router breaks out of the access list comparison. A packet that matches one of the first two configured rules on Router A or Router B will never be compared against the third rule of the access list and will always be encrypted.

To display the access list configuration of each router, issue the **show access-list** command. The result of issuing the **show access-lists** command on Router can be seen in Listing 5.26, and in Listing 5.27 shows the result of issuing it on Router B.

Listing 5.26 Access list configuration of Router A.

```
Router-A#show access-lists
Extended IP access list 100
    permit ip 192.168.10.0 0.0.0.255 192.168.11.0 0.0.0.255
    permit icmp 192.168.10.0 0.0.0.255 192.168.11.0 0.0.0.255
    deny ip 192.168.10.0 0.0.0.255 any
Router-A#
```

Listing 5.27 Access list configuration of Router B.

```
Router-B#show access-lists
Extended IP access list 101
    permit ip 192.168.11.0 0.0.0.255 192.168.10.0 0.0.0.255
    permit icmp 192.168.11.0 0.0.0.255 192.168.10.0 0.0.0.255
    deny ip 192.168.11.0 0.0.0.255 any
Router-B#
```

The next major step in the configuration of Cisco Encryption Technology is to define crypto maps on each router. Crypto maps define a control policy for Cisco Encryption Technology by linking the traffic selection criteria of the access lists, defines the peer routers and defines the DES algorithm to use. To define a crypto map on Router A and Router B, you must use the **crypto map** command and define a name and a sequence number. After the crypto map is defined, the Cisco IOS command parser will move you into crypto map configuration mode. In crypto map configuration mode, you will need to define the peer router that encryption is to take place between, define the access list that will be used for determining which packets are to be encrypted, and define the encryption algorithm to use.

Listing 5.28 shows an example of defining a crypto map and the parameters of the crypto map on Router A, and Listing 5.29 shows an example for Router B.

Listing 5.28   Crypto map configuration of Router A.

```
Router-A#config t
Router-A(config)#crypto map routeramap 10 cisco
% NOTE: This new crypto map will remain disabled until a peer
        and a valid access list have been configured.
Router-A(config-crypto-map)#set peer routerb
Router-A(config-crypto-map)#match address 100
Router-A(config-crypto-map)#set algorithm des
Router-A(config-crypto-map)#end
Router-A#
```

Listing 5.29   Crypto map configuration of Router B.

```
Router-B#config t
Router-B(config)#crypto map routerbmap 10 cisco
% NOTE: This new crypto map will remain disabled until a peer
        and a valid access list have been configured.
Router-B(config-crypto-map)#set peer routera
Router-B(config-crypto-map)#match address 101
Router-B(config-crypto-map)#set algorithm des
Router-B(config-crypto-map)#end
Router-B#
```

After configuring each router's crypto map, use the **show crypto map** command to view the parameters of the crypto map. Verifying the crypto map configuration on each router is crucial to the operation of encryption because no encryption session can be established between peer routers if the encryption policy that is configured on each router is different from the other peer. Listing 5.30 displays the output of issuing the **show crypto map** command on Router A. Listing 5.31 shows the output on Router B.

Listing 5.30   Viewing the crypto map configuration of Router A.

```
Router-A#sh crypto map
Crypto Map "routeramap" 10 cisco
 Peer = routerb
 PE = 192.168.10.0
 UPE = 192.168.11.0
 Extended IP access list 100
 access-list 100 permit ip 192.168.10.0 0.0.0.255 -
  192.168.11.0 0.0.0.255
 access-list 100 permit icmp 192.168.10.0 0.0.0.255 -
  192.168.11.0 0.0.0.255
 access-list 100 deny ip 192.168.10.0 0.0.0.255 any
 Connection Id = UNSET    (0 established, 0 failed)
 Interfaces using crypto map routeramap:

 Router-A#
```

5. Cisco Encryption Technology

Listing 5.31   Viewing the crypto map configuration of Router B.

```
Router-B#sh crypto map
Crypto Map "routerbmap" 10 cisco
 Peer = routera
 PE = 192.168.11.0
 UPE = 192.168.10.0
 Extended IP access list 101
 access-list 101 permit ip 192.168.11.0 0.0.0.255 -
   192.168.10.0 0.0.0.255
 access-list 101 permit icmp 192.168.11.0 0.0.0.255 -
   192.168.10.0 0.0.0.255
 access-list 101 deny ip 192.168.11.0 0.0.0.255 any
 Connection Id = UNSET     (0 established, 0 failed)
 Interfaces using crypto map routerbmap:

Router-B#
```

After configuring the crypto map and verifying that the parameters of the crypto map are correct between each peer, the final step in the configuration of Cisco Encryption Technology is to apply the crypto map to an encryption-terminating interface. To do so, use the **crypto map** command in interface configuration mode. Only one crypto map set can be applied to an interface. If multiple crypto map entries have the same crypto map name but have different sequence numbers, they are considered part of the same crypto set and each one is sequentially assigned to the interface.

Listing 5.32 displays an example of applying the defined crypto map on Router A to its serial interface. Listing 5.33 displays an example of applying the defined crypto map on Router B to its serial interface.

Listing 5.32   Applying the crypto map to Router A.

```
Router-A#config t
Enter configuration commands, one per line.  End with CNTL/Z.
Router-A(config)#int serial0/0
Router-A(config-if)#crypto map routeramap
Router-A(config-if)#end
Router-A#
```

Listing 5.33   Applying the crypto map to Router B.

```
Router-B#config t
Enter configuration commands, one per line. End with CNTL/Z.
Router-B(config)#int serial0/0
Router-B(config-if)#crypto map routerbmap
Router-B(config-if)#end
Router-B#
```

To test the configurations of Router A and Router B, an extended ping will be used on Router A to ping local Ethernet interface of Router B. An extended ping is used so that the source address of the IP packet can be specified. In this case the source of the packet will be Router A's local Ethernet interface. Although the **ping** command is running, the **debug crypto sessmgmt** command is issued to display the connection setup messages. Listing 5.34 displays the output of the **ping** command.

Listing 5.34   The ping command issued on Router A.

```
Router-A#debug crypto sessmgmt
Crypto Session Management debugging is on
Router-A#
Router-A#ping ip
Target IP address: 192.168.11.1
Repeat count [5]: 30
Datagram size [100]:
Timeout in seconds [2]:
Extended commands [n]: y
Source address or interface: 192.168.10.1
Type of service [0]:
Set DF bit in IP header? [no]:
Validate reply data? [no]:
Data pattern [0xABCD]:
Loose, Strict, Record, Timestamp, Verbose[none]:
Sweep range of sizes [n]:
Type escape sequence to abort.
Sending 30, 100-byte ICMP Echos to 192.168.11.1, timeout is 2 -
  seconds:
```

After the ping has started, the output listed in Listing 5.35 is displayed on the console of Router A.

Listing 5.35   DEBUG output from the ping command on Router A.

```
CRYPTO-SDU: get_pet: PET node created
CRYPTO-SDU:Adding new CIB for ACL: 100
CRYPTO-SDU: get_cot: New COT node allocated
CRYPTO: Pending connection = -1
CRYPTO: Dequeued a message: Inititate_Connection
CRYPTO: Allocated conn_id 1 slot 0, swidb 0x0,
CRYPTO: Next connection id = 1
CRYPTO: DH gen phase 1 status for conn_id 1 slot 0:OK
CRYPTO: Sign done. Status=OK
CRYPTO_SM: sending CET message to FastEthernet0/0:192.168.11.1
CRYPTO: ICMP message sent: s=192.168.10.1, d=192.168.11.1
CRYPTO-SDU: send_nnc_req:   NNC Echo Request sent
```

```
CRYPTO: Sign done. Status=OK
CRYPTO: Retransmitting a connection message
CRYPTO: ICMP message sent: s=192.168.10.1, d=192.168.11.1
CRYPTO: Dequeued a message: CRM
CRYPTO: CRM from 192.168.10.0 to 192.168.11.0
CRYPTO: Peer has serial number: 0615EC60
CRYPTO: DH gen phase 2 status for conn_id 1 slot 0:OK
CRYPTO: Syndrome gen status for conn_id 1 slot 0:OK
CRYPTO: Verify done. Status=OK
CRYPTO: Sign done. Status=OK
CRYPTO: ICMP message sent: s=192.168.12.1, d=192.168.12.2
CRYPTO-SDU: recv_nnc_rpy:    NNC Echo Confirm sent.
CRYPTO: Create encryption key for conn_id 1 slot 0:OK
CRYPTO: Replacing -1 in crypto maps with 1 (slot 0)
CRYPTO:old_conn_id=-1, new_conn_id=1, orig_conn_id=1
CRYPTO: Crypto Engine clear dh conn_id 1 slot 0: OK
```

Notice the final highlighted line in the output of Listing 5.35. This line states that the encryption keys are being created because each of the other highlighted lines returned a status message of **OK**.

At this point, the status of the connections can be viewed on Router A by using the commands **show crypto cisco connections** and **show crypto engine connections active**. Listing 5.36 displays the output of the **show** commands.

Listing 5.36   Output of **show** commands on Router A.

```
Router-A#show crypto engine connections active
ID Interface   IP-Address    State  Algorithm      Encrypt Decrypt
1  Serial0/0  192.168.12.1   set    DES_56_CFB64     358     312
!
Router-A#show crypto cisco connections
Connection Table
PE             UPE         Conn_id New_id Algorithm
192.168.10.0 192.168.11.0 1    0         DES_56_CFB64
flags: TIME_KEYS ACL: 100

Router-A#
```

The **show crypto engine connections active** command is used to view the current active encrypted session connections for all crypto engines. The ID field identifies a connection by using a connection ID value, which is **1** in Listing 5.36. The interface field identifies the interface involved in the encrypted session connection, and the IP address field identifies the IP address of the interface. The state field is the most important field in the output of the **show crypto engine connections active** command in Listing 5.36; it specifies the current state of the connection, and a *set* state indicates an established session. The algorithm field indicates the DES algorithm that is used to encrypt and decrypt packets. The final two fields display the number of packets that have been encrypted and decrypted by connection ID number 1.

The **show crypto cisco connections** command displays the connection ID value that is assigned by the Cisco IOS when a new connection is initiated. In Listing 5.36, the connection ID is 1. The PE field represents a protected entity and displays a source IP address as specified in the crypto map's encryption access list, which is access list 100. The UPE field represents an unprotected entity and displays a destination IP address as specified in the crypto map's encryption access list, which again is access list 100. The flag field can display one of five different status messages. Table 5.1 includes each of the flag messages and provides a description of each.

Because the flag field in Listing 5.36 displays **TIME_KEYS**, you can assume that the session is established. The ACL field in Listing 5.36 indicates that the session is using access list 100 for the duration of the connection in order to determine what should and should not be encrypted. The final configurations for Router A and Router B can be seen by issuing the **show running-config** command; they are displayed in Listings 5.37 and Listing 5.38.

Listing 5.37   Final CET configuration of Router A.

```
Router-A#show running-config
Building configuration...
!
version 12.1
```

Table 5.1   Flag field messages.

Flag	Explanation
PEND_CONN	Indicates a pending connection
XCHG_KEYS	Indicates that a connection has timed out and the router must first exchange Diffie-Hellman numbers and generate a new session (DES) key before encrypted communication can take place again
TIME_KEYS	Indicates a session that is in progress and is counting down to key timeout
BAD_CONN	Indicates that no existing or pending connection exists for this entry
UNK_STATUS	Indicates an error condition

```
service timestamps debug uptime
service timestamps log uptime
no service password-encryption
!
hostname Router-A
!
username routera privilege 15 password 0 routera
!
memory-size iomem 10
ip subnet-zero
no ip finger
ip tcp synwait-time 10
no ip domain-lookup
!
!
crypto cisco algorithm des
crypto cisco algorithm des cfb-8
crypto cisco algorithm 40-bit-des
!
!
crypto key pubkey-chain dss
 named-key routerb signature
  serial-number 0615EC60
  key-string
   4B013A5D DB942F8F 556B6F67 13110723 A05F17F9 D7BA15BF -
   74B1C17B D2E5C4A5 ABC0A7DE D1188289 A54C80EC 5BB3B9AE -
   F4366FB1 D5DBB125 C44F904A 62209467
  quit
 !
 crypto map routeramap 10 cisco
 set peer routerb
 set algorithm des
 match address 100
 !
interface Ethernet1/1
 ip address 192.168.10.1 255.255.255.0
 no ip directed-broadcast
 !
interface Serial0/0
 ip address 192.168.12.1 255.255.255.0
 crypto map routeramap
 !
ip classless
ip route 0.0.0.0 0.0.0.0 Serial0/0
no ip http server
!
access-list 100 permit ip 192.168.10.0 0.0.0.255 -
```

```
 192.168.11.0 0.0.0.255
access-list 100 permit icmp 192.168.10.0 0.0.0.255 -
 192.168.11.0 0.0.0.255
access-list 100 deny    ip 192.168.10.0 0.0.0.255 any
!
line con 0
 session-timeout 30
 exec-timeout 30 0
 login local
 transport input none
line aux 0
line vty 0 4
 session-timeout 30
 exec-timeout 30 0
 login local
!
no scheduler allocate
end
```

Listing 5.38   Final CET configuration of Router B.

```
Router-B#show running-config
Building configuration...
!
version 12.1
service timestamps debug uptime
service timestamps log uptime
no service password-encryption
!
hostname Router-B
!
username routerb privilege 15 password 0 routerb
!
memory-size iomem 10
ip subnet-zero
no ip finger
ip tcp synwait-time 10
no ip domain-lookup
!
crypto cisco algorithm des
crypto cisco algorithm des cfb-8
crypto cisco algorithm 40-bit-des cfb-8
!
!
crypto key pubkey-chain dss
 named-key routera signature
   serial-number 6B86ECF4
   key-string
```

```
     CC0438CE 125C2C5E DAE47A2C B47B44EE 4737C1D9 9FDF3164 -
     69CAACA7 82D25416 8CA218AC 644BE782 36966277 BBF437DF -
     1347FFAA F2E3C04E 94CE60E5 5485C539
    quit
   !
   !
   crypto map routerbmap 10 cisco
   set peer routera
   set algorithm des
   match address 101
   !
   !
   !
   !
   !
   !
   interface Ethernet0/1
    ip address 192.168.11.1 255.255.255.0
    no ip directed-broadcast
   !
   interface Serial0/0
    ip address 192.168.12.2 255.255.255.0
    crypto map routerbmap
   !
   ip classless
   ip route 0.0.0.0 0.0.0.0 Serial0/0
   no ip http server
   !
   access-list 101 permit ip 192.168.11.0 0.0.0.255 -
    192.168.10.0 0.0.0.255
   access-list 101 permit icmp 192.168.11.0 0.0.0.255 -
    192.168.10.0 0.0.0.255
   access-list 101 deny   ip 192.168.11.0 0.0.0.255 any
   !
   !
   line con 0
    session-timeout 30
    exec-timeout 30 0
    login local
    transport input none
   line aux 0
   line vty 0 4
    session-timeout 30
    exec-timeout 30 0
    login local
   !
   end
```

Chapter 6

Internet Protocol Security

In Brief

Internet Protocol Security (IPSec) is a framework of open standards for ensuring secure private communications over IP networks. Based on standards developed by the Internet Engineering Task Force (IETF), IPSec ensures confidentiality, integrity, and authenticity of data communications across a public IP network. IPSec provides a necessary component for a standards-based, flexible solution for deploying a networkwide security policy.

The IPSec initiative proposed to offer a standard way of establishing authentication and encryption services between end points. This means not only standard algorithms and transforms, but also standard key negotiation and management mechanisms to promote interoperability between devices by allowing for the negotiation of services between them.

IPSec provides Network layer encryption, and the standards provide several new packet formats. Authentication Header (AH) provides data integrity, and Encapsulating Security Payload (ESP) provides data integrity and confidentiality. The Diffie-Hellman protocol is used to create a shared secret key between two IPSec peers, and Internet Key Exchange (IKE), based on Internet Security Association Key Management Protocol (ISAKMP)/Oakley, is the protocol used to manage the generation and handling of keys. It is also the protocol by which potential peer devices form security associations.

A *security association (SA)* is a negotiated policy or agreed-upon way of handling the data that will be exchanged between two peer devices; the transform used to encrypt data is an example of a policy item. The active SA parameters are stored in the Security Association Database (SAD).

SAs for both IKE and IPSec are negotiated by IKE over various phases and modes. During Phase 1, IKE negotiates IPSec security associations. Two modes can be used for Phase 1:

- Main mode, which is used the majority of the time.

- Aggressive mode, which is used under rare circumstances.

The user cannot control which mode is chosen because the router automatically chooses a mode. The mode chosen depends on the configuration parameters used between each peer.

During Phase 2, IKE negotiates IPSec security associations. The only Phase 2 exchange is quick mode:

- *Phase 1*—During Phase 1, IKE negotiates IPSec security associations. Two modes can be used for Phase 1:
  1. Main mode, which is used the majority of the time.
  2. Aggressive mode, which is used under rare circumstances.

The user cannot control which mode is chosen, because the router automatically chooses a mode. The mode chosen depends on the configuration parameters used between each peer:

- *Phase 2*—During Phase 2, IKE negotiates IPSec security associations and the only Phase 2 exchange is quick mode.

IPSec SAs terminate through deletion or by timing out. When the SAs terminate, the keys are also discarded. When subsequent IPSec SAs are needed for a flow, IKE performs a new Phase 2 and, if necessary, a new Phase 1 negotiation. A successful negotiation results in new SAs and new keys. New SAs can be established before the existing SAs expire so that a given flow can continue uninterrupted.

Security associations are unidirectional, meaning that for each pair of communicating systems there are at least two security connections. The security association is uniquely identified by a randomly chosen unique number called the security parameter index (SPI) and the destination IP address of the IPSec peer. When a system sends a packet that requires IPSec protection, it looks up the security association in its database, applies the specified processing, and then inserts the SPI from the security association into the IPSec header. When the IPSec peer receives the packet, it looks up the security association in its database by destination address and SPI and then processes the packet as required. In summary, the security association is simply a statement of the negotiated security policy between two devices.

IPSec Packet Types

IPSec defines a set of headers that are added to IP packets. These new headers are placed after the IP header and before the Layer 4 protocol. They provide information for securing the payload of the IP packet. The security services are provided by the Authentication Header (AH) and the Encapsulating Security Payload (ESP) protocols. AH and ESP can be used independently or together, although for most applications, just one of them is sufficient. For both of these protocols, IPSec does not define the specific security algorithms to use; instead it provides an open framework for implementing industry-standard algorithms.

Authentication Header

Authentication Header (AH), described in RFC 2402, ensures the integrity and authenticity of the data, including the invariant fields in the outer IP header. It does not provide confidentiality protection, meaning it does not provide encryption. When an AH mode header is added to an IP packet, it provides authentication for as much of the IP header as possible, as well as for all the upper-layer protocols of an IP packet. However, some of the IP header fields may change in transit, and the value of these fields, when the packet arrives at the receiver, may not be predictable by the sender. These fields are known as mutable fields, and their values cannot be protected by AH. Predictable fields are also known as immutable fields.

AH provides authentication and integrity to packets by performing an integrity check, which is a keyed hash using a shared secret value that creates a message digest, when used together they are known as the integrity check value (ICV). The ICV is computed on the following:

- IP header fields that are either immutable in transit or predictable in value upon arrival at the end point for the Authentication Header security association.

- The Authenticated Header, payload length, reserved fields, SPI, sequence number, authentication data, and padding bytes.

- The upper-layer protocol data.

The result of the integrity check value helps the remote peer to determine if the packet has changed in transit. Upon receipt of the packet, the remote peer performs the same integrity check on the packet and compares the integrity check value that it has computed against the value of the integrity check value that the sender provided. The following are immutable fields and are included in the Authentication Header integrity check value computation:

- Version

- Internet header length

- Total length

- Identification

- Protocol

- Source address

- Destination address

AH cannot include in the integrity check any mutable field of the packet that might be modified by other routers within the transmission path of the packet from the source to the destination. The following are mutable fields and are not included in the computation of the AH ICV:

- Type of Service (ToS)
- Flags
- Fragment offset

Encapsulating Security Payload

Encapsulating Security Payload (ESP), described in RFC 2406, ensures the confidentiality, integrity, and optional authenticity of the data, yet ESP does not use the invariant fields in the IP header to validate data integrity. ESP has an optional field used for authentication. It contains an ICV that is computed over the remaining part of the ESP, minus the authentication field. The length of the optional field varies depending on the authentication algorithm that is chosen. If authentication is not chosen, the ICV is omitted. Authentication is always calculated after the encryption is done.

ESP performs encryption at the IP packet layer. It supports a variety of symmetric encryption algorithms. The default algorithm for IPSec is the 56-bit Data Encryption Standard using the cipher block chaining mode transform (DES-CBC). This cipher must be implemented to guarantee interoperability with other IPSec products.

The services that are provided by ESP depend on the options that are configured during the IPSec implementation and after an IPSec SA is established.

IPSec Modes of Operation

The format of the AH and ESP headers and the values contained within each packet vary according to the mode in which each is used. IPSec operates in either tunnel or transport mode.

Transport Mode

Transport mode is used when both peers are hosts. It may also be used when one peer is a host and the other is a gateway if that gateway is acting as a host. Transport mode has an advantage of adding only a few bytes to the header of each packet. When transport mode is used, the original header is not protected. This setup allows the true source and destination addresses to be viewed by intermediate devices implemented based on the contents of the IP header. One advantage of not changing the original header is that Quality of Service (QoS), can be processed from the information in the IP header. One disadvantage is that it is possible to do traffic analysis on the packets. Transport mode can be used only if the two end devices are the ones providing IPSec protection. Transport mode cannot be used if an intermediate device, such as a router or firewall, is providing the IPSec protection. Figure 6.1 displays an example of a normal IP packet.

When Authentication Header (AH) is used in transport mode, the AH services protect the external IP header along with the data payload. It protects all the fields in the header that do not change in transport. The AH header goes after the IP header and, if present before the ESP header, if present, and other higher-layer protocols, like TCP. Figure 6.2 shows an example of using AH in transport mode.

When ESP is used in transport mode, the IP payload is encrypted; however, the original headders are not encrypted. The ESP header is inserted after the IP header and before the upper-layer protocol header, like TCP. The upper-layer protocols are encrypted and authenticated along with the ESP header. ESP does not authenticate the IP header or the higher-layer information, such as TCP port numbers in the Layer 4 header. Figure 6.3 shows an example of using ESP in transport mode.

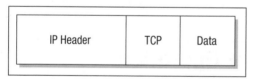

Figure 6.1   IP packet.

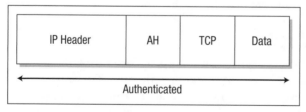

Figure 6.2   AH in transport mode.

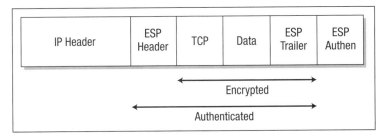

Figure 6.3   ESP in transport mode.

Tunnel Mode

Tunnel mode is used between two gateway devices, such as two PIX firewalls, or between a host and a gateway. In tunnel mode, the entire original IP packet is encrypted and becomes the payload of a new IP packet. The new IP header has the destination address of its IPSec peer. This allows for tunneling of IP packets from a protected host through a router or firewall usually to another router or firewall, which can both be acting as security gateways. One of the advantages of tunnel mode is that intermediate devices, such as routers, can do encryption without any modification to the end system. All the information from the original packet, including the headers, is protected. Tunnel mode protects against traffic analysis because, although the IPSec tunnel end points can be determined, the true source and destination end points cannot be determined because the information in the original IP header has been encrypted.

When Authentication Header (AH) is used in tunnel mode, the original header is authenticated and the new IP header is protected in exactly the same manner it was protected when used in transport mode. Figure 6.4 shows an example of using AH in tunnel mode.

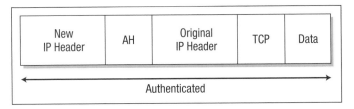

Figure 6.4   AH in tunnel mode.

When ESP is used in tunnel mode, the original IP header is protected because the entire original IP packet is encrypted. When both authentication and encryption are configured, encryption is performed first, before authentication. The reason for this process to take place in this order is that it facilitates rapid detection and rejection of replayed or bogus packets by the receiving node. Prior to decrypting the packet, the receiver can detect the problem and potentially reduce the impact of an attack. Figure 6.5 shows an example of using ESP in tunnel mode.

When you want to make sure that certain data from a known and trusted source gets transferred with integrity and the data does not need confidentiality, use the AH protocol. AH protects the upper-layer protocols and the IP header fields that do not change in transit, such as the source and destination addresses. AH cannot protect those fields that change in transit, such as the Type of Service (TOS) field. When the fields are protected, the values cannot be changed without detection, so the IPSec node will reject any altered IP packet. In summary, AH does not protect against someone sniffing the wire and seeing the headers and data. However, because headers and data cannot be changed without the change being detected, changed packets would get rejected.

If data confidentiality is needed, use ESP. ESP will encrypt the upper-layer protocols in transport mode and the entire original IP packet in tunnel mode so that neither is readable. ESP can also provide authentication for the packets. However, when you use ESP in transport mode, the outer IP original header is not protected; in tunnel mode, the new IP header is not protected. You will probably implement tunnel mode more than transport mode during initial IPSec usage. This mode allows a network device, such as a router to act as an IPSec proxy.

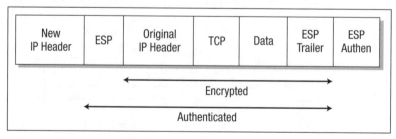

Figure 6.5   ESP in tunnel mode.

Key Management

I'll now discuss Internet Security Association Key Management.

Internet Key Exchange

Internet Key Exchange (IKE) is the facilitator and manager of IPSec-based conversations and is a derivative of Internet Security Association Key Management Protocol/Oakley (ISAKMP/Oakley), specifically for IPSec. IPSec uses the services of IKE to authenticate peers, manage the generation and handling of the keys used by the encryption algorithm, as well as the hashing algorithms between peers. It also negotiates IPSec security associations.

IKE provides three modes for exchanging key information and setting up IKE SAs. The first two modes are Phase 1 exchanges, which are used to set up the initial secure channel; the other mode is the Phase 2 exchange, which negotiates IPSec SAs. The two modes in Phase 1 are main mode and aggressive mode, and the Phase 2 mode is called quick mode. An IKE SA is used to provide a protected pipe for subsequent protected IKE exchanges between the IKE peers and then use Phase 2 quick mode with the IKE SA to negotiate the IPSec SAs.

Main mode has three two-way exchanges between the initiator and receiver. In the first exchange, the algorithms and hashes are agreed upon. The second exchange uses Diffie-Hellman to agree on a shared secret and to pass nonces. (*Nonces* are random numbers sent to the other party and signed and returned to prove their identity. The third exchange verifies the identity of the other peer.

In aggressive mode, fewer exchanges are done using fewer packets than with main mode. On the first exchange, almost everything is squeezed in—the proposed SA. The receiver sends back everything that is needed to complete the exchange. The only thing left is for the initiator to confirm the exchange. The disadvantage of using the aggressive mode is that both sides have exchanged information before there is a secure channel. Therefore, it is possible to snoop the wire and discover who formed the new SA. However, aggressive mode is faster than main mode.

Quick mode occurs after IKE has established the secure tunnel. Every packet is encrypted using quick mode. Both negotiation of the IPSec SA and derivation of the key material needed by IPSec are accomplished in quick mode. Before IKE will proceed, the potential parties are required to agree upon a way to authenticate themselves to each other. This authentication method is negotiated during the IKE Phase 1 main mode exchange.

Before any traffic can be passed using IPSec, each router/firewall/host must be able to verify the identity of its peer. This is accomplished by authenticating each peer, and IKE supports multiple authentication methods as part of the Phase 1 exchange. The two entities must agree on a common authentication protocol through a negotiation process. IPSec supports the following negotiation processes:

- Pre-shared keys
- Public key cryptography (nonces)
- Digital signatures

When pre-shared keys are used, identical keys are configured on each host. IKE peers authenticate each other by computing and sending a keyed hash of data that includes the pre-shared key. If the receiving peer is able to create the same hash using its pre-shared key, then it knows that both parties share the same secret key, thus authenticating the other party. Pre-shared keys do not scale well because each IPSec peer must be configured with the key of every other peer with which the router needs to establish a session.

When using public key cryptography, each party generates a pseudo-random number (a nonce) and encrypts it in the other party's public key. The ability for each party to compute a keyed hash containing the other peer's nonce, decrypted with the local private key as well as other publicly and privately available information, authenticates the parties to each other. This system provides for deniable transactions. That is, either side of the exchange can plausibly deny that it took part in the exchange. Currently, only the RSA public key algorithm is supported.

When digital signatures are used, each device digitally signs a set of data and sends it to the other party. This method is similar to public key cryptography, except that it provides nonrepudiation.

Sharing keys does not scale well for a large network. One method that does scale is encapsulation of the public key in a digital certificate authenticated by a Certificate Authority (CA). A CA is a trusted third party who can bind a public key to an identity. In this case, that includes the identity of devices, especially router and firewall devices.

In summary, when the IKE negotiation begins, IKE looks for an IKE policy that is the same on both peers. The peer that initiates the negotiation will send all its configured policies to the remote peer, and the remote peer will try to find a match. The remote peer looks for a match by comparing its own highest priority policy against the other peer's received policies. The remote peer checks each of its configured policies in the order of its highest priority first until a match is found.

A match is made when both policies from the two peers contain the same encryption, hash, authentication, and Diffie-Hellman parameter values and when the remote peer's policy specifies a lifetime less than or equal to the lifetime in the policy being compared. If no acceptable match is found, IKE refuses negotiation and IPSec will not be established. If a match is found, IKE will complete negotiation and IPSec security associations will be created

Diffie-Hellman Key Agreement

Diffie-Hellman provides a means for two parties to agree upon a shared secret in such a way that the secret will be unavailable to eavesdroppers. *Diffie-Hellman key agreement* requires that both the sender and recipient of a message have key pairs. By combining your private key and the other party's public key, both parties can compute the same shared secret number. This number can then be converted into cryptographic keying material.

Each peer generates a public key and private key pair. The private key that is generated by each peer is never shared; the public key is calculated from the private key by each peer and the result is exchanged with the other peer. Each peer combines the other peer's public key with its own private key and each peer computes the same shared secret number. The shared secret number is then converted into a shared secret key, which is used for encrypting data using the encryption algorithm specified during the security association setup.

The Diffie-Hellman key agreement has two system parameters, p and g. They are both public and may be used by all the users in a system. Parameter p is a prime number and parameter g (usually called a generator) is an integer less than p with the following properties: for every number n between 1 and p-1 inclusive, there is a power k, of g such that $n = g^k$ modulus p. The Diffie-Hellman key agreement can be explained further using the following example:

1. The Diffie-Hellman process begins with each host creating a prime number, p (which is larger than 2) and a base number, g, an integer that is smaller than p.

2. Next, the hosts each secretly generate a private number called x, which is less than p - 1.

3. The hosts next generate the public keys, y. They are created with the following function:

```
y = gx % p
```

4. The two hosts now exchange the public keys (y) and the exchanged numbers are converted into a secret key, z:

```
z = yx % p
```

5. The value z can now be used as the key for the IPSec encryption method used to transfer information between the two hosts. Mathematically, the two hosts should have generated the same value for z.

6. This yields the following:

```
z = (gx % p)x' % p = (gx' % p)x % p
```

On Cisco devices, Diffie-Hellman can be configured to support one of two different group modes on a per-IKE-policy basis: 768-bit groups or 1024-bit groups. The 1024-bit groups are more challenging to break, but they come with the added expense of being more CPU intensive.

Encryption

I'll now discuss encryption.

Data Encryption Standard

IPSec can use either the 56-bit Data Encryption Standard (DES) algorithm or the 168-bit 3DES algorithm for encryption. After two IPSec peers obtain their shared secret key, they can use the key to communicate with each other using the DES encryption algorithm. The 56-bit DES system consists of an algorithm and a key. The key has a length of 64 bits, of which 56 are used as the key. The remaining 8 bits are parity bits used in checking for errors. Even with just 56 bits, there are more than 70 quadrillion possible keys (simply, 2^{56}). The digits in the key must be independently determined to take full advantage of 70 quadrillion possible keys.

The mechanics of DES are relatively simple. DES enciphers data in blocks of 64 bits of binary data. Given a message that needs to be encrypted, one must first pick a 64-bit key and then convert the plaintext into binary form. It takes a string of only 5 bits to describe our alphabet, because $2^5=32$ and the alphabet is 26 letters long. This is relatively easy to do. Now within the blocks or strings of 64 bits, order is very important. The leftmost bit is known as the 1st bit or is in the first position. The rightmost bit is the 64th bit.

The first step in the DES procedure is to change the order within each block. For example, the 52nd bit in the original string becomes the 1st bit in this new block. Bit 40 becomes bit 2 and so forth, as specified by a table. This step is called the initial permutation. Permutation is used in the strict mathematical sense that only order is changed. The results of this initial permutation are broken down into two halves. The first 32 bits become L0. The last 32 bits are called R0. Now the data is subjected to the following transformation 16 times:

```
Ln = Rn-1  where R0 occurs at n=1
Rn = Ln-1 ( ((Rn-1, Kn) where L0 occurs at n=1
```

After the first iteration, we are presented with the following:

```
Ln+1 = Rn     in essence Ln+1 = Ln-1 ( ((Rn, K0)
Rn+1 = Ln ( ((Rn, K0) in essence Rn+1 = Rn-1 ( ((Rn, K0)
```

Cisco's encryption algorithm incorporates cipher feedback (CFB), which further guarantees the integrity of the data received by using feedback. This is the essence of DES. The key and the message become interwoven and inseparable, which makes it difficult to break apart the cipher text into its constituent parts. This procedure is performed 16 times. The expression **Rn = Ln-1 (((Rn+1, Kn)** is simply saying, "Add L, bit by bit in modulo 2, from one iteration ago to the term **((Rn-1, Kn)**." This function is determined by **R**, one iteration ago and **Kn**, which is based on the key. **Kn** is, in turn, given by another formula, **Kn= KS(n, KEY)**. Because this algorithm goes through 16 iterations, **Kn** will be of length 48. The calculation of **Kn** is another operation in which DES looks in a table. The calculation of the function **((Rn+1,Kn)** is likewise simple. First, however, notice that **R** is of 32-bit length and K is 48 bits long. R is expanded to 48 bits using another table. The resulting R is added to K (using bit-by-bit addition in mod base 2). The result of this addition is broken into eight 6-bit strings. One enters into another table that gives the primitive function Sn. There is one S function for each 6-bit block. The result of entering into these S functions is a 32-bit string. After 16 iterations, the result should be, L16 and R16. These two strings are united where R forms the first 32 bits and L forms the last 32. The 64-bit result is entered into the inverse of the initial permutation function. The result of this last step is cipher text. Decoding is accomplished by simply running the process backwards.

Triple DES

When the encryption services provided by the 56-bit DES algorithm are not deemed as being strong enough from a mathematical standpoint for encryption of data, the Triple DES (3DES) symmetrical encryption algorithm can be used. Cisco products support the use of the 168-bit 3DES encryption algorithm with IPSec implementations. 3DES has been standardized by the National Institute of Standards and Technology (NIST) and is a variant of 56-bit DES. 3DES takes data and breaks it into 64-bit blocks just as DES does, yet 3DES processes each block three times. Each time 3DES uses an independent 56-bit key, the encryption strength over 56-bit DES is tripled.

MD5 Message Digest

The *MD5 algorithm*, an extension to the MD4 message digest, can be used to ensure that a message has not been altered. The MD5 algorithm takes as input a message of arbitrary length—for example, a username and password—and after running the message through the algorithm, MD5 produces as output a 128-bit message digest of the input. It is considered computationally infeasible to produce two messages having the same message digest or to produce a message that has a predefined message digest.

IPSec Implementations

Generally, there are two accepted schemes for implementing IPSec. The first is for each end station to perform IPSec directly. This provides the advantage of not having an impact on the network design, topology, or any routing decisions. The disadvantage is that each end station usually must possess special software or needs an upgrade in addition to the added configuration. Complicating the issue is that the user must be aware of when encryption is required. Because users make the decisions, they potentially must make a change to the configuration. When using this scheme, encryption is not transparent to the end user.

The second is for the network devices to provide the service of IPSec. An advantage to this scheme is that the end stations and users are not directly involved. Another consideration is that, when you design a network to use encryption and the end stations won't be doing the encryption, the enrypting end points impose a very simple constraint. All traffic that has security services applied to it must go through the two peering crypto end points. This setup places some limits on asymmetric traffic paths. After a packet is processed by one enrypting end point (one end of the SA), the packets may take any route between the two encrypting end points; however, the route must bring the packet back to the peer encrypting end point for processing. This requirement means that there are single points in a network where IPSec traffic must traverse. For enterprises with multiple access points onto the Internet, care must be taken in how network addresses are advertised to enforce the symmetric relationship between IPSec peers.

The security associations are unique between the two peering encrypting end points and are not shared with other possible encrypting devices. When applying security, make sure that it is indeed secure; that is, make sure that the "state" of any particular data flow in the SAD is restricted to the two peers.

6. Internet Protocol Security

Immediate Solutions

Configuring IPSec Using Pre-Shared Keys

This section details how to configure IPSec on Cisco routers using pre-shared keys. Configuring IPSec encryption can be difficult and complicated. However, with a well-thought-out plan, the challenges associated with configuring IPSec can be overcome. Because IPSec can be configured without IKE (manual key configuration) or with IKE (pre-shared keys, public keys, or digital certificates), and the configuration of each is different, I will begin by configuring IPSec using IKE with pre-shared keys for authentication of IPSec sessions.

To configure IKE, perform the tasks in the following list. The first two tasks are required; the remaining tasks are optional:

1. The first step is to use the **crypto isakmp enable** command to enable IKE globally for the router. If you do not want IKE to be used with your IPSec implementation, use the **no crypto isakmp enable** command. IKE is enabled by default globally on the router and does not need to be enabled on a per-interfaces basis.

2. The next step is to define a suite of IKE policies on the router. The IKE policies define the parameters to be used during IKE negotiation. Use the **crypto isakmp policy** *<priority>* command to uniquely identify and define the policy. The *priority* parameter assigns a priority to the policy and can accept any integer from 1 to 10,000, with 1 being the highest priority and 10,000 being the lowest priority. Multiple IKE policies can be configured for each peer participating in IPSec. Use of this command takes you into IKE policy configuration command mode (**config-isakmp**).

3. In IKE policy configuration command mode, use the **encryption** *<des | 3des>* command to define the encryption algorithm to be used for encryption of packets between IPSec peers. If this command is not defined within the IKE policy, the encryption algorithm defaults to 56-bit DES.

4. In IKE policy configuration command mode, use the **hash** <*sha* | *md5*> command to define the hash algorithm used within the IKE policy. If this command is not defined within the IKE policy, the hash algorithm defaults to SHA1.

5. To specify the authentication method used in the IKE policy, use this command in IKE policy configuration command mode:

```
authentication <rsa-sig | rsa-encr | pre-share>
```

If this command is not defined within the IKE policy, the authentication method defaults to RSA signatures.

6. To specify the Diffie-Hellman identifier used for the IKE policy, use the **group** <*1* | *2*> command in IKE policy configuration command mode. The **group 1** command specifies that the policy should use the 768-bit Diffie-Hellman group. The **group 2** command specifies that the policy should use the 1024-bit Diffie-Hellman group. If this command is not defined within the IKE policy, the 768-bit Diffie-Hellman group will be used.

7. To specify how long the IKE established security association should exist before expiring, use the **lifetime** <*seconds*> command in IKE policy configuration mode. If this command is not defined within the IKE policy, the security associations expire after 86,400 seconds or 1 day.

NOTE: *The default values for configured policies do not show up in the configuration when you issue a **show running** command. To view the default IKE values within the configured policies, use the **show crypto isakmp policy** command.*

The configuration commands in the preceding list are all that are needed to enable and define the IKE policy. Next, you should define the ISAKMP identity for each peer that uses pre-shared keys in an IKE policy. When two peers use IKE to establish IPSec security associations, each peer sends its identity to the remote peer. To configure the ISAKMP identity mode used between peers, use the commands in the following steps:

1. Use this command to define the identity used by the router:

```
crypto isakmp identity <address | hostname>
```

The *address* parameter is used when there is only one interface and only one IP address that is used by the peer for IKE negotiations and the IP address is known. The *hostname* parameter

6. Internet Protocol Security

is used if there is more than one interface that might be used for IKE negotiations or if the IP address is unknown. If this command is not specified, the *identity* parameter will be used by the router.

2. If the crypto identity was configured to use the hostname of the remote peer, the hostname of the remote peer must be defined using the **ip host** *<name> <address>* command to define a static hostname-to-address mapping in the host cache.

After configuring the ISAKMP identity used between peers, you must specify the pre-shared keys to use between each peer. The keys must be configured anytime pre-shared authentication is specified in an IKE policy. The same pre-shared key must be configured on each pair of IPSec peers when you're using pre-shared keys for IKE authentication. Configuration of the pre-shared key can be accomplished by two separate commands and is dependant upon the identity configured in the previous command. Configure the pre-shared key using the following commands. To configure a pre-shared authentication key, use this command:

```
crypto isamkmp key key-string address <peer-address> -
<peer-mask>
```

This command is used if the ISAKMP identity was configured to use the *address* parameter or if the identity was not configured, because the default is to use the peer routers address. If the ISAKMP identity was configured to use the *hostname* parameter, then use this command:

```
crypto isakmp key key-string hostname <peer-hostname>
```

The next task that needs to be performed is to configure the router for IPSec. The first step in configuring IPSec is to define the transform set the router should use. A transform set is an acceptable combination of security protocols, algorithms, and other settings to apply to IPSec-protected traffic. The transform set is agreed upon between peers during the IPSec security association negotiation. It tells the router how to protect data within a particular data flow. During IPSec security association negotiations with IKE, the peers search for a transform set that is the same at both peers. When such a transform set is found, it is selected and will be applied to the protected traffic as part of both peers' IPSec security associations.

To define a transform set, use the following commands starting in global configuration mode (only the first command is required):

1. Define the transform set using the following command:

    ```
    crypto ipsec transform-set transform-set-name <transform1> -
        <transform2> <transform3>
    ```

    Rules exist that define an acceptable combination of security protocols and algorithms that can be used as transforms. Table 6.1 defines the acceptable combinations.

2. To change the mode associated with the transform set, use the **mode** *<tunnel | transport>* command in crypto transport configuration mode. If this command is omitted, the mode will default to tunnel mode.

NOTE: *The IOS command parser will deny you from entering invalid combinations. There is one other possible transform, **comp-lzs**; however, it will not be discussed within this book.*

After defining the transform set that IPSec should use, you must configure an access list. Access lists defined for IPSec are different than regular access lists, which permit or deny traffic from entering into or exiting out of an interface. Access lists are used with IPSec to de-

6. Internet Protocol Security

Table 6.1   Transform combinations.

Type	Transform	Description
AH Authentication Transform	**ah-md5-hmac**	Authentication Header with Message Digest 5 authentication
	ah-sha-hmac	Authentication Header with SHA1 authentication
ESP Encryption Transform	**esp-des**	ESP with 56-bit DES encryption
	esp-3des	ESP with 168-bit DES encryption
	esp-null	Null encryption
ESP Authentication Transform	**esp-md5-hmac**	ESP with Message Digest 5 authentication
	esp-sha-hmac	ESP with SHA1 authentication

fine which IP traffic will be protected by encryption and which will not. To create access lists that define which traffic should be encrypted, use the following command in global configuration mode. To determine which IP packets will be encrypted by IPSec, use this command:

```
access-list access-list-number {deny | permit} <protocol> -
    <source> <source-wildcard> <destination> <destination- -
    wildcard> <log>
```

Cisco recommends that the access list keyword **any** be avoided when specifying the source address or destination address within the access list. It is not recommended because it causes the router to encrypt all outbound or all inbound traffic. Try to be as precise as possible when defining which packets to protect with an access list. It is also recommended that mirrored copies of the access list be configured between each host that is to perform IPSec.

After configuration of the access list(s), you must define IPSec crypto maps to allow the setup of security associations for traffic flows to be encrypted. Crypto map entries contain information for IPSec. When IKE is used to establish security associations, the IPSec peers can negotiate the settings they will use for the new security associations. This allows you to specify the parameters of the crypto map on a per-peer basis. To configure the crypto maps and define the appropriate parameters, use the commands in the following steps (only the first four steps are required):

1. To create the crypto map entry and enter the crypto map configuration mode, use this command:

```
crypto map map-name seq-num ipsec-isakmp
```

The *map-name* parameter defines the name that identifies the crypto map set. The *seq-num* parameter is the number that is assigned to this crypto map; it should not be chosen arbitrarily because this number is used to rank multiple crypto map entries within a crypto map set, and a crypto map entry with a lower *seq-num* is evaluated before a map entry with a higher *seq-num*. Use of this command moves you into crypto map configuration mode. The **ipsec-isakmp** parameter specifies that IKE will be used to establish the security associations for protecting the traffic matched by this crypto map entry.

2. In crypto map configuration mode, use this command to specify an extended access list for a crypto map entry that matches packets that should be protected by encryption:

    ```
    match address <access-list number | name>
    ```

3. To specify an IPSec peer, use the following command in crypto map configuration mode:

    ```
    set peer <ip address | hostname>
    ```

    You can specify the remote IPSec peer by its hostname if the hostname is mapped to the peer's IP address in a domain name server (DNS) or if you manually map the hostname to the IP address with the **ip host** command that was discussed earlier. When using IKE to set up security associations, you can specify multiple peers per crypto map.

4. To specify which transform sets can be used with the crypto map entry, use this command:

    ```
    set transform set <transform-set-name1> <transform-set- -
      name2...transform-set-name6>
    ```

    List multiple transform sets in order of priority with the highest-priority transform set listed first. When using IKE to set up security associations, you can specify multiple transform sets per crypto map.

5. Use the **set pfs** *<group1 | group2>* command to specify that IPSec should ask for perfect forward secrecy when requesting a new sa or should demand **PFS** in requests received from the IPSec peer.

6. To specify that separate IPSec security associations should be requested for each source/destination host pair, use the **set security-association level per-host** command. This command should be omitted if one security association should be requested for each crypto map access list **permit** entry.

7. To override the global lifetime value on a per-crypto-map-list basis, which is used when negotiating IPSec security associations, use this command:

    ```
    set security-association lifetime <seconds seconds | -
      kilobytes kilobytes>
    ```

After configuring the router for IPSec, the last step in IPSec configuration is to apply the configured crypto map to an interface. As soon as the crypto map is applied to an interface, the security associations are set up in the Security Association Database (SAD). Only one crypto map can be applied to an interface, and multiple crypto map entries with the same crypto name and different sequence numbers are permitted. To apply a previously defined crypto map set to an interface, use the commands in these steps:

1. To apply a previously defined crypto map to an interface, use the following command to move into interface configuration mode:

    ```
    interface <interface type> <interface number>
    ```

2. To apply a previously defined crypto map set to an interface, use the **crypto map** *map-name* command. A crypto map set must be applied to an interface before that interface can provide IPSec services.

I'll begin with the network shown in Figure 6.6. This network contains two routers, which must communicate with one another via the use of IPSec. Router A is the corporate gateway router and Router B is the branch office router for the remote location. Remote users communicate with the corporate office via the wide area network (WAN), and when users at the branch office communicate with the corporate office, their traffic should be protected with IPSec. This configuration will use all the security services provided by both IKE and IPSec, and Router A and Router B will be configured to exchange pre-shared keys.

Listing 6.1 displays the configuration of Router A, and Listing 6.2 displays the configuration of Router B.

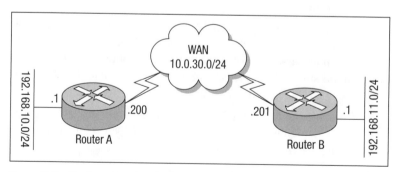

Figure 6.6   Basic network using IPSec.

Listing 6.1 IPSec configuration of Router A.

```
hostname Router-A
!
username ipsec privilege 15 password 0 ipsec
memory-size iomem 10
ip subnet-zero
ip tcp synwait-time 10
no ip domain-lookup
!
crypto isakmp policy 11
 hash md5
 encryption des
 group 2
 authentication pre-share
!
crypto isakmp key ouripseckey address 10.0.30.201
!
crypto ipsec transform-set remote esp-des esp-md5-hmac
!
crypto map encrypt 11 ipsec-isakmp
 set peer 10.0.30.201
 set transform-set remote
 match address 120
!
interface Ethernet0/0
 description Internet Connection
 ip address 10.0.30.200 255.255.255.0
 no ip directed-broadcast
 ip nat outside
 no ip route-cache
 no ip mroute-cache
 crypto map encrypt
!
interface Ethernet0/1
 ip address 192.168.10.1 255.255.255.0
 no ip directed-broadcast
 ip nat inside
!
ip nat pool pat 10.0.30.203 10.0.30.203 network 255.255.255.0
ip nat inside source route-map donotnat pool pat overload
!
ip classless
ip route 0.0.0.0 0.0.0.0 Ethernet0/0
!
access-list 120 permit ip 192.168.10.0 0.0.0.255 -
   192.168.11.0 0.0.255.255
```

```
access-list 130 deny    ip 192.168.10.0 0.0.0.255 -
   192.168.11.0 0.0.255.255
access-list 130 permit ip 192.168.10.0 0.0.0.255 any
!
route-map donotnat permit 10
 match ip address 130
 !
```

Listing 6.2   IPSec configuration of Router B.

```
hostname Router-B
!
username ipsec privilege 15 password 0 ipsec
memory-size iomem 10
ip subnet-zero
ip tcp synwait-time 10
no ip domain-lookup
!
crypto isakmp policy 10
 hash md5
 encryption des
 group 2
 authentication pre-share
!
crypto isakmp key ouripseckey address 10.0.30.200
!
crypto ipsec transform-set remote esp-des esp-md5-hmac
!
crypto map encrypt 10 ipsec-isakmp
 set peer 10.0.30.200
 set transform-set remote
 match address 120
!
interface Ethernet1/0
 description Internet Connection
 ip address 10.0.30.201 255.255.255.0
 no ip directed-broadcast
 ip nat outside
 crypto map encrypt
!
interface Ethernet0/1
 ip address 192.168.11.1 255.255.255.0
 no ip directed-broadcast
 ip nat inside
!
ip nat pool pat 10.0.30.204 10.0.30.204 network 255.255.255.0
ip nat inside source route-map donotnat pool pat overload
!
```

```
ip classless
ip route 0.0.0.0 0.0.0.0 Ethernet1/0
!
access-list 120 permit ip 192.168.11.0 0.0.0.255 -
  192.168.10.0 0.0.255.255
access-list 130 deny   ip 192.168.11.0 0.0.0.255 -
  192.168.10.0 0.0.255.255
access-list 130 permit ip 192.168.11.0 0.0.0.255 any
!
route-map donotnat permit 10
 match ip address 130
!
```

The configurations in Listing 6.1 and Listing 6.2 configure each router to use the benefits of IPSec, but the configurations utilize the services of PAT.

PAT (NAT could have been configured in place of PAT) makes use of a route map within this configuration. The route map is needed to discriminate between packets that have a destination address that matches an address within the enterprise's IP address space or packets that could be destined to the Internet. Each router has been configured with an IKE policy using the **crypto isakmp policy** command. Within each IKE policy, the encryption algorithm is set at the default 56-bit DES.

NOTE: *Default commands used for configuring IPSec and IKE are not displayed in the configuration output of the **show running** command. The default commands used to configure IPSec and IKE are listed in this chapter for completeness.*

Each router's Diffie-Hellman group has been changed from the default 768-bit group 1 to the stronger 1024-bit group 2, and the IKE authentication method has been defined to use pre-shared keys. Each router is then configured with the pre-shared key used for authentication; the pre-shared key is specified by using the **crypto isakmp key** command. In Listing 6.1 and Listing 6.2, the key is defined as **ouripeckey**. This concludes the configuration of IKE on Router A and Router B.

Next, IPSec support must be configured on Router A and Router B. The first step used in Listing 6.1 and Listing 6.2 to configure IPSec support is to define a transform set that defines the security protocols and algorithms used between the two peers; this was done using the **crypto ipsec transform-set** command, which is named remote.

6. Internet Protocol Security

A crypto map is then defined that indicates that IKE will be used to establish the IPSec security associations for protecting the traffic specified by this crypto map entry, using the **ipsec-isakmp** parameter. The IPSec peer is identified and the transform set is defined for communication between the peers. An access list is defined, which specifies whether or not IPSec should provide encryption services for packets that are matched by access list entry.

To begin testing the configurations of Router A and Router B, an extended Ping will be issued with the packet sourced from the Ethernet0/1 interface of Router B; the packet's destination is the Ethernet0/1 interface of Router A. On Router B, I have issued the **debug crypto ipsec**, **debug crypto isakmp**, and **debug crypto engine** commands. Each of these commands can be used to view event messages for IPSec and IKE. The packets from the Ping request will match the access list entry and require the encryption services of IPSec. Listing 6.3 displays the Ping request and the **debug** commands.

Listing 6.3   Enabling the debug commands and the Ping request.

```
#debug crypto ipsec
Crypto IPSEC debugging is on
#debug crypto isakmp
Crypto ISAKMP debugging is on
#debug crypto engine
Crypto Engine debugging is on
#ping ip
Target IP address: 192.168.10.1
Repeat count [5]: 100
Datagram size [100]:
Timeout in seconds [2]:
Extended commands [n]: y
Source address or interface: 192.168.11.1
Type of service [0]:
Set DF bit in IP header? [no]:
Validate reply data? [no]:
Data pattern [0xABCD]:
Loose, Strict, Record, Timestamp, Verbose[none]:
Sweep range of sizes [n]:
Type escape sequence to abort.
Sending 100, 100-byte ICMP Echos to 192.168.10.1, -
  timeout is 2 seconds:
```

After the Ping request sends the first packet, Router B determines that the packet matches the access list—in this case, access list 120, configured under the IPSec crypto map—and begins the security association setup by offering to Router A all of its configured transform sets. This can be verified by displaying the output of the **debug crypto ipsec** command. Listing 6.4 shows the security association request.

Listing 6.4   Security association request.

```
: IPSEC(sa_request): ,
    (key eng. msg.) src= 10.0.30.201, dest= 10.0.30.200,
    src_proxy= 192.168.11.0/255.255.255.0/0/0 (type=4),
    dest_proxy= 192.168.10.0/255.255.255.0/0/0 (type=4),
    protocol= ESP, transform= esp-des esp-md5-hmac,
    lifedur= 120s and 4608000kb,
    spi= 0x0(0), conn_id= 0, keysize= 0, flags= 0x4004
```

The debug output in Listing 6.4 shows that, upon security association setup, Router B offers to Router A all of its configured transform sets. It is at this point that the final verification of the IKE security association takes place. The IKE security association verification messages can be seen by displaying the output of the **debug crypto isakmp** command. Listing 6.5 shows the IKE verification process.

Listing 6.5   IKE verification process.

```
!
: ISAKMP (6): beginning Main Mode exchange
: ISAKMP (6): sending packet to 10.0.30.200 (I) MM_NO_STATE
: ISAKMP (6): received packet from 10.0.30.200 (I) MM_NO_STATE
: ISAKMP (6): processing SA payload. message ID = 0
: ISAKMP (6): Checking ISAKMP transform 1 against priority 10 -
              policy
: ISAKMP:        encryption DES-CBC
: ISAKMP:        hash MD5
: ISAKMP:        default group 2
: ISAKMP:        auth pre-share
: ISAKMP:        Open
: ISAKMP:        life duration (basic) of 120
: ISAKMP (6): atts are acceptable. Next payload is 0
: ISAKMP (6): SA is doing pre-shared key authentication using -
              id type ID_IPV4_ADDR
: ISAKMP (6): sending packet to 10.0.30.200 (I) MM_SA_SETUP
: ISAKMP (6): received packet from 10.0.30.200 (I) MM_SA_SETUP
: ISAKMP (6): processing KE payload. message ID = 0
: ISAKMP (6): processing NONCE payload. message ID = 0
: ISAKMP (6): SKEYID state generated
: ISAKMP (6): processing vendor id payload
: ISAKMP (6): speaking to another IOS box!
: ISAKMP (6): ID payload
        next-payload : 8
        type         : 1
```

6. Internet Protocol Security

```
              protocol    : 17
              port        : 500
              length      : 8
: ISAKMP (6): Total payload length: 12
: ISAKMP (6): sending packet to 10.0.30.200 (I) MM_KEY_EXCH
: ISAKMP (6): received packet from 10.0.30.200 (I) MM_KEY_EXCH
: ISAKMP (6): processing ID payload. message ID = 0
: ISAKMP (6): processing HASH payload. message ID = 0
: ISAKMP (6): SA has been authenticated with 10.0.30.200
!
```

After the security associations are set up, IKE begins IPSec negotiation. You can see the process of IKE negotiation of IPSec by again viewing the output of the **debug crypto ipsec** and **debug crypto isakmp** commands. Listing 6.6 displays the IKE negotiation.

Listing 6.6   IKE negotiation.

```
!
: IPSEC(key_engine): got a queue event...
: IPSEC(spi_response): getting spi 559422693 for SA
     from 10.0.30.200  to 10.0.30.201  for prot 3
!
: ISAKMP (6): beginning Quick Mode exchange, M-ID of 121737022
: ISAKMP (6): sending packet to 10.0.30.200 (I) QM_IDLE
: ISAKMP (6): received packet from 10.0.30.200 (I) QM_IDLE
: ISAKMP (6): processing SA payload. message ID = 121737022
: ISAKMP (6): Checking IPSec proposal 1
: ISAKMP: transform 1, ESP_DES
: ISAKMP:    attributes in transform:
: ISAKMP:        encaps is 1
: ISAKMP:        SA life type in seconds
: ISAKMP:        SA life duration (basic) of 120
: ISAKMP:        SA life type in kilobytes
: ISAKMP:        SA life duration (VPI) of  0x0 0x46 0x50 0x0
: ISAKMP:        authenticator is HMAC-MD5
: ISAKMP (6): atts are acceptable.
!
```

The final display shows the security association completing the setup process. When the security association setup process is complete, traffic can begin to flow from source to destination using the security services of IPSec. Listing 6.7 displays the completion of the security association setup process.

Listing 6.7   Completion of security association setup process.

```
: IPSEC(validate_proposal_request): proposal part #1,
   (key eng. msg.) dest= 10.0.30.200, src= 10.0.30.201,
```

```
          dest_proxy= 192.168.10.0/255.255.255.0/0/0 (type=4),
          src_proxy= 192.168.11.0/255.255.255.0/0/0 (type=4),
          protocol= ESP, transform= esp-des esp-md5-hmac,
          lifedur= 0s and 0kb,
          spi= 0x0(0), conn_id= 0, keysize= 0, flags= 0x4
: IPSEC(key_engine): got a queue event...
: IPSEC(initialize_sas): ,
  (key eng. msg.) dest= 10.0.30.201, src= 10.0.30.200,
          dest_proxy= 192.168.11.0/255.255.255.0/0/0 (type=4),
          src_proxy= 192.168.10.0/255.255.255.0/0/0 (type=4),
          protocol= ESP, transform= esp-des esp-md5-hmac,
          lifedur= 120s and 4608000kb,
          spi= 0x21581CE5(559422693), conn_id= 2, keysize= 0, -
            flags= 0x4
: IPSEC(initialize_sas): ,
  (key eng. msg.) src= 10.0.30.201, dest= 10.0.30.200,
: ISAKMP (6): processing NONCE payload. message ID = 121737022
: ISAKMP (6): processing ID payload. message ID = 121737022
: ISAKMP (6): unknown error extracting ID
: ISAKMP (6): processing ID payload. message ID = 121737022
: ISAKMP (6): unknown error extracting ID
: ISAKMP (6): Creating IPSec SAs
:         inbound SA from 10.0.30.200 to 10.0.30.201 -
          (proxy 192.168.10.0 to 192.168.11.0)
:         has spi 331813658 and conn_id 7 and flags 4
:         lifetime of 120 seconds
:         lifetime of 4608000 kilobytes
:         outbound SA from 10.0.30.201 to 10.0.30.200 -
          (proxy 192.168.11.0 to 192.168.10.0)
:         has spi 306250407 and conn_id 8 and flags 4
:         lifetime of 120 seconds
:         lifetime of 4608000 kilobytes
: ISAKMP (6): sending packet to 10.0.30.200 (I) QM_IDLE
: src_proxy= 192.168.11.0/255.255.255.0/0/0 (type=4),
          dest_proxy= 192.168.10.0/255.255.255.0/0/0 (type=4),
          protocol= ESP, transform= esp-des esp-md5-hmac,
          lifedur= 120s and 4608000kb,
          spi= 0x1472092E(343017774), conn_id= 3, keysize= 0, -
            flags= 0x4
: IPSEC(create_sa): sa created,
  (sa) sa_dest= 10.0.30.201, sa_prot= 50,
      sa_spi= 0x21581CE5(559422693),
      sa_trans= esp-des esp-md5-hmac , sa_conn_id= 2
: IPSEC(create_sa): sa created,
  (sa) sa_dest= 10.0.30.200, sa_prot= 50,
      sa_spi= 0x1472092E(343017774),
      sa_trans= esp-des esp-md5-hmac , sa_conn_id= 3
```

**6. Internet
Protocol Security**

After the security association is set up and complete, you can view the settings of each security association within the database (SAD) by issuing the **show crypto ipsec sa** command. Listing 6.8 displays the output of the security association database of Router B.

Listing 6.8   Security association database on Router B.

```
Router-B#sh crypto ipsec sa
interface: Ethernet0/0
    Crypto map tag: encrypt, local addr. 10.0.30.201
    local  ident (addr/mask/prot/port): -
    (192.168.11.0/255.255.255.0/0/0)
    remote ident (addr/mask/prot/port): -
    (192.168.10.0/255.255.255.0/0/0)
    current_peer: 10.0.30.200
      PERMIT, flags={origin_is_acl,}
    #pkts encaps: 5, #pkts encrypt: 5, #pkts digest 5
    #pkts decaps: 4, #pkts decrypt: 4, #pkts verify 4
    #send errors 5, #recv errors 0
      local crypto endpt.: 10.0.30.201, remote crypto endpt.: -
      10.0.30.200
      path mtu 1500, media mtu 1500
      current outbound spi: 20DB2311
!
    inbound esp sas:
      spi: 0x22900598(579863960)
        transform: esp-des esp-md5-hmac,
        in use settings ={Tunnel, }
        slot: 0, conn id: 2, crypto map: encrypt
        sa timing: remaining key lifetime (k/sec): (4607999/71)
        IV size: 8 bytes
        replay detection support: Y
!
    inbound ah sas:
!
    outbound esp sas:
      spi: 0x20DB2311(551232273)
        transform: esp-des esp-md5-hmac,
        in use settings ={Tunnel, }
        slot: 0, conn id: 3, crypto map: encrypt
        sa timing: remaining key lifetime (k/sec): (4607999/71)
        IV size: 8 bytes
        replay detection support: Y
!
    outbound ah sas:
Router-B#
```

It appears that Router B has two security associations; however, in "In Brief" earlier in this chapter, it was mentioned that security associations are unidirectional. This causes Router B to set up two security associations, one for inbound ESP packets and one for outbound ESP packets. The Security Association Database (SAD) for IKE can be viewed as well by issuing the **show crypto isakmp sa** command. Issuing the command on Router B displays the output seen in Listing 6.9.

Listing 6.9 IKE security association database.

```
#show crypto isakmp sa
    dst            src           state     conn-id   slot
10.0.30.200    10.0.30.201     QM_IDLE      16        0
!
```

The connection state of an IKE security association, displayed in state field, can vary depending on which Phase and mode the security association was negotiated over. All security association states for each entry contained within the database are listed in Table 6.2.

Table 6.2 Security association states.

Phase	Mode	State	Description
Phase 1	Main	**MM_NO_STATE**	The IKE SA has been created, yet nothing else has happened.
		MM_SA_SETUP	Parameters of the IKE SA have been agreed upon by each peer.
		MM_KEY_EXCH	Each peer has exchanged Diffie-Hellman public keys and have generated a shared secret.
		MM_KEY_AUTH	The IKE SA has been authenticated. If this router initiated the exchange, the state transitions immediately to **QM_IDLE** and a quick mode exchange begins.
	Aggressive	**AG_NO_STATE**	The IKE SA has been created, yet nothing else has happened.
		AG_INIT_EXCH	Peers have completed first aggressive mode exchange.
		AG_AUTH	The IKE SA has been authenticated. If this router initiated the exchange, the state transitions immediately to **QM_IDLE** and a quick mode exchange begins.

(continued)

Table 6.2   Security association states *(continued)*.

Phase	Mode	State	Description
Phase 2	Quick	**QM_IDLE**	The IKE SA is in a quiescent state; it will remain authenticated with its peer and may be used for subsequent quick mode exchanges.

The entire security association setup can take up to a minute or longer to complete, which caused the Ping request in Listing 6.3 fail. After the security associations are complete, the Ping, or any traffic that matched an entry in the access list, would flow as normal.

The network in Figure 6.7 displays three routers connected to each other using a WAN connection. The layer 2 media of exchange is configured as a full mesh, allowing full communication between each host within each network. Hosts in the 192.168.10.0 network behind Router A are configured to communicate with the hosts in both the 192.168.11.0 network behind Router B and the 192.168.12.0 network behind Router C. Hosts within the 192.168.11.0 and 192.168.12.0 networks are configured in the same manner. The company that owns these routers has determined that all traffic between hosts that is exchanged via the WAN is to be protected by the services of IKE and IPSec. To meet the requirements of the company, a creative configuration of IPSec must be used.

Both IPSec and IKE permit the configuration of multiple crypto policies and maps. This is accomplished through the effective use of the *sequence-number* parameter. Listings 6.10 through Listing 6.12 display the configuration of each router to the requirements outlined earlier.

Listing 6.10   IPSec configuration of Router A.

```
hostname Router-A
!
username ipsec privilege 15 password 0 ipsec
memory-size iomem 10
ip subnet-zero
ip tcp synwait-time 10
no ip domain-lookup
!
crypto isakmp policy 10
hash md5
encryption des
groups 2
```

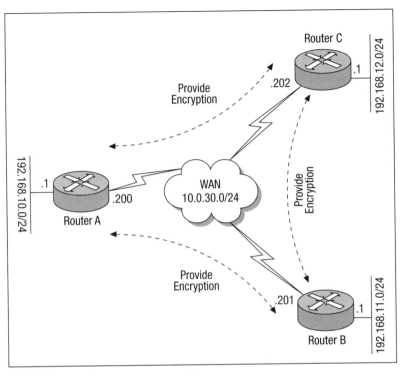

Figure 6.7   Full mesh IPSec network.

```
authentication pre-share
!
crypto isakmp key AandBkey address 10.0.30.201
crypto isakmp key AandCkey address 10.0.30.202
!
crypto ipsec transform-set routerb esp-des esp-md5-hmac
crypto ipsec transform-set routerc esp-des esp-md5-hmac
!
crypto map mesh 10 ipsec-isakmp
set peer 10.0.30.201
set transform-set routerb
match address 100
!
crypto map mesh 11 ipsec-isakmp
set peer 10.0.30.202
set transform-set routerc
match address 101
!
interface Ethernet0/1
ip address 192.168.10.1 255.255.255.0
no ip directed-broadcast
```

```
ip nat inside
!
interface Serial0
ip address 10.0.30.200 255.255.255.0
no ip directed-broadcast
ip nat outside
no ip mroute-cache
no fair-queue
crypto map mesh
!
ip nat inside source route-map donotnat interface Serial0 -
 overload
ip classless
ip route 192.168.11.0 255.255.255.0 10.0.30.201
ip route 192.168.12.0 255.255.255.0 10.0.30.202
no ip http server
!
access-list 100 permit ip 192.168.10.0 0.0.0.255 192.168.11.0 -
 0.0.0.255
access-list 101 permit ip 192.168.10.0 0.0.0.255 192.168.12.0 -
 0.0.0.255
access-list 102 deny ip 192.168.10.0 0.0.0.255 192.168.11.0 -
 0.0.0.255
access-list 102 deny ip 192.168.10.0 0.0.0.255 192.168.12.0 -
 0.0.0.255
access-list 102 permit ip 192.168.10.0 0.0.0.255 any
!
route-map donotnat permit 10
  match ip address 102
```

Listing 6.11   IPSec configuration of Router B.

```
hostname Router-B
!
username ipsec privilege 15 password 0 ipsec
ip subnet-zero
ip tcp synwait-time 10
no ip domain-lookup
!
crypto isakmp policy 11
hash md5
encryption des
groups 2
authentication pre-share
!
crypto isakmp key AandBkey address 10.0.30.200
```

```
crypto isakmp key BandCkey address 10.0.30.202
!
crypto ipsec transform-set routera esp-des esp-md5-hmac
crypto ipsec transform-set routerc esp-des esp-md5-hmac
!
crypto map mesh 11 ipsec-isakmp
set peer 10.0.30.200
set transform-set routera
match address 100
!
crypto map mesh 12 ipsec-isakmp
set peer 10.0.30.202
set transform-set routerc
match address 101
!
interface Ethernet0/1
ip address 192.168.11.1 255.255.255.0
no ip directed-broadcast
ip nat inside
!
interface Serial0/0
ip address 10.0.30.201 255.255.255.0
no ip directed-broadcast
ip nat outside
no ip mroute-cache
no fair-queue
crypto map mesh
!
ip nat inside source route-map donotnat interface Serial0/0 -
 overload
ip classless
ip route 192.168.10.0 255.255.255.0 10.0.30.200
ip route 192.168.12.0 255.255.255.0 10.0.30.202
no ip http server
!
access-list 100 permit ip 192.168.11.0 0.0.0.255 192.168.10.0 -
 0.0.0.255
access-list 101 permit ip 192.168.11.0 0.0.0.255 192.168.12.0 -
 0.0.0.255
access-list 102 deny ip 192.168.11.0 0.0.0.255 192.168.10.0 -
 0.0.0.255
access-list 102 deny ip 192.168.11.0 0.0.0.255 192.168.12.0 -
 0.0.0.255
access-list 102 permit ip 192.168.11.0 0.0.0.255 any
!
route-map donotnat permit 11
  match ip address 102
```

Listing 6.12   IPSec configuration of Router C.

```
hostname Router-C
!
username ipsec privilege 15 password 0 ipsec
memory-size iomem 10
ip subnet-zero
ip tcp synwait-time 10
no ip domain-lookup
!
crypto isakmp policy 12
hash md5
encryption des
groups 2
authentication pre-share
!
crypto isakmp key BandCkey address 10.0.30.201
crypto isakmp key AandCkey address 10.0.30.200
!
crypto ipsec transform-set routera esp-des esp-md5-hmac
crypto ipsec transform-set routerb esp-des esp-md5-hmac
!
crypto map mesh 12 ipsec-isakmp
set peer 10.0.30.200
set transform-set routera
match address 110
!
crypto map mesh 13 ipsec-isakmp
set peer 10.0.30.201
set transform-set routerb
match address 111
!
interface Ethernet1
ip address 192.168.12.1 255.255.255.0
no ip directed-broadcast
ip nat inside
!
interface Serial1/0
ip address 10.0.30.202 255.255.255.0
no ip directed-broadcast
ip nat outside
no ip mroute-cache
no fair-queue
crypto map mesh
!
ip nat inside source route-map donotnat interface Serial1/0 -
overload
ip classless
```

```
ip route 192.168.10.0 255.255.255.0 10.0.30.200
ip route 192.168.11.0 255.255.255.0 10.0.30.201
no ip http server
!
access-list 110 permit ip 192.168.12.0 0.0.0.255 192.168.10.0 -
  0.0.0.255
access-list 111 permit ip 192.168.12.0 0.0.0.255 192.168.11.0 -
  0.0.0.255
access-list 112 deny ip 192.168.12.0 0.0.0.255 192.168.10.0 -
  0.0.0.255
access-list 112 deny ip 192.168.12.0 0.0.0.255 192.168.11.0 -
  0.0.0.255
access-list 112 permit ip 192.168.12.0 0.0.0.255 any
!
route-map donotnat permit 12
  match ip address 112
```

These configurations define multiple crypto maps with different sequence numbers defined for each crypto map. This allows each router to configure IPSec parameters accordingly on a per-host basis. To view the security associations that IKE has set up for each router, issue the **show crypto isakmp sa** command on each router. Issuing the command on Router B displays the following output.

```
#show crypto isakmp sa
      dst            src          state    conn-id   slot
10.0.30.200    10.0.30.201      QM_IDLE      16       0
10.0.30.202    10.0.30.201      QM_IDLE      17       0
!
```

Related solution:	*Found on page:*
Configuring Network Address Translation (NAT)	138

Configuring IPSec Using Manual Keys

The use of IKE enhances IPSec by providing additional features, flexibility, and ease of configuration for IPSec standards. Some network equipment may not support IKE, and in these instances, IPSec can be configured without IKE. If IKE is not used for establishing the security associations, there is no negotiation of security associations, so the configuration information in both systems must be the same in order for traffic to be processed successfully by IPSec.

IKE provides for the dynamic creation of SAs and is the preferred method to use with IPSec. This section covers manual configuration. Manual keying involves a direct exchange of keys between IPSec peers, and this method of key exchange is not a very scalable solution for IPSec. A benefit of manual keying is that it allows Cisco networking equipment to work with other vendors' networking equipment when the services of IPSec are needed and IKE cannot be used. The process of configuring manual IPSec involves the configuration of remote keys during the initial IPSec configuration of the routers. Each crypto map requires multiple keys. For AH authentication, there is a key for both the outbound and inbound sessions. For ESP, there is a cipher and authentication key for both the outbound and inbound sessions.

To configure manual IPSec keys between IPSec peers, follow these steps:

1. To create the crypto map entry and enter the crypto map configuration mode, use the following command:

   ```
   crypto map map-name seq-num ipsec-manual
   ```

   The **map-name** defines the name that identifies the crypto map set. The **seq-num** parameter is the number that is assigned to this crypto map; it should not be chosen arbitrarily because this number is used to rank multiple crypto map entries within a crypto map set, and a crypto map entry with a lower **seq-num** is evaluated before a map entry with a higher **seq-num**. The **ipsec-manual** parameter specifies that IKE will not be used to establish the security associations for traffic that is matched by this crypto map and the security associations will be created by a manual process. Use of this command moves you into crypto map configuration mode.

2. In crypto map configuration mode, use the following command to specify an extended access list for a crypto map entry that matches packets for which encryption should be performed:

   ```
   match address <access-list number | name>
   ```

3. To specify an IPSec peer, use this command in crypto map configuration mode:

   ```
   set peer <ip address | hostname>
   ```

You can specify the remote IPSec peer by its hostname if the hostname is mapped to the peer's IP address in a domain name server (DNS) or you manually map the hostname to the IP address with the **ip host** command that was discussed earlier. When configuring manual IPSec to set up security associations, you can specify only one peer per crypto map.

4. To specify which transform sets can be used with the crypto map entry, use the following command:

```
set transform set <transform-set-name1> -
  <transform-set-name2…. transform-set-name6>
```

List multiple transform sets in order of priority with the highest-priority transform set listed first. When configuring manual IPSec to set up security associations, you can specify one transform set per crypto map.

5. Use one of the following commands to manually specify the session keys for AH or ESP. The **ah** parameter sets the session key for the Authentication Header protocol:

```
set session-key <inbound | outbound> ah <spi> <hex-key-string>
```

The **esp** parameter sets the session key for the Encapsulating Security Protocol:

```
set session-key <inbound | outbound> esp <spi> cipher -
  <hex-key-string> authenticator <hex-key-string>
```

When defining the session key for either the AH protocol or the ESP protocol, both an inbound and outbound key must be configured for each peer. Figure 6.8 displays a network with two routers separated by a WAN that must protect data via the use of IPSec. The routers will be configured to use IPSec with manual keys.

Because the configuration of manual IPSec is different when using the Authentication Header protocol as opposed to the Encapsulating Security Payload within a transform set, each configuration will be discussed separately. Listing 6.13 and Listing 6.14 display the manual IPSec configurations of Router 1 and Router 2 in Figure 6.8 using AH transform sets.

NOTE: *The configurations in Listing 6.13 and Listing 6.14 are not recommended for a production environment because each configuration provides authentication services only for the IP packet.*

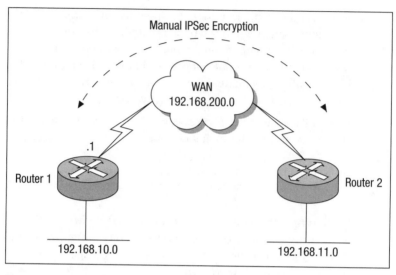

Figure 6.8 Network using manual IPSec keys.

Listing 6.13 Manual AH configuration of Router 1.

```
hostname Router-1
!
username ipsec privilege 15 password 0 ipsec
memory-size iomem 10
ip subnet-zero
ip tcp synwait-time 10
no ip domain-lookup
!
crypto ipsec transform-set manual ah-sha-hmac

!
crypto map toR2 10 ipsec-manual
set peer 192.168.200.2
set transform-set manual
match address 110
set session-key inbound ah 3073 -
   CCCC1234567890CCCC1234567890CCCC1234567890CCCC
set session-key outbound ah 3072 -
   DDDD1234567890DDDD1234567890DDDD1234567890DDD1
!
interface Ethernet1
ip address 192.168.10.1 255.255.255.128
no ip directed-broadcast

!
interface Serial1/0
```

```
ip address 192.168.200.1 255.255.255.0
no ip directed-broadcast

no ip mroute-cache
no fair-queue
crypto map mesh
!
ip classless
!
access-list 110 permit ip 192.168.10.0 0.0.0.255 192.168.11.0 -
   0.0.0.255
!
```

Listing 6.14   Manual AH configuration of Router 2.

```
hostname Router-2
!
username ipsec privilege 15 password 0 ipsec
memory-size iomem 10
ip subnet-zero
ip tcp synwait-time 10
no ip domain-lookup
!
crypto ipsec transform-set manual ah-sha-hmac
!
crypto map toR1 10 ipsec-manual
set peer 192.168.200.1
set transform-set manual
match address 101
set session-key inbound ah 3072 -
   DDDD1234567890DDDD1234567890DDDD1234567890DDD1
set session-key outbound ah 3073 -
   CCCC1234567890CCCC1234567890CCCC1234567890CCCC
!
interface Ethernet1/0
ip address 192.168.11.1 255.255.255.128
no ip directed-broadcast

!
interface Serial0/0
ip address 192.168.200.2 255.255.255.0
no ip directed-broadcast

no ip mroute-cache
no fair-queue
crypto map mesh
!
```

6. Internet Protocol Security

```
ip classless
!
access-list 101 permit ip 192.168.11.0 0.0.0.255 192.168.10.0 -
  0.0.0.255
!
```

Access lists are read in sequential order by a router; as such, any packet in Listing 6.14 that has a source IP address that is within the **192.168.11.0** subnet with a destination IP address within the **192.168.10.0** subnet will match access list 101 (which is defined under **crypto map toR1**) and create a match rule for IPSec, thus allowing IPSec to provide authentication services on the packet. Any other packet that does not match the permit statement within access list 101 will not be protected by IPSec because of the **implicit deny any** at the end of the access list. Security associations established via the use of manual IPSec do not expire (whereas security associations established via IKE do), and an inbound session key configured on one IPSec peer must match the outbound session key configured on the remote IPSec peer. To view the manual security associations established on each router, you must issue the **show crypto ipsec sa** command. Issuing the **show crypto ipsec sa** command on Router 2 displays the output in Listing 6.15.

Listing 6.15   Manual security associations on Router 2.

```
Router-2#sh crypto ipsec sa

interface: Serial0/0
Crypto map tag: toR1, local addr. 192.168.200.2
!
local  ident: (192.168.11.0/255.255.255.0/0/0)
remote ident: (192.168.10.0/255.255.255.0/0/0)
current_peer: 192.168.200.1
PERMIT, flags={origin_is_acl,}
pkts encaps: 117, pkts encrypt: 49, pkts digest 117
pkts decaps: 116, pkts decrypt: 48, pkts verify 116
pkts compressed: 0, pkts decompressed: 0
pkts not compressed: 0, pkts compr. failed: 0, -
  pkts decompress failed: 0
send errors 1, recv errors 0
!
local crypto endpt.: 192.168.200.2, -
  remote crypto endpt.: 192.168.200.1
path mtu 1500, media mtu 1500
current outbound spi: C01
!
```

```
inbound esp sas:
!
inbound ah sas:
spi: 0xC00(3072)
transform: ah-sha-hmac ,
in use settings ={Tunnel,}
slot: 0, conn id: 2001, flow_id: 1, crypto map: toR1
no sa timing
replay detection support: Y
!
inbound pcp sas:
!
outbound esp sas:
!
outbound ah sas:
spi: 0xC01(3073)
transform: ah-sha-hmac,
in use settings ={Tunnel,}
slot: 0, conn id: 2000, flow_id: 2, crypto map: toR1
no sa timing
replay detection support: Y
!
outbound pcp sas:
!
Router-2#
!
```

Notice the highlighted lines in Listing 6.15; each of these lines state that the security association for inbound and outbound traffic do not timeout, unlike security associations created using IKE. During the configuration of Router 2 in Listing 6.14, the **debug crypto ipsec**, **debug crypto engine**, and **debug crypto key-exchange** commands were used to verify that both routers were configured correctly. The output from those commands can be seen in Listing 6.16.

Listing 6.16   Security association process on Router 2.

```
Router-2#debug crypto ipsec
Crypto IPSEC debugging is on
Router-2#debug crypto engine
Crypto Engine debugging is on
Router-2#debug crypto key-exchange
Crypto Key Exchange debugging is on
!
: IPSEC(sa_request): ,
  (key eng. msg.) src= 192.168.200.2, dest= 192.168.200.1,
   src_proxy= 192.168.11.0/255.255.255.0/0/0 (type=4),
```

```
          dest_proxy= 192.168.10.0/255.255.255.0/0/0 (type=4),
          protocol= AH, transform= ah-sha-hmac,
          lifedur= 3600s and 4608000kb,
          spi= 0x173715C3(389486019), conn_id= 0, keysize= 0,
          flags= 0x4004
    : IPSEC(key_engine): got a queue event...
    : IPSEC(initialize_sas):,
          (key eng. msg.) src= 192.168.200.2, dest= 192.168.200.1,
          src_proxy= 192.168.11.0/255.255.255.0/0/0 (type=4),
          dest_proxy= 192.168.10.0/255.255.255.0/0/0 (type=4),
          protocol= AH, transform= ah-sha-hmac,
          lifedur= 3600s and 4608000kb,
          spi= 0xC01(3073), conn_id= 2000, keysize= 0, flags= 0x4
    : IPSEC(initialize_sas):,
          (key eng. msg.) dest= 192.168.200.2, src= 192.168.200.1,
          dest_proxy= 192.168.11.0/255.255.255.0/0/0 (type=4),
          src_proxy= 192.168.10.0/255.255.255.0/0/0 (type=4),
          protocol= AH, transform= ah-sha-hmac,
          lifedur= 3600s and 4608000kb,
          spi= 0xC00(3072), conn_id= 2001, keysize= 0, flags= 0x4
    : IPSEC(create_sa): sa created,
          (sa) sa_dest= 192.168.200.1, sa_prot= 51,
          sa_spi= 0xC01(3073),
          sa_trans= ah-sha-hmac, sa_conn_id= 2000
    : IPSEC(create_sa): sa created,
          (sa) sa_dest= 192.168.200.2, sa_prot= 51,
          sa_spi= 0xC00(3072),
          sa_trans= ah-sha-hmac, sa_conn_id= 2001
```

The manual IPSec configurations of Router 1 and Router 2 in Listings 6.13 and 6.14, which used AH only to provide authentication services, do not provide the strongest form of encryption services. In fact, the configurations did not provide any encryption services; they provided only authentication. To provide the encryption services, the use of ESP is needed.

Router 1 and Router 2 in Figure 6.8 will be configured to provide the security services of both AH and ESP. The crypto map that is defined for each router will make use of a transform set that includes an ESP encryption protocol, and as such, each router will define IPSec keys for ESP encryption for both inbound and outbound traffic. The transform set will also include an ESP authentication protocol, so an IPSec key for ESP authentication for inbound and outbound traffic must be defined as well. The configuration of the AH protocol will remain the same as they are in Listing 6.13 and 6.14. The manual AH and ESP configuration of Router 1 and Router 2 are displayed in Listing 6.17 and Listing 6.18.

Listing 6.17   Manual AH and ESP configuration of Router 1.

```
hostname Router-1
!
username ipsec privilege 15 password 0 ipsec
memory-size iomem 10
ip subnet-zero
ip tcp synwait-time 10
no ip domain-lookup
!
crypto ipsec transform-set manual ah-sha-hmac esp-des -
esp-sha-hmac

!
crypto map toR2 10 ipsec-manual
set peer 192.168.200.2
set transform-set manual
match address 110
set session-key inbound esp 4096 cipher -
BBBB1234567890BBBB1234567890BBBB1234567890BBB0 authenticator -
1234567890BBBB1234567890BBBB1234567890BBBB1234
set session-key outbound esp 4098 cipher -
AAAA1234567890AAAA1234567890AAAA1234567890AAA0 authenticator -
1234567890AAAA1234567890AAAA1234567890AAAA1234
set session-key inbound ah 3073 -
CCCC1234567890CCCC1234567890CCCC1234567890CCCC
set session-key outbound ah 3072 -
DDDD1234567890DDDD1234567890DDDD1234567890DDD1
!
interface Ethernet1
ip address 192.168.10.1 255.255.255.128
no ip directed-broadcast
ip nat inside
!
interface Serial1/0
ip address 192.168.200.1 255.255.255.0
no ip directed-broadcast
ip nat outside
no ip mroute-cache
no fair-queue
crypto map mesh
!
ip nat inside source route-map donotnat interface Serial1/0 -
overload
ip classless
!
access-list 110 permit ip 192.168.10.0 0.0.0.255 192.168.11.0 -
0.0.0.255
```

```
access-list 112 deny ip 192.168.10.0 0.0.0.255 192.168.11.0 -
0.0.0.255
access-list 112 permit ip 192.168.10.0 0.0.0.255 any
!
route-map donotnat permit 10
  match ip address 112
```

Listing 6.18   Manual AH and ESP configuration of Router 2.

```
hostname Router-2
!
username ipsec privilege 15 password 0 ipsec
memory-size iomem 10
ip subnet-zero
ip tcp synwait-time 10
no ip domain-lookup
!
crypto ipsec transform-set manual ah-sha-hmac esp-des -
 esp-sha-hma
!
crypto map toR1 10 ipsec-manual
set peer 192.168.200.1
set transform-set manual
match address 101
set session-key inbound esp 4098 cipher -
 AAAA1234567890AAAA1234567890AAAA1234567890AAA0 authenticator -
 1234567890AAAA1234567890AAAA1234567890AAAA1234
set session-key outbound esp 4096 cipher -
 BB1234567890BBBB1234567890BBBB1234567890BBB0 authenticator -
 1234567890BBBB1234567890BBBB1234567890BBBB1234
set session-key inbound ah 3072 -
 DDDD1234567890DDDD1234567890DDDD1234567890DDD1
set session-key outbound ah 3073 -
 CCCC1234567890CCCC1234567890CCCC1234567890CCCC
!
interface Ethernet1/0
ip address 192.168.11.1 255.255.255.128
no ip directed-broadcast
ip nat inside
!
interface Serial0/0
ip address 192.168.200.2 255.255.255.0
no ip directed-broadcast
ip nat outside
no ip mroute-cache
no fair-queue
crypto map mesh
```

```
!
ip nat inside source route-map donotnat interface Serial0/0 -
overload
ip classless
!
access-list 101 permit ip 192.168.11.0 0.0.0.255 192.168.10.0 -
0.0.0.255
access-list 102 deny ip 192.168.10.0 0.0.0.255 192.168.11.0 -
0.0.0.255
access-list 102 permit ip 192.168.10.0 0.0.0.255 any
!
route-map donotnat permit 10
  match ip address 102
```

Again, security associations established via the use of manual IPSec do
not expire (whereas security associations established via IKE do) and
an inbound session key configured on one IPSec peer must match the
outbound session key configured on the remote IPSec peer. To view
the manual security associations established on each router, you must
issue the **show crypto ipsec sa** command. Issuing the **show crypto
ipsec sa** command on Router 1 displays the output in Listing 6.19.

Listing 6.19   Manual security associations on Router 1.

```
Router-1#sh crypto ipsec sa

interface: Ethernet0/0
    Crypto map tag: toR2, local addr. 192.168.200.1
local  ident: (192.168.10.0/255.255.255.0/0/0)
remote ident: (192.168.11.0/255.255.255.0/0/0)
current_peer: 192.168.200.2
PERMIT, flags={origin_is_acl,}
pkts encaps: 705, pkts encrypt: 705, pkts digest 705
pkts decaps: 699, pkts decrypt: 699, pkts verify 699
pkts compressed: 0, pkts decompressed: 0
pkts not compressed: 0, pkts compr. failed: 0,
pkts decompress failed: 0
send errors 0, #recv errors 0
!
local crypto endpt.: 192.168.200.1,
remote crypto endpt.: 192.168.200.2
path mtu 1500, media mtu 1500
current outbound spi: 1002
!
inbound esp sas:
spi: 0x1000(4096)
transform: esp-des esp-sha-hmac,
```

6. Internet
Protocol Security

```
in use settings ={Tunnel,}
slot: 0, conn id: 2003, flow_id: 1, crypto map: toR2
no sa timing
IV size: 8 bytes
replay detection support: Y
!
inbound ah sas:
spi: 0xC01(3073)
transform: ah-sha-hmac,
in use settings ={Tunnel,}
slot: 0, conn id: 2002, flow_id: 1, crypto map: toR2
no sa timing
replay detection support: Y
inbound pcp sas:
!
outbound esp sas:
spi: 0x1002(4098)
transform: esp-des esp-sha-hmac,
in use settings ={Tunnel,}
slot: 0, conn id: 2001, flow_id: 2, crypto map: toR2
no sa timing
IV size: 8 bytes
replay detection support: Y
!
outbound ah sas:
spi: 0xC00(3072)
transform: ah-sha-hmac,
in use settings ={Tunnel,}
slot: 0, conn id: 2000, flow_id: 2, crypto map: toR2
no sa timing
replay detection support: Y
!
outbound pcp sas:
Router-1#
```

One other useful command that can be used to verify that all security associations are configured properly and that each one is active is the **show crypto engine connection active** command. This command will display the current active encrypted session connections. Issuing the command on Router 2 displays the following output:

```
Router-2#sh crypto en conn ac
!
ID   Interface    IP-Address     State Algorithm             Enc  Dec
2000 Serial0/0    192.168.200.2  set   HMAC_SHA              612  0
2001 Serial0/0    192.168.200.2  set   HMAC_SHA+DES_56_CB    612  0
2002 Serial0/0    192.168.200.2  set   HMAC_SHA              0    612
2003 Serial0/0    192.168.200.2  set   MAC_SHA+DES_56_CB     0    612
```

The ID field is the connection ID number, and each active encrypted session connection is identified by an ID number. The Interface field identifies the interface that is involved in the encrypted session connection. The IP-Address field identifies the IP address of the interface involved in the encrypted session. The State field identifies the state of the connection. The Algorithm field identifies the algorithm that is used to encrypt or to decrypt the packets. The Enc field displays the total number of outbound encrypted packets, and the Dec field displays the total number of inbound encrypted packets.

Although manual IPSec configurations allow a security administrator to have strict control over the implementation of IPSec VPNs, as well provide interoperability with any device that does not support the IPSec utility services of IKE, these advantages come with an added cost. The overhead associated with maintaining strict control over the IPSec VPNs can become burdensome as the number of VPNs the company has begins to grow. Security administrators should always be aware that when configuring manual IPSec, each router should contain a mirror copy IPSec configuration of its peer router. One of the problems associated with manual IPSec configurations is incorrectly configured keys between peers.

For instance, changing the keys on Router 2 in Listing 6.18 will result in encryption not taking place and error messages being displayed on Router 2. Listing 6.20 displays the new, incorrectly configured keys on Router 2.

Listing 6.20 Changing keys on Router 2.

```
crypto map toR1 10 ipsec-manual
no set session-key inbound esp 4098 cipher -
 AAA1234567890AAAA1234567890AAAA1234567890AAA0 authenticator -
 1234567890AAAA1234567890AAAA1234567890AAAA1234
no set session-key outbound esp 4096 cipher -
 BBBB1234567890BBBB1234567890BBBB1234567890BBB0 authenticator -
 1234567890BBBB1234567890BBBB1234567890BBBB1234
no set session-key inbound ah 3072 -
 DDD1234567890DDDD1234567890DDDD1234567890DDD1
no set session-key outbound ah 3073-
 CCCC1234567890CCCC1234567890CCCC1234567890CCCC
!
set session-key inbound esp 4098 cipher -
 11111111111111111111111111111111111111111111111111 authenticator -
 11111111111111111111111111111111111111111111111111
set session-key outbound esp 4096 cipher -
 22222222222222222222222222222222222222222222222222 authenticator -
 22222222222222222222222222222222222222222222222222
set session-key inbound ah 3072 -
```

```
3333333333333333333333333333333333333333333333
set session-key outbound ah 3073 -
4444444444444444444444444444444444444444444444
```

First, the original keys were deleted using the **no form the set session-key** command, and then the new keys were added into the configuration. As the keys are being changed, Router 2 begins to delete each security association it had configured. This can be seen in Listing 6.21 by issuing the **debug crypto ipsec** and **debug crypto engine** commands.

Listing 6.21   Router 2 deleting security associations.

```
: IPSEC(delete_sa): deleting SA,
  (sa) sa_dest= 192.168.200.1, sa_prot= 51,
    sa_spi= 0xC01(3073),
    sa_trans= ah-sha-hmac, sa_conn_id= 2000
: IPSEC(delete_sa): deleting SA,
  (sa) sa_dest= 192.168.200.1, sa_prot= 50,
    sa_spi= 0x1000(4096),
    sa_trans= esp-des esp-sha-hmac, sa_conn_id= 2001
: IPSEC(delete_sa): deleting SA,
  (sa) sa_dest= 192.168.200.2, sa_prot= 51,
    sa_spi= 0xC00(3072),
    sa_trans= ah-sha-hmac , sa_conn_id= 2002
: IPSEC(delete_sa): deleting SA,
  (sa) sa_dest= 192.168.200.2, sa_prot= 50,
    sa_spi= 0x1002(4098),
    sa_trans=esp-des esp-sha-hmac, sa_conn_id=2003
```

Router 2 at this point has deleted each of the existing security associations it had configured for its peer IPSec router. After the new keys (which are incorrect) are configured on Router 2 under the crypto map and a packet that matches the encryption access list is received on the router, Router 2 should attempt to set a security association with Router 1. However, the security association attempt should fail because of incorrectly configured keys between the routers. This process can be seen in the output in Listing 6.22.

Listing 6.22   Router 2's failed attempt to set a security association.

```
: IPSEC(sa_request): ,
  (key eng. msg.) src= 192.168.200.2, dest= 192.168.200.1,
    src_proxy= 192.168.11.0/255.255.255.0/0/0 (type=4),
    dest_proxy= 192.168.10.0/255.255.255.0/0/0 (type=4),
    protocol= AH, transform= ah-sha-hmac,
    lifedur= 3600s and 4608000kb,
    spi= 0x1028254B(271066443), conn_id= 0, keysize= 0,
```

```
        flags= 0x4004
: IPSEC(sa_request):,
  (key eng. msg.) src= 192.168.200.2, dest= 192.168.200.1,
    src_proxy= 192.168.11.0/255.255.255.0/0/0 (type=4),
    dest_proxy= 192.168.10.0/255.255.255.0/0/0 (type=4),
    protocol= ESP, transform= esp-des esp-sha-hmac,
    lifedur= 3600s and 4608000kb,
    spi= 0x2360B83(37096323), conn_id= 0, keysize= 0,
    flags= 0x4004
: IPSEC(manual_key_stuffing): keys missing for -
  addr 192.168.200.2/prot 50/spi 0.
: IPSEC(sa_request):,
  (key eng. msg.) src= 192.168.200.2, dest= 192.168.200.1,
    src_proxy= 192.168.11.0/255.255.255.0/0/0 (type=4),
    dest_proxy= 192.168.10.0/255.255.255.0/0/0 (type=4),
    protocol= AH, transform= ah-sha-hmac,
    lifedur= 3600s and 4608000kb,
    spi= 0xB2C0887(187435143), conn_id= 0, keysize= 0,
    flags= 0x4004
: IPSEC(sa_request):,
  (key eng. msg.) src= 192.168.200.2, dest= 192.168.200.1,
    src_proxy= 192.168.11.0/255.255.255.0/0/0 (type=4),
    dest_proxy= 192.168.10.0/255.255.255.0/0/0 (type=4),
    protocol= ESP, transform= esp-des esp-sha-hmac,
    lifedur= 3600s and 4608000kb,
    spi= 0x4AD1EE4(78454500), conn_id= 0, keysize= 0,
    flags= 0x4004
: IPSEC(manual_key_stuffing): keys missing for -
    addr 192.168.200.2/prot 50/spi 0.
```

Configuring Tunnel EndPoint Discovery

The ability to automate as much of the configuration and maintenance of IPSec VPNs as possible is important for administrators who are challenged to minimize their administrative and operations costs and at the same time layer sophisticated IP services, such as IPSec. One IPSec enhancement that helps simplify VPN configuration is Tunnel EndPoint Discovery (TED), which was available beginning in Cisco IOS software version 12.0(5)T. Tunnel EndPoint Discovery allows IPSec to scale to large networks by reducing multiple encryption schemes, reducing the setup time, and allowing for simple configurations on participating peer routers. Each IPSec-enabled router has a simple configuration that defines the local network that the router is protecting and the IPSec transforms that are required. Tunnel

EndPoint Discovery is recommended for use with networks in which the IPSec peers are not always predetermined.

To understand how Tunnel EndPoint Discovery works, I will use Figure 6.9 as an example for the rest of this discussion. In Figure 6.9, Host A behind Router A attempts to establish a session with Host B behind Router B. If Router A has not initiated encryption services before with Router B (meaning no security association is set up), it compares the IP address of the destination host, Host B in this case, to an access list that defines a range of IP addresses that determine which network devices are members of the IPSec VPN group. This is accomplished via the use of a permit statement within the access list. Upon receipt of the packet from Host A that is destined to Host B, Router A drops the packet and then sends a TED probe packet to Router B. Upon receipt, Router B drops the TED packet and sends a TED reply packet to Router A with its own IP address in the payload of the packet. When Router A receives the TED reply packet, it initiates dynamic Internet Key Exchange (IKE), which enables Router A to establish a secure network session.

To configure Tunnel EndPoint Discovery, use the following commands:

1. Configure the IKE process as explained in "Configuring IPSec using Pre-Shared Keys" earlier in this chapter.

2. Use the following command to create a dynamic crypto map entry:

```
crypto dynamic-map <dynamic-map-name> <seq-num>
```

   Use of this command places you in dynamic crypto map configuration command mode.

3. To specify which transform sets can be used with the dynamic crypto map entry, use the following command:

```
set transform set <transform-set-name1> -
    <transform-set-name2....transform-set-name6>
```

   List multiple transform sets in order of priority with the highest-priority transform set listed first.

4. In dynamic crypto map configuration mode, use this command to specify an extended access list for a crypto map entry that matches packets that should be protected by encryption:

```
match address <access-list number | name>
```

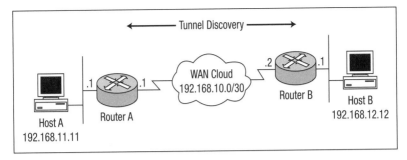

Figure 6.9   Tunnel EndPoint Discovery.

5. Use the following command to add one or more dynamic crypto map sets into a crypto map set via crypto map entries that reference the dynamic crypto map sets:

```
crypto map <map-name> <seq-num> ipsec-isakmp –
    dynamic <dynamic-map-name> discover
```

The **discover** parameter defined on the dynamic crypto map enables peer discovery.

6. Apply the crypto map to an interface using the **crypto map** *<map-name>* command. The map name specified with this command is the name of the crypto map that was created in Step 5.

Listing 6.23 and Listing 6.24 display the configuration needed to enable TED on both Router A and Router B (use Figure 6.9 as a reference).

Listing 6.23   Tunnel EndPoint Discovery configuration of Router A.

```
hostname Router-A
!
username ipsec privilege 15 password 0 ipsec
ip subnet-zero
ip tcp synwait-time 10
no ip domain-lookup
!
crypto isakmp policy 10
 authentication pre-share
 group 2
 hash sha
!
crypto isakmp key aandbkey address 0.0.0.0
!
crypto ipsec transform-set discovery esp-des esp-md5-hmac
```

```
!
crypto dynamic-map discovery-map 10
 set transform-set ted-transforms
 match address 100
!
crypto map tunnelend 10 ipsec-isakmp dynamic discovery-map -
 discover
!
interface Ethernet1
 ip address 192.168.11.1 255.255.255.0
 no ip directed-broadcast
!
interface Serial0/0
 ip address 192.168.10.1 255.255.255.0
 no ip directed-broadcast
 crypto map tunnelend
!
ip classless
ip route 0.0.0.0 0.0.0.0 192.168.10.2
no ip http server
!
access-list 100 permit ip 192.168.11.0 0.0.0.255 192.168.12.0 -
 0.0.0.255
access-list 100 permit icmp 192.168.11.0 0.0.0.255 192.168.12.0 -
 0.0.0.255
!
line con 0
login local
transport input none
line aux 0
line vty 0 4
login local
```

Listing 6.24   Tunnel EndPoint Discovery configuration of Router B.

```
hostname Router-B
!
username ipsec privilege 15 password 0 ipsec
ip subnet-zero
ip tcp synwait-time 10
no ip domain-lookup
!
crypto isakmp policy 10
 authentication pre-share
 group 2
 hash sha
!
crypto isakmp key aandbkey address 0.0.0.0
!
```

```
crypto ipsec transform-set discovery esp-des esp-md5-hmac
!
crypto dynamic-map discovery-map 10
 set transform-set discovery
 match address 110
!
crypto map tunnelend 10 ipsec-isakmp dynamic discovery-map -
 discover
!
interface Ethernet1/0
 ip address 192.168.12.1 255.255.255.0
 no ip directed-broadcast
!
interface Serial0/0
 ip address 192.168.10.2 255.255.255.0
 no ip directed-broadcast
   crypto map tunnelend
!
ip classless
ip route 0.0.0.0 0.0.0.0 192.168.10.1
no ip http server
!
access-list 100 permit ip 192.168.12.0 0.0.0.255 192.168.11.0 -
 0.0.0.255
access-list 100 permit icmp 192.168.12.0 0.0.0.255 192.168.11.0 -
 0.0.0.255
!
line con 0
login local
transport input none
line aux 0
line vty 0 4
login local
```

After Host A behind Router A attempts to initiate a connection to Host B behind Router B, dynamic IPSec security association takes place. Because Router A has not initiated encryption services before with Router B (meaning no security association is set up), Router A compares the IP address of the destination host, Host B in this case, against access list 100, which defines a range of IP addresses that determine which network devices are members of the IPSec VPN group. Upon receipt of the packet from Host A that is destined to Host B, Router A drops the packet and then sends a TED probe packet to Router B. Upon receipt, Router B drops the TED packet and sends a TED reply packet to Router A with its own IP address in the payload of the packet. When Router A receives the TED reply packet, it initiates dynamic Internet Key Exchange (IKE), which enables Router A to establish a secure network session. You can verify that a secure session has been set up by issuing the **debug crypto ipsec**, **debug crypto isakmp**, and **debug crypto engine** commands on Router A and having Host A attempt to connect Host B. Listing 6.25 displays the complete output of the Tunnel EndPoint Discovery process.

Listing 6.25   Complete Tunnel EndPoint process for Router A.

```
: IPSEC(tunnel discover request):,
(key eng. msg.) src= 192.168.11.1, dest= 192.168.12.1,
 src_proxy= 192.168.11.0/255.255.255.0/0/0 (type=4),
 dest_proxy= 192.168.10.1/255.255.255.255/0/0 (type=1),
 protocol= ESP, transform= esp-des esp-md5-hmac,
 lifedur= 3600s and 4608000kb,
 spi= 0x0(0), conn_id= 0, keysize= 0, flags= 0x4004
dest=Ethernet0/0:192.168.10.2
: ISAKMP: received ke message (1/1)
: ISAKMP: GOT A PEER DISCOVERY MESSAGE FROM THE SA MANAGER!!!
: src = 192.168.11.1 to 192.168.12.1, protocol 3, transform 2,
 hmac 1
: proxy source is 192.168.11.0/255.255.255.0 and my address
 (not used now) is 192.168.10.1
: ISAKMP: local port 500, remote port 500
: ISAKMP (2): ID payload
        next-payload : 5
        type         : 1
        protocol     : 17
        port         : 500
        length       : 8
: ISAKMP (2): Total payload length: 12
: 1st ID is 192.168.10.1
: 2nd ID is 192.168.11.0    /255.255.255.0
: ISAKMP (0:2): beginning peer discovery exchange
: ISAKMP (2): sending packet to 192.168.12.1 (I) PEER_DISCOVERY
 via Ethernet0/0:192.168.10.2
: ISAKMP (2): received packet from 192.168.10.2(I)PEER_DISCOVERY
: ISAKMP (0:2): processing vendor id payload
: ISAKMP (0:2): speaking to another IOS box!
: ISAKMP (0:2): processing ID payload. message ID = 0
: ISAKMP (0:2): processing ID payload. message ID = -1594735024
: ISAKMP (2): ID_IPV4_ADDR_SUBNET dst 192.168.12.0/255.255.255.0
 prot 0 port 0
: ISAKMP (2): received response to my peer discovery probe!
: ISAKMP: initiating IKE to 192.168.10.2 in response to probe.
: ISAKMP: local port 500, remote port 500
: ISAKMP (0:2): created new SA after peer-discovery
 with 192.168.10.2
```

```
: ISAKMP (3): sending packet to 192.168.10.2 (I) MM_NO_STATE
: ISAKMP (0:2): deleting SA reason "delete_me flag/throw" state
  (I) PEER_DISCOVERY   (peer 192.168.12.1) input queue 0
: ISAKMP (3): received packet from 192.168.10.2 (I) MM_NO_STATE
: ISAKMP (0:3): processing SA payload. message ID = 0
: ISAKMP (0:3): Checking ISAKMP transform 1 against priority
  10 policy
: ISAKMP:        encryption DES-CBC
: ISAKMP:        hash SHA
: ISAKMP:        default group 2
: ISAKMP:        auth pre-share
: ISAKMP (0:3): atts are acceptable. Next payload is 0
: CryptoEngine0: generate alg parameter
: CRYPTO_ENGINE: Dh Phase 1 status: 0
: CRYPTO_ENGINE: Dh Phase 1 status: 0
: ISAKMP (0:3): SA is doing pre-shared key authentication
: ISAKMP (3): SA is doing pre-shared key authentication
  using id type ID_IPV4_ADDR
: ISAKMP (3): sending packet to 192.168.10.2 (I) MM_SA_SETUP
: ISAKMP (3): received packet from 192.168.10.2 (I) MM_SA_SETUP
: ISAKMP (0:3): processing KE payload. message ID = 0
: CryptoEngine0: generate alg parameter
: ISAKMP (0:3): processing NONCE payload. message ID = 0
: CryptoEngine0: create ISAKMP SKEYID for conn id 3
: ISAKMP (0:3): SKEYID state generated
: ISAKMP (0:3): processing vendor id payload
: ISAKMP (0:3): speaking to another IOS box!
: ISAKMP (3): ID payload
        next-payload : 8
        type         : 1
        protocol     : 17
        port         : 500
        length       : 8
: ISAKMP (3): Total payload length: 12
: CryptoEngine0: generate hmac context for conn id 3
: ISAKMP (3): sending packet to 192.168.10.2 (I) MM_KEY_EXCH
: ISAKMP (0:2): purging SA.
: CryptoEngine0: delete connection 2
: ISAKMP (3): received packet from 192.168.10.2 (I) MM_KEY_EXCH
: ISAKMP (0:3): processing ID payload. message ID = 0
: ISAKMP (0:3): processing HASH payload. message ID = 0
: CryptoEngine0: generate hmac context for conn id 3
: ISAKMP (0:3): SA has been authenticated with 192.168.10.2
: ISAKMP (0:3): beginning Quick Mode exchange, M-ID of 699308944
: ISAKMP (0:3): asking for 1 spis from ipsec
: ISAKMP (0:3): had to get SPI's from ipsec.
: CryptoEngine0: clear dh number for conn id 1
```

```
:  IPSEC(key_engine): got a queue event...
:  IPSEC(spi_response): getting spi 560995998 for SA
   from 192.168.10.2    to 192.168.10.1    for prot 3
:  ISAKMP: received ke message (2/1)
:  CryptoEngine0: generate hmac context for conn id 3
:  ISAKMP (3): sending packet to 192.168.10.2 (I) QM_IDLE
:  ISAKMP (3): received packet from 192.168.10.2 (I) QM_IDLE
:  CryptoEngine0: generate hmac context for conn id 3
:  ISAKMP (0:3): processing SA payload. message ID = 699308944
:  ISAKMP (0:3): Checking IPSec proposal 1
:  ISAKMP: transform 1, ESP_DES
:  ISAKMP:    attributes in transform:
:  ISAKMP:       encaps is 1
:  ISAKMP:       SA life type in seconds
:  ISAKMP:       SA life duration (basic) of 3600
:  ISAKMP:       SA life type in kilobytes
:  ISAKMP:       SA life duration (VPI) of  0x0 0x46 0x50 0x0
:  ISAKMP:       authenticator is HMAC-MD5
:  validate proposal 0
:  ISAKMP (0:3): atts are acceptable.
:  IPSEC(validate_proposal_request): proposal part #1,
     (key eng. msg.) dest= 192.168.10.2, src= 192.168.10.1,
       dest_proxy= 192.168.12.0/255.255.255.0/0/0 (type=4),
       src_proxy= 192.168.11.0/255.255.255.0/0/0 (type=4),
       protocol= ESP, transform= esp-des esp-md5-hmac,
       lifedur= 0s and 0kb,
       spi= 0x0(0), conn_id= 0, keysize= 0, flags= 0x4
:  validate proposal request 0
:  ISAKMP (0:3): processing NONCE payload. message ID = 699308944
:  ISAKMP (0:3): processing ID payload. message ID = 699308944
:  ISAKMP (0:3): processing ID payload. message ID = 699308944
:  CryptoEngine0: generate hmac context for conn id 3
:  ipsec allocate flow 0
:  ipsec allocate flow 0
:  ISAKMP (0:3): Creating IPSec SAs
:  inbound SA from 192.168.10.2 to 192.168.10.1
   (proxy 192.168.12.0    to 192.168.11.0)
:  has spi 560995998 and conn_id 2000 and flags 4
:          lifetime of 3600 seconds
:          lifetime of 4608000 kilobytes
:          outbound SA from 192.168.10.1    to 192.168.10.2
           (proxy 192.168.11.0    to 192.168.12.0)
:          has spi 104538836 and conn_id 2001 and flags 4
:          lifetime of 3600 seconds
:          lifetime of 4608000 kilobytes
:  ISAKMP (3): sending packet to 192.168.10.2 (I) QM_IDLE
:  ISAKMP (0:3): deleting node 699308944 error FALSE reason ""
```

```
: IPSEC(key_engine): got a queue event...
: IPSEC(initialize_sas):,
  (key eng. msg.) dest= 192.168.10.1, src= 192.168.10.2,
    dest_proxy= 192.168.11.0/255.255.255.0/0/0 (type=4),
    src_proxy= 192.168.12.0/255.255.255.0/0/0 (type=4),
    protocol= ESP, transform= esp-des esp-md5-hmac,
    lifedur= 3600s and 4608000kb,
    spi= 0x21701E9E(560995998), conn_id= 2000,
    keysize= 0, flags= 0x4
: IPSEC(initialize_sas):,
  (key eng. msg.) src= 192.168.10.1, dest= 192.168.10.2,
    src_proxy= 192.168.11.0/255.255.255.0/0/0 (type=4),
    dest_proxy= 192.168.12.0/255.255.255.0/0/0 (type=4),
    protocol= ESP, transform= esp-des esp-md5-hmac,
    lifedur= 3600s and 4608000kb,
    spi= 0x63B22D4(104538836), conn_id= 2001, keysize= 0,
    flags= 0x4
: IPSEC(create_sa): sa created,
  (sa) sa_dest= 192.168.10.1, sa_prot= 50,
    sa_spi= 0x21701E9E(560995998),
    sa_trans= esp-des esp-md5-hmac, sa_conn_id= 2000
: IPSEC(create_sa): sa created,
  (sa) sa_dest= 192.168.10.2, sa_prot= 50,
    sa_spi= 0x63B22D4(104538836),
    sa_trans= esp-des esp-md5-hmac, sa_conn_id= 2001
Router-A#
```

**6. Internet
Protocol Security**

Chapter 7

Additional Access List Features

In Brief

In this chapter, I'll discuss IP access list security features. Two are slight deviations of the commonly used numbered access lists and will be discussed in detail: session filtering using reflexive access lists and lock and key security using dynamic access lists. I'll also address enhancements to access list configurations using named access lists, access list comments, and time-based access lists.

An access list is a sequential series of filters. Each filter is made up of some sort of matching criteria and action. The action within the filter is always either a permit or a deny. The criteria by which the access list matches upon can be as simple as a source address or as complex as a source address, a destination address, a protocol, a port, and flags. When access lists are configured, a packet is compared against the filter rules contained within the access list. At the first filter rule, a matching criteria is applied. If a match occurs at this rule, the packet is permitted or denied based on the configured action of the filter rule. If a match does not occur, the packet is compared against the second rule configured within the filter and the matching process is again applied. If a packet is compared against all the rules configured within the filter and a match does not occur, the router must have some default action method of determining what should happen to the packet. The configured default action for the Cisco implementation of access lists is to deny any packet that is subjected to each filter rule contained within an access list and does not match any of them. This filter rule does not display in any configured access list and is the default action for an access list. This is referred to as an **implicit deny any**.

NOTE: *Routers compare addresses against the access list conditions one by one. The order of the conditions is critical for proper operation of the access list because the first match in an access list is used. If the router does not find a match, the packet is denied because of the* **implicit deny any** *at the end of each access list.*

The two primary uses of access lists in security-related implementations are for packet filtering and traffic selection. Packet filtering helps to control a packet or flow of packets through an internetwork. This allows the router to limit network traffic, thus providing a finer granularity of control for restricting network access. Traffic selection is used to determine what traffic the router should consider "interesting" in order to invoke a certain feature or security operation.

Table 7.1   Access list type and numbers.

Access List Type	Range
Standard IP access list, Standard Vines	1–99
Extended IP access list, Extended Vines	100–199
Ethernet Type Code, Transparent Bridging Protocol Type, Source Route Bridging Protocol Type, Simple Vines	200–299
DECnet and Extended DECnet	300–399
XNS	400–499
Extended XNS	500–599
AppleTalk	600–699
Transparent Bridging Vendor Code, Source Route Bridging Vendor Code, Ethernet Address	700–799
Standard IPX	800–899
Extended IPX	900–999
IPX SAP	1000–1099
Extended Transparent Bridging	1100–1199
NLSP Route Summary	1200–1299

Access list types may be identified by either a number or a name. Table 7.1 shows the access list types and the number range available for each.

When determining whether or not to configure access lists on a production router, take the following rules into consideration prior to applying the configuration change to the router:

- *Organization*—Organization of your access lists should be such that the more specific access entries are configured first and the more general entries are listed toward the bottom of the list.

- *Precedence*—Configure your access list such that the more frequently matched conditions are placed before less frequently matched conditions. This alleviates load on the router's CPU.

- *Implicit action*—If the purpose of your access list is to deny a few devices and permit all others, you must remember to add the **permit any** statement because the access list has at the end an **implicit deny any** that will not appear in the configuration.

- *Additions*—New access list entries are always added to the end of the existing access list. When you're using numbered access, it is best to copy the access list configuration to a text editor, make the necessary changes to the access list, and then reapply the access list to the router. Access list entries cannot be selectively deleted with numbered access lists; however, they can be selectively deleted with named access lists.

Wildcard Masks

To fully understand access lists, you must first understand inverse masks, known more commonly as wildcard masks. A wildcard mask specifies which bits in an IP address should be ignored when that address is compared with another IP address. Normal IP masks that are used for subnetting use a Boolean **AND** operation to derive a network mask or a subnet address. To perform the Boolean **AND** operation, you **AND** a value of 0 to another value of 0 or 1, and the result is a value of 0. Only a value of 1 **AND**ed with another value of 1 will result in a value of 1, resulting in a value of 1 if and only if both bits are 1. A Boolean **OR** operation, which is used for wildcard masks, is the exact opposite of the **AND** operation. To perform a Boolean **OR** operation, you **OR** a value of 1 to another value of 1 or 0 and the result is a value of 1. Only a 0 **OR**ed with another 0 value will result in a 0 value, resulting in a value of 0 if and only if both bits are 0. Wildcard masks set a 0 for each bit of the address that should be matched exactly and a 1 for each bit where anything will match; the 1 bits are frequently referred to as *don't care bits* and the 0 bits are referred to as *do care* bits.

In order to define the difference between the Boolean **AND** operation and the Boolean **OR** operation, we will create a truth table. Figure 7.1 displays a truth table for the Boolean **AND** operation and the Boolean **OR** operation.

```
Boolean AND (used for subnet masks)
192.168.10.10  =  11000000101010000000101000001010
255.255.255.0  =  11111111111111111111111100000000
-------------------------------------------------
192.168.10.0   =  11000000101010000000101000000000
```

Boolean "AND"			Boolean "OR"		
	0	1		0	1
0	0	0	0	0	1
1	0	1	1	1	1

Figure 7.1   Truth table for Boolean operations.

```
Boolean OR (used for wildcard masks)
192.168.10.10   =   11000000101010000000101000001010
    0.0.0.255   =   00000000000000000000000011111111
------------------------------------------------------
192.168.10.255 =   11000000101010000000101011111111
```

Subnet masks make use of the Boolean **AND** operation to derive a network or subnet. Access lists make use of the Boolean **OR** operation, which is the inverse of the **AND** operation, to come to the same conclusion. The **AND** operation derives a network or subnet address from the host address and mask. A 1 is set in the mask to correspond to each bit of the network address, and a 0 is set for each bit of the host address. The Boolean **AND** operation is performed on each bit, and the result is the network or subnet number. The **OR** operation derives a network from the host address and inverse mask. A 0 is set in the mask to correspond to each bit of the network address, and a 1 is set for each bit of the host address. The Boolean **OR** operation is performed on each bit, and the result is the network or subnet number. In IP terms, the result of using the inverse mask is that all hosts within the 192.168.10.0 subnet are matched. Any address within the range of 192.168.10.1 through 192.168.10.254 will match that particular wildcard mask combination.

Standard Access Lists

An access list defined with a number ranging from 1 to 99 is a *standard access list*. A standard access list is used to permit or deny packets based solely on the source IP address. The source address is the number of the network or host from which the packet is being sent. The source address is followed by a wildcard mask, which is used to specify the bit positions that must match. Standard access lists can be used as either an inbound or outbound filter, or as both. When a standard access list is used as an inbound filter, the router checks the source address of the packet and compares that address with each entry within the access list. If the access list is configured with a permit statement for that source IP address, the router breaks out of the access list and processes the packet accordingly. If the access list is configured with a deny statement or does not match any other filter rule defined within the access list, the packet is dropped. When a standard access list is used as an outbound packet filter, the packet is received by the router and switched to the proper outbound interface. At this point the router will compare the source address against the filter rules contained within the access list. If the access list permits that packet, the router forwards the packet out to the interface toward its final destination, and if the packet matches a deny statement or does not match any other filter rule defined within the access list, the packet is dropped.

Standard access lists also support a feature known as *implicit masks*. Implicit masks can be used by not issuing a wildcard mask after the IP address specified within the access list. Implicit masks use a mask of 0.0.0.0, and as mentioned earlier in the section "Wildcard Masks," a mask of all 0s instructs the router to match all bits within the address in order to permit or deny the packet.

One more thing you should know about standard access lists is that they should be placed as close to the intended destination as possible.

Extended Access Lists

Extended access lists provide more flexibility in the specification of what is to be filtered. An access list defined with a number ranging from 100 to 199 is an extended IP access list. An extended access list can be configured to be static or dynamic; the default is static. An extended access list is used to permit or deny packets based on multiple factors such as protocol, source IP address, destination IP address, precedence, Type-of-Service (TOS), and port. An extended access list also supports the use of logging, which creates an informational logging message about any packet that matches a filter rule within the list.

Extended access lists can filter according to protocol and protocol features. When configuring an extended access list for different protocols, you will notice the command syntax for the extended access list for each protocol is different; these changes must be taken into consideration prior to configuring the access list or you could inadvertently open a security hole. Different IP protocol configurations will be discussed in "Immediate Solutions" later in this chapter. Protocols that can be matched upon when configuring extended access lists are listed in Table 7.2.

Extended access lists should be placed as close to the source as possible, in part because of their capability to filter packets using a finer granularity of controls. This also prevents wasting unnecessary bandwidth and processing power on packets that are to be dropped anyway.

Reflexive Access Lists

For another form of security, you can use reflexive access lists. Based on session parameters, they permit IP packets for sessions that originate from within a network but deny packets that originate from outside your network.

Table 7.2   Protocols available with extended access lists.

Name	Description
0–255	Any IP protocol number
ahp	Authentication Header Protocol
eigrp	Cisco Systems Enhanced Interior Gateway Routing Protocol
esp	Encapsulated Security Payload
gre	Cisco Systems Generic Route Encapsulation Tunneling
icmp	Internet Control Message Protocol
igmp	Internet Gateway Message Protocol
igrp	Cisco Systems Interior Gateway Routing Protocol
ip	Any Internet Protocol
ipinip	IP in IP Tunneling
nos	KA9Q NOS Compatible IP over IP Tunneling
ospf	Open Shortest Path First Routing Protocol
pcp	Payload Compression Protocol
pim	Protocol Independent Multicast
tcp	Transmission Control Protocol
udp	User Datagram Protocol

Using reflexive access lists is commonly referred to as session filtering. Reflexive access lists are most often configured on routers, which border between two different networks. They provide a certain level of security against spoofing and denial-of-service (DoS) attacks. You would typically implement reflexive access lists on a customer edge Internet router or firewall router.

Reflexive access lists share many of the features that normal access lists possess. Rules are created and evaluated in a sequential order until a match occurs, at which time no further entry evaluation takes place. There are also some differences between a reflexive access list and a normal access list. Reflexive access lists use a feature referred to as "nesting," meaning you can place them within another named extended access list. Reflexive access lists do not have an **implicit deny any** statement at the end of the list configuration, and the access list entries are created on a temporary basis.

Fundamentals of Reflexive Access Lists

Reflexive access lists are triggered when an IP packet is sent from within the inside secure network to an external destination network. If this packet is the first in the session, a temporary access list entry is

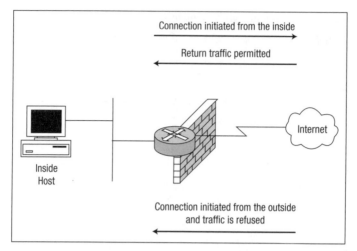

Figure 7.2   Example of traffic initiated on an internal network with reflexive access lists configured.

created. This entry will permit or deny traffic to enter back into the network if the traffic received on the interface is deemed to be part of the original session created from within the inside network; it will deny all other traffic that is not part of the original session. Figure 7.2 details the operation of reflexive access lists.

After the session has completed, the temporary access list entry is removed. If the session was opened with a TCP packet, two methods are used to tear it down. The first method will tear down the session 5 seconds after two set FIN bits are detected within the packet or the detection of a RST bit being set within the packet. The second method tears down the session if no packets for that session have been detected within a configurable timeout period. Because UDP is a connectionless-oriented protocol that does not maintain session services, if the session was opened with a UDP packet or other protocols with similar characteristics, the session is torn down when no packets for the session have been detected within a configurable timeout period. Reflexive access lists can be configured on internal interfaces or external interfaces.

Dynamic Access Lists

Dynamic access lists, commonly referred to as Lock and Key security, are a form of traffic filtering that can dynamically allow external users IP traffic that would normally be blocked by a router, to gain temporary access through the router such that it can reach its final destination. In order for this to happen, a user must first telnet to the router. The dynamic access list will then attempt to authenticate the user. If the credentials the user supplies during the authentication phase are correct, the user will be disconnected from her Telnet session and the access list will dynamically reconfigure the existing access list on the interface such that the user is allowed temporary access through the router. After a specified timeout period—either an idle timeout period or an absolute timeout period—the access list reconfigures the interface such that it returns to its original state.

NOTE: *After the user passes the authentication phase, the dynamic access list creates a temporary opening in the router by reconfiguring the interface to allow access through the router. This can potentially allow a user to spoof the source address of the legitimate user and gain unauthorized access into the internal network. IPSec termination at the router performing Lock and Key security is recommended.*

Typically, you would configure dynamic access lists when you want a specific remote host or a subset of remote hosts to be allowed access to a host or a subset of hosts within your network. This can take place via the Internet or through dedicated circuits between your network and the remote network. Dynamic access lists are also configured when you want a host or a subset of hosts within your network to gain access to a remote host or subset of remote hosts protected with a firewall.

As mentioned earlier, in order for the user to gain access through the router, she first must pass the authentication phase. Authentication can take many forms, but the most commonly used are maintaining a local user database within the router or performing authentication from a central security server such as a TACACS+ or RADIUS server. The central security server method of authentication is recommended. Dynamic access lists make use of the **autocommand** and the **access-enable** commands; these commands allow the creation of the temporary access list. There are some caveats to configuring dynamic access lists:

- You can configure only one dynamic access list for each access list.
- You cannot associate a dynamic access list to more than one access list.
- An idle timeout or an absolute timeout must be configured. The idle timeout is defined within the **autocommand** command, and the absolute timeout is configured within the **access-list** command. If neither is configured, the temporary access entry will remain indefinitely and must be cleared manually. The idle timeout value must be less than the absolute timeout value.

7. Additional Access List Features

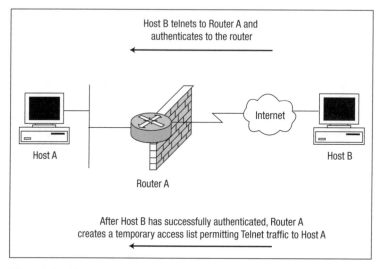

Figure 7.3 Example of Host B accessing Host A through Router A configured with dynamic access lists.

Fundamentals of Lock and Key Security

Figure 7.3 details the steps involved when a host on an outside network would like to gain authorized access to a host behind a router configured with Lock and Key security. Host B would like to access Host A behind the perimeter router, Router A, but first must be authenticated using Lock and Key Security. The steps are as follows:

1. Host B opens a Telnet session to the virtual terminal port of Router A.

2. Router A receives the Telnet request and opens a Telnet session with Host B.

3. Depending on the authentication method Router A is configured to perform, Router A asks Host B to provide the proper authentication credentials (configured on a security access server or within the local authentication database).

4. After Host B passes the authentication phase, Router A logs Host B out of the Telnet session. At this time Router A creates a temporary access list entry within the dynamic access list.

5. Host B now has a dynamic access list entry within Router A, allowing access to Host A.

6. Finally, Router A will delete the temporary access entry after the configured idle timeout period or absolute timeout period is reached.

Additional Access List Features

Prior to Cisco IOS 11.2 code, IP access list configuration was somewhat limited. However, many enhancements have since been added within the IOS. Named access lists, time-based access lists, and access lists comments are just a few.

Named Access Lists

Typical numbered access lists have a finite number of lists that can be created. As of Cisco IOS 11.2 you can identify IP access lists with an alphanumeric string rather than a number. When you use named access lists, you can configure more IP access lists in a router than you could if you were to use numbered access lists. Another advantage to using a named access list is that descriptive names can make large numbers of access lists more manageable. If you identify your access list with a name rather than a number, the mode and command syntax is slightly different. Keep a few things in mind when configuring named access lists: Not all access lists that accept a number will accept a name, and a standard access list and an extended access list cannot have the same name.

Time-Based Access Lists

Cisco IOS 12.0(1) introduced *timed-based access lists*, which are implemented based on the time range specified within the list configuration. Prior to the introduction of this feature, access lists that were defined were in effect for an infinite period of time or until they were deleted by the administrator. With time-based access list configured, administrators can control traffic according to service provider rates (which might vary during certain times of the day) and have finer granularity of control when permitting or denying certain traffic within their network.

NOTE: *The time-based access list feature is dependant on a reliable clock source. It is therefore recommended that the router be configured to utilize the features of the Network Time Protocol (NTP).*

Commented Access Lists

Commented access lists give security administrators the opportunity to configure a remark within the access list. This feature allows for ease of identification when defining an access list. The commented access list feature is configurable within both named and numbered access lists. Commented remarks within the access list are limited to 100 characters.

Immediate Solutions

Configuring Standard IP Access Lists

Standard IP access lists provide selection of packets only according to the source IP address contained within the header of the IP packet. To configure a standard IP access list to filter user traffic, use the following steps:

1. Use the following command to define the subnets or host addresses that should either be permitted or denied:

    ```
    access-list <access-list number> <permit | deny> <source
    <source wildcard mask> | any> log
    ```

    The *<access-list number>* parameter is the identification number of the access list; the number for a standard IP access list can be any number from 1 to 99. The *<source>* identifies the source IP address of the packet. The *<source wildcard>* is an optional parameter that indicates the wildcard bits that should be applied to the source; if this parameter is omitted, a mask of 0.0.0.0 is assumed. The parameter **any** can be used as an abbreviation for the **source**, which represents 0.0.0.0 255.255.255.255 in dotted decimal notation. The optional **log** parameter will generate an informational syslog message about a packet that matches the filter rule.

2. Use this command to select the input interface under which the access list will be applied:

    ```
    interface <interface name> <interface number>
    ```

3. Use the following command to apply the access list to the interface:

    ```
    ip access-group <access-list-number> <in | out>
    ```

    When the **in** parameter is defined and the router receives a packet, the router checks the source address of the packet against the access list. If the access list permits the address, the router will continue to process the packet. If the access list rejects the address, the router discards the packet and returns an "ICMP host unreachable" message. When the access list is using the **out** parameter, after receiving and routing a packet to a controlled interface, the router checks the source address of the packet against the access list. If the access list permits the address, the router forwards the packet out the interface to its final destination. If the access list rejects the address, the router discards the packet and returns an "ICMP host unreachable" message.

NOTE: *Any access list defined under an interface without a matching access list entry is interpreted by the router as a permit. This is sometimes called an undefined access list.*

Figure 7.4 displays a network with two routers, Router Raul and Router Chris. The routers will be configured to provide packet filtering using standard access lists. Router Raul should be configured to permit only traffic from the 192.168.20.0 network and deny traffic from all other networks. Router Chris will be configured to permit traffic only from 192.168.40.0 and deny traffic from all other networks.

An inbound access list filter will be applied to the FastEthernet interfaces of each router that permit packets from only the networks mentioned in the preceding paragraph and deny all other packets. The configuration of each router is shown in the following listings: Router Raul's configuration is shown in Listing 7.1 followed by Router Chris's configuration in Listing 7.2.

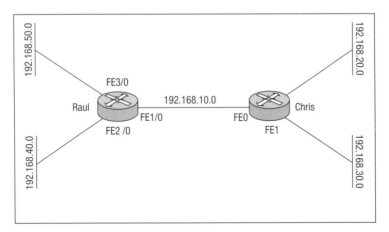

Figure 7.4   Standard access list network.

Listing 7.1   Raul's numbered access list configuration.

```
hostname Raul
!
interface FastEthernet1/0
ip address 192.168.10.2 255.255.255.0
no ip directed-broadcast
ip access-group 20 in
!
interface FastEthernet2/0
ip address 192.168.40.1 255.255.255.0
no ip directed-broadcast
!
interface FastEthernet3/0
ip address 192.168.50.1 255.255.255.0
no ip directed-broadcast
!
ip route 192.168.20.0 255.255.255.0 192.168.10.1
ip route 192.168.30.0 255.255.255.0 192.168.10.1
!
access-list 20 permit 192.168.20.0 0.0.0.255
```

Listing 7.2   Chris's numbered access list configuration.

```
hostname Chris
!
interface FastEthernet0
ip address 192.168.10.1 255.255.255.0
no ip directed-broadcast
ip access-group 40 in
!
interface Ethernet1
ip address 192.168.20.1 255.255.255.0
no ip directed-broadcast
!
interface FastEthernet1
ip address 192.168.30.1 255.255.255.0
no ip directed-broadcast
!
ip route 192.168.40.0 255.255.255.0 192.168.10.2
ip route 192.168.50.0 255.255.255.0 192.168.10.2
!
access-list 40 permit 192.168.40.0 0.0.0.255
```

To test the configuration, you can issue the **ping IP** global command. Raul is configured to accept only inbound packets with a source address within the 192.168.20.0 subnet, and Chris is configured to accept only inbound packets with a source address of 192.168.40.1. From Raul you can issue the **ping IP** command to test the configuration.

First, the configuration will be tested by using an extended ping to verify connectivity to Chris's FastEthernet1 interface. The packet will be sourced on Raul from its FastEthernet2/0 interface. Because Chris is configured to accept packets from Raul's 192.168.40.0 network, one would think that configuration would work. To verify this, the **debug IP packet** command has been issued to display the results of each packet. The output from the ping is shown in Listing 7.3.

Listing 7.3   Issuing the **ping** command on Raul.

```
Raul#debug ip packet
ip packet debugging is on
Raul#ping ip
Target ip address: 192.168.30.1
Repeat count [5]:
Datagram size [100]:
Timeout in seconds [2]:
Extended commands [n]: y
Source address or interface: 192.168.40.1
Type of service [0]:
Set DF bit in ip header? [no]:
Validate reply data? [no]:
Data pattern [0xABCD]:
Loose, Strict, Record, Timestamp, Verbose[none]:
Sweep range of sizes [n]:
Type escape sequence to abort.
Sending 5,100-byte ICMP Echo to 192.168.30.1, -
   timeout is 2 seconds:
.....
Success rate is 0 percent (0/5)
```

The output in Listing 7.3 shows that the **ping** command was not successful. To see why, you can examine the results that are returned by the **debug IP packet** command. Listing 7.4 displays the results of the command for the ping attempt in Listing 7.3.

Listing 7.4   Results of the **debug IP packet** command.

```
ip: s=192.168.40.1, d=192.168.30.1, len 100, sending
ip: s=192.168.30.1, d=192.168.40.1, len 100, access denied
ip: s=192.168.10.2, d=192.168.30.1, len 56, sending.
!
ip: s=192.168.40.1, d=192.168.30.1, len 100, sending
ip: s=192.168.30.1, d=192.168.40.1, len 100, access denied
ip: s=192.168.10.2, d=192.168.30.1, len 56, sending.
!
ip: s=192.168.40.1, d=192.168.30.1, len 100, sending
ip: s=192.168.30.1, d=192.168.40.1, len 100, access denied
ip: s=192.168.10.2, d=192.168.30.1, len 56, sending.
```

7. Additional Access List Features

In the first line of the output, the packet is sourced from IP address 192.168.40.1, and its destination is 192.168.30.1; the router tells you that it is sending the packet. The second line of the output displays the problem. The return packet is sourced from 192.168.30.1 and its destination is to IP address 192.168.40.1, but the router denies the packet. If you look back at Raul's configuration in Listing 7.1, you'll see that its access list only allows packets from the 192.168.20.0 subnet and not the 192.168.30.0 subnet.

If you were to try the **ping** command again and time source the packet from the 192.168.40.1 interface with a destination of Chris's 192.168.20.1 interface, everything should work. Listing 7.5 displays the output of issuing the **ping** command again on router Raul.

Listing 7.5   Issuing the ping command again on Raul.

```
Raul#ping ip
Target ip address: 192.168.20.1
Repeat count [5]:
Datagram size [100]:
Timeout in seconds [2]:
Extended commands [n]: y
Source address or interface: 192.168.40.1
Type of service [0]:
Set DF bit in ip header? [no]:
Validate reply data? [no]:
Data pattern [0xABCD]:
Loose, Strict, Record, Timestamp, Verbose[none]:
Sweep range of sizes [n]:
Type escape sequence to abort.
Sending 5,100-byte ICMP Echo to 192.168.20.1, -
  timeout is 2 seconds:
!!!!!
Success rate is 100 percent (5/5)
```

This time the ping worked. Listing 7.6 displays the results of the **debug IP packet** command on Raul.

Listing 7.6   Results of the debug IP packet command on Raul.

```
ip: s=192.168.40.1, d=192.168.20.1, len 100, sending
ip: s=192.168.20.1, d=192.168.40.1, len 100, rcvd 4
!
ip: s=192.168.40.1, d=192.168.20.1, len 100, sending
ip: s=192.168.20.1, d=192.168.40.1, len 100, rcvd 4
!
ip: s=192.168.40.1, d=192.168.20.1, len 100, sending
ip: s=192.168.20.1, d=192.168.40.1, len 100, rcvd 4
```

Just as expected, the router sourced the ping packet from the 192.168.40.1 interface (which is the IP address that Chris is configured to accept), and the return traffic was sourced from the 192.168.20.1 interface on Chris.

Configuring Extended IP Access Lists

Extended IP access lists match a packet according to the source and destination addresses, and optional protocol type information for finer granularity of control as opposed to standard access lists, which are only matched by the source IP address. This allows for greater flexibility in terms of packet-matching characteristics for deciding whether or not to forward a packet.

Except for configuring the packet-matching features of the access list, the process used to configure an extended IP access list is the same process used to configure a standard IP access list. To configure an extended access list, follow these steps:

1. Use the following command to define the extended access list:

   ```
   access-list <access-list-number> <deny | permit> protocol -
     <source source-wildcard> <destination destination-wildcard>-
     <precedence precedence-value> <tos tos-value> -
     <log | log-input>
   ```

2. Use this command to select the input interface under which the access list will be applied:

   ```
   interface <interface name> <interface number>
   ```

3. Use the following command to apply the access list to the interface:

   ```
   ip access-group <access-list-number> <in | out>
   ```

   When applied inbound or outbound, the access list functions the same as it does in a standard access list configuration (see Step 3 in the section "Configuring Standard IP Access Lists").

NOTE: *Any access list defined under an interface without a matching access list entry is interpreted by the router as a permit. This is sometimes called an undefined access list.*

In Step 1, the ***access-list number*** parameter is the identification number of the access list; the number range for an extended IP access list can be any number from 100 to 199. The ***protocol*** specifies either the name or number of an IP protocol that is passed in the header of the packet. The values that can be used for this field are listed in Table 7.2. The ***source*** and ***destination*** fields specify the number of the network or host in a 32-bit format. The keywords **any** and **host** may be used to simplify the configuration. The ***source-wildcard*** and the ***destination-wildcard*** fields specify the number of wildcard bits that should be applied to the source or destination. The wildcard field can be populated by specifying a 32-bit value, where the value of 1 is not counted. If the keyword **any** is used for specification of the ***source*** or ***destination***, a wildcard mask of all 1s is assumed. If the keyword **host** is used for specification of the ***source*** or ***destination***, a wildcard mask of all 0s is assumed.

Specification of the **precedence** value is optional and allows for filtering based on the configured precedence value of the packet. The ***precedence-value*** field may be populated by either a name or a number. The values that can be used to specify the precedence are listed in Table 7.3.

Table 7.3   Precedence values for extended access lists.

Name	Number
routine	0
priority	1
immediate	2
flash	3
flash-override	4
critical	5
internet	6
network	7

Specification of the **type-of-service (tos)** value configures the router to filter packets based on the **type-of-service** level configured. The ***tos-value*** field may be populated by either a name or number as well, and each of the values may be used in combination. The values that can be used to specify the **type-of-service** are listed in Table 7.4.

Table 7.4   Type-of-service values for extended access lists.

Name	Number
normal	0
min-monetary-cost	1
max-reliability	2
max-throughput	4
min-delay	8

The optional **log** parameter will generate an informational syslog message about a packet that matches the filter. Figure 7.5 displays a network in which packet filtering using extended access lists may be used. Raul should be configured to allow only connection requests to 192.168.50.50 from 192.168.30.30 and to allow only connection request from 192.168.20.21 to 192.168.40.41. Listing 7.7 shows the configuration for Raul, and Listing 7.8 shows the configuration for Chris.

Listing 7.7   Extended access list configuration of Raul.

```
!
interface FastEthernet1/0
ip address 192.168.10.2 255.255.255.0
no ip directed-broadcast
ip access-group 101 in
!
interface FastEthernet2/0
ip address 192.168.40.1 255.255.255.0
```

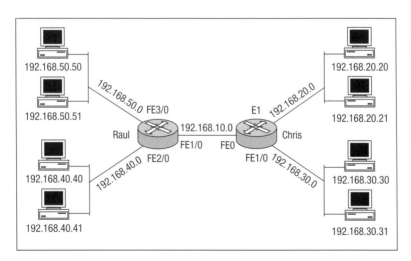

Figure 7.5   Two routers configured for extended access lists.

7. Additional Access List Features

```
no ip directed-broadcast
!
interface FastEthernet3/0
ip address 192.168.50.1 255.255.255.0
no ip directed-broadcast
!
ip route 192.168.20.0 255.255.255.0 192.168.10.1
ip route 192.168.30.0 255.255.255.0 192.168.10.1
!
access-list 101 permit ip host 192.168.30.30 host 192.168.50.50 -
    log
access-list 101 permit ip host 192.168.20.21 host 192.168.40.41 -
    log
!
```

Listing 7.8   Extended access list configuration of Chris.

```
hostname Chris
!
interface FastEthernet0
ip address 192.168.10.1 255.255.255.0
no ip directed-broadcast
!
interface Ethernet1
ip address 192.168.20.1 255.255.255.0
no ip directed-broadcast
!
interface FastEthernet1
ip address 192.168.30.1 255.255.255.0
no ip directed-broadcast
!
ip route 192.168.40.0 255.255.255.0 192.168.10.2
ip route 192.168.50.0 255.255.255.0 192.168.10.2
!
```

The configuration of Raul in Listing 7.7 makes use of the keyword **host** in the access list configuration. When the **host** parameter is used, there is no need to specify a wildcard mask because an all 0s mask is assumed by the router. To make sure the configuration is correct and that Raul is allowing only the connections the access list is configured for, you must do some testing. Using the **debug IP packet** command on Raul will help you to determine the effects of the access list. If you try to ping host 192.168.50.50 from the workstation with the IP address 192.168.30.31, the ping should fail. Listing 7.9 shows an attempt to ping from 192.168.30.31 to 192.168.50.50.

Listing 7.9   Ping attempt to 192.168.50.50 from 192.168.30.31.

```
C:\>ping 192.168.50.50

Pinging 192.168.50.50 with 32 bytes of data:

Reply from 192.168.10.2: Destination net unreachable
Reply from 192.168.10.2: Destination net unreachable
Reply from 192.168.10.2: Destination net unreachable
Reply from 192.168.10.2: Destination net unreachable
```

When you look at Raul, which has the **debug IP packet** command running, you will note that it is denying the ping packet request. In the output in Listing 7.10, you can see the ping packet being denied.

Listing 7.10   Output of the debug IP packet command on Raul.

```
ip: s=192.168.10.2, d=192.168.30.31, len 56, sending
ip: s=192.168.30.31, d=192.168.50.50, len 100, access denied
!
ip: s=192.168.10.2, d=192.168.30.31, len 56, sending
ip: s=192.168.30.31, d=192.168.50.50, len 100, access denied
!
ip: s=192.168.10.2, d=192.168.30.31, len 56, sending
ip: s=192.168.30.31, d=192.168.50.50, len 100, access denied
!
ip: s=192.168.10.2, d=192.168.30.31, len 56, sending
ip: s=192.168.30.31, d=192.168.50.50, len 100, access denied
```

The connection request to 192.168.50.50 was denied at Raul because the source of the packet was not configured with a permit statement in the access list. However, if you try to access 192.168.50.50 from 192.168.30.30 using the **ping** command, everything should work. Listing 7.11 displays the output of the **ping** command issued on 192.168.30.30.

Listing 7.11   Ping attempt to 192.168.50.50 from 192.168.30.30.

```
C:\>ping 192.168.50.50

Pinging 192.168.50.50 with 32 bytes of data:

Reply from 192.168.50.50: bytes=32 time=126ms TTL=233
Reply from 192.168.50.50: bytes=32 time=117ms TTL=233
Reply from 192.168.50.50: bytes=32 time=117ms TTL=233
Reply from 192.168.50.50: bytes=32 time=116ms TTL=233
```

The ping request worked, so now you can look again at the debug output on Raul, as displayed in Listing 7.12.

7. Additional Access List Features

Listing 7.12   Output of the debug IP packet command on Raul.

```
ip: s=192.168.30.30, d=192.168.50.50, len 100, rcvd 4
ip: s=192.168.50.50, d=192.168.30.30, len 100, sending
!
ip: s=192.168.30.30, d=192.168.50.50, len 100, rcvd 4
ip: s=192.168.50.50, d=192.168.30.30, len 100, sending
!
ip: s=192.168.30.30, d=192.168.50.50, len 100, rcvd 4
ip: s=192.168.50.50, d=192.168.30.30, len 100, sending
!
ip: s=192.168.30.30, d=192.168.50.50, len 100, rcvd 4
ip: s=192.168.50.50, d=192.168.30.30, len 100, sending
```

Another troubleshooting command to issue is the **show IP access-lists** command, which will display each access list configured on the router; if the optional **log** parameter is specified in the configuration of the access list, the **show IP access-lists** command will display the number of matches the access list has encountered. Issuing the **show IP access-lists** command on Raul displays the number of packets that have matched access list 101:

```
Raul#sh access-lists

Extended ip access list 101
 permit ip host 192.168.30.0 host 192.168.50.0 log -
 (13222 matches)
 permit ip host 192.168.20.0 host 192.168.40.0 log
```

Configuring Extended TCP Access Lists

In the preceding section, you learned how to configure IP-specific access lists. The Cisco IOS also gives security administrators the ability to configure extended access lists using more specific protocol-dependent options for filtering packets; for example, you can configure TCP access lists. The steps for configuring extended TCP access lists are the same as the steps for configuring extended IP access lists with the exception of the additional parameters that TCP extended access lists permit:

1. Use the following command to define the extended TCP access list:

```
access-list <access-list-number> <deny | permit> tcp -
  <source source-wildcard> <operator port> <destination -
  destination-wildcard> <operator port> <established> -
  <precedence precedence-value> <tos tos-value> <log>
```

2. Use this command to select the input interface under which the access list will be applied:

```
interface <interface name> <interface number>
```

3. Use the following command to apply the access list to the interface:

```
ip access-group <access-list-number> <in | out>
```

In the command in Step 1, the **operator** parameter specifies a condition of qualifications for packets that match the source and destination of the access list. The possible values for the operator include less than (**lt**), greater than (**gt**), equal (**eq**), not equal (**nq**), and an inclusive range (**range**). The *port* parameter specifies a number from 0 to 65535 or a name that represents a TCP port number. The **established** parameter is TCP-specific and indicates an established session if the TCP packet has the ACK or RST bit set. The **established** option should be used if you have implemented an inbound access list to prevent TCP sessions from being established into your network, but you must ensure that the access list will allow legitimate response packets back to your inside hosts from hosts with which the inside network users have attempted to establish a session.

The simple network that is shown in Figure 7.6 will be used in this example. Router C should be configured to deny all inbound connection requests to the 192.168.10.0 network. However, it should also be configured to allow responses to connection requests that were initiated from the inside network to pass through the access list. Listing 7.13 shows the configuration of Router C to accomplish this.

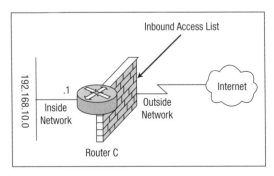

Figure 7.6   TCP access list for Router C.

Listing 7.13   TCP established configuration of Router C.

```
hostname Router-C
!
interface FastEthernet0/0
ip address 192.168.10.1 255.255.255.0
no ip directed-broadcast
!
interface Serial/0
ip address 172.16.200.1 255.255.255.0
ip access-group 101 in
no ip directed-broadcast
!
ip route 0.0.0.0 0.0.0.0 172.116.200.2
!
access-list 101 permit tcp any 192.168.10.0 0.0.0.255 -
  established log
access-list 101 deny ip any any log
```

In Listing 7.13, Router C is configured to permit packets regardless of the source address if the packets' destination is in the 192.168.40.0 subnet and the ACK or RST bit is set within the packet. The next line of the configuration is not needed due to the **implicit deny any**, but it is included so that any packet that fails to meet the requirements of the first access list statement can be logged. Of note also is that the access list is bounded to the external Serial interface of Router C for packets that are incoming on that interface.

To test the configuration, you can establish a Telnet session from a host on the 192.168.10.0 network to a host on the external network of Router C. On Router C, use the **debug IP packet detail** command to monitor packets that are coming into or leaving Router C. Here is the Telnet request from 192.168.10.212:

```
C:\>telnet 172.16.146.73
Connecting to 172.16.146.73...open
```

Examining the debug output on Router C, you can see that the request is considered valid because the flag fields the access list is configured to look for are set. Listing 7.14 shows the output of the **debug** command on Router C.

Listing 7.14   Established TCP connection output.

```
Router-C#debug ip packet detail
 ip packet debugging is on (detailed)
 .....
ip: s=192.168.10.212, d=172.16.146.73, len 44, sending
TCP src=11001, dst=23, seq=1697250670, ack=0, win=4128 SYN
```

```
IP: s=172.16.146.73, d=192.168.10.212, len 44, rcvd 4
TCP src=23, dst=11001, seq=1724867633, ack=1697250671, -
  win=4128 ACK SYN
!
ip: s=192.168.10.212, d=172.16.146.73, len 40, sending
TCP src=11001, dst=23, seq=1697250671, ack=1724867634, -
  win=4128 ACK
!
ip: s=192.168.10.212, d=172.16.146.73, len 52, sending
TCP src=11001, dst=23, seq=1697250671, ack=1724867634, -
  win=4128 ACK PSH
!
ip: s=192.168.10.212, d=172.16.146.73, len 40, sending
TCP src=11001, dst=23, seq=1697250683, ack=1724867634, -
  win=4128 ACK
!
IP: s=172.16.146.73, d=192.168.10.212, len 52, rcvd 4
TCP src=23, dst=11001, seq=1724867634, ack=1697250671, -
  win=4128 ACK PSH
!
ip: s=192.168.10.212, d=172.16.146.73, len 43, sending
TCP src=11001, dst=23, seq=1697250683, ack=1724867646, -
  win=4116 ACK PSH

!
```

NOTE: *Because of the format limitations of this book, some lines of the code in Listing 7.14 have been broken with a hyphen.*

The highlighted lines display that the ACK or RST bit is set on the packets from 172.16.146.73 to 192.168.10.212. The initial TCP access list configuration defined the **log** parameter to the end of the access list. The following example shows the output from the **log** parameter, which generates an informational log message regarding any packet that matches the parameters of the extended TCP access list. Notice that the response packets from 172.16.146.73 match all parameters of access list 101, and is therefore, permitted:

```
%SEC-6-IPACCESSLOGP: list 101 permitted tcp 172.16.146.73(23)-> -
  192.168.10.212(11001), 1 packet
!
%SEC-6-IPACCESSLOGP: list 101 permitted tcp 172.16.146.73(23)-> -
  192.168.10.212(11001), 24 packets
```

NOTE: *Because of the format limitations of this book, some lines of code listed above have been broken with a hyphen.*

The **show IP access-lists** command is another troubleshooting command you can issue. It will display each access list configured on the router, and because the optional **log** parameter was specified in the configuration of the access list, the command will display the number of matches that the access list has encountered. Issuing the **show IP access-lists** command on Router C displays the number of packets that have matched access list 101:

```
Router-C#show access-lists

Extended ip access list 101
permit tcp any 192.168.10.0 0.0.0.255 established log(427 -
  matches)
deny ip any any log(11924 matches)
Router-C#
```

Configuring Named Access Lists

Because of the numeric limitations of numbered standard and extended access lists, in IOS release 11.2, Cisco included a feature known as named access lists, which extend the numeric limit of numbered access lists. To configure a named access list, follow these steps:

1. Use the following configuration command to define a named access list:

    ```
    ip access-list <standard | extended> name
    ```

    The **standard** command option configures a standard access list and the **extended** command option configures an extended access list. The *name* parameter defines the name of the access list. The name of the access list cannot contain a space and must begin with a letter, not a number.

2. Use this command to define the filter rules for a standard named access list:

    ```
    <deny | permit> source source-wildcard
    ```

    Use this command to define the filter rules for an extended access list:

    ```
    <deny | permit> <protocol> <source source-wildcard> -
      <destination destination-wildcard> <precedence precedence> -
      <tos tos> log
    ```

3. Use the following command to select the input interface under which the access list will be applied:

```
interface <interface name> <interface number>
```

4. Use this command to bind the access list to the interface and to apply the filter to packets entering into or exiting the interface:

```
ip access-group name {in | out}
```

In the beginning of "Immediate Solutions," I began with a basic standard access list configuration. In Listing 7.1 and Listing 7.2, Routers Raul and Chris were configured to provide packet filtering using standard numbered access lists. You can also configure routers to use named access lists to provide packet filtering. In Listing 7.15, **Raul** is configured to permit traffic from only the 192.168.20.0 network and deny traffic from all other networks. Router **Chris** will be configured in Listing 7.16 to permit traffic from only 192.168.40.0 and deny traffic from all other networks. Instead of using a standard numbered access list, this time I will use a standard named access list. Refer back to Figure 7.4 for a description of the network that will be used to configure the routers.

Listing 7.15 Named access list configuration of Raul.

```
hostname Raul
!
interface FastEthernet1/0
ip address 192.168.10.2 255.255.255.0
no ip directed-broadcast
ip access-group permit-20 in
!
interface FastEthernet2/0
ip address 192.168.40.1 255.255.255.0
no ip directed-broadcast
!
interface FastEthernet3/0
ip address 192.168.50.1 255.255.255.0
no ip directed-broadcast
!
ip route 192.168.20.0 255.255.255.0 192.168.10.1
ip route 192.168.30.0 255.255.255.0 192.168.10.1
!
ip access-list standard permit-20
 permit 192.168.20.0 0.0.0.255
 deny any
```

Listing 7.16   Named access list configuration of **Chris.**

```
hostname Chris
!
interface FastEthernet0
ip address 192.168.10.1 255.255.255.0
no ip directed-broadcast
ip access-group permit-40 in
!
interface Ethernet1
ip address 192.168.20.1 255.255.255.0
no ip directed-broadcast
!
interface FastEthernet1
ip address 192.168.30.1 255.255.255.0
no ip directed-broadcast
!
ip route 192.168.40.0 255.255.255.0 192.168.10.2
ip route 192.168.50.0 255.255.255.0 192.168.10.2
!
ip access-list standard permit-40
 permit 192.168.40.0 0.0.0.255
 deny any
```

You can issue the **show access-lists** command on **Chris** to verify the proper configuration of the access list:

```
Chris#show access-lists
Standard ip access list permit-40
    permit 192.168.40.0, wildcard bits 0.0.0.255
    deny    any
```

You can also use the **show IP interface** command to verify the access list. Issuing this command displays any and all access lists that are configured on an interface. Issuing the command on Chris displays the output listed in Listing 7.17.

Listing 7.17   Output of the **show IP interface** command on **Chris.**

```
Chris#sh ip int e0/0
FastEthernet0 is up, line protocol is up
  Internet address is 192.168.10.1/24
  Broadcast address is 255.255.255.255
  Address determined by non-volatile memory
  MTU is 1500 bytes
  Helper address is not set
  Directed broadcast forwarding is disabled
  Outgoing access list is not set
  Inbound  access list is permit-40
  Proxy ARP is enabled
```

Configuring Commented Access Lists

When you use named access lists, you are able to provide a small description of the access list within the name, as shown in Listing 7.15 and Listing 7.16. Sometimes, though, the name of an access list does not provide enough information about what the access list does or what function each line within the access list provides. In 12.0.2 code, Cisco released a feature known as commented access lists. In Listings 7.1 and 7.15, Raul has an access list configured that permits the 192.168.20.0 network and denies all others. In Listing 7.15, a name was used to define the access list instead of a number; I attempted to give the access list a name that was relevant to the function that it provided. In Listing 7.1, a standard numbered access list was used to define the same access lists; however, no descriptive information about the access list could be made with the numbered access list. You can add a comment to standard and extended access lists as well as to numbered and named access lists. Follow these steps to configure comments within a name-based access list:

1. Use the following configuration command to define a named access list:

   ```
   ip access-list <standard | extended> name
   ```

2. Use the **remark** command to define the comment on an access list basis or on a per-filter-rule basis. The *remark* parameter is limited to 100 characters, including spaces.

3. Use this command to select the input interface under which the access list will be applied:

   ```
   interface <interface name> <interface number>
   ```

4. Use the following command to bind the access list to the interface and to apply the filter to packets entering into or exiting the interface:

   ```
   ip access-group name {in | out}
   ```

Follow these steps to configure comments within a numbered access:

1. Use the following configuration command to define the numbered access list and to define the comment on an access list basis:

   ```
   access-list access-list-number remark remark
   ```

7. Additional Access List Features

2. Use this command to select the input interface under which the access list will be applied:

```
interface <interface name> <interface number>
```

3. Use this command to bind the access list to the interface and to apply the filter to packets entering into or exiting the interface:

```
ip access-group access list number {in | out}
```

Figure 7.7 displays a router with two networks directly attached to it. The router, Router C, has a large access list configuration defined, and if remarks weren't used, the access list would be fairly complicated to fully understand. To add clarity to the access list, remarks have been defined within the list. Router C will be configured with a name-based access list and the appropriate remarks will be added within the access list. Listing 7.18 displays the configuration of Router C.

Listing 7.18   Commented named access list on Router C.

```
hostname Router-C
!
interface FastEthernet0/0
ip address 172.16.15.1 255.255.255.0
no ip directed-broadcast
!
interface Serial1/0
ip address 10.10.10.1 255.255.255.0
ip access-group Commented in
no ip directed-broadcast
!
ip access-list extended Commented
 remark Deny any inbound request unless initiated from inside
 permit tcp any 172.16.0.0 0.0.255.255 established
 remark Permit mail traffic to this host
 permit tcp any host 172.16.15.83 eq smtp
```

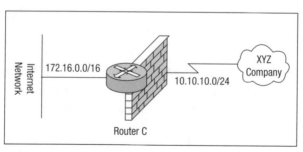

Figure 7.7   Router C permitting and denying traffic.

```
remark Permit telnet from XYZ company to our company
permit tcp 10.10.10.0 0.0.0.255 172.16.0.0 0.0.255.255 -
    eq telnet
remark Permit FTP from XYZ company to our company
permit tcp 10.10.10.0 0.0.0.255 172.16.0.0 0.0.255.255 eq ftp
remark Allow DNS traffic to the internal DNS server
permit udp any host 172.16.15.84 eq domain
remark Deny all other traffic
deny ip any any
```

Router C has been configured with an extended name-based access list. Within the access list remarks provide clarity on the function of each filter rule statement. As mentioned earlier, comments can also be listed for numbered access lists. Using the same requirements that were listed with Listing 7.18, Router C can now be configured with a numbered access list that contains remarks for each filter rule. An extended numbered access list is used to accomplish the same thing Listing 7.18 accomplishes. Listing 7.19 displays the configuration of Router C using numbered access lists.

Listing 7.19   Commented numbered access list on Router C.

```
hostname Router-C
!
interface FastEthernet0/0
ip address 172.16.15.1 255.255.255.0
no ip directed-broadcast
!
interface Serial1/0
ip address 10.10.10.1 255.255.255.0
ip access-group 121 in
no ip directed-broadcast
!
access-list 121 remark Deny any inbound request
access-list 121 permit tcp any 172.16.0.0 0.0.255.255 -
  established
access-list 121 remark Permit mail traffic to this host
access-list 121 permit tcp any host 172.16.15.83 eq smtp
access-list 121 remark Permit telnet from XYZ company
access-list 121 permit tcp 10.10.10.0 0.0.0.255 -
  172.16.0.0 0.0.255.255 eq telnet
access-list 121 remark Permit FTP from XYZ company to our -
  company
access-list 121 permit tcp 10.10.10.0 0.0.0.255 -
  172.16.0.0 0.0.255.255 eq ftp
access-list 121 Allow DNS traffic to the internal DNS server
access-list 121 permit udp any host 172.16.15.84 eq domain
```

7. Additional Access List Features

347

```
access-list 121 remark Deny all other traffic
access-list 121 deny ip any any
```

NOTE: *Because of the format limitations of this book, some lines of code listed above have been broken with a hyphen.*

Configuring Dynamic Access Lists

Dynamic access lists permit or deny traffic based on user credentials that are passed to the Lock and Key router for user authentication. To be permitted access to a host behind a router configured for Lock and Key security, a user must first telnet to the router and pass an authentication phase. If authentication is successful, a temporary access list is created; it will enable the user to connect to the intended destination. To configure a router to provide Lock and Key security services for hosts, follow these steps:

1. Use the following global configuration command to define a dynamic access list:

    ```
    access-list <access-list-number> <dynamic dynamic-name> -
       <timeout minutes> <deny | permit> telnet <source -
       source-wildcard> <destination destination-wildcard> -
       <precedence precedence> <tos tos> <established> <log>
    ```

2. Optionally, use the **access-list dynamic-extend** command to extend the absolute timer of the dynamic ACL by six minutes when another Telnet session is opened into the router.

3. Use this command to configure user authentication:

    ```
    username name password secret
    ```

4. Use the following command to select the input interface under which the access list will be applied:

    ```
    interface <interface name> <interface number>
    ```

5. Use the following command to bind the access list to the interface and to apply the dynamic filter to packets entering into the interface:

    ```
    ip access-group name <in>
    ```

6. Use this command to define one or more virtual terminal (vty) ports:

```
line vty <line-number> <ending-line-number>
```

7. Use the **login local** command to specify that user authentication should use the locally configured security database.

8. Use the following command in line configuration mode to enable the creation of temporary access list entries:

```
autocommand access-enable host [timeout minutes]
```

The network displayed in Figure 7.8 will demonstrate dynamic access list security. Router 1 and Router 2 are each configured with two loopback interfaces. When Router 2 attempts to connect to one of the loopback interfaces on Router 1, it must first telnet to Router 1 and will be asked to authenticate via the local security database. If authentication takes place correctly, Router 2 will be disconnected from Router 1 and then will be allowed to communicate with the host on the loopback interface. The configuration of Router 1 is shown in Listing 7.20, and the configuration of Router 2 is shown in Listing 7.21.

Listing 7.20   Configuration of Router 1 for dynamic access lists.

```
hostname Router-1
!
username R2 password 0 R2
!
interface Loopback0
```

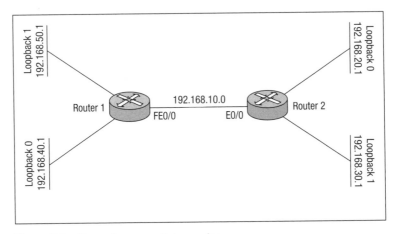

Figure 7.8   Dynamic access list security.

349

```
  ip address 192.168.40.1 255.255.255.0
  no ip directed-broadcast
 !
 interface Loopback1
  ip address 192.168.50.1 255.255.255.0
  no ip directed-broadcast
 !
 interface FastEthernet0/0
  ip address 192.168.10.2 255.255.255.0
  ip access-group 101 in
  no ip directed-broadcast
 !
 ip classless
 ip route 192.168.20.0 255.255.255.0 192.168.10.1
 ip route 192.168.30.0 255.255.255.0 192.168.10.1
 no ip http server
 !
 access-list 101 permit tcp any host 192.168.10.2 eq telnet
 access-list 101 dynamic PermitR2 permit tcp -
    host 192.168.20.1 host 192.168.40.1
 access-list 101 dynamic PermitR2 permit tcp -
    host 192.168.20.1 host 192.168.50.1
 !
 line con 0
  session-timeout 30
  exec-timeout 30 0
  login local
  transport input none
 line aux 0
 line vty 0 4
  session-timeout 30
  exec-timeout 30 0
  login local
  autocommand access-enable timeout 5
 !
```

Listing 7.21   Configuration of Router 2 for dynamic access lists.

```
hostname Router-2
!
username R1 password 0 R1
ip telnet source-interface Loopback1
!
interface Loopback1
 ip address 192.168.20.1 255.255.255.0
 no ip directed-broadcast
!
```

```
interface Loopback2
 ip address 192.168.30.1 255.255.255.0
 no ip directed-broadcast
!
interface Ethernet0/0
 ip address 192.168.10.1 255.255.255.0
 no ip directed-broadcast
!
ip classless
ip route 192.168.40.0 255.255.255.0 192.168.10.2
ip route 192.168.50.0 255.255.255.0 192.168.10.2
!
line con 0
 session-timeout 30
 exec-timeout 30 0
 login local
 transport input none
line aux 0
line vty 0 4
 session-timeout 30
 exec-timeout 30 0
 login local
!
```

NOTE: *Because of the format limitations of this book, some lines of code listed above have been broken with a hyphen.*

As you can probably tell, there is nothing special about Router 2's configuration. It is Router 1's configuration that matters. The only special command configured on Router 2 is the **IP telnet source-interface** command, which is used to have Router 2 source the Telnet packet from the specified loopback interface because, by default, the router will source the packet with the output interface's IP address as the source of the packet.

You can first try to establish a Telnet connection to the 192.168.40.1 loopback interface of Router 1 from Router 2 to verify that the access list is not allowing access. The following code displays the output of a Telnet connection request from Router 2 to the loopback interface of Router 1. To verify that the access list is denying access, Router 1 is configured to debug packets using the **debug IP packet detail** command and is configured to log all events to the internal buffer using the **logging buffered** command.

```
Router-2#telnet 192.168.40.1
Trying 192.168.40.1 ...
% Destination unreachable; gateway or host down

Router-2#
```

As you can see, Router 1 has denied Router 2 access to the 192.168.40.1 interface. Looking back at the log information on Router 1 will in fact show that the packet request was made for access to 192.168.40.1 but was denied. The following output can be seen by issuing the **show logging** command on Router 1:

```
Router-1#show logging
Syslog logging: enabled(1 messages dropped, 0 flushes, -
 0 overruns)
    Console logging: level debugging, 81 messages logged
    Monitor logging: level debugging, 0 messages logged
    Buffer logging: level debugging, 9 messages logged
    Trap logging: level informational, 24 message lines logged
Log Buffer (2000000 bytes):

IP: s=192.168.20.1, d=192.168.40.1, len 44, access denied
TCP src=11007, dst=23, seq=3683728902, ack=0, win=4128 SYN
ip: s=192.168.10.2, d=192.168.20.1, len 56, sending
ICMP type=3, code=13
Router-1#
```

Router 1 has in fact denied the connection request. Now I'll go back to Router 2 and attempt a Telnet connection to the 192.168.10.2, Fast Ethernet0/0 interface of Router 1. The Telnet connection request from Router 2 to Router 1 can be seen in the following output. Router 1 is still configured with the **debug IP packet detail** command so that the connection request can be verified:

```
Router-2#telnet 192.168.10.2
Trying 192.168.10.2 ... Open


User Access Verification

Username: R2
Password: R2
[Connection to 192.168.10.2 closed by foreign host]
Router-2#
```

After Router 2 makes the connection request to Router 1 and is authenticated via the local security database, Router 1 disconnects the Telnet session with Router 2 and creates the temporary access list entries in access list 101, permitting traffic from 192.168.20.1 to 192.168.40.1. The output in Listing 7.22 displays the creation of the temporary access lists on Router 1. To display the information, issue the **show IP access-lists** command.

Listing 7.22 Temporary access list entries on Router 1.

```
Router-1#show ip access-lists
Extended ip access list 101
permit tcp any host 192.168.10.2 eq telnet log (38 matches)
Dynamic PermitR2 permit tcp host 192.168.20.1 host 192.168.40.1 -
    log
permit tcp host 192.168.20.1 host 192.168.40.1 log -
(time left 293)
Dynamic PermitR2 permit tcp host 192.168.20.1 host 192.168.50.1 -
    log
permit tcp host 192.168.20.1 host 192.168.40.1 log -
    (time left 293)
Router-1#
```

It should also be helpful to take a look at the logging information. The output in Listing 7.23 displays the output from the **show logging** command.

Listing 7.23 **Show logging** on Router 1.

```
Router-1#show logging
Syslog log: enabled (1 messages dropped, 0 flushes, 0 overruns)
    Console logging: level debugging, 679 messages logged
    Monitor logging: level debugging, 0 messages logged
    Buffer logging: level debugging, 607 messages logged
    Trap logging: level informational, 27 message lines logged

Log Buffer (2000000 bytes):

%SEC-6-IPACCESSLOGP: list 101 permitted tcp 192.168.20.1 -
    (11010) -> 192.168.10.2(23), 1 packet
ip: s=192.168.20.1, d=192.168.10.2, len 44, rcvd 3
TCP src=11010, dst=23, seq=1082833484, ack=0, win=4128 SYN
ip: s=192.168.10.2, d=192.168.20.1, len 44, sending
TCP src=23,dst=11010,seq=2196401629,ack=1082833485,win=4128 ACK
SYN
ip: s=192.168.20.1, d=192.168.10.2, len 40, rcvd 3
TCP src=11010,dst=23,seq=1082833485,ack=2196401630,win=4128 ACK
ip: s=192.168.20.1, d=192.168.10.2, len 52, rcvd 3
```

7. Additional Access List Features

```
TCP src=11010, dst=23, seq=1082833485, ack=2196401630, win=4128
ACK PSH
```

At this point, I have been authenticated and Router 1 has created the temporary access list entries to allow connectivity to Router 2. I should now be able to connect to the loopback interface of Router 1 because the temporary access list entry has been created to allow for the connectivity from 192.168.20.1 to 192.168.40.1. The following output details the connection request to Router 1's loopback interface:

```
Router-2#telnet 192.168.40.1
Trying 192.168.40.1 ... Open


User Access Verification

Username: R2
Password:
Router-1#
```

After the connection request is made to Router 1, you can look again at the access list configuration and see that packets have matched the temporary access lists. The following output displays the information from the **show IP access-lists** command:

```
Router-1#show ip access-lists
Extended ip access list 101
permit tcp any host 192.168.10.2 eq telnet (40 matches)
Dynamic PermitR2 permit tcp host 192.168.20.1 host 192.168.40.1
permit tcp host 192.168.20.1 host 192.168.40.1 (38 matches) -
  (time left 275)
Dynamic PermitR2 permit tcp host 192.168.20.1 host 192.168.50.1
permit tcp host 192.168.20.1 host 192.168.40.1 (38 matches) -
  (time left 275)
Router-1#
```

NOTE: *Because of the format limitations of this book, some lines of code listed above have been broken with a hyphen.*

Of particular note in the preceding output is the **time left 275** field; this field displays the amount of idle time remaining before the timeout period is reached and the router tears down the temporary access list entry. In Listing 7.20, the timeout period was configured to three minutes using the **autocommand access-enable** command. This configured all dynamic access lists' idle timeout period to five minutes. If the idle timeout value is reached and the dynamic entry is deleted, any user that authenticated to Router 1 using the username R2 will have to reauthenticate before gaining access again. Sometimes security administrators need a finer granularity of control on a per-user basis. One user may need to have a longer idle timeout value than another user; however, with the preceding configuration, all users have the same idle timeout value. Router 1's configuration in Listing 7.20 can be altered to provide different timeout values on the basis of local database users. Listing 7.24 displays Router 1's new configuration, which has defined multiple local security database entries and configured a specific idle timeout value for each local database entry.

Listing 7.24   New configuration of Router 1.

```
hostname Router-1
!
username R2 password 0 R2
uername R2 autocommand access-enable timeout 3
username Cisco password 0 Cisco
username Cisco autocommand access-enable timeout 5
username Systems password 0 Systems
username Systems autocommand access-enable timeout 7
!
interface Loopback0
 ip address 192.168.40.1 255.255.255.0
 no ip directed-broadcast
!
interface Loopback1
 ip address 192.168.50.1 255.255.255.0
 no ip directed-broadcast
!
interface FastEthernet0/0
 ip address 192.168.10.2 255.255.255.0
 ip access-group 101 in
 no ip directed-broadcast
!
ip classless
ip route 192.168.20.0 255.255.255.0 192.168.10.1
ip route 192.168.30.0 255.255.255.0 192.168.10.1
no ip http server
!
access-list 101 permit tcp any host 192.168.10.2 eq telnet log
access-list 101 dynamic PermitR2 permit tcp -
  host 192.168.20.1 host 192.168.40.1 log
access-list 101 dynamic PermitR2 permit tcp -
  host 192.168.20.1 host 192.168.50.1 log
```

```
!
line con 0
 session-timeout 30
 exec-timeout 30 0
 login local
 transport input none
line aux 0
line vty 0 4
 session-timeout 30
 exec-timeout 30 0
 login local
```

Configuring Reflexive Access Lists

To define a reflexive access list, you must create an entry in an extended named IP access list. This entry must use the **reflect** keyword and is nested inside of another access list. To define reflexive access lists, follow these steps:

1. Use this command to define an extended named access list:

   ```
   ip access-list extended name
   ```

   If the reflexive access list is configured for an external interface, the extended named IP access list should be one that is applied to outbound traffic, and if the reflexive access list is configured for an internal interface, the extended named IP access list should be one that is applied to inbound traffic. This command moves you into access list configuration mode.

2. In access list configuration mode, use this configuration command to define the reflexive access list:

   ```
   permit protocol any any reflect name <timeout timeout-seconds>
   ```

   The *protocol* parameter should be specified for each upper-layer protocol that should be permitted.

3. Use the **IP access-list extended** *name* command to define another extended named access list. The name of this access list must be different from the name that was used to create the access list in Step 1. If the access list that was created in Step 1 was for inbound packets, then the access list that is created during this step is created for outbound packets. This command moves you into access list configuration mode.

4. Use **permit** statements to permit any traffic that should not be subjected to the reflexive access list, and then use the **evaluate** *name* command to create an entry that references the reflect statement that was created in Step 2. The *name* parameter defined in this step should match the *name* parameter that was created in Step 2 with the **reflect** *name* parameter.

5. Apply the extended named IP access list to the interface, using this command:

```
ip access-group name {in | out}
```

When previous access lists were configured, this command was somewhat simple, but when applying reflexive access lists, each **in** or **out** option must be used. This will be further explained in the following paragraphs.

6. Optionally, use this command to change the default idle timeout for each temporary access list entry (the default idle timeout period is 300 seconds):

```
ip reflexive-list timeout seconds
```

A brief discussion is needed in order to provide clarity to the preceding configuration steps. Reflexive access lists are normally configured on external interfaces, which will prevent IP traffic from entering the router and the internal network unless the traffic is part of a session already established from within the internal network. If the reflexive access list is not configured on the external interface and more than two interfaces are in use, then more than likely it will be configured on the internal interface, which prevents IP traffic from entering your internal network unless the traffic is part of a session already established from within the internal network.

If reflexive access lists are being configured and applied to an external interface, the extended named IP access list should be applied to outbound traffic. If reflexive access lists are being configured and applied to an internal interface, the extended named IP access list should be applied to inbound traffic. After the reflexive access list has been defined (Step 1), the access list must be "nested" within the second access list that is created in Step 4. If reflexive access lists are being configured and applied to an external interface, nest the reflexive access list within an extended named IP access list applied to inbound traffic. If reflexive access lists are being configured and applied to an internal interface, nest the reflexive access list within an extended named IP access list applied to outbound traffic.

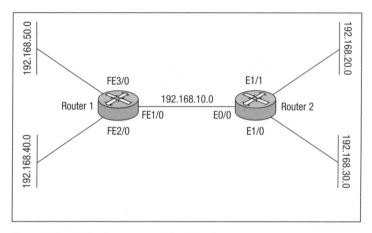

Figure 7.9   Reflexive access list network.

Figure 7.9 displays a network in which reflexive access lists may be used. In this example, reflexive access lists are configured on the Ethernet0/0 interface of Router 2 for outbound traffic that is originated from the internal networks. The reflexive access list configuration of Router 2 is shown in Listing 7.25.

Listing 7.25   Reflexive access list configuration of Router 2.

```
hostname Router-2
!
ip reflexive-list timeout 100
!
interface Ethernet1/1
 ip address 192.168.20.1 255.255.255.0
 no ip directed-broadcast
!
interface Ethernet1/0
 ip address 192.168.30.1 255.255.255.0
 no ip directed-broadcast
!
interface Ethernet0/0
 ip address 192.168.10.1 255.255.255.0
 ip access-group in-filter in
 ip access-group out-filter out
 no ip directed-broadcast
!
ip classless
ip route 192.168.40.0 255.255.255.0 192.168.10.2
ip route 192.168.50.0 255.255.255.0 192.168.10.2
!
!
```

```
ip access-list extended out-filter
 permit icmp any any
 evaluate protect
ip access-list extended in-filter
permit icmp any any
permit tcp any any reflect protect
permit udp any any reflect protect
!
```

The configuration in Listing 7.26 defines two access lists and each is applied to the Ethernet0/0 interface. The reflexive access list has been named "protect," and before there is any packet movement through the router, you can view the access list by using the **show IP access-lists** command. Using this command on Router 2 prior to any packet movement through the router displays the output listed in Listing 7.27.

Listing 7.26 Display of the access lists defined on Router 2.

```
Router-2#show access-lists

Extended ip access list out-filter
    permit icmp any any (40008 matches)
    permit tcp any any reflect protect
    permit udp any any reflect protect
Extended ip access list in-filter
    permit icmp any any
    evaluate protect
Router-2#
```

Notice that no information regarding the reflexive access list is displayed in the output in Listing 7.27; no traffic has triggered the access list yet. There is, however, ping traffic moving through the router, but ping traffic is not subjected to the reflexive access list filters. To trigger the reflexive access list, initiate a Telnet session from Router 2 to Router 1. After the Telnet session has started, you can issue the **show access-lists** command again to view the reflexive access list. Issuing the command on Router 2 displays the output in Listing 7.28.

Listing 7.27 Displaying the reflexive access list on Router 2.

```
Router-2#sh access-lists

Extended ip access list out-filter
permit icmp any any (70006 matches)
permit tcp any any reflect protect
permit udp any any reflect protect
!
Extended ip access list in-filter
```

7. Additional Access List Features

```
permit icmp any any
evaluate protect
!
Reflexive ip access list protect
permit tcp host 192.168.20.1 eq 11003 host 192.168.50.1 -
  eq telnet -
  (49 matches) (time left 95)
permit tcp host 192.168.30.1 eq 11002 host 192.168.40.1 -
  eq telnet -
  (49 matches) (time left 62)
permit tcp host 192.168.30.2 eq 11001 host 192.168.40.1 -
  eq telnet -
  (69 matches) (time left 18)
Router-2#
```

The configuration that has been examined in this section so far has been for reflexive access lists on an internal interface basis. Configuring reflexive access lists on an external interface basis is just the opposite of the configuration in Listing 7.26. Figure 7.10 displays a network in Router 2 should be configured for a reflexive access list that should be placed on an external interface. Listing 7.28 displays Router 2's configuration.

Listing 7.28   External reflexive access list on Router 2.

```
hostname Router-2
!
ip reflexive-list timeout 100
!
interface Ethernet1
 ip address 192.168.20.1 255.255.255.0
 no ip directed-broadcast
!
```

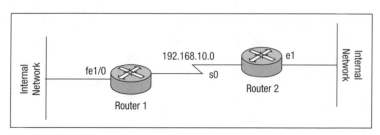

Figure 7.10   External reflexive access list.

```
interface Serial0
 ip address 192.168.10.1 255.255.255.0
 ip access-group in-filter in
 ip access-group out-filter out
 no ip directed-broadcast
!
ip classless
ip route 0.0.0.0 0.0.0.0 serial0
!
ip access-list extended in-filter
 permit icmp any any
 evaluate protect
ip access-list extended out-filter
 permit icmp any any
 permit tcp any any reflect protect
 permit udp any any reflect protect
!
```

Configuring Time-Based Access Lists

To configure time-based access lists, perform the following steps:

1. Use the **time-range** *name* command to define the name of the timed access list. Issuing this command moves you into time-range configuration mode.

2. Use either of the following commands to specify when the timed access list should be in effect:

    ```
    absolute <start time date> <end time date>
    periodic <days-of-the-week> hh:mm to <days-of-the-week> hh:mm
    ```

    When using the **periodic** parameter, you may define multiple ranges. When using the **absolute** parameter, only one range may be defined. The *day(s)-of-the-week* parameter can be specified as any day of the week or a combination of days using the *Monday, Tuesday, Wednesday, Thursday, Friday, Saturday*, or *Sunday* keyword. There are also three other options that may be used: The daily keyword represents Monday through Sunday. The weekend keyword specifies Saturday and Sunday, and the weekday keyword specifies Monday through Friday.

7. Additional Access List Features

3. Define an extended numbered access list as described earlier using the command and bind the time range to the access list:

```
access-list <access-list-number> <deny | permit> protocol -
<source source-wildcard> <destination destination-wildcard>-
<precedence precedence-value> <tos tos-value> -
<log | log-input>
```

4. Use this command to apply the access list to the interface:

```
ip access-group <access-list-number> <in | out>
```

In the first example, I will configure time-based access lists using only periodic statements with extended numbered access lists. In this configuration, I would like to permit FTP traffic only on the weekdays from 7:00 A.M. to 6:00 P.M., deny all HTTP traffic on the weekend, permit TFTP traffic only on the weekend from noon to 8:00 P.M., and permit Telnet traffic only on Saturday from noon to 8:00 P.M. Listing 7.29 displays the configuration needed to meet these requirements.

Listing 7.29   Timed access list using numbered access list.

```
time-range permit-ftp
periodic weekdays 07:00 to 18:00
!
time-range deny-http
periodic weekend 00:00 to 23:59
!
time-range permit-tftp
periodic weekend 12:00 to 20:00
!
time-range permit-telnet
periodic saturday 12:00 to 20:00
!
access-list 120 permit tcp any any eq 21 time-range permit-ftp
access-list 120 deny tcp any any eq 80 time-range deny-http
access-list 120 permit udp any any eq 69 time-range permit-tftp
access-list 120 permit tcp any any eq 23 time-range -
  permit-telnet
!
interface fast0/0
ip access-group 120 in
```

To monitor the access list, issue the **show access-lists** command. This will display results that tell you whether the access list is active or inactive. An active state means the access list is currently in use, and an inactive state means the access list is currently not in use. Here are the results of issuing this command to monitor the access list configured in Listing 7.30:

```
ACL-Router#sh access-lists

Extended ip access list 120
    permit tcp any any eq 21 time-range permit-ftp (inactive)
    deny tcp any any eq 80 time-range deny-http (inactive)
    permit udp any any eq 69 time-range permit-tftp (inactive)
    permit tcp any any eq 23 time-range permit-telnet (inactive)
ACL-Router#
```

Time-based access lists can also be configured using the **absolute** argument with extended numbered access lists or with extended named access lists. The next example shows how to configure a time-based access list using the **absolute** argument and binding the time range to an extended named access list. This access list should deny HTTP traffic during a preplanned Web-server outage within the year, and it should permit FTP traffic to a different server for the entire year of 2004. It should also permit TFTP traffic from the time the access list applied until the 11th of February 2004 and permit Telnet traffic until the end of the year 2004. Listing 7.30 displays the configuration needed to meet these requirements.

Listing 7.30   Timed access list using named access list.

```
time-range permit-ftp
absolute start 06:00 1 January 2004 end 23:59 31 December 2004
!
time-range deny-http
absolute start 00:00 24 November 2004 end 06:00 26 November 2004
!
time-range permit-tftp
absolute end 17:50 11 February 2004
!
time-range permit-telnet
absolute end 23:59 31 December 2004
!
ip access-list extended absolute-list
 permit tcp any host 192.168.10.234 eq 21 time-range permit-ftp
 deny tcp any host 192.168.10.233 eq 80 time-range deny-http
 permit udp any any eq 69 time-range permit-tftp
 permit tcp any any eq 23 time-range permit-telnet
!
interface fast0/0
ip access-group absolute-list in
```

As with the numbered access list, you can monitor the time-based named access list by issuing the **show access-lists** command. This will display results that tell you whether the access list is active or inactive. An active state means the access list is currently in use, and an inactive state means the access list is currently not in use. Here are the results of issuing this command to monitor the access list defined in Listing 7.30:

```
ACL-Router#show access-lists
.....
Extended ip access list absolute-list
deny tcp any host 192.168.10.233 eq 80 time-range -
 deny-http (inactive)
permit udp any any eq 69 time-range permit-tftp (active)
permit tcp any any eq 23 time-range permit-telnet (active)
permit tcp any host 192.168.10.234 eq 21 time-range -
 permit-ftp (inactive)
ACL-Router#
```

NOTE: *Because of the format limitations of this book, some lines of code listed above have been broken with a hyphen.*

IOS Firewall Signature List

This appendix includes a complete list of Cisco IOS Firewall IDS signatures. A signature detects patterns of misuse in network traffic. The 59 intrusion-detection signatures included in the Cisco IOS Firewall software represent the most common network attacks and information-gathering scans that should be considered intrusive activity in an operational network.

The signatures in Table A.1 are listed in numerical order by their signature number in the Cisco Secure IDS Network Security Database (NSD).

Table A.1   IOS Firewall Network Security Database signatures.

NSD Number	Description	Type
1000 IP options-Bad Option List	Signature is triggered by receipt of an IP datagram in which the list of IP options in the IP datagram header is incomplete.	Info, Atomic
1001 IP options-Record Packet Route	Signature is triggered by receipt of an IP datagram with the Record Packet Route chosen or option 7.	Info, Atomic
1002 IP options-Timestamp	Signature is triggered by receipt of an IP datagram with the timestamp option chosen.	Info, Atomic
1003 IP options-Provide s,c,h,tcc	Signature is triggered by receipt of an IP datagram in which the IP option list for the datagram includes security options.	Info, Atomic
1004 IP options-Loose Source Route	Signature is triggered by receipt of an IP datagram where the IP option list for the datagram includes Loose Source Route.	Info, Atomic
1005 IP options-SATNET ID	Signature is triggered by receipt of an IP datagram where the IP option	Info, Atomic

(continued)

Table A.1   IOS Firewall Network Security Database signatures (*continued*).

NSD Number	Description	Type
1005 IP options-SATNET ID (continued)	list for the datagram includes SATNET stream identifier.	Info, Atomic
1006 IP options-Strict Source Route	Signature is triggered by receipt of an IP datagram in which the IP option list for the datagram includes Strict Source Route.	Info, Atomic
1100 IP Fragment Attack	Signature is triggered when any IP datagram is received with the "more fragments" flag set to 1 or if there is an offset indicated in the offset field.	Attack, Atomic
1101 Unknown IP Protocol	Signature is triggered when an IP datagram is received with the protocol field set to 101 or greater, which are undefined or reserved protocol types.	Attack, Atomic
1102 Impossible IP Packet	Signature is triggered when an IP packet arrives with the source address equal to the destination address.	Attack, Atomic
2000 ICMP Echo Reply	Signature is triggered when an IP datagram is received with the "protocol" field in the IP header set to 1 (ICMP) and the type field in the ICMP header set to 0 (Echo Reply).	Info, Atomic
2001 ICMP Host Unreachable	Signature is triggered when an IP datagram is received with the "protocol" field in the IP header set to 1 (ICMP) and the type field in the ICMP header set to 3 (Host Unreachable).	Info, Atomic
2002 ICMP Source Quench	Signature is triggered when an IP datagram is received with the "protocol" field in the IP header set to 1 (ICMP) and the type field in the ICMP header set to 4 (Source Quench).	Info, Atomic
2003 ICMP Redirect	Signature is triggered when an IP datagram is received with the "protocol" field in the IP header set to 1 (ICMP) and the type field in the ICMP header set to 5 (Redirect).	Info, Atomic

(continued)

Table A.1   IOS Firewall Network Security Database signatures (*continued*).

NSD Number	Description	Type
2004 ICMP Echo Request	Signature is triggered when an IP datagram is received with the "protocol" field in the IP header set to 1 (ICMP) and the type field in the ICMP header set to 8 (Echo Request).	Info, Atomic
2005 ICMP Time Exceeded for a Datagram	Signature is triggered when an IP datagram is received with the "protocol" field in the IP header set to 1 (ICMP) and the type field in the ICMP header set to 11 (Time Exceeded for a Datagram).	Info, Atomic
2006 ICMP Parameter Problem on Datagram	Signature is triggered when an IP datagram is received with the "protocol" field in the IP header set to 1 (ICMP) and the type field in the ICMP header set to 12 (Parameter Problem on Datagram).	Info, Atomic
2007 ICMP Timestamp Request	Signature is triggered when an IP datagram is received with the "protocol" field in the IP header set to 1 (ICMP) and the type field in the ICMP header set to 13 (Timestamp Request).	Info, Atomic
2008 ICMP Timestamp Reply	Signature is triggered when an IP datagram is received with the "protocol" field in the IP header set to 1 (ICMP) and the type field in the ICMP header set to 14 (Timestamp Reply).	Info, Atomic
2009 ICMP Information Request	Signature is triggered when an IP datagram is received with the "protocol" field in the IP header set to 1 (ICMP) and the type field in the ICMP header set to 15 (Information Request).	Info, Atomic
2010 ICMP Information Reply	Signature is triggered when an IP datagram is received with the "protocol" field in the IP header set to 1 (ICMP) and the type field in the ICMP header set to 16 (Information Reply).	Info, Atomic
2011 ICMP Address Mask Request	Signature is triggered when an IP datagram is received with the "protocol" field in the IP header set to 1 (ICMP) and the type field in the ICMP header set to 17 (Address Mask Request).	Info, Atomic

(continued)

Table A.1   IOS Firewall Network Security Database signatures (*continued*).

NSD Number	Description	Type
2012 ICMP Address Mask Reply	Signature is triggered when an IP datagram is received with the "protocol" field in the IP header set to 1 (ICMP) and the type field in the ICMP header set to 18 (Address Mask Reply).	Info, Atomic
2150 Fragmented ICMP Traffic	Signature is triggered when an IP datagram is received with the "protocol" field in the IP header set to 1 (ICMP) and either the More Fragments Flag set to 1 (ICMP) or an offset indicated in the offset field.	Info, Atomic
2151 Large ICMP Traffic	Signature is triggered when an IP datagram is received with the "protocol" field in the IP header set to 1 (ICMP) and the IP length greater than 1024.	Info, Atomic
2154 Ping of Death Attack	Signature is triggered when an IP datagram is received with the protocol field in the IP header set to 1 (ICMP), the Last Fragment bit is set, and (IP offset * 8) + (IP data length) > 65535. Where the IP offset (which represents the starting position of this fragment in the original packet, and which is in 8-byte units) plus the rest of the packet is greater than the maximum size for an IP packet.	Attack, Atomic
3040 TCP-no bits set in flags	Signature is triggered when a TCP packet is received with no bits set in the flags field.	Attack, Atomic
3041 TCP-SYN and FIN bits set	Signature is triggered when a TCP packet is received with both the SYN and FIN bits set in the flag field.	Attack, Atomic
3042 TCP-FIN bit with no ACK bit in flags	Signature is triggered when a TCP packet is received with the FIN bit set but with no ACK bit set in the flags field.	Attack, Atomic

(continued)

Table A.1   IOS Firewall Network Security Database signatures (*continued*).

NSD Number	Description	Type
3050 Half-open SYN Attack/ SYN Flood	Signature is triggered when multiple TCP sessions have been improperly initiated on any of several well-known service ports. Detection of this signature is currently limited to FTP, Telnet, HTTP, and email servers.	Attack, Compound
3100 Smail Attack	Signature is triggered on the "smail" attack against SMTP-compliant email servers.	Attack, Compound
3101 Sendmail Invalid Recipient	Signature is triggered on any mail message with a pipe symbol (I) in the recipient field.	Attack, Compound
3102 Sendmail Invalid Sender	Signature is triggered on any mail message with a pipe symbol (I) in the "From:" field.	Attack, Compound
3103 Sendmail Reconnaissance	Signature is triggered when **expn** or **vrfy** commands are issued to the SMTP port.	Attack, Compound
3104 Archaic Sendmail Attacks	Signature is triggered when **wiz** or **debug** commands are issued to the SMTP port.	Attack, Compound
3105 Sendmail Decode Alias	Signature is triggered on any mail message with ": decode@" in the header.	Attack, Compound
3106 Mail Spam	Signature counts number of Rcpt to: lines in a single mail message and sends an alarm after a user-definable maximum has been exceeded (default is 250).	Attack, Compound
3107 Majordomo Execute Attack	Signature when a bug in the Majordomo program allows remote users to execute arbitrary commands at the privilege level of the server.	Attack, Compound
3150 FTP Remote Command Execution	Signature is triggered when someone tries to execute the FTP SITE command.	Attack, Compound

(continued)

Table A.1   IOS Firewall Network Security Database signatures (*continued*).

NSD Number	Description	Type
3151 FTP SYST Command Attempt	Signature is triggered when someone tries to execute the **FTP SYST** command.	Attack, Compound
3152 FTP CWD ~root	Signature is triggered when someone tries to execute the **CWD ~root** command.	Attack, Compound
3153 FTP Improper Address Specified	Signature is triggered if a port command is issued with an address that is not the same as the requesting host's address.	Attack, Atomic
3154 FTP Improper Port Specified	Signature is triggered if a port command is issued with a data port specified that is less than 1024 or greater than 65535.	Attack, Atomic
4050 UDP Bomb	Signature is triggered when the UDP length specified is less than the IP length specified.	Attack, Atomic
4100 Tftp Passwd File	Signature is triggered on an attempt to access the passwd file via TFTP.	Attack, Compound
6100 RPC Port Registration	Signature is triggered when attempts are made to register new RPC services on a target host.	Info, Atomic
6101 RPC Port Unregistration	Signature is triggered when attempts are made to unregister existing RPC services on a target host.	Info, Atomic
6102 RPC Dump	Signature is triggered when an RPC dump request is issued to a target host.	Info, Atomic
6103 Proxied RPC Request	Signature is triggered when a proxied RPC request is sent to the portmapper of a target host.	Attack, Atomic
6150 ypserv Portmap Request	Signature is triggered when a request is made to the portmapper for the YP server daemon (ypserv) port.	Info, Atomic
6151 ypbind Portmap Request	Signature is triggered when a request is made to the portmapper for the YP bind daemon (ypbind) port.	Info, Atomic
6152 yppasswdd Portmap Request	Signature is triggered when a request is made to the portmapper for the YP password daemon (yppasswdd) port.	Info, Atomic

(continued)

Table A.1   IOS Firewall Network Security Database signatures (*continued*).

NSD Number	Description	Type
6153 ypupdated Portmap Request	Signature is triggered when a request is made to the portmapper for the YP update daemon (ypupdated) port.	Info, Atomic
6154 ypxfrd Portmap Request	Signature is triggered when a request is made to the portmapper for the YP transfer daemon (ypxfrd) port.	Info, Atomic
6155 mountd Portmap Request	Signature is triggered when a request is made to the portmapper for the mount daemon (mountd) port.	Info, Atomic
6175 rexd Portmap Request	Signature is triggered when a request is made to the portmapper for the remote execution daemon (rexd) port.	Info, Atomic
6180 rexd Attempt	Signature is triggered when a call to the rexd program is made.	Info, Atomic
6190 statd Buffer Overflow	Signature is triggered when a large statd request is sent. This could be an attempt to overflow a buffer and gain access to system resources.	Attack, Atomic
8000 FTP Retrieve Password File SubSig ID: 2101	Signature is triggered on the string "passwd" issued during an FTP session.	Attack, Atomic

Securing Ethernet Switches

This appendix covers security features that are available and can be used on the Catalyst series Ethernet switches. Security topics for the Catalyst switches are configuring management access to the switch, controlling Telnet, and Simple Network Management Protocol (SNMP) access, configuring the switch to support the AAA architecture, and configuring private virtual local area networks (VLANS) and port security.

The Catalyst line of Ethernet switches has multiple command-line interfaces (CLI); each has a different look and feel depending on which model of switch you are working on. The two most predominant versions of operating system code in use today are the CatOS XDI version and the Native IOS mode version. An in-depth discussion of each of these versions is beyond the scope of this book; however, configuration command examples for each version will be displayed where applicable.

Configuring Management Access

When a Catalyst switch is first received from Cisco, it does not have any passwords configured. This can present a major security risk because anyone with physical access to the switch can establish a connection to it simply by plugging into the console port and pressing the Enter key.

NOTE: *The password configured on a switch by default is the Enter key. This is true for both EXEC mode and privileged mode.*

The first step any administrator should perform when configuring a Catalyst switch is to configure passwords for both the EXEC mode and privileged mode access on the switch. This helps to complement any other physical security measures that have been taken as a result of the enterprise's security policy. To configure management passwords on the Catalyst switch using CatOS XDI code, use the following commands:

1. Use the **set password** command to define a password for EXEC mode access into the switch. The password that is configured using this command can be from 0 to 30 characters in length.

2. Use the **set enablepass** command to define a password for
    privileged mode access on the switch. The password that is
    configured using this command can be from 0 to 30 characters
    in length.

The following listing displays an example of configuring the EXEC
mode password and the privileged mode password for a Catalyst
switch using CatOS code:

```
Cat-6509> (enable) set password
Enter old password:
Enter new password:
Retype new password:
Password changed.
!
Cat-6509> (enable) set enablepass
Enter old password:
Enter new password:
Retype new password:
Password changed.
Cat-6509> (enable)
```

The Native IOS mode code that runs on many newer switches is a
blend of Layer 2 code and Layer 3 code all rolled up into one version.
The Native IOS mode code creates an environment in which Catalyst
switches can be configured and managed through the familiar IOS
user interface that runs on most routers.

To configure a password on a Catalyst switch that is using Native IOS
use the commands in the following steps:

1. Use this command to enter into line configuration mode:

    ```
    line <con | aux | vty> line-number
    ```

2. Use the **password** *<password>* command to define the pass-
    word for each line on the router.

3. To configure enable mode access you can use one of two
    commands, **enable password** *<password>* or **enable secret
    level** *<level> <password>*. Both commands accomplish the
    same thing; they allow access to enable mode. However, the
    enable secret password is considered to be more secure
    because it uses a one-way encryption scheme based on the
    MD5 hashing function.

The following listing displays an example of configuring the line password and enable passwords on a Catalyst switch using Native IOS:

```
Cat-6509#config t
Cat-6509(config)#enable secret Secret@Password
Cat-6509(config)#line con 0
Cat-6509(config-line)#login
Cat-6509(config-line)#password thisissecure
```

Configuring Port Security

Port security is used to block input to an Ethernet, FastEthernet, or Gigabit Ethernet port when the MAC address of the station attempting to access the port is different from any of the MAC addresses specified for that port. When a packet is received on a port with port security enabled, the source MAC address of the packet is compared with the secure MAC address configured for the port. If the MAC address of the device attached to the port differs from the secure MAC address configured for the port, a security violation occurs and the port can be configured to go into shutdown mode or restrictive mode. If the security violation is configured to transition the port into shutdown mode, the port is permanently disabled or disabled for only a specified time. The default action of shutdown mode is for the port to shut down permanently. If the security violation is configured to transition the port into restrictive mode, the port will remain enabled during the security violation and only drop packets that are coming in from insecure hosts.

WARNING: *If you configure a port in restrictive mode and the MAC address on a device that is connected to the port is already configured as a secure MAC address on another port on the switch, the port in restrictive mode shuts down instead of restricting traffic from that device.*

The secure MAC address of the port can be configured statically, or the port can be configured to dynamically learn the MAC address of the device connected to the switch via the port. There are a few restrictions to configuring port security. Certain rules exist that pertain to configuring port security on a Cisco Catalyst switch:

- Port security cannot be enabled on a port that is performing trunking.
- Port security cannot be enabled on a destination Switched Port Analyzer (SPAN) port.

- Content-Addressable Memory (CAM) entries cannot be configured for a port on which port security is enabled. Use the **set cam** *<dynamic | static | permanent>* command to enter CAM entries into the switch.

To configure port security for a switch using CatOS code, use the following commands:

1. Use this command to enable dynamic port security on the specified port:

```
set port security <mod_num/port_num> enable
```

2. Use this command to statically define the MAC address of the device connected via the secure port:

```
set port security mod_num/port_num enable <mac_address>
```

3. Use this command to define the length of time a dynamically learned address on the port specified within the command is secured:

```
set port security <mod_num/port_num> age <time>
```

4. Use this command to define the action a port should take when a security violation occurs:

```
set port security <mod_num/port_num> violation <shutdown | -
    restrict>
```

The *shutdown* parameter disables the port permanently or for a specified period time that is configured with the next command. The *restrict* parameter drops all packets from an insecure source but the port remains enabled.

5. Use this command to define the amount of time a port remains disabled as a result of a security violation:

```
set port security <mod_num/port_num> shutdown <time>
```

If this command is not configured, the default time is set to permanent and the port must be manually reenabled.

Here is an example of configuring port security on a switch that is using CatOS code:

```
Cat-6509 (enable) set port security 4/48 enable
Cat-6509 (enable) set port security 5/3 enable 00-d0-b7-53-40-bb
Cat-6509 (enable) set port security 4/48 age 360
Cat-6509 (enable) set port security 4/48 violation restrict
Cat-6509 (enable) set port security 5/3 violation shutdown
Cat-6509 (enable) set port security 5/3 shutdown 360
```

The commands used to enable port security for Catalyst switches that are using Native IOS code are not as robust as the commands available via the CatOS code. To configure port security for a switch that is using Native IOS code, use the following commands:

1. Use this command to select the interface on which port security should be configured:

    ```
    interface <ethernet | fastethernet | gigEthernet> <slot/port>
    ```

2. Use this command to define the action the port should take in the event of a violation condition:

    ```
    port security action <shutdown | trap>
    ```

    The *shutdown* parameter will disable the port in the event of a security violation. The *trap* parameter will send an SNMP trap message in the event of a security violation.

3. Use this command to define the maximum MAC address count for the port:

    ```
    port security max-mac-count <count>
    ```

The following code is an example of configuring port security on a switch that is using Native IOS code:

```
Cat-6509#config t
Cat-6509(config)#interface fast0/42
Cat-6509(config-if)#port security action shutdown
Cat-6509(config-if)#port security max-mac-count 1
Cat-6509(config-if)#end
```

Configuring Permit Lists

The IP permit list is a feature of the CatOS that permits authorized Telnet and SNMP access to the switch only from authorized source IP addresses. IP permit lists do not affect traffic that is transiting the switch or that is locally originated by the switch. IP permit lists only affect inbound Telnet and SNMP traffic with a destination address as that of the management address of the switch.

Each IP permit entry consists of an IP address and subnet mask pair that is permitted Telnet or SNMP access. If a mask for an IP permit list entry is not specified, or if a hostname is entered instead of an IP address, the mask has an implicit value equal to all 1s, which effectively means match according to host address. There is a limit on the number of permit entries that can be configured on the switch; the maximum is 100 entries.

To configure IP permit lists on a switch running CatOS code, use the following commands:

1. Use this command to enable the IP permit list for Telnet, SNMP, or SSH access:

   ```
   set ip permit enable <telnet | snmp | ssh>
   ```

2. Use this command to specify the IP addresses that are added to the permit list:

   ```
   set ip permit <ip_address> <mask> <telnet | snmp | ssh | all>
   ```

Figure B.1 displays a small network that has devices, which need network management access to the switch. Telnet access into the switch should be allowed from any machine within the network. The following code is an example of configuring an IP permit list for the Catalyst switch in Figure B.1 using CatOS code:

```
set ip permit enable telnet
set ip permit enable snmp
set ip permit 192.168.0.0 255.255.0.0 telnet
set ip permit 192.168.24.12  snmp
set ip permit 192.168.24.15  snmp
set ip permit 192.168.24.16  snmp
set ip permit 192.168.40.250  snmp
```

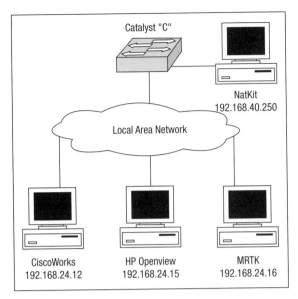

Figure B.1   Catalyst switch using IP permit lists.

Configuring AAA Support

Cisco Catalyst switches support the use of the AAA architecture that was discussed in Chapter 2. Catalyst switches allow for the configuration of any combination of these authentication methods to control access to the switch:

- *Local authentication*—Uses the locally configured login and enable passwords to authenticate login attempts.

- *RADIUS authentication*—Uses the AAA server to authenticate login attempts using the RADIUS protocol.

- *TACACS+ authentication*—Uses the AAA server to authenticate login attempts using the TACACS+ protocol.

- *Kerberos authentication*—Uses a trusted Kerberos server to authenticate login attempts.

NOTE: *All configurations in this section are related to switches that use the CatOS software. To configure for AAA support a Catalyst that uses Native IOS software, please refer to Chapter 2.*

Use the following commands to enable authorization for the Catalyst switch (local login and enable authentication are enabled for both console and Telnet connections by default):

```
set authentication login tacacs disable console
set authentication login tacacs enable telnet primary
```

```
set authentication login tacacs enable http primary
set authentication enable tacacs disable console
set authentication enable tacacs enable telnet primary
set authentication enable tacacs disable http
set authentication login local enable console
set authentication login local enable telnet
set authentication login local enable http
set authentication enable local enable console
set authentication enable local enable telnet
set authentication enable local enable http
```

To view the results of enabling authorization on the switch, issue the **show authentication** command. The following output is an example of issuing the **show authentication** command:

```
Cat-6509> (enable) sh authentication

Login :   Console          Telnet              Http
-------   -------          ------              ----
tacacs    disabled         enabled(primary)    enabled(primary)
radius    disabled         disabled            disabled
kerberos  disabled         disabled            disabled
local     enabled(primary) enabled             enabled

Enable:   Console          Telnet              Http
-------   -------          ------              ----
tacacs    disabled         enabled(primary)    disabled
radius    disabled         disabled            disabled
kerberos  disabled         disabled            disabled
local     enabled(primary) enabled             enabled(primary)
```

Authorization is also supported in the Catalyst model switches. It controls the functions that are permitted by an authenticated user on the switch. Authorization is supported on the Catalyst Ethernet switches for the following:

- *Commands*—User must supply username and password that is verified by the AAA server to EXECute certain commands. Authorization for all commands can be enabled only for enable mode commands.

- *EXEC mode*—User must supply a valid username and password that is verified by the AAA server to gain access to EXEC mode.

- *Enable mode*—User must supply a valid username and password that is verified by the AAA server to gain access to enable mode.

Authentication is supported for three different connections attempts; however, authorization is supported for only two, Console and Telnet:

- *Console*—Authorization is performed for all console sessions.
- *Telnet*—Authorization is performed for all Telnet sessions.

Just as with routers, switches can be configured to support the use of methods to provide authorization services. The methods are sometimes referred to as options, and the option configured is known as the primary option. Any option configured after the primary option is known as a fallback option. Fallback options are used only in the event of an error condition or failure of the primary option. The Catalyst switches support the use the following options:

- *TACACS+*—Uses a defined TACACS+ server to provide authorization services.
- *If-Authenticated*—If authentication has already taken place for a session, authorization succeeds.
- *Deny*—If the authentication server fails to respond to a request for authorization, the authentication request fails.
- *None*—If the authentication server fails to respond, authentication succeeds.

Use the following commands to enable authorization for the Catalyst switch:

1. Use this command to enable authorization for EXEC mode access:

   ```
   set authorization exec enable <option><fallbackoption> -
      <console | telnet>
   ```

2. Use this command to enable authorization for privileged mode access to the switch:

   ```
   set authorization enable enable <option> <fallbackoption>
      <console | telnet>
   ```

3. Use this command to enable authorization of configuration commands:

   ```
   set authorization commands enable <config | all> <option> -
      <fallbackoption> <console | telnet>
   ```

The following output displays an example of enabling authorization on the Catalyst switch:

```
set authorization exec disable console
set authorization exec enable tacacs+ if-authenticated telnet
set authorization enable disable console
set authorization enable disable telnet
set authorization commands disable console
set authorization commands enable config tacacs+ -
if-authenticated telnet
```

To view the results of enabling authorization on the switch, issue the **show authorization** command. The following output displays an example of issuing the **show authorization** command:

```
Cat-6509> (enable) sh authorization

Telnet:
-------
                Primary             Fallback
                -------             --------
exec:           tacacs+             if-authenticated
enable:         -                   -
commands:
  config:       tacacs+             if-authenticated
  all:          -                   -


Console:
--------
                Primary             Fallback
                -------             --------
exec:           -                   -
enable:         -                   -
commands:
  config:       -                   -
  all:          -                   -
```

Accounting allows you to track user activity to a specified host, suspicious connection attempts in the network, and unauthorized changes. The accounting information is sent to the accounting server where it is saved in the form of a record. Accounting information typically consists of the user's action and the duration for which the action lasted. You can use the accounting feature for security, billing, and resource allocation purposes.

Accounting on the Catalyst switches can be configured for the following types of events:

- *EXEC mode*—Accounting information about EXEC mode sessions on the switch is recorded when this mode of accounting is configured.
- *Connect*—All outbound connection requests made from the switch are accounted for when this mode of accounting is performed.
- *System*—Accounting information on system events that are not user related is recorded. This information includes system reset, system boot, and user configuration of accounting.
- *Command*—Accounting information for each command entered into the switch by a user is recorded when this mode of accounting is configured.

After the switch is configured for accounting of services on the switch, accounting records are created. There are two types of accounting records: start records and stop records. Start records include information that pertains to the beginning of an event and stop records include the complete information of the event. To configure the switch for accounting, perform the following steps:

1. Use this command to enable accounting for connection events:

```
set accounting connect enable <start-stop | stop-only> -
    <tacacs+ | radius>
```

2. Use this command to enable accounting for EXEC mode events:

```
set accounting exec enable <start-stop | stop-only> -
    <tacacs+ | radius>
```

3. Use this command to enable accounting for system events:

```
set accounting system enable <start-stop | stop-only> -
    <tacacs+ | radius>
```

4. Use this command to enable accounting of all configuration commands:

```
set accounting commands enable <config | all> <stop-only> -
    <tacacs+>
```

5. Use this command to enable suppression of unknown user events:

```
set accounting suppress null-username enable
```

It is best to use the following command to disable this command so that information about unknown user events is accounted for:

```
set accounting suppress null-username disable
```

An example of configuring a Catalyst switch for accounting service is shown here:

```
set accounting exec enable stop-only tacacs+
set accounting connect disable
set accounting system enable stop-only tacacs+
set accounting commands enable config stop-only tacacs+
set accounting suppress null-username disable
```

To view the results of enabling authorization on the switch, issue the **show accounting** command. The following output is an example of issuing the **show accounting** command:

```
GC05-6509A> (enable) sh accounting
Event     Method  Mode
-----     ------  ----
exec:     tacacs+ stop-only
connect:  -       -
system:   tacacs+ stop-only
commands:
config:   tacacs+ stop-only
all:      -       -


TACACS+ Suppress for no username: disabled
Update Frequency: new-info

Accounting information:
----------------------
Active Accounted actions on tty0, User (null) Priv 0
Active Accounted actions on tty-2106106732, -
User testuser Priv 15
 Task ID 807, exec Accounting record, 0,00:00:44 Elapsed
 task_id=807 start_time=1011372975 timezone=CST service=shell

Overall Accounting Traffic:
          Starts  Stops  Active
          ------  -----  ------
Exec         0     489     1
Connect      0       0     0
Command      0       0     0
System       0      43     0
```

Index